陈奕奕◎著

# 涉外刑事案件
# 办案手册

**中英对照** ///

A HANDBOOK FOR HANDLING
FOREIGNER-RELATED CRIMINAL CASES

中国政法大学出版社

2022·北京

**图书在版编目（ＣＩＰ）数据**

涉外刑事案件办案手册：汉英对照/陈奕奕著. —北京：中国政法大学出版社，2022.9
ISBN 978-7-5764-0653-5

Ⅰ.①涉… Ⅱ.①陈… Ⅲ.①涉外案件－刑事诉讼－审判－中国－手册－汉、英
Ⅳ.①D925.2-62

中国版本图书馆 CIP 数据核字(2022)第 169386 号

---------------------------------------------------------------------------------------------

| | |
|---|---|
| 出 版 者 | 中国政法大学出版社 |
| 地 　 址 | 北京市海淀区西土城路 25 号 |
| 邮寄地址 | 北京 100088 信箱 8034 分箱　邮编 100088 |
| 网 　 址 | http://www.cuplpress.com (网络实名：中国政法大学出版社) |
| 电 　 话 | 010-58908586(编辑部) 58908334(邮购部) |
| 编辑邮箱 | zhengfadch@126.com |
| 承 　 印 | 北京朝阳印刷厂有限责任公司 |
| 开 　 本 | 720mm×960mm　　1/16 |
| 印 　 张 | 23 |
| 字 　 数 | 380 千字 |
| 版 　 次 | 2022 年 9 月第 1 版 |
| 印 　 次 | 2022 年 9 月第 1 次印刷 |
| 定 　 价 | 99.00 元 |

# 自序及说明

首先感谢家人和朋友的支持、恩师的指教和同事的启发，没有他们我不可能完成本书。说来惭愧，本书从疫情前就开始写，写完正文部分正好是 2022 年第一天。如果没有居家隔离的日子，这本书可能永远写不出来。

我从 2016 年实习开始，就专做刑事案件。因为之前的本硕都是翻译专业，加上中英翻译和英语老师的职业背景，所里的涉外刑事案件我一般都会参与。刑事律师常被问：你为什么要替坏人说话？到我这里就成了：你替坏人说话就算了，为什么还要替坏的外国人说话？就差说出"汉奸"俩字了，这时我干脆推说所里指定的。

我接触的涉外刑事案件中，有外国人在中国犯罪，也有中国人在国外犯罪，或涉及外国人在国外侵害中国人权益的案件，但主要是外国人在中国境内犯罪。2016 年来我参与的这类案件数量稳步上升，直到 2020 年初，国内外国人数量明显下降，案件量随之也少了很多。但相信未来还会上升。故本书以外国人在华犯罪为代表，展示涉外刑事案件的办理要点及涉外刑事法律英语的主要应用场景，共 50 个。

有些同仁很好奇，问我仅做外国人刑事案件业务量大不大。当然不够养家糊口，还要加上其他国内刑事案件。但我从实习开始到现在，接触的外国人犯罪数量已足够我复盘很多次，这本书便是其中一个方面的小结。

本书中不仅有司法机关使用的主要文书、高频对话的中英对照版本，例如提审、判决书等；书中还包括律师办理外国人犯罪案件中的高频对话、文书材料的中英文对照版本，例如接待、会见、委托合同、委托书等。但是一些不需要翻译的场景则没有收录，例如律师与国内司法机关的沟通、辩护意见等。一些通知性的文书例如取保候审决定书也省略，因内容较简单，不具有典型性。本书有以下功能：

1. 可以为法律翻译提供参考。

2. 涉外刑事律师可以现学现用，翻到相关场景的高频问答，总能用到几处。

3. 外语专业学生可以用作法律英语的学习材料，模拟真实的使用场景。

4. 如有做这块业务意愿的同仁可提前感受一下工作环境

本人在写作、翻译过程中也学到了很多，更新了知识系统，比如知道了看守所的最佳对应是 jail。因为 jail 的英文解释是"a correctional institution used to detain persons who are in the lawful custody of the government（either accused persons awaiting trial or convicted persons serving a sentence）"，即既关押已决犯又关押未决犯的地方，就比 detention house（centre），或者 prison 更为贴切。

本书的内容源于我个人的办案经验和记忆，基本包含了外国人犯罪案件办理需要用到翻译的所有场景。限于本人语言水平和法律实践，难免有错漏，望广大读者朋友和同仁不吝指正。

最后感谢系友帮助整理刑诉法和刑法单词的中文意思和音标。

本书使用的几点说明：

1. 本书高频问答选取的是外国人常见的程序性问题，不包含实体问题。具体案件千人千面，故涉及具体案情的部分都做了省略。

2. 虽然拘留逮捕等是诉前保障的强制措施，但方便起见，本书将看守所监管规定归在刑事执行阶段。

3. 律师接待有两种形式——面谈和电话，两者大同小异，故本书将其合二为一。

4. 司法机关与当事人之间的对话用 Q（question）和 A（answer）简化；律师实务英语中，嫌疑人、家属和客户等用 Client 代替，律师也用 Lawyer 简化处理。

5. 每个单元后的相关英文表达以常用词组或搭配为主，纯英语单词在附表中的刑法和刑诉法词汇中。

6. 裁判文书仅选取有罪和维持的，无罪的省略。

7. 一退与二退后的会见记录中，选二退作为代表。二审仅收录不开庭审理的场景。

8. 本书内容来自本人办理的不同案件，同一阶段内各内容无关联，不存在时间或逻辑关系。例如在取保候审注意事项后，后文还会出现被逮捕的内容。

9. 本书根据 2021 年 7 月 1 日实施的最高人民法院、最高人民检察院《关于常见犯罪的量刑指导意见（试行）》等司法文件编写，结合疫情等时事对办案的影响。

10. 为统一格式，所有应用场景的中英对照都是中文在左、英文在右，相关英文表达都是英文在左、中文在右，主要是为了提取英语表达。

## 目　录

◦CONTENTS

目 录

# 司法机关办案常用语中英对照

## 侦查阶段

### 嫌疑人诉讼权利义务告知书

| 中文版 | 英文版 |
| --- | --- |
| **嫌疑人诉讼权利义务告知书** | **Notification of Rights and Obligations to Criminal Suspect** |
| 根据《中华人民共和国刑事诉讼法》和《中华人民共和国刑法》的规定，在公安机关对案件进行侦查期间，犯罪嫌疑人有如下诉讼权利和义务： | Under *Criminal Procedure Law of the People's Republic of China and Criminal Law of the People's Republic of China*, during the phase of investigation by public security authority, suspects have the following rights and obligations： |
| 一、不通晓当地通用的语言文字时有权要求配备翻译人员，有权用本民族语言文字进行诉讼。 | 1. You have the right to request for an interpreter and use your native languages in litigation if you are not familiar with the commonly used local language. |
| 二、对于公安机关及其侦查人员侵犯其诉讼权利和人身侮辱的行为，有权提出申诉或者控告。 | 2. You have the right to file accusations against public security authority and investigators who infringe upon their procedural rights or inflict personal insult on them. |

三、对于侦查人员、鉴定人、记录人、翻译人员有下列情形之一的，有权申请他们回避：

（一）是本案的当事人或者是当事人的近亲属的；

（二）本人或者他的近亲属和本案有利害关系的；

（三）担任过本案的证人、鉴定人、辩护人、诉讼代理人的；

（四）与本案当事人有其他关系，可能影响公正处理案件的。对于驳回申请回避的决定，可以申请复议一次。

四、自接受第一次讯问或者被采取强制措施之日起，有权委托律师作为辩护人。经济困难或者有其他原因没有委托辩护人的，可以向法律援助机构提出申请。

五、在接受传唤、拘传、讯问时，有权要求饮食和必要的休息时间。

3. You have the right to demand the withdrawal of an investigator, appraiser, clerk or interpreter under any of the following circumstances：

（1）If he is a party to the case or a close relative of a party to the case；

（2）If he or his close relative is an interested party to the case；

（3）If he once served as a witness, identification or evaluation expert, defender, or litigation representative in the case；or

（4）If he has any other relationship with a party, which may affect the just handling of the case. Against a decision that dismisses a request for disqualification, you may apply for reconsideration once.

4. You have the right to retain a defender from the day when you are interrogated by a criminal investigation authority for the first time or from the day when a compulsory measure is taken against you. In the case that you have not retained a defender for financial hardship or other reasons, you may file an application with a legal aid agency.

5. During the period of interrogation by summons or forced appearance, you have the right to have meals and necessary rest time.

六、对于采取强制措施超过法定期限的，有权要求解除强制措施。

6. You have the right to require termination of a compulsory measure taken by public security authority when the term of the compulsory measure expires.

七、对于侦查人员的提问，应当如实回答。但是对与本案无关的问题，有拒绝回答的权利。在接受讯问时有权为自己辩解。如实供述自己罪行的，可以从轻处罚；因如实供述自己罪行，避免特别严重后果发生的，可以减轻处罚。

7. You shall truthfully answer the questions of the investigators, but you have the right to refuse to answer questions irrelevant to the case. During interrogation, you have the right to defend yourself. Where you truthfully confesses to the facts of the crime, you may be given a lighter penalty; and you may be given a mitigated penalty if any especially serious consequence is avoided for your truthful confession.

八、自愿如实供述自己的罪行，承认指控的犯罪事实，愿意接受处罚的，可以依法从宽处理。

8. If you voluntarily and truthfully confess to your crime, admit to the facts of the crime that you are charged with, and are willing to accept punishment, you may be granted leniency in accordance with Chinese law.

九、你有核对讯问笔录的权利，如果笔录记载有遗漏或者差错，可以提出补充或者改正。

9. You have the right to confirm your interrogation transcripts. If there are any omissions or errors in the transcripts, you may suggest supplements or corrections.

十、犯罪嫌疑人请求自行书写供述的，应当准许。

10. You shall be permitted to personally write a confession, if you so request.

十一、未满 18 周岁的犯罪嫌疑人在接受讯问时有要求通知其法定代理人到场的权利。

11. During the interrogation and trial of a juvenile criminal case, the legal representative of a criminal suspect under 18

十二、如果你有聋或哑的情形，在讯问时有要求通晓聋、哑手势的人参加的权利。

十三、你应当依法接受拘传、取保候审、监视居住、拘留、逮捕等强制措施和人身检查、搜查、扣押、鉴定等侦查措施。

十四、公安机关送达的各种法律文书经确认无误后，你应当签名、捺指印。

十五、你有权知道用作证据的鉴定意见的内容，并可以申请补充鉴定或重新鉴定。

本告知书在对犯罪嫌疑人依法进行第一次讯问或采取强制措施时交犯罪嫌疑人。

签字　手印：

日期：

years old shall be notified to be present.

12. If you suffer hearing or speech impairment when you are interrogated, you have the right to request a person who is familiar with the sign language for hearing- or speech-impaired persons.

13. You shall, in accordance with Chinese law, accept compulsory measures such as forced appearance, bail, residential confinement, detain or arrest and investigation measures such as physical examination, search, impoundment, identification or evaluation according to law.

14. After confirming that the legal documents are free of error, you shall sign the documents and press your inked thumbprint on your signature.

15. You have the right to know the expert opinion to be used as evidence. And you may apply for a supplementary evaluation or re-evaluation.

This document shall be given to you in your first interrogation or the first compulsory measure adopted against you.

Please sign and press your inked thumbprint on your signature here：

Date of signing：（day/month/year）

# 被害人诉讼权利义务告知书

| 中文版 | 英文版 |
|---|---|
| **被害人诉讼权利义务告知书** | **Victim Notification of Rights and Obligations** |
| 　　根据《中华人民共和国刑事诉讼法》和《中华人民共和国刑法》的规定，在公安机关对案件进行侦查期间，被害人有如下权利和义务。权利： | 　　Under *Criminal Procedure Law of the People's Republic of China* and *Criminal Law of the People's Republic of China*, during the phase of investigation by public security authority, victims have the following rights and obligations: |
| 　　一、用本民族的语言文字进行诉讼的权利。 | 　　1. You have the right to use your native language in litigation. |
| 　　二、对公安机关及其侦查人员侵犯其诉讼权利或者进行人身侮辱的行为，有权提出控告。 | 　　2. You have the right to file accusations against public security authority and investigators who infringe upon your procedural rights or inflict personal insult on you. |
| 　　三、对于侦查人员、鉴定人、记录人、翻译人员有下列情形之一的，被害人及其法定代理人有权申请回避： | 　　3. You have the right to demand the withdrawal of an investigator, appraiser, clerk or interpreter under any of the following circumstances: |
| 　　（一）是本案的当事人或者是当事人的近亲属的； | 　　（1）If he is a party to the case or a close relative of a party to the case; |
| 　　（二）本人或者其近亲属与本案有利益关系的； | 　　（2）If he or his close relative is an interested party to the case; |
| 　　（三）担任过本案的证人、鉴定人、辩护人、诉讼代理人的； | 　　（3）If he once served as a witness, identification or evaluation expert, defender, or litigation representative in the case; or |

（四）与本案当事人有其他关系，可能影响公正处理案件的。对驳回申请回避的决定，可以申请复议一次。

四、被害人由于被告人的犯罪行为而遭受物质损失的，在刑事诉讼过程中，有权提起附带民事诉讼。

五、对于被害人的报案，公安机关作出不予立案决定的，被害人如果不服，可以申请复议。

六、被害人认为公安机关对应当立案侦查的案件而不立案侦查的，有权向人民检察院提出。

七、被害人有权核对询问笔录。被害人没有阅读能力的，侦查人员应当向其宣读。如果记载有遗漏或者差错，被害人可以提出补充或者改正。被害人有权自行书写被害人陈述。

八、有权知道用作证据的鉴定意

(4) If he has any other relationship with a party, which may affect the just handling of the case. Against a decision that dismisses a request for disqualification, you may apply for reconsideration once.

4. Where you have suffered any material loss as a result of the defendant's crime, you shall have the right to institute an incidental civil action during criminal procedures.

5. Against a decision of not opening a case by a public security authority after examining the materials regarding a reported crime, the accuser may apply for reconsideration.

6. If you deem that a public security authority fails to file a case that shall be otherwise filed for criminal investigation, you have the right to report to a people's procuratorate.

7. You have the right to confirm your interview transcripts, and, if you are unable to read, the transcripts shall be read out to you. If there are any omissions or errors in the transcripts, you may suggest supplements or corrections. You shall be permitted to personally write a statement, if you so request.

8. You have the right to be informed

见的内容，可以申请补充鉴定或重新鉴定。

about the the expert opinion to be used as evidence. Upon application of you, a supplementary identification or evaluation or a re-identification or re-evaluation may be conducted.

九、应当如实地提供证据、作出陈述，捏造事实诬告陷害他人或者隐匿罪证应负法律责任。

9. You shall truthfully provide evidence and testimony, and be subject to legal liability for perjury or concealing criminal evidence.

本告知书在第一次询问被害人时交被害人。

This document shall be given to you in your first interview.

签字　手印：

Please sign and press your inked thumbprint here:

日期：

Date of signing：（day/month/year）

# 证人诉讼权利义务告知书

| 中文版 | 英文版 |
|---|---|
| **证人诉讼权利义务告知书** | **Witness Notification of Rights and Obligations** |
| 　　根据《中华人民共和国刑事诉讼法》和《中华人民共和国刑法》的规定，在公安机关对案件进行侦查期间，证人有如下权利和义务： | 　　Under *Criminal Procedure Law of the People's Republic of China* and *Criminal Law of the People's Republic of China*, during the phase of investigation by public security authority, suspects have the following rights and obligations： |
| 　　一、你有用本民族的语言文字进行诉讼的权利。 | 　　1. You have the right to use your native language in litigation. |

二、你对侦查人员侵犯你的诉讼权利或者对你进行人身侮辱的行为，有权提出控告。

三、你有权要求侦查机关保障你自身及你近亲属的安全。

四、你有权核对询问笔录。如果你没有阅读能力，侦查人员应当向你宣读。如果记载有遗漏或者差错，你可以提出补充或者改正。你有权自行书写亲笔证词。

五、凡是知道案件情况的人，都有作证的义务。

六、你应当如实地提供证据、证言，有意作伪证或隐匿罪证应负相当的法律责任。

本告知书在第一次询问证人时交证人。

签字　手印：

日期：

2. You have the right to file accusations against investigators who infringe upon their procedural rights or inflict personal insult on you.

3. You have the right to request the criminal investigation authority to ensure the safety of yourself and your close relatives.

4. You have the right to confirm your interview transcripts. If you are unable to read, the transcripts shall be read out to you. If there are any omissions or errors in the transcripts, you may suggest supplements or corrections. You have the right to write a statement personally.

5. Any person who has information regarding a case shall have the obligation to testify.

6. You shall truthfully provide evidence and testimony, and be subject to legal liability for perjury or concealing criminal evidence.

This document shall be given tothe you in your first interview.

Please sign and press your inked thumbprint here：

Date of signing：（day/month/year）

# 取保候审权利义务告知书

| 中文版 | 英文版 |
|---|---|
| **取保候审权利义务告知书** | **Notification of Rights and Obligations for Bailed Criminal Suspect or Defendant** |
| 一、未经执行机关批准，你不得离开所居住的市、县。 | 1. You are not allowed to leave the city or county where you reside without the approval of the execution authority. |
| 二、住址、工作单位和联系方式发生变动的，在 24 小时以内向执行机关报告。 | 2. You shall report any change of your residence address, employer, or contact information to the execution authority within 24 hours of such change. |
| 三、在传讯的时候及时到案。 | 3. You shall appear before court in a timely manner when summoned. |
| 四、不得以任何形式干扰证人作证。 | 4. You shall not interfere in any way with the testimony of witnesses. |
| 五、不得毁灭、伪造证据或者串供。 | 5. You shall not destroy or forge evidence or make a false confession in collusion. |
| 六、不得进入××等场所。 | 6. You may not enter ＊ ＊ ＊ （particular places）. |
| 七、不得与××会见或者通信。 | 7. You may not meet or communicate with ＊ ＊ ＊ （particular persons）. |
| 八、不得从事××等活动。 | 8. You may not engage in ＊ ＊ ＊ （particular activities）. |
| 九、将××证件交执行机关保存。 | 9. Your passport and other international travel credentials and driver's license shall be preserved by the execution |

| | |
|---|---|
| 　　被取保候审人在取保候审期间违反上述规定，已交纳保证金的，由公安机关没收部分或者全部保证金，并且区别情形，责令被取保候审人具结悔过，重新交纳保证金、提出保证人，或者监视居住、予以逮捕。 | authority.<br><br>　　Where a bailed criminal suspect or defendant violates any provision of the preceding paragraphs, if a bond has been paid, part or all of the bond shall be forfeited, and, based on the actual circumstances, the criminal suspect or defendant shall be ordered to make a statement of repentance, pay a bond or provide a surety again, or be placed under residential confinement or arrested. |
| 被取保候审人：<br><br>日期： | Signature of the person bailed：<br><br>Date of signing：(day/month/year) |

## 监视居住权利义务告知书

| 中文版 | 英文版 |
|---|---|
| **监视居住权利义务告知书** | **Notification of Rights and Obligations for Criminal Suspect or Defendant under Residential Confinement** |
| 　　一、未经执行机关批准不得离开执行监视居住的处所。 | 　　1. You are not allowed to leave the residence where residential confinement is executed without the approval of the execution authority. |
| 　　二、未经执行机关批准不得会见他人或者通信。 | 　　2. You shall not meet or communicate with others without the approval of the |

三、在传讯的时候及时到案。

四、不得以任何形式干扰证人作证。

五、不得毁灭、伪造证据或者串供。

六、将护照等出入境证件、身份证件、驾驶证件交执行机关保存。

被监视居住的犯罪嫌疑人、被告人违反前款规定，情节严重的，可以予以逮捕；需要予以逮捕的，可以对犯罪嫌疑人、被告人先行拘留。

被监视居住人：

日期：

execution authority.

3. You shall appear before court in a timely manner when summoned.

4. You shall not interfere in any way with the testimony of witnesses.

5. You shall not destroy or forge evidence or making a false confession in collusion.

6. Your passport and other international travel credentials, ID card and driver's license shall be preserved by the execution authority.

Wherea criminal suspect or defendant under residential confinement who seriously violates any provision of the preceding paragraphs may be arrested; and if arrest is necessary, you may be detained first.

Signature of the personunder residential confinement：

Date of signing：（day/month/year）

# 公安讯问嫌疑人高频问答

| 中文版 | 英文版 |
| --- | --- |
| 问：我们是××公安局民警（出示证件），现在你被依法传唤，对你进行讯问，你要如实回答我们的问题，对与本案无关的内容，你有拒绝回答的权利，你听清楚了吗？ | Q：We are from ＊＊ police station (showing of officer ID). Now you are legally summoned and questioned. You need to answer our questions truthfully, but you have the right to refuse to answer questions irrelevant to the case. Is that all clear? |
| 答：听清楚了。 | A：Clear. |
| 问：根据《中华人民共和国刑事诉讼法》的规定，你在被讯问期间有相应的权利和义务（递上嫌疑人权利义务告知单）。因为你是外国人，我们聘请了××先生作为此次讯问的翻译。现在由翻译向你宣读《讯问期间权利义务告知单》，你清楚了吗？ | Q：Under *Criminal Procedure Law of the People's Republic of China*, you enjoy procedural right and assume obligation accordingly (hand over the Suspect Notification of Rights and Obligations). Because you are a foreigner, we have retained Mr. ＊＊ as your interpreter. Now he will read to you the notification of your rights and obligations. Are you clear? |
| 答：我清楚了。 | A：Clear. |
| 问：（仅针对需要同步录音录像的情形）我们将对整个审讯过程进行同步录音录像，你听明白了吗？ | Q：(for cases requiring an audio-visual record) we will keep an audio-visual record of the interrogation process. Is that clear? |
| 答：明白了。 | A：Clear. |
| 问：你能否使用英语进行正常的表达？能否听懂英语？ | Q：Can you express yourself normally in English? Can you understand English? |

答：英语虽然不是我的母语，但是我能用英语表达和沟通。

问：你是否申请翻译回避？

答：不申请。

问：你是否申请侦查人员及记录人员回避？

答：不申请。

问：你的身体是否有疾病？

答：没有的/有的，我有×××

问：（针对被羁押的女性犯罪嫌疑人）你是否怀孕或者正在哺乳自己的婴儿？

答：没有/有的，我×××。

问：你现在可否正常表达？

答：可以的。

问：根据中国法律规定，你有权委托辩护人，你是否委托？

答：我要考虑考虑。

问：如果你经济困难，可以申请法律援助，你是否申请？

答：我需要，我没有钱。

问：你是什么时候入境中国的？

答：×××。

A：English is not my first language, but I can use it to express myself and communicate.

Q：Do you apply for your interpreter's disqualification?

A：No.

Q：Do you apply for the disqualification of your investigators and recorders?

A：No.

Q：Do you have any disease?

A：No. /Yes, I have * *.

Q：（to female suspect）Are you pregnant or breastfeeding your own baby?

A：No. /Yes, I am * *.

Q：Can you correctly express yourself?

A：Yes, I can.

Q：Under Chinese law, you have the right to retain a defender. Do you like to retain one?

A：I need to think about it.

Q：If you has not retained a defender for financial hardship, you could file an application with a legal aid agency. Do you need so?

A：I need it badly because I have no money.

Q：Since when you entered into China?

A：* * * （year/month/day）.

问：你的签证种类和停留期限？

答：商务签证，停留×日。

问：你在中国有什么联系人？

答：××，他是××。

问：你是否是外交人员？

答：不是。/是，我是××使/领馆的××。

问：你的详细居住地址？

答：×××。

问：你的文化程度？

答：大学/高中/初中/小学毕业/肄业。

问：你有无前科？

答：没有的/有的，我曾经因××被判处××。

问：你的工作单位和职务？

答：我是××的××，负责××。

问：你的家庭情况。

答：家里有一个妻子，×个孩子，分别为×岁的儿子和×岁的女儿。

问：你有无曾用名？

答：没有的/有，是××。

问：你是否知晓为何将你传讯？

Q：What's your visa type and your permitted length of stay?

A：Business visa, I am allowed to stay for ＊＊days.

Q：Do you have any contacts in China?

A：＊＊, he is my ＊＊.

Q：Are you a diplomat?

A：No. /yes, I am ＊＊from ＊＊ embassy/consulate.

Q：Your detailed living address?

A：＊＊＊.

Q：What's your educational level?

A：University graduate/high school/secondary school/elementary school/uncompleted ＊＊.

Q：Do you have any criminal record?

A：No. /yes, I was sentenced to ＊＊ years in prison for ＊＊＊.

Q：What's your employer and post?

A：I am ＊＊in ＊＊, in charge of ＊＊.

Q：Tell us about your family.

A：My wife, ＊ kids, ＊ year old boy and ＊ year old daughter.

Q：Do you have any former name?

A：I don't have one. /Yes, it's ＊＊.

Q：Do you know why you are summoned and questioned today?

答：我不清楚。

问：你在中国是否有违法犯罪行为？

答：我觉得是没有的／有的，我觉得我×××。

问：根据《中华人民共和国刑事诉讼法》，嫌疑人有如实供述的义务，没有沉默权，你是否知晓？

答：我明白了。

问：有无检举揭发？（宣读《中华人民共和国刑法》第68条：犯罪分子有揭发他人犯罪行为，查证属实的，或者提供重要线索，从而得以侦破其他案件等立功表现的，可以从轻或者减轻处罚；有重大立功表现的，可以减轻或者免除处罚。）

答：无／有，×××。

问：根据《中华人民共和国刑事诉讼法》的规定，犯罪嫌疑人愿如实供述自己的罪行，承认指控的犯罪事实愿意接受处罚的，可以依法从宽处理。

A：I have no idea.

Q：Do you think you have broken the law in China?

A：I don't think so. ／I think I have, I * *.

Q：Under *Criminal Procedure Law of the People's Republic of China*, a suspect shall truthfully answer the questions from the investigators, and have no right to keep silent. Are you clear?

A：Clear.

Q：Do you have any crimes of others to expose? （read criminal law Article 68. Criminals who perform meritorious service by exposing other people's crimes that can be verified or who provide important clues leading the cracking of other cases may be given a lesser punishment or a mitigated punishment. Those who performed major meritorious service may be given a mitigated punishment or may be exempted from punishment. ）

A：No/Yes, it's * * *.

Q：According to theCriminal Procedure Law of the People's Republic of China, Where a criminal suspect or defendant voluntarily and truthfully confesses to his or her crime, admits to the facts of the crime that he or she is charged with, and

| | |
|---|---|
| 答：我认罪认罚／我不认罪，我觉得我没有犯罪。<br><br>问：有无其他补充？<br><br>答：无／有，×××。<br><br>问：上述我们问你的这些问题你是否都如实回答了？<br><br>答：是的。<br><br>问：因你不懂中文，上述笔录由翻译人员××向你宣读一遍，你听一下，是否与你所讲一致？<br><br>答：我听过了，与我所讲一致。<br><br>问：请在笔录上签名按指印。<br><br>答：好的。 | is willing to accept punishment, the criminal suspect or defendant may be granted leniency in accordance with Chinese law.<br><br>A：I confess to my crime. ／I don't confess. I am innocent.<br><br>Q：Anything else to say?<br><br>A：Nothing. ／Yes, ＊＊＊.<br><br>Q：Your above answers are all truthful, right?<br><br>A：Yes.<br><br>Q：Because you cannot understand Chinese, your statement will be read out by your interpreter. Please listen and tell us if it's consistent with what you said.<br><br>A：I listened. It's consistent with what I said.<br><br>Q：Please sign and press your inked thumbprint here.<br><br>A：OK. |

## 公安询问外籍证人高频问答

| 中文版 | 英文版 |
|---|---|
| 问：我们是××公安局民警（出示证件），现依法对你进行询问。你应当如实回答我们的询问并协助调查，不得提供虚假证言，不得伪造、隐匿、毁灭证据，否则将承担法律责任。你有权就被询问事项自行提供书面材料， | Q：We are from ＊＊ police station (showing of officer ID) and we are going to interview you in accordance with Chinese law. You need to answer our questions truthfully and assist the investigation, but you have the right to refuse to |

有权拒绝回答与案件无关的问题，有权核对询问笔录，对笔录记载有无或者遗漏之处提出更正或者补充意见，如果你回答的内容涉及国家秘密、商业秘密或者个人隐私，公安机关将予以保密。以上内容你是否听清楚了？

答：听清楚了。

问：你是否申请回避？

答：不申请回避。

问：你是否能够听懂中文？

答：我不会中文。

问：你平时主要使用什么语言？

答：我用英文。

问：我们聘请××先生作为此次询问的翻译，你有无意见。

答：没有意见。

问：现由××先生向你宣读《证人权利义务告知书》。

答：他读的我听懂了，没有意见。

问：那请你根据自己所见，说说事发时的情况。

答：好的……

answer questions irrelevant to the case. You aresubject to legal liability for perjury or concealing criminal evidence. You have the right to provide written material related to the questions asked, and confirm the transcripts. If there are any omissions or errors in the transcripts, you may suggest supplements or corrections. If your answer involves state secret, trade secret, or personal privacy, we shall keep confidential. Is everything above clear to you?

A：Clear.

Q：Do you apply for disqualification?

A：No.

Q：Can you understand Chinese?

A：No, I cannot understand Chinese.

Q：What's the language you use most?

A：English.

Q：We retain Mr. ＊＊ as your interpreter for this interview, do you agree?

A：I agree.

Q：Now Mr. ＊＊ will read to you the notification of your rights and obligations.

A：I heard it and agree.

Q：So please tell us about what happened during that event according to your real experience.

A：OK...

| | |
|---|---|
| 问：还有什么要补充的吗？ | Q：Do you have anything else to say about the event? |
| 答：没有。 | A：No. |
| 问：上述我们问你的这些问题你是否都如实回答了？ | Q：Are your previous answers truthful and based on actual facts? |
| 答：是的。 | A：Yes. |
| 问：上述笔录由翻译人员××向你宣读一遍，你听一下，是否与你所讲一致？ | Q：Your statement will be read out by your interpreter. Please listen and tell us if it's consistent with what you said. |
| 答：我听过了，与我所讲一致。 | A：I listened. It's consistent with what I said. |
| 问：请在笔录上签名。按指引。 | Q：Please sign and use your inked thumbprint here. |
| 答：好的。 | A：OK. |

## 公安询问外籍被害人高频问答

| 中文版 | 英文版 |
|---|---|
| 问：我们是××公安局民警（出示证件），现依法对你进行询问。你应当如实回答我们的询问并协助调查，不得提供虚假陈述，不得伪造、隐匿、毁灭证据，否则将承担法律责任。你有权就被询问事项自行提供书面材料，有权拒绝回答与案件无关的问题，有权核对询问笔录，对笔录记载有无或者遗漏之处提出更正或者补充意见，如果你回答的内容涉及国家秘密、商业秘密或者个人隐私，公安机关将予 | Q：We are from ＊＊ police station (showing of officer ID) and we are going to interview you in accordance with Chinese law. You need to answer our questions truthfully and assist the investigation, but you have the right to refuse to answer questions irrelevant to the case. You are subject to legal liability for perjury or concealing criminal evidence. You have the right to provide written material related to the questions asked, and con- |

以保密。以上内容你是否听清楚了？

答：听清楚了。

问：你是否申请回避？

答：不申请回避。

问：你是否能够听懂中文？

答：我不会中文。

问：你平时主要使用什么语言？

答：我用英文。

问：我们聘请××先生作为此次询问的翻译，你有无意见。

答：没有意见。

问：现由××先生向你宣读《被害人权利义务告知书》。

答：他读的我听懂了，没有意见。我是否能聘请律师？

问：根据《中华人民共和国刑事诉讼法》，公诉案件的被害人及其法定代理人或者近亲属，附带民事诉讼的当事人及其法定代理人，自案件移送审查起诉之日起，有权委托诉讼代理人。

firm the transcripts. If there are any omissions or errors in the transcripts, you may suggest supplements or corrections. If you answer involves state secret, trade secret, or personal privacy, we shall keep confidential. Is everything above clear to you?

A：Clear.

Q：Do you apply for our disqualification?

A：No.

Q：Can you understand Chinese?

A：No, I cannot understand Chinese.

Q：What's the language you use most?

A：English.

Q：We retain Mr. * * as your interpreter for this interview, do you agree?

A：I agree.

Q：Now Mr. * * will read to you the notification of your rights and obligations.

A：I heard it and agree. May I retain my own lawyer?

Q：Under *Criminal Procedure Law of the People's Republic of China*, a victim or his or her legal representative or close relative in a case of public prosecution or a party or his or her legal representative in an incidental civil action shall have the right to retain a litigation representative from the day when the case is transferred for examination and prosecution.

| | |
|---|---|
| 问：还有什么要补充的吗？ | Q：Do you have anything else to say about the event? |
| 答：没有。 | A：No. |
| 问：上述我们问你的这些问题你是否都如实回答了？ | Q：Are your previous answers truthful and based on actual facts? |
| 答：是的。 | A：Yes. |
| 问：上述笔录由翻译人员××向你宣读一遍，你听一下，是否与你所讲一致？ | Q：Your statement will be read out by your interpreter. Please listen and tell us if it's consistent with what you said. |
| 答：我听过了，与我所讲一致。 | A：I listened. It's consistent with what I said. |
| 问：请在笔录上签名按指印。 | Q：Please sign and use your inked thumbprint here. |
| 答：好的。 | A：OK. |

## 检察院批捕前讯问外籍嫌疑人高频问答

| 中文版 | 英文版 |
|---|---|
| 问：我们是×××人民检察院的工作人员（出示证件），你所涉嫌的×××一案现在进入审查批捕阶段，审查批捕期限为×年×月×日至×年×月×日，今天我们依法向你进行讯问，希望你能如实回答问题，对与本案无关的内容，你有拒绝回答的权利，你听清楚了吗？ | Q：We are from ＊＊＊ Procuratorate（showing prosecutor ID）. Now your case of ＊＊＊ is in the period of approval of arrest, lasting from ＊＊＊（date/month/year）to ＊＊＊（date/month/year）. We are here, in accordance with Chinese law, to ask you several questions, you shall answer them truthfully, but you have the right to refuse to answer questions irrelevant to the case. Is that all clear? |

答：好的。

问：我们将对整个审讯过程进行同步录音录像，你听明白了吗？

答：明白了。

问：根据《中华人民共和国刑事诉讼法》的规定，你在被讯问期间有相应的权利和义务（递上嫌疑人权利义务告知单）。因为你是外国人，我们聘请了××先生作为此次讯问的翻译。你能否使用英语进行正常的表达以及理解？

答：英语虽然不是我的母语，但是我能用英语表达和沟通。

问：你是否申请翻译回避？

答：不申请。

问：现在由翻译向你宣读《讯问期间权利义务告知单》，你清楚了吗？

答：我清楚了。

问：你是否申请检察人员及记录人员回避？

答：不申请。

问：你的身体是否有疾病？

答：没有的／有的，我有×××。

问：（发问被羁押的女性犯罪嫌

A: Clear.

Q: We will keep an audio‑visual record of the interrogation process. Is that clear?

A: Clear.

Q: Under *Criminal Procedure Law of China of the People's Republic*, you enjoy procedural right and assume obligation accordingly (hand over the suspect notification of rights and obligations). Because you are a foreigner, we have retained Mr. * * as your interpreter. Can you express yourself normally in English? Can you understand English?

A: English is not my first language, but I can use it to express myself and communicate.

Q: Do you apply for your interpreter's disqualification?

A: No.

Q: Now he will read to you the notification of your rights and obligations. Are you clear?

A: Clear.

Q: Do you apply for the disqualification of prosecutors and recorders?

A: No.

Q: Do you have any disease?

A: No. /Yes, I have...

Q: (to female suspect) Are you pr-

疑人）你是否怀孕或者正在哺乳自己的婴儿？

答：没有/有的，我×××。

问：你现在可否正常表达？

答：可以的。

问：根据法律规定，你有权委托辩护人，你是否委托？

答：我会考虑的。

问：如果你经济困难，可以申请法律援助？你是否申请？

答：我需要，我没有钱。

问：你是什么时候入境中国的？

答：×××。

问：你的签证种类和拘留期限？

答：商务签证，停留×日。

问：你在中国有什么联系人？

答：××，他是××。

问：你是否是外交人员？

答：不是。/是，我是××使/领馆的××。

问：你的详细居住地址。

答：×××。

egnant or breastfeeding your own baby?

A：No. /Yes, I am. . .

Q：Can you correctly express yourself?

A：Yes, I can.

Q：Under Chinese law, you have the right to retain a defender. Do you like to retain one?

A：I need to think about it.

Q：If you has not retained a defender for financial hardship, you could file an application with a legal aid agency. Do you need so?

A：I need it badly because I have no money.

Q：Since when you entered into China?

A：＊＊＊（year/month/day）.

Q：What's your visa type and your permitted length of stay?

A：Business visa, I am allowed to stay for ＊＊days.

Q：Do you have any contacts in China?

A：＊＊, he is my ＊＊.

Q：Are you a diplomat?

A：No. /yes, I am ＊＊from ＊＊ embassy/consulate.

Q：Your detailed living address.

A：＊＊＊.

问：你的文化程度？

答：大学/初中/高中/小学毕业/肄业。

问：你有无前科？

答：没有的/有的，我曾经因××被判处××。

问：你在你自己国家和中国的工作单位和职务？

答：我是××的××，负责××。

问：你的家庭情况。

答：家里有一个妻子，×个孩子，分别为×岁的儿子和×岁的女儿。

问：你有无曾用名？

答：没有的/有的，是××。

问：你是何时因何罪被采取何种强制措施？

答：××时我被××。

问：你是如何归案的？

答：我在××被抓获/我自首的。

问：你的第一份笔录是在何时、何地制作的？

答：我第一份笔录是在×××做的。

问：你是于何时被送到看守所羁

Q：What's your educational level?

A：University graduate/high school/secondary school/elementary school/uncompleted ＊＊.

Q：Do you have any criminal record?

A：No. /yes, I was sentenced to ＊＊ years in prison for ＊＊＊.

Q：What's your employer and post back in your own country and in China?

A：I am ＊＊in＊＊, in charge of ＊＊.

Q：Tell us about your family.

A：My wife, ＊kids, ＊ year old boy and ＊ year old daughter.

Q：What's your former name?

A：I don't have one. /It's ＊＊.

Q：When and what compulsory measure was taken against you and for what crime?

A：I was detained at ＊＊＊ because I was suspected of ＊＊＊.

Q：How were you captured?

A：I was captured at ＊＊＊/I voluntarily surrendered myself.

Q：When and where was your first statement being taken?

A：My first statement was taken at ＊＊＊.

Q：When were you delivered to de-

押的？

答：×××。

问：你所供述的内容是否反映你的真实意思？

答：是的/不是的，我没有说过××，我的意思是××。

问：到目前为止你被讯问过多少次？每次供述的时间、地点？

答：××次，地点分别是在××。

问：你在侦查机关的供述是否属实？

答：是的。

问：翻译是否向你宣读过并经确认后再签字？

答：有的/没有，翻译没有宣读过。

问：检察机关对侦查活动有监督职责。侦查机关的侦查活动有无违法情形？

答：什么样的情形算违法？

问：比如侦查人员在讯问过程中有无对你采用刑讯逼供、暴力、威胁、诱供等非法方法？

答：没有。

tention house?

A: * * *.

Q: Do you mean what's in your statement?

A: Yes. /No, I didn't say * * *, I meant * * *.

Q: How many times have you been interrogated so far? When and where were your interrogations taken?

A: * * times. The locations were * *.

Q: Are your confession truthful so far?

A: Yes.

Q: Has the interpreter read your interrogation transcripts out to you for you to confirm before you sign on them?

A: Yes/no, the interpreter has not read them out to me.

Q: People's procuratorate shall conduct legal supervision over investigation procedure. Is there any circumstance against the law during the investigation?

A: What kind of circumstance is against the law?

Q: For instance, have the investigators extorted your confessions by torture, violence, threat, enticement, or other illegal means?

A: Not that I can remember.

问：你有无涉案物品被查封、扣押？

答：有的，我的××被警察查封/扣押。

问：你对公安机关的查封、扣押，有无异议？

答：没有/有的，我认为不应该扣押我的××。

问：公安机关是否告知过你享有聘请律师的权利？

答：有的/没有。

问：公安机关是否已告知鉴定意见的情况，你有无异议？

答：没有/有异议，我认为不应该××。

问：《中华人民共和国刑法》第67条第3款"犯罪嫌疑人虽不具有前两款规定的自首情节，但是如实供述自己罪行的，可以从轻处罚；因其如实供述自己罪行，避免特别严重后果发生的，可以减轻处罚"的规定，你清楚了吗？

答：清楚了。

问：《中华人民共和国刑事诉讼法》规定，对一切案件的判处都要重证据，重调查研究，不轻信口供。只有被告人供述，没有其他证据的，不

Q：Do you have anything involved in the case being seized or impounded?

A：Yes, my ＊ ＊ ＊ is at the police.

Q：Do you raise an objection to the seizure or impoundment by the police?

A：No objection. /Yes, I think they shouldn't seize my ＊ ＊ ＊.

Q：Has the police informed you about your right of retaining a lawyer?

A：Yes. /No.

Q：Has the police informed you about expert opinion? Do you raise an objection?

A：No. /Yes, I don't think ＊ ＊ ＊.

Q：According to the Paragraph 3, Article 67 of *Criminal Law of the People's Republic of China*, "A criminal suspect who truthfully confesses to his crime may be given a lighter penalty although there is no voluntary surrender as mentioned in the preceding two paragraphs; and may be given a mitigated penalty if any especially serious consequence is avoided for his truthful confession". You heard me?

A：Loud and clear.

Q：According to *Criminal Procedure Law of the People's Republic of China*, in deciding each case, a people's court shall focus on evidence, investigation, and re-

能认定被告人有罪和处以刑罚；没有被告人供述，证据确实、充分的，可以认定被告人有罪和处以刑罚。你听明白了吗？

答：听明白了。检察官，我是否会被批准逮捕？能不能不要逮捕我，让我取保候审？

答：根据《中华人民共和国刑事诉讼法》第81条的规定：对有证据证明有犯罪事实，可能判处徒刑以上刑罚的犯罪嫌疑人、被告人，采取取保候审尚不足以防止发生下列社会危险性的，应当予以逮捕：

（一）可能实施新的犯罪的；

（二）有危害国家安全、公共安全或者社会秩序的现实危险的；

（三）可能毁灭、伪造证据，干扰证人作证或者串供的；

search, and credence shall not be readily provided for confessions. A defendant shall not be convicted and sentenced to a criminal punishment merely based on the defendant's confession without other evidence; a defendant may be convicted and sentenced to a criminal punishment based on hard and sufficient evidence even without his or her confession. Is it clear?

A: Yes. Prosecutor, will you approve my arrest? Could you please not arrest me and bail me out?

Q: According to the Article 81 of *Criminal Procedure Law of the People's Republic of China*, where there is evidence to prove the facts of a crime and a criminal suspect or defendant may be sentenced to imprisonment or a heavier punishment, if residential confinement is insufficient to prevent any of the following dangers to society, the criminal suspect or defendant shall be arrested:

(1) The criminal suspect or defendant may commit a new crime;

(2) There is an actual danger to national security, public security, or social order;

(3) The criminal suspect or defendant may destroy or forge evidence, interfere with the testimony of a witness, or make

（四）可能对被害人、举报人、控告人实施打击报复的；

（五）企图自杀或者逃跑的。

批准或者决定逮捕，应当将犯罪嫌疑人、被告人涉嫌犯罪的性质、情节、认罪认罚等情况，作为是否可能发生社会危险性的考虑因素。

对有证据证明有犯罪事实，可能判处十年有期徒刑以上刑罚的，或者有证据证明有犯罪事实，可能判处徒刑以上刑罚，曾经故意犯罪或者身份不明的，应当予以逮捕。

被取保候审、监视居住的犯罪嫌疑人、被告人违反取保候审、监视居住规定，情节严重的，可以予以逮捕。

a false confession in collusion;

（4）The criminal suspect or defendant may retaliate against a victim, informant, or accuser; or

（5）The criminal suspect or defendant attempts to commit suicide or escape.

In the process of approving ordeciding an arrest, factors like the nature and circumstances of the suspected crime, the admission of guilt and the acceptance of punishment of a criminal suspect or defendant shall be considered to evaluate the danger to the society.

Where there is evidence to prove the facts of a crime and a criminal suspect or defendant may be sentenced to fixed-term imprisonment of 10 years or a heavier punishment or there is evidence to prove the facts of a crime and a criminal suspect or defendant who once committed an intentional crime or has not been identified may be sentenced to imprisonment or a heavier punishment, the criminal suspect or defendant shall be arrested.

Where a criminal suspect or defendant waiting for trial on bail or under residential confinement seriously violates the provisions on bail or residential confinement, the criminal suspect or defendant may be arrested.

我们今天来提审你主要是想了解一下你的情况，我们回去后会对相关问题进行讨论，综合所有因素作出不批捕或者批捕的决定。

问：你之前并未认罪，为何现在又供述有犯罪行为？

答：因为我之前害怕/之前记不清楚，现在想起来了。

问：你之前为何要作有罪供述？你翻供不认罪的理由是什么？

答：我当时不太了解这里的法律，所以一时冲动认罪了。现在我想清楚了，我的行为不是犯罪，我不认罪。

问：有无道歉赔偿并取得被害人自愿谅解等情节？

答：我准备道歉赔偿以取得谅解/我准备道歉赔偿，谅解的事我的家属正在帮我联系。

问：根据《中华人民共和国刑事诉讼法》第 15 条的规定：犯罪嫌疑人、被告人自愿如实供述自己的罪行，承认指控的犯罪事实，愿意接受处罚的，可以依法从宽处理。

We are here today to get to know your particular situation, and then we go back to discuss over relevant issues and make a decision on whether or not to arrest you.

Q：Why you plead not guilty before but confess to your crime this time?

A：Because I freaked out. /I couldn't remember clearly but now it's coming back to me.

Q：Why did you confess to your crime before but plead not guilty now?

A：I did not understand the law here so I admitted it on impulse. I have thought it over and it's not a criminal of fense to me so I don't admit it.

Q：Have you made compensation or an apology to the victim, and has the victim voluntarily agreed on a settlement?

A：I am preparing for making compensation and an apology to them. /I am ready to make compensation and an apology to them and my family are working on it.

Q：According to the Article 15 of *Criminal Procedure Law of the People's Republic of China*, where a criminal suspect or defendant voluntarily and truthfully confesses to his or her crime, admits to the facts of the crime that he or she is charged with, and is willing to accept punishment, the criminal suspect or def-

答：我认罪认罚/我不认罪，我觉得我没有犯罪。

问：有无检举揭发？（宣读《中华人民共和国刑法》第68条：犯罪分子有揭发他人犯罪行为，查证属实的，或者提供重要线索，从而得以侦破其他案件等立功表现的，可以从轻或者减轻处罚；有重大立功表现的，可以减轻或者免除处罚。）

答：没有/有的，××。

问：有无其他补充？

答：没有。

问：今天你讲的是不是事实，是否是你真实意思的表达？

答：是的。

问：上述笔录由翻译人员××向你宣读一遍，你听一下，是否与你所讲一致？如果记载有遗漏或者差错，你可以提出补充或者改正。确认笔录没有错误后，请签名、捺印。

答：好的。

endant may be granted leniency in accordance with Chinese law.

A: I plead guilty/not guilty, I don't think I have broken the law.

Q: Do you have any crimes of others to expose? (read criminal law Article 68 of *Criminal Law of People's Republic of China*. Criminals who perform meritorious service by exposing other people's crimes that can be verified or who provide important clues leading the cracking of other cases may be given a lesser punishment or a mitigated punishment. Those who performed major meritorious service may be given a mitigated punishment or may be exempted from punishment.

A: No. /Yes, it's ＊＊.

Q: Do you have anything else to say?

A: No.

Q: Are your previous answers truthful and do you mean them?

A: Yes.

Q: This transcript will be read out by your interpreter. Please listen and tell us if it's consistent with what you said. If there are any omissions or errors in the transcripts, you may suggest supplements or corrections. After you have confirmed it, you may sign and press your inked thumbprint on it.

A: OK.

# 相关英文表达

| 英文表达 | 中文意思 |
| --- | --- |
| native language | 母语 |
| file accusations against | 针对某人提出控告 |
| infringe upon | 侵犯（权利等） |
| inflict personal insult | 进行人身侮辱 |
| withdrawal/disqualification | 回避 |
| under any of the following circumstances | 以下情形 |
| just handling | 公正处理 |
| apply for reconsideration | 申请复议 |
| compulsory measure | 强制措施 |
| financial hardship | 经济困难 |
| file an application | 提出申请 |
| forced appearance | 拘传 |
| termination of a compulsory measure | 解除强制措施 |
| mitigated penalty | 减轻处罚 |
| juvenile criminal case | 未成年人犯罪案件 |
| hearing or speech impairment | 聋或哑 |
| residential confinement | 监视居住 |
| inked thumbprint | 指印 |
| legal liability for perjury | 伪证的法律责任 |
| conceal criminal evidence | 隐瞒刑事证据 |
| execution authority | 执行机关 |
| in a timely manner | 及时地 |
| forge evidence | 伪造证据 |
| international travel credentials | 出境旅游证件 |
| preceding paragraphs | 前款 |

续表

| 英文表达 | 中文意思 |
|---|---|
| statement of repentance | 悔过书 |
| length of stay | 停留时长 |
| confess to my crime | 认罪 |
| granted leniency | 从宽处理 |
| state secret | 国家秘密 |
| trade secret | 商业秘密 |
| personal privacy | 个人隐私 |
| examination and prosecution | 审查起诉 |
| legal aid agency | 法援机构 |
| interrogation transcripts | 提审笔录 |
| seizure or impoundment | 查封或扣押 |
| hard and sufficient evidence | 证据确实、充分 |
| testimony of a witness | 证人作证 |
| make a false confession in collusion | 串供 |
| retaliate against | 报复（某人） |
| intentional crime | 故意犯罪 |
| meritorious service | 立功表现 |
| omissions or errors | 遗漏或者差错 |

# 审查起诉阶段

## 检察院审查起诉阶段讯问外籍嫌疑人高频问答

| 中文版 | 英文版 |
|---|---|
| 问：我们是×××人民检察院的工作人员（出示工作证），你所涉嫌的×××一案现在进入审查起诉环节，审查起诉期限为×年×月×日至×年×月×日，今天我们依法向你进行讯问，希望你能如实回答问题，对与本案无关的内容，你有拒绝回答的权利，你听清楚了吗？ | Q：We are from ＊＊＊ Procuratorate（showing prosecutor ID）. Now your case of ＊＊＊ is in the period of Public Prosecution, lasting from ＊＊＊（date/month/year）to ＊＊＊（date/month/year）. We are here, in accordance with Chinese law, to ask you several questions, but you have the right to refuse to answer questions irrelevant to the case. Is that all clear? |
| 答：好的。 | A：Clear. |
| 问：我们将对整个审讯过程进行同步录音录像，你听明白了吗？ | Q：We will keep an audio-visual record of the interrogation process. Is that clear? |
| 答：明白了。 | A：Clear. |
| 问：根据《中华人民共和国刑事诉讼法》的规定，你在被讯问期间有相应的权利和义务（递上讯问期间权利义务告知单）。因为你是外国人，我们聘请了××先生作为此次讯问的翻译。你能否使用英语进行正常的表达以及理解？ | Q：Under *Criminal Procedure Law of the People's Republic of China*, you enjoy procedural right and assume obligation accordingly（hand over the suspect notification of rights and obligations）. Because you are a foreigner, we have retained Mr. ＊＊ as your interpreter. Can you express yourself normally in English? Can you understand English? |

答：英语虽然不是我的母语，但是我能用英语表达和沟通。

问：你是否申请翻译回避？

答：不申请。

问：现在由翻译向你宣读《讯问期间权利义务告知单》，你清楚了吗？

答：我清楚了。

问：你的身体是否有疾病？

答：没有的／有的，我有×××。

问：（发问被羁押的女性犯罪嫌疑人）你是否怀孕或者正在哺乳自己的婴儿？

答：没有／有的，我×××。

问：你现在可否正常表达？

答：可以的。

问：根据法律规定，你有权委托辩护人，你是否委托？

答：我要考虑一下。

问：如果你经济困难，可以申请法律援助。你是否申请？

答：我不需要／我需要的，我很穷。

问：你是什么时候入境中国的？

A：English is not my first language, but I can use it to express myself and communicate.

Q：Do you apply for your interpreter's disqualification?

A：No.

Q：Now he will read to you the notification of your rights and obligations. Are you clear?

A：Clear.

Q：Do you have any disease?

A：No. /Yes, I have * *.

Q：(to female suspect) Are you pregnant or breastfeeding your own baby?

A：No. /Yes, I am * *.

Q：Can you correctly express yourself?

A：Yes, I can.

Q：Under Chinese law, you have the right to retain a defender. Do you like to retain one?

A：I need to think about it.

Q：If you has not retained a defender for financial hardship, you could file an application with a legal aid agency. Do you need so?

A：Not now. /I need it badly because I have no money.

Q：Since when you entered into China?

答：×××。

问：你的签证种类和拘留期限？

答：商务签证，停留×日。

问：你在中国有什么联系人？

答：××，他是××。

问：你是否是外交人员？

答：不是。/是，我是××使/领馆的××。

问：你的详细居住地址？

答：×××。

问：你有无前科？

答：没有的/有的，我曾经因××被判处××。

问：你在你自己国家和中国的工作单位和职务？

答：我是××的××，负责××。

问：你是何时因何罪被采取何种强制措施？

答：××时我被××。

问：你是如何归案的？

答：我在××被抓获/我自首的。

问：你在侦查阶段所供述的内容是否反映你的真实意思？

A：* * *（year/month/day）

Q：What's your visa type and your permitted length of stay?

A：Business visa, and I am allowed to stay for * * days.

Q：Do you have any contacts in China?

A：* *, he is my * *.

Q：Are you a diplomat?

A：No. /yes, I am * * from * * embassy/consulate.

Q：Your detailed living address?

A：* * *.

Q：Do you have any criminal record?

A：No. /yes, I was sentenced to * * years in prison for * * *.

Q：What's your employer and post back in your own country and in China?

A：I am * * in * *, in charge of * *.

Q：When and what compulsory measure was taken against you and for what crime?

A：I was detained at * * * because I was suspected of * * *.

Q：How were you captured?

A：I was captured at * * *. /I voluntarily surrendered myself.

Q：Do you mean what's in your statement during investigation?

答：是的/不是的，我没有说过××，我的意思是××。

问：到目前为止你被讯问过多少次？每次供述的时间、地点？

答：××次，地点分别是在××。

问：你在侦查机关的供述是否属实？

答：是的。

问：翻译是否向你宣读过并经确认后再签字？

答：有的/没有，翻译没有宣读过。

问：检察机关是国家法律监督机关，对侦查活动有监督职责。侦查机关的侦查活动有无违法情形？

答：什么样的情形算违法？

问：比如侦查人员在讯问过程中有无对你采用刑讯逼供、暴力、威胁、诱供等非法方法？

答：没有的/有的，××时候他们××。

问：你有无涉案物品被查封、扣押？

答：有的，我的××在警察那里。

A: Yes. /No, I didn't say * * *, I meant * * *.

Q: How many times have you been interrogated so far? When and where were your interrogations taken?

A: * * times. The locations were * * *.

Q: Are your confession truthful so far?

A: Yes.

Q: Has the interpreter read your interrogation transcripts out to you for you to confirm before you sign on them?

A: Yes. /No, the interpreter has not read them out to me.

Q: People's Procuratorates shall conduct legal supervision over investigation procedure. Is there any circumstance against the law during the investigation?

A: What kind of circumstances are against the law?

Q: For instance, have the investigators extorted your confessions by torture, violence, threat, enticement, or other illegal means?

A: Not that I can remember. /Yes, they once * * *.

Q: Do you have anything involved inthe case being seized or impounded?

A: Yes, my * * * is at the police.

问：你对公安机关的查封、扣押，有无异议？

答：没有/有的，我认为不应该××。

问：公安机关是否告知过你享有聘请律师的权利？

答：有的/没有。

问：公安机关是否已告知你鉴定意见的情况，你有无异议？

答：没有/有异议，我认为不应该是××。

问：《中华人民共和国刑法》第67条第3款规定："犯罪嫌疑人虽不具有前两款规定的自首情节，但是如实供述自己罪行的，可以从轻处罚；因其如实供述自己罪行，避免特别严重后果发生的，可以减轻处罚。"你清楚了吗？

答：清楚了。

问：《中华人民共和国刑事诉讼法》规定，对一切案件的判处都要重证据，重调查研究，不轻信口供。只有被告人供述，没有其他证据的，不能认定被告人有罪和处以刑罚；没有被告人供述，证据确实、充分的，可以认定被告人有罪和处以刑罚。你听明白了吗？

Q：Do you raise an objection to the seizure or impoundment by the police?

A：No objection. /Yes, I think they shouldn't seize my ＊＊＊.

Q：Has the police informed you about your right of retaining a lawyer?

A：Yes. /No.

Q：Has the police informed you about expert opinion? Do you raise an objection?

A：No. /Yes, I don't think ＊＊＊.

Q：According to the Paragraph 3, Article 67 of *Criminal Law of the People's Republic of China*, "A criminal suspect who truthfully confesses to his crime may be given a lighter penalty although there is no voluntary surrender as mentioned in the preceding two paragraphs; and may be given a mitigated penalty if any especially serious consequence is avoided for his truthful confession." You heard me?

A：Loud and clear.

Q：According to *Criminal Procedure Law of the People's Republic of China*, in deciding each case, a people's court shall focus on evidence, investigation, and research, and credence shall not be readily provided for confessions. A defendant shall not be convicted and sentenced to a criminal punishment merely based on the

答：听明白了。检察官，我能不能办取保候审？在我们国家都可以取保，只要我付保证金。

问：根据《中华人民共和国刑事诉讼法》第67条的规定：人民检察院对有下列情形之一的犯罪嫌疑人、被告人，可以取保候审：

（一）可能判处管制、拘役或者独立适用附加刑的；

（二）可能判处有期徒刑以上刑罚，采取取保候审不致发生社会危险性的；

（三）患有严重疾病、生活不能自理，怀孕或者正在哺乳自己婴儿的妇女，采取取保候审不致发生社会危险性的；

（四）羁押期限届满，案件尚未

defendant's confession without other evidence; a defendant may be convicted and sentenced to a criminal punishment based on hard and sufficient evidence even without his or her confession. Is it clear?

A: Yes. Prosecutor, can I get bailed out? You know in our country, I can get bailed out if I pay a surety bond.

Q: According to the Article 67 of *Criminal Procedure Law of the People's Republic of China*, apeople's procuratorate may grant bail to a criminal suspect or defendant under any of the following circumstances:

（1）The criminal suspect or defendant may be sentenced to supervision without incarceration, limited incarceration, or an accessory penalty only;

（2）The criminal suspect or defendant may be sentenced to fixed-term imprisonment or a heavier penalty but will not cause danger to the society if granted bail;

（3）The criminal suspect or defendant suffers a serious illness, cannot take care of himself or herself or is a pregnant woman or a woman who is breastfeeding her own baby, and will not cause danger to the society if granted bail; or

（4）The term of custody of the cri-

办结，需要采取取保候审的。

我们今天来提审你主要是想了解一下你的情况。你可以书面提出取保候审的申请，我们回去后会对这个问题进行讨论，再作出同意取保或不同意取保的决定。

答：好的，我知道了。我会提出申请的。

问：根据《中华人民共和国刑事诉讼法》第 15 条的规定：犯罪嫌疑人、被告人自愿如实供述自己的罪行，承认指控的犯罪事实，愿意接受处罚的，可以依法从宽处理。

答：我认罪认罚/我不认罪，我觉得我没有犯罪。

问：你之前并未认罪，为何现在又供述有犯罪行为？

答：因为我之前害怕/之前记不清楚。

问：（针对翻供）你之前为何要作有罪供述？你翻供不认罪的理由是什么？

minal suspect or defendant has expired but the case has not been closed, and a bail is necessary.

We are here today to know your specific situation. You may apply for a bailout in writing and then we go back to discuss over this issue and make a decision on whether or not to bail you out.

A: Got it. I will apply for it.

Q: According to the Article 15 of *Criminal Procedure Law of the People's Republic of China*, where a criminal suspect or defendant voluntarily and truthfully confesses to his or her crime, admits to the facts of the crime that he or she is charged with, and is willing to accept punishment, the criminal suspect or defendant may be granted leniency in accordance with Chinese law.

A: I plead guilty/not guilty, I don't think I have broken the law.

Q: Why you pleaded not guilty before but confess to your crime this time?

A: Because I freaked out/I can't remember clearly but now it's coming back to me.

Q: (in case of withdrawing a confession) Why did you confess to your crime before but plead not guilty now?

答：我当时不太了解这里的法律，所以一时冲动认罪了。现在我想清楚了，我的行为不是犯罪，我不认罪。

问：你之前向检察机关交代的是否属实？

答：是的。

问：有无退赃、退赔、取得被害人谅解等情节？

答：我准备退赃，以取得谅解/我准备退赃，赔偿并向他们道歉，我的家属正在帮我联系。

问：有无检举揭发？（宣读《中华人民共和国刑法》第68条：犯罪分子有揭发他人犯罪行为，查证属实的，或者提供重要线索，从而得以侦破其他案件等立功表现的，可以从轻或者减轻处罚；有重大立功表现的，可以减轻或者免除处罚。）

答：没有/有的，××。

A: I did not understand the law here so I admitted it on impulse. I have thought it over and it's not a criminal of fense to me so I don't admit it.

Q: Are your previous statements to the procuratorate truthful?

A: Yes.

Q: Have you surrendered all ill-obtained gains, made compensation or an apology to the victim, and has the victim voluntarily agreed on a settlement?

A: I am preparing for surrendering all ill-obtained gains, making compensation and an apology to them. /I am ready to surrender all ill-obtained gains, make compensation and an apology to them and my family are working on it.

Q: Do you have any crimes of others to expose? (read Article 68 of *Criminal Law of the People's Republic of China*. Criminals who perform meritorious service by exposing other people's crimes that can be verified or who provide important clues leading the cracking of other cases may be given a lesser punishment or a mitigated punishment. Those who performed major meritorious service may be given a mitigated punishment or may be exempted from punishment.

A: No. /Yes, it's ＊＊.

问：你的案件审查起诉需要延期15日，请签字确认。

答：好的/我不签字。

问：你的案件需要退回进行补充侦查，因此你需要被延长羁押，请再次签字确认。

答：好的/我不签字。

问：有无其他补充？

答：没有

问：今天你讲的是不是事实，是否是你真实意思的表达？

答：是的。

问：上述笔录由翻译人员向你宣读一遍，你听一下，是否与你所讲一致？如果记载有遗漏或者差错，你可以提出补充或者改正。确认笔录没有错误后，请签名、捺印。

答：好的。

Q：The period of examination of prosecution for your case needs to be extended by 15 days. Please confirm and sign here.

A：OK. /I'd rather not sign.

Q：Your case needs to go back for additional investigation, so your term of custody needs to be extended. Please confirm and sign here.

A：OK. /I'd rather not sign.

Q：Do you have anything else to say?

A：No.

Q：Are your previous answers truthful and do you mean them?

A：Yes.

Q：This transcript will be read out by your interpreter. Please listen and tell us if it's consistent with what you said. If there are any omissions or errors in the transcripts, you may suggest supplements or corrections. After you have confirmed it, you may sign and press your inked thumbprint on it.

A：OK.

# 不起诉决定书

| 中文版 | 英文版 |
|---|---|
| **××省××市××区人民检察院**<br><br>不起诉决定书<br><br>××检××刑不诉〔20××〕×号<br><br><br>被不起诉人……（姓名、性别、出生日期、国籍、护照号码、职业、工作单位、职务及强制措施的情况）<br><br><br><br><br><br><br><br><br><br><br>辩护人……（写姓名、单位） | **The People's Procuratorate of ＊＊ District of ＊＊ City, ＊＊ Province**<br>Written Decision of Non-prosecution<br><br>Case No. 〔20＊＊〕＊＊Procuratorate ＊＊Criminal Non-Prosecution No. ＊＊<br><br>Name：＊＊＊（the person who is not prosecuted）<br>Gender：＊＊＊<br>Date of birth：＊＊＊<br>Nationality：＊＊＊<br>Passport Number：＊＊＊<br>Occupation：＊＊＊<br>Employer：＊＊＊<br>Post：＊＊＊<br>On suspicion of his involvement in this case, suspect ＊＊＊ was detained in ＊＊＊ Detention House till ＊＊＊ (day/month/year) and on bail now.<br>The defenders for ＊＊＊ (the person who is not prosecuted)：＊＊＊ and ＊＊＊, lawyers with ＊＊＊＊ Law Firm. |

本案由×××（写侦查机关名称）侦查终结，以被不起诉人×××涉嫌××罪，于×年×月×日向本院移送审查起诉。

The criminal Investigation of this case is closed by ＊＊＊（name of the investigation organ）. ＊＊＊, who is suspected of ＊＊＊, is not prosecuted. This case is transferred for examination and prosecution on ＊＊＊（day/month/year）.

（针对补充侦查的情形）本案经×次退回补充侦查，于×年×月×日再次移送审查起诉。

（for the case with supplementary investigation）This case has been returned for supplementary investigation once/twice, and transferred to the people's procuratorate for examination and prosecution on ＊＊＊（day/month/year）.

经本院依法审查查明：
…………

Based on the examination in accordance with Chinese law, this procuratorate finds that...

本院认为，×××实施了《中华人民共和国刑法》第××条规定的行为，因自愿如实供述涉嫌犯罪的事实，情节显著轻微、危害不大，符合相对不起诉条件，决定对×××依法不起诉。

This procuratorate holds as follows: The conduct of ＊＊＊ constituted the Article ＊＊＊ of *Criminal Law of the People's Republic of China* , and since the criminal suspect voluntarily and truthfully confesses to his crime, and the circumstances of the alleged conduct are obviously minor, causing no serious harm, which meets the conditions of relative non-prosecution. Therefore, This pr-

查封、扣押、冻结的涉案款物的处理情况：

被不起诉人如不服本决定，可以自收到本决定书后 7 日内向本院申诉。

被害人如不服本决定，可以自收到本决定书后 7 日以内向上一级人民检察院申诉，请求提起公诉；也可以不经申诉，直接向×××人民法院提起自诉。

（院印）

××年×月×日

ocuratorate, in accordance with Chinese law, makes a decision not to initiate a prosecution against ***.

The handling of the seized, impounded, or frozen property of ***:

Against the decision, the person not prosecuted may file a petition with the people's procuratorate within seven days after receiving the written decision.

Against the decision, the victim may, within seven days after receiving the written decision, file a petition with the people's procuratorate at the next higher level for initiation of a public prosecution; the victim may also institute an action directly in a people's court without undergoing the petition procedure.

Stamp of thisprocuratorate

*** (day/month/year)

# 认罪认罚案件起诉书

| 中文版 | 英文版 |
|---|---|
| **××省××市××区人民检察院** | **The People's Procuratorate of ＊＊＊ District of ＊＊＊ City, ＊＊＊ Province** |
| 起诉书 | Bill of Indictment |
| ××检××刑诉〔20××〕×号 | Case No. 〔20＊＊〕＊＊＊ Procuratorate ＊＊ Criminal Prosecution No. ＊＊ |
| 被告人……（姓名、性别、出生日期、国籍、护照号码、职业、工作单位、职务及强制措施的情况） | Name：＊＊＊（Defendant）<br>Gender：＊＊＊<br>Date of birth：＊＊＊<br>Nationality：＊＊＊<br>Passport Number：＊＊＊<br>Occupation：＊＊＊<br>Employer：＊＊＊<br>Post：＊＊＊<br>On suspicion of his involvement in this case, defendant ＊＊＊ was detained in ＊＊＊ Detention House on ＊＊＊（day/month/year）till now. |
| 辩护人……（姓名、单位） | The defenders for ＊＊＊（defendant）：＊＊＊ and ＊＊＊, lawyers with ＊＊＊ Law Firm. |

本案由×××（侦查机关）侦查终结，以被告人×××涉嫌×××罪，于×××年××月××日向本院移送审查起诉。

本院受理后，于×××年××月××日已告知被告人有权委托辩护人和认罪认罚可能导致的法律后果，×××年××月××日已告知被害人及其法定代理人（近亲属）、附带民事诉讼的当事人及其法定代理人有权委托诉讼代理人，依法讯问了被告人，听取了被告人及其辩护人（或值班律师）、被害人及其诉讼代理人的意见，审查了全部案件材料。在辩护人（或值班律师）的见证下与被告人签署认罪认罚具结书并进行证据开示，被告人同意本案适用简易/速裁程序审理。

The criminal Investigation of this case is closed by ＊＊＊ (name of the investigation organ), with ＊＊＊ suspected of ＊＊＊ (particular crime). This case is transferred for examination and prosecution on ＊＊＊ (day/month/year).

After accepting this case, this procuratorate has informed the defendant on ＊＊＊ (day/month/year) that he has the right to retain a defender and the legal effect if he admits guilt and accepts the punishment, and the victim or his legal representative or close relative and the party or his legal representative in an incidental civil action on ＊＊＊ (day/month/year) that they have the right to retain a litigation representative, interrogated the defendant in accordance with Chinese law, heard the opinion of the defendant and his defense lawyer (or duty lawyer), the victim and his litigation representative, examined all case files. Witnessed by his defense lawyer (or duty lawyer), the defendant signed a recognizance to admit guilt and accept punishment with disclosure of the evidence, and agreedwith the summary procedure/fast - track sentencing procedure for this case.

（变更管辖的情形）×××人民检察院于×××年××月××日转至（交由）本院审查起诉。本院受理后，于×××年××月××日已告知被告人有权……

经依法审查查明：

…………

（写明被告人到案后自愿如实供述自己的罪行，与被害人达成和解协议或者赔偿被害人损失，取得被害人谅解等量刑情节）

本院认为……（被告人行为概述），其行为触犯了《中华人民共和国刑法》第××条，犯罪事实清楚，证据确实、充分，应当以×××罪追究其刑事责任……（法定、酌定量刑情节及相关法律条款），建议判处被告人×××……（具体量刑建议）。根据《中华人民共和国刑法》第176条的规定，提起公诉，请依法判处。

（for the case with changed jurisdiction) The People's Procuratorate of * * * District has transferred this case to the people's procuratorate of * * * on * * * （day/month/year）. The defendant was informed on * * * （day/month/year) that he has the right to. . .

Based on the examination in accordance with Chinese law, this procuratorate finds that. . .

（including but not limited to the sentencing circumstances that the defendant voluntarily and truthfully confesses to his or her crime, a settlement agreement is reached and compensation is made to the victim, and forgiveness from the victim is obtained)

This procuratorate holds as follows：. . . (overview of the conduct of the defendant)，which constituted the Article * * * of *Criminal Law of the People's Republic of China* , and the facts are clear and evidence is hard and sufficient. Therefore, the defendant shall be held criminally liable. In accordance with . . . （the legal and discretionary sentencing circumstances and relevant legal provisions），here offers a sentencing recommendation of . . . （specific sentencing recommendation）. In accordance with the

此致

××省××市××区人民法院

检察员：×××

（院印）

××年××月××日

附：

1. 被告人现在处所……（在押被告人的羁押场所或监视居住、取保候审的处所）

2. 案卷材料和证据××册。

3. 有关涉案款物情况。

4. 被害人（单位）附带民事诉讼情况。

5.《认罪认罚从宽制度告知书》《认罪认罚具结书》《刑事案件证据开示清单》各一份。

6.《适用速裁程序/简易程序建议书》一份。

7. 其他需要附注的事项。

Article 176 of *Criminal Procedure Law of the People's Republic of China*, this procuratorate initiates a public prosecution for the people's court to sentence by law.

To

The People's Court of ＊＊＊ District of ＊＊＊ City, ＊＊＊ Province

Procurator：＊＊＊

Stamp of thisprocuratorate

＊＊＊（day/month/year）

Appendix：

1. The compulsory measure of the defendant ...（held in custody, under residential confinement or bail）

2. Case file in ＊＊ volumes.

3. List of property involved in the case.

4. Incidental civil actions of a victim.

5. One *Notification of leniency system on admission of guilt and acceptance of punishment*, one *Recognizance to admit guilt and accept punishment*, and one *List of evidence for criminal case*.

6. One *Recommendation for Summary Procedure/Fast－Track Sentencing Procedure*.

7. Others.

# 认罪认罚具结书

| 中文版 | 英文版 |
|---|---|
| **认罪认罚具结书** | **Recognizance to Admit Guilt and Accept Punishment** |
| 一、犯罪嫌疑人身份信息<br>本人姓名××，……（其他详细信息）<br>二、权利知悉<br>本人已阅读《认罪认罚从宽制度告知书》，且理解并接受其全部内容，本人××自愿适用认罪认罚从宽制度，同意适用简易程序/速裁程序/普通程序。 | 1. Personal information of the suspect<br>My name is... （other detailed information）<br>2. Awareness of legal rights<br>I have read the *Notification of Leniency System on Admission of Guilt and Acceptance of Punishment* , and I have fully understood and accepted the contents therein. I voluntarily agree with the application of leniency system on admission of guilt and acceptance of punishment, and summary procedure/ fast-track sentencing procedure/ ordinary procedure. |
| 三、认罪认罚内容<br><br>本人××知悉并认可如下内容：<br><br>1.××区/县人民检察院指控本人×××的犯罪事实，构成××××罪。<br><br>2.××区/县人民检察院提出的有期徒刑××至××的量刑建议。 | 3. The contents on admission of guilt and acceptance of punishment<br>I am aware of and agree with the contents of the following subparagraphs：<br>3.1. The facts of the crime charged by the People's Procuratorate of ＊＊＊ district against me constitute the crime of ＊＊＊.<br>3.2. The People's Procuratorate of ＊＊＊ district makes a sentencing recommendation of a fixed-term imprisonment from ＊＊＊ to ＊＊＊ years. |

3. 本案适用简易程序/速裁程序/普通程序。

四、自愿签署声明

本人学历××，我已获得翻译服务，因此我已完全清楚理解本文内容。

本人就具结书内容已经听取辩护人/值班律师的法律意见，知悉认罪认罚可能导致的法律后果。

本《认罪认罚具结书》是本人在知情和自愿的情况下签署的，未受任何暴力、威胁或任何其他形式的非法影响，亦未受任何可能损害本人理解力和判断力的毒品、药物或酒精物质的影响，除了本《认罪认罚具结书》载明的内容，本人没有获得其他任何关于案件处理的承诺。

本人已阅读、理解并认可本《认罪认罚具结书》的每一项内容，上述内容真实、准确、完整。

3. 3. A summary procedure/fast－track sentencing procedure/ordinary procedure shall be applied for this case.

4. Voluntary declaration

My education background is ＊＊＊, and I have received translation service, therefore I have fully understood the contents in Chinese of this document.

Regarding the article 3, I have received the advice from my defender/the duty lawyer, and I am aware of the legal consequence of admission of guilt and acceptance of punishment.

This *Recognizance to Admit Guilt and Accept Punishment* is signed by myself voluntarily, free from by any illegal means such as violence, threats or others, and from any drugs or alcoholic substances that may impair my understanding and judgment. Besides the contents on this *Recognizance to Admit Guilt and Accept Punishment*, I do not have any other promises on the handling of this case.

I have read all parts of this *Recognizance to Admit Guilt and Accept Punishment*, and fully understood and accepted the contents herein. The content above is true, accurate and complete.

| | |
|---|---|
| 本人签名：×× | Signature（Criminal Suspect or Defendant）： |
| ×× 年 ×× 月 ×× 日 | *＊＊（day/month/year） |
| 本人是犯罪嫌疑人、被告人××的辩护人/值班律师，本人证明，犯罪嫌疑人、被告人××已经阅读了《认罪认罚具结书》及《认罪认罚从宽制度告知书》，犯罪嫌疑人、被告人××系自愿签署了上述《认罪认罚具结书》。 | I am the defender/the duty lawyer of *＊＊（Criminal Suspect or Defendant）. I, hereby, certify that *＊＊（Criminal suspect or defendant）has read this *Recognizance to Admit Guilt and Accept Punishment* and *Notification of Leniency System on Admission of Guilt and Acceptance of Punishment*, and signed this *Recognizance to Admit Guilt and Accept Punishment* voluntarily. |
| 签名：×× | Signature（the defender or the duty lawyer）： |
| 日期： | Date of signing：*＊＊（day/month/year） |

## 认罪认罚从宽制度告知书

| 中文版 | 英文版 |
|---|---|
| **认罪认罚从宽制度告知书** | **Notification of Leniency System on Admission of Guilt and Acceptance of Punishment** |
| 一、适用认罪认罚从宽制度，犯罪嫌疑人、被告人应当书面签署本《认罪认罚从宽制度告知书》及《认罪认罚具结书》。该《认罪认罚具结书》 | 1. Where a leniency system on admission of guilt and acceptance of punishment is applied, the criminal suspect or defendant shall sign this *Notification of* |

应经辩护人或值班律师签字确认，方为有效。

二、《认罪认罚具结书》载明：犯罪嫌疑人基本信息、认罪认罚情况、被指控的罪名及适用的条款、检察机关对犯罪嫌疑人拟提出的从轻、减轻或者免除处罚等从宽处罚的建议；认罪认罚后案件处理适用的程序及其他需要听取意见的情形。

三、检察机关根据犯罪嫌疑人、被告人的犯罪情节、认罪情形拟出量刑建议。犯罪嫌疑人、被告人如有其他法定、酌定从轻、减轻处罚情节，应适当调整量刑幅度。具体量刑幅度，犯罪嫌疑人、被告人或其辩护人／值班律师可以向检察机关提出意见。

*Leniency System on Admission of Guilt and Acceptance of Punishment* and a *Recognizance to Admit Guilt and Accept Punishment*. This *Recognizance to Admit Guilt and Accept Punishment* shall be signed and confirmed by the defender or duty lawyer to be effective.

2. This *Recognizance to Admit Guilt and Accept Punishment* shall have following contents: basic information of the criminal suspect, information on admission of guilt and acceptance of punishment, charges filed and applicable provisions of law, sentencing recommendation on lenient punishment, such as lighter punishment, mitigated punishment, and exemption from punishment from the people's procuratorate, procedures applicable to the trial of the case after the criminal suspect admits guilt and accepts punishment and other matters requiring their opinions.

3. Procuratorates shall offer a sentencing recommendation to the criminal suspect or defendant on the circumstances of a crime and the information on admission of guilt. Where a criminal suspect or defendant has othercircumstances of a lesser punishment or a mitigated punishment of either legal or discretionary nature,

四、犯罪嫌疑人、被告人签署《认罪认罚具结书》后，人民法院一般将直接依据《认罪认罚具结书》及相应《起诉书》载明的内容认定其犯罪事实，且人民法院对人民检察院作出的量刑建议一般应予采纳。

五、《认罪认罚具结书》签署后，犯罪嫌疑人、被告人可以要求撤回，但应书面向办案机关提出申请，人民检察院将重新作出量刑建议。犯罪嫌疑人、被告人未提出书面撤回申请，但对《认罪认罚具结书》确认的及《起诉书》载明的主要犯罪事实、罪名和认罪表述提出异议或变更的，视为撤回《认罪认罚具结书》。

procuratorates shall adjust sentencing range accordingly. The defender/the duty lawyer of a criminal suspect or defendant may offer opinions on concrete sentencing range to procuratorates.

4. When the criminal suspect or defendant has signed the *Recognizance to Admit Guilt and Accept Punishment*, people's court generally finds criminal facts based on the contents in the *Recognizance to Admit Guilt and Accept Punishment* and the *Bill of Indictment*, and people's court generally adopts the sentencing recommendation from the people's procuratorate.

5. When a *Recognizance to Admit Guilt and Accept Punishment* is signed, the criminal suspect or defendant may file a withdrawal request, but the application to the handling authority should be in writing, and the people's procuratorate shall renew the sentencing recommendation. Where the criminal suspect or defendant has not filed a withdrawal request, but raises any objection or applies for modification to the main facts of a crime, the charges or the statement of the admission of guilt, the *Recognizance to Admit Guilt and Accept Punishment* is treated as withdrawn.

六、犯罪嫌疑人、被告人撤回《认罪认罚具结书》，犯罪嫌疑人、被告人已签署过的《认罪认罚具结书》不能作为本人认罪认罚的依据，但仍可能作为其曾作有罪供述的证据，由人民法院结合其他证据对本案事实进行认定。

七、犯罪嫌疑人、被告人撤回《认罪认罚具结书》后，经人民检察院同意重新签署《认罪认罚具结书》的，人民检察院应基于新签署的《认罪认罚具结书》重新作出量刑建议；犯罪嫌疑人、被告人撤回《认罪认罚具结书》，后又重新确认该《认罪认罚具结书》内容的，仍应重新签署《认罪认罚具结书》。

八、经协商，犯罪嫌疑人、被告人如不同意检察机关的量刑建议，有权不签署《认罪认罚具结书》，不适用本制度。

6. Where the criminal suspect or defendant has withdrawn the *Recognizance to Admit Guilt and Accept Punishment*, it cannot be used as the evidence of admission of guilt and acceptance of punishment hereof, but shall be considered as an evidence of confession of guilt. The people's court shall find the facts in light of this and other evidence.

7. Where the criminal suspect or defendant has withdrawn the *Recognizance to Admit Guilt and Accept Punishment*, but agrees to re-sign it with the permission of the people's procuratorate, the people's procuratorate shall renew the sentencing recommendation based on the updated *Recognizance to Admit Guilt and Accept Punishment*. Where the criminal suspect or defendant has withdrawn the *Recognizance to Admit Guilt and Accept Punishment* but reconfirmed the same one later, he or she shall re-sign the *Recognizance to Admit Guilt and Accept Punishment*.

8. After negotiation, if the criminal suspect or defendant disagrees with the sentencing recommendation from people's procuratorates, he or she has the right not to sign the *Recognizance to Admit Guilt and Accept Punishment*, and is not subject to

| | |
|---|---|
| 　　本人已阅读并完全理解上述《认罪认罚从宽制度告知书》，并由本人签署后附卷留存。<br><br><br><br><br>　　签名：<br><br><br>　　日期： | this leniency system on admission of guilt and acceptance of punishment.<br>　　I have read and fully understood this *Notification of Leniency System on Admission of Guilt and Acceptance of Punishment*, and the copy hereof signed by me shall be attached to the case file and well-preserved.<br><br><br>　　Signature（Criminal Suspect or Defendant）：<br><br>　　＊＊＊（day/month/year） |

# 相关英文表达

| 英文表达 | 中文意思 |
|---|---|
| in accordance with Chinese law | 根据中国法律 |
| audio-visual record | 录音录像 |
| assume obligation accordingly | 承担相应的义务 |
| non-prosecution | 不起诉 |
| cause no serious harm | 危害不大 |
| initiate a prosecution against | 起诉某人 |
| file a petition | 申诉 |
| at the next higher level | 上一级 |
| institute an action directly | 提起自诉 |
| legal effect | 法律后果 |
| disclosure of the evidence | 证据开示 |

续表

| 英文表达 | 中文意思 |
| --- | --- |
| summary procedure | 简易程序 |
| fast-track sentencing procedure | 速裁程序 |
| incidental civil action | 附带民事诉讼 |
| recognizance to admit guilt and accept punishment | 认罪认罚具结书 |
| leniency system on admission of guilt and acceptance of punishment | 认罪认罚从宽制度 |
| alcoholic substances | 酒精物质 |
| impair understanding and judgment | 影响理解力和判断力 |
| duty lawyer | 值班律师 |
| exemption from punishment | 免除处罚 |
| sentencing range | 量刑幅度 |
| in light of | 鉴于…… |
| be subject to | 受……约束 |

# 一审阶段

## 被告人权利义务告知书

| 中文版 | 英文版 |
| --- | --- |
| **被告人权利义务告知书**<br><br>被告人：<br>　　人民检察院诉你犯罪一案，现已进入审判程序，根据《中华人民共和国刑事诉讼法》及其他有关法律的规定，被告人在刑事诉讼中既享有权利， | **Notification of Rights and Obligations to Defendant**<br>Defendant of this case,<br>　　Thecriminal case against you prosecuted by the People's Procuratorate, has now entered the trial procedure. In accordance with the *Criminal Procedure Law of* |

也承担相应的义务。现将被告人在第一审程序中享有的权利义务的主要内容告知如下：

一、被告人的权利

1. 有要求用本民族语言文字进行诉讼的权利，不通晓当地通用语言的被告人有权要求人民法院提供翻译。

2. 有权获得辩护，人民法院有义务保证被告人获得辩护：

（1）被告人除自己行使辩护权以外，还可以委托1人至2人作为辩护人。下列的人可以被委托为辩护人：律师；人民团体或者犯罪嫌疑人、被告人所在单位推荐的人；犯罪嫌疑人、被告人的监护人、亲友；正在被执行刑罚或者依法被剥夺、限制人身自由的人，不得担任辩护人。

（2）人民法院自受理案件之日起

the People's Republic of China and other relevant laws, the defendant in criminal procedure enjoys rights and assumes corresponding obligations. The rights and obligations at the first instance are notified as follows：

1. Rights of Defendant

1. 1. You shall have the right to use your native language in litigation. Litigation participants who are not familiar with the commonly used local language shall have rights to request people's courts to provide interpretation.

1. 2. You shall have the right to defense, and the people's court shall have the duty to ensure that a defendant acquires defense：

1. 2. 1. In addition to defending himself or herself, a defendant may retain one or two defenders. The following persons may serve as defenders：a lawyer; a person recommended by a people's organization or the employer of a criminal suspect or defendant; and a guardian, relative, or friend of a criminal suspect or defendant. A person who is serving a criminal sentence or whose personal freedom is deprived of or restricted in accordance with the law shall not serve as a defender.

1. 2. 2. A people's court shall, within

3日以内，应当告知被告人有权委托辩护人。被告人在押期间要求委托辩护人的，人民法院、人民检察院和公安机关应当及时转达其要求。被告人在押的，也可以由其监护人、近亲属代为委托辩护人。

（3）被告人因经济困难或者其他原因没有委托辩护人的，本人及其近亲属可以向法律援助机构提出申请。对符合法律援助条件的，法律援助机构应当指派律师为其提供辩护。

被告人是盲、聋、哑人，或者是尚未完全丧失辨认或者控制自己行为能力的精神病人，没有委托辩护人的，人民法院、人民检察院和公安机关应当通知法律援助机构指派律师为其提供辩护。

被告人可能被判处无期徒刑、死刑，没有委托辩护人的，人民法院、人民检察院和公安机关应当通知法律援助机构指派律师为其提供辩护。

three days after accepting a case, inform a defendant that the defendant has the right to retain a defender. If a defendant in custody files a request for retaining a defender, the people's court, people's procuratorate, and public security authority shall convey such a request in a timely manner. For a defendant in custody, his or her guardian or close relative may retain a defender on his or her behalf.

1.2.3. Where a defendant has not retained a defender for financial hardship or other reasons, the defendant or his or her close relative may file an application with a legal aid agency. If the legal aid conditions are met, the legal aid agency shall designate a lawyer to defend him or her.

Where a defendant suffers vision, hearing, or speech impairment or is a mental patient who has not completely lost the ability to recognize or control his or her behavior, if he or she has not retained a defender, the people's court, people's procuratorate, and public security authority shall notify a legal aid agency to designate a lawyer to defend him or her.

Where a defendant who may be sentenced to life imprisonment or death penalty has not retained a defender, the people's court, people's procuratorate,

（4）在审判过程中，被告人可以拒绝辩护人继续为其辩护，也可以另行委托辩护人辩护。

3. 未经人民法院依法判决，不得被确定为有罪。

4. 对审判人员、检察人员和侦查人员侵犯其诉讼权利和人身侮辱的行为有控告的权利。

5. 有要求具有下列情形之一的审判人员、检察人员、侦查人员、翻译人员、书记员、鉴定人回避的权利：

（1）是本案的当事人或者是当事人的近亲属的。

（2）本人或者其近亲属和本案有利害关系的。

（3）担任过本案的证人、鉴定人、辩护人、诉讼代理人的。

（4）与本案当事人有其他利害关系，可能影响公正处理案件的。

and public security authority shall notify a legal aid agency to designate a lawyer to defend him or her.

1.2.4. At trial, a defendant may refuse to continue retaining a defender and may retain another defender.

1.3. No person shall be found guilty without being judged so by a people's court in accordance with the law.

1.4. You have the right to file accusations against judges, prosecutors, and investigators who infringe upon their procedural rights or inflict personal insult on them.

1.5. You have the right to request the disqualification of a judge, prosecutor, or investigator, court clerks, interpreters, and identification or evaluation experts any of the following circumstances：

1.5.1. Any thereof is a party to the case or a close relative of a party to the case.

1.5.2. Any thereof is an interested party to the case.

1.5.3. Any thereof once served as a witness, identification or evaluation expert, defender, or litigation representative in the case.

1.5.4. Any thereof has any other relationship with a party, which may affect the just handling of the case.

（5）接受当事人及其委托的人请客送礼的。

（6）违反规定会见当事人及其委托的人的。

对驳回申请回避的决定，被告人及其法定代理人可以申请复议一次。

6. 有不被强迫证实自己有罪的权利，即公诉案件中被告人有罪的举证责任由人民检察院承担，自诉案件中被告人有罪的举证责任由自诉人承担，审判人员、检察人员、侦查人员不得强迫任何人证实自己有罪。

7. 有申请人民法院对以非法方法收集的证据依法予以排除的权利。申请排除以非法方法收集的证据的，应当提供相关线索或者材料。

8. 被告人及其法定代理人、近亲属或者辩护人有申请变更强制措施的权利。人民法院、人民检察院和公安机关收到申请后，应当在 3 日以内作出决定；不同意变更强制措施的，应

1.5.5. Any thereof accepts treats and gifts from the parties and their agents.

1.5.6. Any thereof meets the parties and their agents in violation of relevant legal provisions.

Against a decision that dismisses a request for disqualification, the party or his or her legal representative may apply for reconsideration once.

1.6. You have the right not to be forced to commit self-incrimination. The burden of proof of guilty of the defendant in a public prosecution case shall fall on the people's procuratorate, while that in a private prosecution case shall fall on the private prosecutor. Judges, prosecutors, and criminal investigators must, under no circumstances, force anyone to commit self-incrimination.

1.7. You have the right to apply to a people's court for excluding illegally obtained evidence. Relevant clues or materials shall be provided for an application for excluding illegally obtained evidence.

1.8. A defendant or his or her legal representative, close relative, or defender has the right to apply for modifying a compulsory measure. A people's court, people's procuratorate, or public security

当告知申请人，并说明不同意的理由。

authority shall make a decision within three days after receiving such an application; and, if a disapproval decision is made, the applicant shall be informed of the decision and reasons for disapproval.

9. 被告人及其法定代理人、近亲属对于人民法院、人民检察院或者公安机关采取强制措施法定期限届满的，有权要求解除强制措施。

1.9. A defendant or his or her legal representative, close relative, or defender shall have the right to requiretermination of a compulsory measure taken by a people's court, a people's procuratorate, or a public security authority when the term of the compulsory measure expires.

10. 对司法机关及其工作人员的下列行为有申诉或控告的权利：

1.10. You have the right to file a petition or accusation with a judicial authority regarding any of the following conduct of the judicial authority or any of its personnel:

（1）采取强制措施法定期限届满，不予以释放，解除或者变更的。

1.10.1. Refusing to release a criminal suspect or defendant or terminate or modify a compulsory measure taken, when the statutory term of the compulsory measure expires.

（2）应当退还取保候审保证金不退还的。

1.10.2. Refusing to refund a bail bond that shall be refunded.

（3）对与案件无关的财物采取查封、扣押，冻结措施的。

1.10.3. Seizing, impounding, or freezing any property irrelevant to a case.

（4）应当解除查封、扣押、冻结不解除的。

1.10.4. Refusing to terminate a measure of seizing, impounding, or freezing property that shall be terminated.

（5）贪污，挪用，私分，调换，违反规定使用查封、扣押、冻结的财物的。

受理申诉或者控告的机关应当及时处理。对处理不服的，可以向同级人民检察院申诉；人民检察院直接受理的案件，可以向上一级人民检察院申诉。人民检察院对申诉应当及时进行审查，情况属实的，通知有关机关予以纠正。

11. 对涉及商业秘密的案件有申请不公开审理的权利。

12. 对用作证据的鉴定意见有被告知和申请补充鉴定、重新鉴定的权利。

13. 有要求出示物证并对物证进行辨认的权利，有要求对未到庭的证人的证言笔录、鉴定人的鉴定意见、勘验笔录和其他作为证据的文书当庭

1. 10. 5. Embezzling, misappropriating, distributing in private, replacing, or illegally using any seized, impounded, or frozen property.

The authority accepting the petition or accusation shall handle it in a timely manner. Against the handling result, the party or the defender or litigation representative thereof or the interested party may file a petition with the people's procuratorate at the same level; or, if the case is directly accepted by the people's procuratorate, may file a petition with the people's procuratorate at the next higher level. The people's procuratorate shall examine the petition in a timely manner and, if it is true, notify the relevant authority to make correction.

1. 11. You have the right to apply forthe case involving any trade secret not be heard in open court.

1. 12. You have the right to be informed of the expert opinion to be used as evidence and apply for a supplementary identification or evaluation or a supplementary evaluation or re-evaluation.

1. 13. You have the right to request the adducing and identification of physical evidence, and the reading out of a statement of a witness who is not in court, an

宣读，并要求审判人员听取自己意见的权利。

14. 在法庭审理过程中，有申请通知新的证人到庭、调取新的物证，申请重新鉴定或者勘验的权利。有申请法庭通知有专门知识的人出庭，就鉴定人作出的鉴定意见提出意见的权利。

15. 在法庭审理过程中，有对证据和案件情况发表意见并进行相互辩论的权利。

16. 在辩论终结后，有最后陈述的权利。

17. 有要求核对、补充或者改正法庭笔录的权利。

18. 自诉案件的被告人在诉讼过程中有提起反诉的权利。

19. 对人民法院第一审的判决、裁定有上诉和上诉不加刑的权利。

expert opinion of an identification or evaluation expert who is not in court, transcripts of crime scene investigation and other documentation serving as evidence. You have the right to request the judge to hear your opinions thereupon.

1.14. During a court session, you have the right to request that a new witness be called to the court, that new physical evidence be submitted, or that a new forensic identification or evaluation or crime scene investigation be conducted. You have the right to request the court to call a person with expertise to appear before court to offer an opinion on the expert opinion of an identification or evaluation expert.

1.15. During a court session, you have the right to present opinions on the evidence and merits of a case and debate with opposing parties.

1.16. You have the right to present a closing statement an end of debate.

1.17. You have the right to request confirmation, supplements or corrections of the court transcripts.

1.18. During litigation of a case of private prosecution, the defendant may file a counterclaim against the private prosecutor.

1.19. Against a sentence or ruling of a people's court at first instance, you

20. 对已经发生法律效力的判决、裁定，有向人民法院、人民检察院申诉的权利。

21. 犯罪的时候不满 18 周岁，被判处五年有期徒刑以下刑罚的被告人，享有犯罪记录封存的权利。

22. 被告人的人身权利和财产权利因行使侦查、检察、审判职权的机关以及看守所、监狱管理机关及其工作人员违法行使职权而受到侵犯的，有获得国家赔偿的权利。

二、被告人的义务

1. 被告人有接受符合法定条件和程序的拘传、取保候审、监视居住、拘留、逮捕等强制措施，接受符合法定条件和程序的讯问、勘验、检查、搜查、查封、扣押、冻结、技术侦查等司法行为的义务。

have the right to appeal.

1. 20. You may file a petition with a people's court or a people's procuratorate against an effective sentence or ruling.

1. 21. Where a juvenile has not attained the age of 18 when committing a crime and is sentenced to fixed-term imprisonment of five years or a lighter punishment, the related criminal records shall be sealed for preservation.

1. 22. Where the personal rights and property rights of a defendant are violated by criminal investigation authority, procuratorial authority, people's court, detention centers, or prison administration, and personnel thereof who illegally exercise their powers, he or she has the right to state compensation.

2. Obligations of Defendant

2. 1. A defendant has the obligation to accept forced appearance, bail, residential confinement, detention, arrest and other compulsory measures which meets legal conditions and procedures, and interrogation, crime scene investigation, examination, search, seizure, impoundment, freezing of property, technical investigation and other judicial acts which meets legal conditions and procedures.

2. 被取保候审的被告人有提出保证人或者交纳保证金的义务。

3. 被取保候审的被告人有遵守下列规定的义务：

（1）未经执行机关批准不得离开所居住的市、县。

（2）住址、工作单位和联系方式发生变动的，在24小时以内向执行机关报告。

（3）在传讯的时候及时到案。

（4）不得以任何形式干扰证人作证。

（5）不得毁灭、伪造证据或者串供。

人民法院还可以根据案件情况，责令被取保候审的被告人遵守以下一项或多项规定：

（1）不得进入特定的场所。

（2）不得与特定的人员会见或者通信。

（3）不得从事特定的活动。

（4）将护照等出入境证件、驾驶证件交执行机关保存。

2.2. A bailed defendant has the right to provide a surety or pay a bond.

2.3. A bailed defendant shall comply with the following provisions：

2.3.1. Not leaving the city or county where he or she resides without the approval of the execution authority.

2.3.2. Reporting any change of his or her residence address, employer, or contact information to the execution authority within 24 hours of suchchange.

2.3.3. Appearing before court in a timely manner when summoned.

2.3.4. Not interfering in any way with the testimony of witnesses.

2.3.5. Not destroying or forging evidence or making a false confession in collusion.

Based on the circumstances of a case, a people's court may order a bailed criminal suspect or defendant to comply with one or more of the following provisions：

2.3.6. Not entering particular places.

2.3.7. Not meeting or communicating with particular persons.

2.3.8. Not engaging in particular activities.

2.3.9. Delivering his or her passport and other international travel credentials

4. 被监视居住的被告人有遵守下列规定的义务：

（1）未经执行机关批准不得离开执行监视居住的处所。

（2）未经执行机关批准不得会见他人或者通信。

（3）在传讯的时候及时到案。

（4）不得以任何形式干扰证人作证。

（5）不得毁灭、伪造证据或者串供。

（6）将护照等出入境证件、身份证件、驾驶证件交执行机关保存。

签字　手印：

日期：

and driver's license to the execution authority for preservation.

2.4. A criminal suspect or defendant under residential confinement shall comply with the following provisions：

2.4.1. Not leaving the residence where residential confinement is executed without the approval of the execution authority.

2.4.2. Not meeting or communicating with others without the approval of the execution authority.

2.4.3. Appearing before court in a timely manner when summoned.

2.4.4. Not interfering in any way with the testimony of witnesses.

2.4.5. Not destroying or forging evidence or making a false confession in collusion.

2.4.6. Delivering his or her passport and other international travel credentials and driver's license to the execution authority for preservation.

Please sign and press your inked thumbprint on your signature here（Defendant）：

＊＊＊（day/month/year）

# 人民法院法庭纪律

| 中文版 | 英文版 |
|---|---|
| **人民法院法庭纪律**　　为落实公开审判制度，除法律规定的不公开审理的案件外，本院所有案件一律公开审理、公开宣判。审判法庭是人民法院行使审判权、审理各类案件的场所，为维护法庭秩序，保障审判活动的正常进行，根据诉讼法及《中华人民共和国人民法院法庭规则》等有关规定，特规定如下：　　一、诉讼参与人需凭传票等法律文书进入法庭，旁听人员需持有效身份证件参加旁听，人大代表、政协委员可持代表证、委员证参加旁听。学校、机关等单位需要集体旁听的，应当事先与法院办公室联系，领取旁听证后在指定时间、地点参加旁听。 | **Court Discipline of the People's Court**　　In order to implement the open court system, except for cases that shall not be heard in open court in accordance with the law, a people's court of first instance shall hear cases openly. Trial courts are places where people's courts exercise judicial powers and try various cases. In order to maintain the court order and ensure the normal legal proceedings, according to the *Procedural Law and the Rules of the People's Courts of the People's Republic of China* and other relevant provisions, the court discipline is as follows:　　1. Litigation participants may enter a court on the basis of a subpoena or other legal documents, and observers of a court must have a valid ID, and NPC deputies and CPPCC members can may observe a court with NPC deputy certificates and CPPCC member certificates. Where schools, government departments or other organizations need to observe a court, they need to contact the court office in advance and receive observation tickets prior to observing the court at a designated time and place. |

二、下列人员不得旁听：

1. 未成年人（经法院批准的除外）；

2. 精神病人和醉酒的人；

3. 其他不宜旁听的人。

三、诉讼参与人、旁听人员应自觉接受司法警察的安全检查，禁止将枪支、弹药、刀具、火种及易燃易爆等危险品带入法庭。

四、诉讼参与人、旁听人员必须在指定的区域活动，不准进入办公区，不得在楼内大声喧哗。

五、诉讼参与人发言、陈述和辩论，须经审判长或者独任审判员许可，并不得使用辱骂、讽刺、中伤等不文明语言。

六、诉讼参与人、旁听人员进入法庭应关闭随身携带的移动通信工具或将其调至静音模式。

七、旁听人员必须遵守下列纪律：

1. 不得录音、录像和摄影；

2. The following persons shall not observe a court：

2. 1. Juveniles（unless approved by the people's court）；

2. 2. Mental patients or intoxicated-person；or

2. 3. Other persons that are not inappropriate to observe a court.

3. Litigation participants or observers shall be subject to the security check by judicial police，carrying hazardous articles like guns，ammunition，knives，kindling or explosive and combustible products is prohibited in a court.

4. Litigation participants or observers shall be at designated places and keep quiet，and are not allowed to enter office area.

5. With the permission of the presiding judge，the litigation participants may present opinions，make a statement or debate，any of the abusing，satiric or slanderous or other rude language is prohibited.

6. Litigation participants or observers shall switch off all the mobile devices or turn them to mute.

7. Observers shall observe the following rules：

7. 1. Do not record, film or take photos；

2. 不得随意走动和进入审判区；

3. 不得发言、提问，如对审判活动有意见，可在休庭或闭庭后书面向法庭提出；

4. 不得鼓掌、喧哗、哄闹和实施其他妨害审判活动的行为。

八、诉讼参与人和旁听人员应保持法庭整洁，不准吸烟、吃零食、随地吐痰和乱扔纸屑。

九、新闻记者参加旁听进行采访需经法院办公室核准登记，并配发专用采访证；未经审判长许可，不得在庭审过程中录音、录像和摄影。

十、对于违反法庭纪律的人，审判长可以口头警告、训诫，也可以没收录音、录像和摄影器材，责令退出法庭或者经院长批准予以罚款、拘留。

7. 2. Do not walk around without permission or enter the trial area;

7. 3. If any observer had any opinions on the trial activities, he or she may present them to the court in writing after the adjournment or closure of the court; or

7. 4. Do not applaud, make noise, clamor or commit other acts that disrupt the order of the courtroom.

8. Litigation participants or observers shall keep tidy of the courtroom, and not smoke, eat snacks, spit on the floor or litter.

9. Presses need to be verified by and register in the court office and obtain special interview pass prior to the observation; without the approval of the presiding judge, no one is allowed torecord, film or take photographs during a court session.

10. Where any litigation participant or observer violates the order of the courtroom, the presiding judge shall verbally warn the person and order admonishment, or confiscate audio-visual recording or photographic equipment, force the person out of the court or fine and detain the person. The fine or detention must be subject to the approval of the president of the people's court.

| | |
|---|---|
| 　　对哄闹、冲击法庭，侮辱、诽谤、威胁、殴打审判人员等严重扰乱法庭秩序的人，依法追究刑事责任；情节较轻的，予以罚款、拘留。 | 　　Whoever interrupts or impacts a court session or insults, defames, intimidates, or batters judicial personnel or litigation participants, seriously disturbing the order of the courtroom and constituting a crime, shall be subject to criminal liability in accordance with the law; for those whose circumstances are minor, fine or detention shall be executed. |

# 延长审限问答示例

| 中文版 | 英文版 |
|---|---|
| 　　问：根据《中华人民共和国刑事诉讼法》第 208 条，你的案件需要延长审限 2 个月，因此你需要被延长羁押，请在这个通知书上签字确认。 | 　　Q: According to the Article 208 of the *Criminal Procedure Law of the People's Republic of China*, the period of the trial for this case may be extended for three months. Please sign your name on this notification hereof. |
| 　　答：好的/我不签字。 | 　　A：OK. /I am not signing on it. |
| 　　问：无论你签字与否，审限都会延长。我只是来通知你的。 | 　　Q: You need to know that it will be extended no matter you sign or not. I am here only to notify you about it. |
| 　　答：好吧。 | 　　A：Fine. |

# 一审法院当庭高频问答

| 中文版 | 英文版 |
|---|---|
| 问：下面核对被告人身份。你的全名叫什么？ | Q：Now I am going to verify the identity of the defendant. What is your full name？ |
| 答：我叫×××。 | A：My full name is . . . |
| 问：有无曾用名？ | Q：Do you have any former name？ |
| 答：有，叫×××/没有。 | A：Yes, it was. . ./No. |
| 问：你的生日？ | Q：When is your birthday？ |
| 答：××年××月××日。 | A：it's . . . |
| 问：你的住址？ | Q：Where is your address？ |
| 答：…… | A：. . . |
| 问：《起诉书》收到没有？ | Q：Have you received the *Bill of Indictment*？ |
| 答：收到了。 | A：Yes. |
| 问：何时收到的起诉书？ | Q：When did you receive it？ |
| 答：…… | A：. . . |
| 问：你是否申请回避？ | Q：Do you apply for disqualification？ |
| 答：不申请/我申请回避，理由是…… | A：No. /Yes, I apply for disqualification of . . . . the reason is. . . |
| 问：你对检察院起诉指控的犯罪事实有无异议？ | Q：Do you raise an objection to the facts of the crime that you are charged with？ |
| 答：没有异议/有的，…… | A：No. /Yes, . . . |
| 问：你在侦查阶段作的供述是否属实？ | Q：Are your confessions truthful during investigation？ |
| 答：属实。 | A：Yes. |

问：你是否自愿认罪？

答：我认罪/我不认罪，我是无辜的。

问：你是否愿意退出犯罪所得？

答：愿意的/我没有犯罪，为什么要退？

问：被告人，以上证据要不要阅看？

答：我需要阅看/不需要。

问：法警，向被告人展示该证据。

…………

问：被告人，对以上证据有无意见？

答：我有意见……/我没有意见。

问：被告人的辩护人，对以上证据有无意见？

答：有的……/我没有意见。

问：公诉人，继续举证……

答：尊敬的法官，我记性不好，能否给我一张纸、一支笔？我不想漏掉重要的细节。

问：法警，给他纸笔。

问：被告人，你有无证据要提交？

Q：Do you confess to your crime?

A：I confess to my crime./I don't confess. I am innocent.

Q：Are you willing to return the illegally obtained money?

A：Yes, I am willing to return it./I am innocent. Why should I return it?

Q：Defendant, do you want to verify the evidence yourself?

A：Yes, please./no.

Q：Court police, show defendant this piece of evidence.

…

Q：Defendant, do you hold any opinions to this piece of evidence.

A：Yes, my opinions are …/I have no opinion.

Q：Defense lawyer, do you have any opinions to it?

A：Yes, my opinions are …/I have no opinion.

Q：Prosecutor, keep going. . .

A：Your honor, I have a memory like a sieve. Can I have a pen and paper in order not to miss anything important?

Q：Court police, bring him pen and paper.

Q：Defendant, do you have any evidence to submit?

| 中文版 | 英文版 |
|---|---|
| 答：有的，我这有份……/我没有。 | A：Yes, I have this . . ./No, I don't have any. |
| 问：被告人的辩护人，你有无证据要提交？ | Q：Defense lawyer, do you have any evidence to submit? |
| 答：有的……/我没有。 | A：Yes, . . ./No, I don't have any. |
| 问：被告人，你有无辩护意见要发表吗？ | Q：Defendant, do you have any defending opinions to present? |
| 答：有的……/我没话可说。 | A：Yes, . . ./No, I don't have any. |
| 问：被告人的辩护人，你有无辩护意见要发表？ | Q：Defense lawyer, do you have any defending opinions to present? |
| 答：有的……/我没话可说。 | A：Yes, . . ./No, I don't have any. |
| 问：被告人，根据法律规定，你有发表最后陈述的权利。你现在可以发表。 | Q：Defendant, according to law, you have the right to make a closing statement. Now you may begin. |
| 答：谢谢审判长…… | A：Thank you . . . |

## 一审有罪判决书

| 中文版 | 英文版 |
|---|---|
| **广东省广州市越秀区人民法院<br>刑 事 判 决 书** | **People's Court of Yuexiu District, Guangzhou City, Guangdong Province** |
| ［2021］粤0×××刑初×××号 | Case No. ［2021］Yue ＊ ＊ ＊ ＊ Xing Chu No. ＊ ＊ ＊ |
| 公诉机关：广东省广州市越秀区人民检察院 | Prosecution Institution：The People's Procuratorate of Yuexiu District, Guangzhou City, Guangdong Province |
| 被告人×××，男，××年××月××日出生，×国公民，护照号××××，文化 | Defendant Name：＊ ＊ ＊<br>Gender：Male |

程度小学，住广东省广州市海珠区。

Date of Birth：＊＊＊

Nationality：＊＊＊

Passport Number：＊＊＊＊

Education Background：Primary School level

Address：Haizhu District, Guangzhou City, Guangdong Province

××年××月××日因本案被羁押，××年××月××日被刑事拘留，××年××月××日被逮捕，现羁押于广州市第三看守所。

On suspicion of his involvement in this case, defendant was kept in custody for investigative purposes on ＊＊, and was arrested on ＊＊. He is now held in custody in the Third Detention Center of Guangzhou.

庭审译员：×××, ×××翻译公司

Court Interpreter：＊＊＊, English interpreter with ＊＊Translation Services Co., Ltd.

辩护人×××, ×××律师事务所。

被告人……

公诉机关以××××号起诉书指控被告人×××犯×××罪，于××年××月××日向本院提起公诉。

Defense lawyer：＊＊＊, ＊＊＊Law Firm

Defendant ...

The ＊＊＊ case filed by the prosecution institution against defendant ＊＊＊ with the *Bill of Indictment* of ＊＊＊, was delivered in this court on ＊＊＊ for initiation of a public prosecution.

本院依法受理后，依法组成合议庭，公开开庭审理了本案。广州市越秀区人民检察院指派检察员×××出庭支持公诉，被告人×××及辩护人×××到庭参加诉讼。本案现已审理终结。

After accepting this case in accordance with law, this court formed a in accordance with law, and tried the case in open court. Prosecutors ＊＊＊, assigned by the People's Procuratorate of Yuexiu District, Guangzhou City, appeared in court to support the public prosecution.

公诉机关指控：……

公诉机关提供了相关证据证实上述指控的事实，认为被告人×××无视国家法律……

其行为触犯了《中华人民共和国刑法》第××条第×款、第×款之规定，犯罪事实清楚，证据确实、充分，应当以××××罪追究其刑事责任。被告人×××归案后如实供述自己的罪行，根据《中华人民共和国刑法》第67条第3款之规定，可以从轻处罚。被告人×××自愿认罪认罚，根据《中华人民共和国刑事诉讼法》第15条的规定，可以从宽处理。根据本案的具体情节，建议对被告人×××在有期徒刑10个月。

Defendant, his defense lawyer ××× and the court interpreter ××× participated in the court proceedings. The trial of this case has now been concluded.

The prosecution institution charges the criminal fact as follows：...

The prosecution institution provided relevant evidence to prove the facts charged above, and found that the defendant * * * ignored national laws and...

His conduct violated the provisions of paragraphs * of Article * of the *Criminal Law of the People's Republic of China*. The fact of the crime is clear, and the evidence is hard and sufficient. The defendant shall be subject to criminal liability of ... The defendant truthfully confessed his crime after appearing in court, can be given a lighter punishment in accordance with the provisions of Paragraph 3 of Article 67 of the *Criminal Law of the People's Republic of China*. The defendant voluntarily admits guilt and accepts punishment. According to Article 15 of the *Criminal Procedure Law of the People's Republic of China*, he can be punished with leniency. Based on the specific circumstances of the case, the sentencing recommendation for the defendant * * * is ten-month imprisonment.

被告人×××对公诉机关指控的事实及罪名均无异议，认罪认罚。其辩护人提出：被告人是民警通过电话要求其到派出所投案，是自首；被告人如实供述自己的罪行，自愿认罚；被告人患有艾滋病、肺结核、脉管炎等多种疾病。综上，请求法庭给予被告人适用缓刑。

经审理查明的事实与公诉机关指控的事实一致，本院予以确认。

上述事实，被告人×××在开庭审理时均无异议，并有……证据证实，证据确实、充分，足以认定。

本院认为，被告人×××无视国家法律……其行为已构成……，依法应予以惩处。公诉机关指控被告人×××犯×××罪事实清楚，证据确实充分，指控的罪名成立，本院予以支持。被

Defendant ＊ ＊ ＊ has no objection to the facts of crime and charges filed by the prosecution institution and admits guilt and accepts punishment. The defense lawyer presents opinions that the defendant was summoned by the police to surrender himself over the phone to the police station, which is voluntary surrender; the defendant truthfully confesses to his crime, and voluntarily accepts punishment; the defendant has many diseases such as AIDS, tuberculosis, vasculitis and other diseases. Based on the foregoing reasons, the defense lawyer requests probation for the defendant.

This court confirmed that the facts found on the trial of this case are consistent with the facts charged by the public prosecution institution.

The Defendant ＊ ＊ ＊ had no objections to the above facts during the trial, and was confirmed by evidences like... and others. The evidence is hard and sufficient to ascertain the fact of the crime.

This court holds as follows, the defendant ＊ ＊ ＊ ignored national laws and..., which constituted the crime of ..., shall be punished in accordance with the law. The fact of crime charged by the

告人×××自愿认罪认罚，根据《中华人民共和国刑事诉讼法》第15条，可以从宽处罚。依照《中华人民共和国刑法》第×××条之规定，判决如下：

一、被告人×××犯×××罪，判处有期徒刑10个月，并处罚金人民币1000元。（刑期从判决执行之日起计算。判决执行以前先行羁押的，羁押一日折抵刑期一日。罚金自本判决发生法律效力第二日起10日内一次性向本院缴纳，上缴国库。）

二、依法扣押的作案工具如手机等物品（详见扣押清单），予以没收。

如不服本判决，可在接到判决书

public institution against the defendant was clear and the evidence is hard and sufficient, this court supports the charge herein. The defendant * * * voluntarily admits guilt and accepts punishment. According to Article 15 of the *Criminal Procedure Law of the People's Republic of China*, he can be punished with leniency. In accordance with Article * * * of the *Criminal Law of the People's Republic of China*, this court ruled as follows:

1. The defendant, convicted of * * *, should be sentenced to 10 years imprisonment, together with a fine of 1 thousand RMB. (The term of fixed-term imprisonment is counted as commencing on the date the judgment begins to be executed; where custody has been employed before the judgment begins to be executed, the term is to be shortened by one day for each day spent in custody. Fine shall be paid to this court in one lump sum within ten days from the second day after the effectiveness of this judgment, and handed over to the national treasury.)

2. The seized tools for committing the crime shall be forfeited (see the seizure list for details).

If you disagree with this judgment,

的第二日起10日内，通过本院或者直接向广东省广州市中级人民法院提出上诉。书面上诉的，应当提交上诉状正本1份，副本2份。

审 判 长 ×××
人民陪审员 ×××
人民陪审员 ×××
××××年×月×日
本件与原本核对无异

书 记 员 ×××

you can appeal through this court or directly to the Intermediate People's Court of Guangzhou City, Guangdong Province within ten days from the second day of receipt of this judgment. Where appeal is in written form, one original and two copies of the appeal petition shall be submitted.

Presiding Judge：＊＊＊
People's assessor 1：＊＊＊
People's assessor 2：＊＊＊
　＊＊＊（day/month/year）
This duplicate is verified to be identical with the original.
　Clerk：＊＊＊

# 相关英文表达

| 英文表达 | 中文意思 |
| --- | --- |
| corresponding obligations | 相应的义务 |
| personal freedom is deprived of or restricted | 人身自由被剥夺或限制 |
| life imprisonment | 无期徒刑 |
| death penalty | 死刑 |
| file accusations against | 控告（某人） |
| interested party | 有利害关系的一方 |
| litigation representative | 诉讼代理人 |
| dismisses a request | 驳回申请 |
| commit self-incrimination | 自证其罪 |

续表

| 英文表达 | 中文意思 |
| --- | --- |
| private prosecutor | 自诉人 |
| exclude illegally obtained evidence | 排除非法证据 |
| forensic evaluation | 法医鉴定 |
| crime scene investigation | 勘验 |
| appear before court | 出庭 |
| present a closing statement | 最后陈述 |
| effective sentence or ruling | 生效判决或裁定 |
| be sealed for preservation | 封存 |
| detention center | 看守所 |
| state compensation | 国家赔偿 |
| exercise judicial power | 刑事审判权 |
| court discipline | 法庭纪律 |
| combustible product | 易燃易爆物 |
| litigation participant | 诉讼参与人 |
| presiding judge | 审判长 |
| switch off | 关闭 |
| trial area | 审判区 |
| adjournment or closure of the court | 休庭或闭庭 |
| verbally warn | 口头警告 |
| order admonishment | 训诫 |
| photographic equipment | 摄影器材 |
| force someone out of the court | 责令某人退出法庭 |
| verify the identity of the defendant | 核对被告人身份 |
| former name | 曾用名 |
| Bill of Indictment | 起诉书 |
| raise an objection | 有异议 |

| 英文表达 | 中文意思 |
|---|---|
| have a memory like a sieve | 记性不好 |
| court police | 法警 |
| be kept in custody | 被拘留 |
| court interpreter | 庭审译员 |
| ignored national laws | 无视国家法律 |
| punished with leniency | 从宽处罚 |
| surrender oneself | 自首 |
| ascertain the fact of the crime | 证实犯罪事实 |
| support the charge | 支持指控 |
| one lump sum | 一次性 |
| the effectiveness of this judgment | 判决发生法律效力 |
| be handed over to the national treasury | 上缴国库 |
| appeal is in written form | 书面上诉 |

# 二审阶段

## 延长审限问答示例

| 中文版 | 英文版 |
|---|---|
| 问：根据《中华人民共和国刑事诉讼法》第 243 条，你的案件需要延长审限 2 个月，因此你需要被延长羁押，请在这个通知书上签字确认。<br><br>答：好的/我不签字。 | Q：According to the Article 243 of the *Criminal Procedure Law of the People's Republic of China*, the period of the trial for this case may be extended for two months. Please sign your name on this notification hereof.<br><br>A：OK. / I am not signing on it. |

| | |
|---|---|
| 问：无论你签字与否，审限都会延长。我只是来通知你的。<br><br>答：好吧。 | Q：You need to know that it will be extended no matter you sign or not. I am here only to notify you about it.<br>A：Fine. |

## 二审法院提审高频问答（不开庭审理）

| 中文版 | 英文版 |
|---|---|
| 问：下面核对被告人身份。你的全名叫什么？ | Q：Now I am going to verify the identity of the defendant. What is your full name? |
| 答：我叫…… | A：My full name is ... |
| 问：有无曾用名？ | Q：Do you have any former name? |
| 答：有，叫×××/没有。 | A：Yes, it was... /No. |
| 问：你的生日？ | Q：When is your birthday? |
| 答：××年××月××日。 | A：It's ＊＊. |
| 问：你的住址？ | Q：Where is your address? |
| 答：…… | A：... |
| 问：一审判决书收到没有？ | Q：Have you received the written sentence at the first instance? |
| 答：收到了。 | A：Yes. |
| 问：何时收到的一审判决书？ | Q：When did you receive it? |
| 答：…… | A：... |
| 问：你是否申请回避？ | Q：Do you apply for disqualification? |
| 答：不申请/我申请回避，理由是…… | A：No. /Yes, I apply for disqualification of .... the reason is... |
| 问：你是否提起上诉？ | Q：Have you appealed? |
| 答：我不上诉/我要上诉。 | A：No. /Yes. |

（如要上诉）

问：你对一审判决中认定的事实有无异议？

答：有的……/没有。

问：你对一审判决中适用的法律有无异议？

答：有的……/没有。

问：你是否自愿认罪？

答：我认罪/我不认罪，我是无辜的。

问：你是否愿意退出犯罪所得？

答：愿意的/我没有犯罪，为什么要退？

问：你有无其他证据要提交？

答：有的……/我没有。

问：你可以自我辩护。

答：有的……/我没话可说。

（in case of appeal）

Q：Do you have any objection to the fact of crime found at the first instance?

A：Yes... /No.

Q：Do you have any objection to the applicable provisions of law at the first instance?

A：Yes... /No.

Q：Do you confess to your crime?

A：I confess to my crime. /I don't confess. I am innocent.

Q：Are you willing to return the illegally obtained money?

A：Yes, I am willing to return it. /I am innocent. Why should I return it?

Q：Do you have any other evidence to submit?

A：Yes, I have this ... /No, I don't have any.

Q：You may defend yourself now.

A：OK, ... /No, I don't have anything to say.

# 二审维持原判刑事裁定书

| 中文版 | 英文版 |
| --- | --- |
| **广州市中级人民法院** | **The Intermediate People's Court of Guangzhou City** |
| 刑事判决书<br>［2021］穗中法刑二终字第×××号 | Criminal Ruling<br>Case No. ［2021］ Sui Zhong Fa Xing Er Zhong Zi No. ＊＊＊ |
| 原公诉机关：广东省广州市越秀区人民检察院。 | Prosecution Institution at First Instance：The People's Procuratorate of Yuexiu District, Guangzhou City, Guangdong Province |
| 上诉人（原审被告人）×××（外文名×××，以下简称×××），男，×年×月×日出生，×××国籍，护照号码×××。因本案于×年×月×日被刑事拘留，同年×月×日被逮捕。现押于广州市第三看守所。 | Appellant（Defendant at the First Instance）<br>Name：＊＊＊<br>Gender：Male<br>Date of Birth：＊＊＊<br>Nationality：＊＊＊<br>Passport Number：＊＊＊<br>On suspicion of his involvement in this case, defendant at First Instance was kept in custody for investigative purposes on ＊＊＊ and was arrested on ＊＊＊ of the same year. He is now held in custody in the Third Detention Center of Guangzhou. |
| 辩护人×××，广东×××律师事务所律师。 | Defense lawyer：＊＊＊ from Guangdong ＊＊＊ Law Firm. |

翻译员×××，广州市×××翻译服务有限公司英语翻译员。

广东省广州市越秀区人民法院审理广东省广州市越秀区人民检察院指控原审被告人×××涉嫌×××罪一案，于×年×月×日日作出［2021］粤×××刑初×××号判决。

原审被告人×××不服，提出上诉。本院受理后，依法组成合议庭，于×年×月×日在本院审判法庭公开开庭进行了审理。广州市人民检察院指派代理检察员×××、×××出庭履行职务。上诉人×××及其辩护人×××以及翻译员×××到庭参加诉讼。现已审理终结。

原判认定：
…………

Court Interpreter：＊＊＊, English interpreter from Guangzhou ＊＊＊ Translation Services Co. , Ltd.

People's Court of Yuexiu District, Guangzhou City, Guangdong Province tried the ＊＊＊ case filed by The People's Procuratorate of Yuexiu District, Guangzhou City, Guangdong Province against the defendant ＊＊＊ at the first Instance and rendered the Criminal Judgment ［2021］Yue ＊＊＊ Xing Chu No. ＊＊＊.

On ＊＊＊（day/month/year）, the defendant ＊＊＊ at the first instance made an objection to the judgment and appealed. After accepting this case, this court formed a collegial panel in accordance with the law and tried the case in open court on ＊＊＊（day/month/year）. Acting prosecutors ＊＊＊ and ＊＊＊, assigned by the Intermediate People's Procuratorate of Guangzhou City, appeared in court to perform their duties. The appellant, his defense lawyer ＊＊＊ and the court interpreter ＊＊＊ participated in the court proceedings. The trial of this case has now been concluded.

In the first-instance judgment, the fact was ascertained as follows：…

原判认定上述事实，采纳了原公诉机关在原审庭审中出示质证的……证据。

原判认为，原审被告人×××的行为已构成×××罪。依照《中华人民共和国刑法》第×××条，作出判决：

一、被告人×××犯×××罪，判处有期徒刑 10 个月，并处罚金人民币1000 元。

二、依法扣押的作案工具如手机等物品，予以没收。

上诉人×××提出……要求二审法院对其改判无罪。

上诉人×××的辩护人提出……综上，请二审法院撤销对×××的×××判决，在查明事实后依法改判其无罪。

In the first instance, the fact was ascertained by adopting the following evidence presented by the prosecution institution and cross-examined at the first instance：...

Based on the above-said evidence, the original judgment found conducts of the defendant at the first Instance constituted the crime of ＊＊＊. In accordance with Article ＊＊＊ of the *Criminal Law of the People's Republic of China*, the original court judged as follows：

1. The defendant, convicted of ＊＊＊, should be sentenced to 10 years imprisonment, together with a fine of 1 thousand RMB.

2. The seized tools for committing the crime shall be forfeited.

The appellant presented opinions that ... By foregoing reasons, he pleaded with this court for a judgment of innocence.

The defense lawyer presented opinions that ... Based on foregoing reasons, he requested this court to render a ruling to revoke the original sentence and modify the original sentence to a judgment of innocence after the case facts are ascertained in accordance with the law.

广东省人民检察院出庭检察员意见：现有证据足以证实……一审认定事实清楚，证据确实、充分，定罪量刑均正确，建议二审法院裁定驳回上诉，维持原判。

经审理查明：

…………

1. 认定上述事实，有经一审、二审庭审质证的如下证据证实：……

2. 原判认定上诉人……的证据确实、充分：……

3. 上述各证据之间相互印证，不存在无法排除的矛盾，足以认定……

4. 鉴于……原审被告人×××依法被判处有期徒刑 10 个月，并处罚金 1000 元人民币，并无不当。上诉人×××及其辩护人要求二审改判无罪，不予采纳。

Acting Prosecutors appeared in court on behalf of the Intermediate People's Procuratorate of Guangzhou City presented opinions as follows: The existing evidence was sufficient to prove .... In the original judgment, the fact was clear, and the evidence was hard and sufficient; the conviction and sentencing were both correct. The acting prosecutors suggested the court at the second instance render a ruling to dismiss the appeal and uphold the original sentence.

Based on the trial of this case, this court found the fact as follows: ...

1. The above-said fact was ascertained by the following evidence presented and cross-examined in the first-instance and second-instance court proceedings: ...

2. At the first instance, the evidence proving that the appellant ... was hard and sufficient: ...

3. The above-said evidence can confirm each other without any contradiction that could not be ruled out, which is sufficient to ascertain that ...

4. Considering that..., it was not improper for the defendant at the first instance to be sentenced to 10 years imprisonment, together with a fine of 1 thousand RMB in accordance with the law. The

appeal by the appellant and his defense lawyer that the second-instance court should modify the original judgment to innocence should be dismissed.

5. 本院认为，上诉人×××无视我国法律，……原判认定事实清楚，证据确实、充分，定罪准确，量刑适当，审判程序合法。上诉人×××及其辩护人所提上诉理由和辩护意见，经查不能成立，不予采纳。依照《中华人民共和国刑法》第×××条以及《中华人民共和国刑事诉讼法》第×××条之规定，裁定如下：

5. This court holds as follows, the defendant * * * ignored national laws ... In the first-instance judgment, the fact was clearly ascertained; the evidence was hard and sufficient; The defendant was correctly convicted and the sentence was proper; the trial procedure was legal. Upon examination, the appellant's reasons for appeal and opinions of his defense lawyer are unfounded and should thus be dismissed. In accordance with Article * * * of *the Criminal Law of the People's Republic of China*, and Article * * * of *the Criminal Procedure Law of the People's Republic of China*, this court hereby rules as follows：

驳回上诉，维持原判。

The appeal shall be dismissed, and the original sentence was upheld.

本裁定为终审裁定。

This ruling is final.

审 判 长 ×××

审判员 ×××

审判员 ×××

×年 ×月 × 日

本件与原本核对无异

书 记 员 ×××

Presiding Judge：* * *

Judge：* * *

Judge：* * *

* * *（day/month/year）

This duplicate is verified to be identical with the original.

Clerk：* * *

# 相关英文表达

| 英文表达 | 中文意思 |
| --- | --- |
| return the illegally obtained money | 退出违法所得 |
| Intermediate People's Court | 中级人民法院 |
| make an objection to | 对……不服 |
| perform one's duty | 履行职责 |
| accept this case | 受理本案 |
| acting prosecutor | 代理检察员 |
| prosecution institution | 公诉机关 |
| cross-examined | 交叉质证 |
| uphold the original sentence | 维持原判 |

# 执行阶段

## 看守所监管规定

| 中文版 | 英文版 |
| --- | --- |
| **看守所监管规定**<br><br>为了保证监所安全，使监管工作有秩序地进行。特制订本监规。<br><br>一、认真学习国家法律和党的政策，深挖犯罪根源，努力改造思想，重新做人。<br><br>二、遵守学习、生活、作息等各项规章制度，服从管教人员的管理教 | **Jail Rule**<br><br>To ensure safety of detention facility and orderly supervision and management, this rule is formulated.<br><br>1. Study national laws and CPC policies hard, reflect deeply upon the roots of crimes, strive to correct wrong thoughts and thoroughly reform oneself.<br><br>2. Comply with the rules andregulations on learning, living and rest, obey management personnel. No person shall |

育。不得妨碍管教人员依法执行公务。严禁侮辱、漫骂、殴打管教人员。

三、保持监所正常秩序，不准高声喧哗、煽动哄闹、打架斗殴、欺压他人；不准索要他人物品；不准教唆犯罪；不准散布反动、淫秽言行；不准携带、制作、隐藏危及监所和人身安全的违禁物品。

四、爱护国家财产，不准损坏监所设施。

五、搞好个人和监所卫生，保持内务整洁，患病要服从治疗，不准伪装病情。

六、彻底交代罪行，检举揭发犯罪，不准串通案情，不准策划抗审。

七、必须互相监督，发现有违反监规和企图逃跑、行凶、自杀、破坏等行为的应立即报告，不准隐瞒包庇，严禁打击报复检举人。

八、在押人员享有的法定权利受法律保护。一经受到侵犯即可揭发控

impede the lawful duty of management personnel. No person is allowed to insult, abuse and beat management personnel.

3. Keep order of the jail, no loud noises, incitement, fights, bullying are allowed; asking for belongings from others or instigating crimes are prohibited; do not spread reactionary or obscene words and deeds; do not carry, make, or hide prohibited items that endanger the prison and personal safety.

4. Take good care of state property and do not damage prison facilities.

5. Keep hygiene of personal and prison cell, keep cell tidy and clean; accept treatment if you are sick, and do not pretend to be sick.

6. Confess your crime thoroughly and report other crimes; do not collude with others; no person shall plan to fight against the court trial.

7. You must supervise each other; if you find anyone who violates the rules or attempts to escape, assault or commit suicide or sabotage, you shall report immediately. No person is allowed to hide or conceal any criminal acts, or retaliate against the informant.

8. The legal rights enjoyed by detainees are protected by law. Being infringed,

| | |
|---|---|
| 告，但不得诬告、诽谤。 | you have the right to report it, but false accusation or defamation is prohibited. |
| 九、在押人员必须严格遵守本监规，对违反监规者将视情节轻重分别给予训诫、责令反省、上械具；对构成犯罪者，将依法从严惩处；对有立功表现者，将酌情依法从轻处理。 | 9. This rule must be strictly obeyed by detainees. Any violators of this rule will be given admonitions, introspection, and restraint measure depending on the circumstance; those who constitute a crime shall be punished in accordance with the law; those who commit meritorious acts shall have lesser punishment in light of the actual circumstances. |

## 社区矫正人员权利义务告知书
### （适用于管制、宣告缓刑、假释或暂予监外执行）

| 中文版 | 英文版 |
|---|---|
| **社区矫正人员权利义务告知书** | **Notification of Rights and Obligations to A Convict under Community Correction** |
| 一、社区矫正人员应当定期向司法所报告遵纪守法，接受监督管理，参加教育学习、社区服务和社会活动的情况。 | 1. Any convict under community correction shall report regularly to the judicial office their compliance with laws, acceptance of supervision and management, participation in education and learning, community services, and social activities. |
| 二、发生居所变化、工作变动、家庭重大变故以及接触对其矫正产生不利影响人员的，社区矫正人员应当及 | 2. In the case of the change of residence or occupation, major change of family or contact with persons who have |

时报告。

三、保外就医的社区矫正人员还应当每个月向司法所报告本人身体情况，每3个月向司法所提交病情复查情况。

四、对于人民法院禁止令确定需经批准才能进入的特定区域或者场所，社区矫正人员确需进入的，应当经县级司法行政机关批准，并告知人民检察院。

五、社区矫正人员未经批准不得离开所居住的县。

六、社区矫正人员因就医、家庭重大变故等原因，确需离开所居住的县，在7日以内的，应当报经司法所批准；超过7日的，应当由司法所签署意见后报经县级司法行政机关批准。返回居住地时，应当立即向司法所报告。社区矫正人员离开所居住县不得超过1个月。

an adverse effect on their corrections, the convict under community corrections shall report in a timely manner.

3. The convict under community corrections because of medical parole shall report to the judicial office every month their physical condition, and submit their health review to the judicial office every three months.

4. Where the people's court prohibits a convict from entering certain areas or places but the convict really needs to enter, the approval from the judicial administrative agency at the county level shall be obtained, and people's procuratorate shall be informed.

5. A convict under community corrections shall not leave the county where he or she resides.

6. Where a convict under community corrections has to leave the county where he or she resides because of medical care or of family major change, in case of no more than seven days, he or she should report to the judicial of fice for approval; in case of more than seven days, the judicial office shall state an opinion and report to the county-level judicial administrative agency. When returning to their places of residence, they should report to

七、社区矫正人员未经批准不得变更居住的县。社区矫正人员因居所变化确需变更居住地的，应当提前1个月提出书面申请，由司法所签署意见后报经县级司法行政机关审批。县级司法行政机关在征求社区矫正人员新居住地县级司法行政机关的意见后作出决定。

八、社区矫正人员应当参加公共道德、法律常识、时事政策等教育学习活动，增强法治观念、道德素质和悔罪自新意识。社区矫正人员每月参加教育学习时间不少于8小时。

九、有劳动能力的社区矫正人员

the judicial office immediately. A convict under community corrections shall not leave the county where they live for more than one month.

7. A convict under community corrections shall not change the county of residence without approval. Where a convict really needs to change their place of residence due to the change of their accommodation, he or she must submit a written application in advance, on which the judicial office shall state an opinion and report to the county – level judicial administrative agency for approval. The county – level judicial administrative agency shall make a decision after taking the opinions of the county – level judicial administrative agency of his new residence of the convict under community corrections.

8. A convict under community corrections must participate in education and learning activities on social ethics, basics of law, current affairs and policies, etc., to enhance the concept of law, moral quality and sense of repentance. A convict under community corrections should take no less than eight hours of education every month.

9. Any convict with the ability to labor

应当参加社区服务，修复社会关系，培养社会责任感、集体观念和纪律意识。社区矫正人员每月参加社区服务时间不少于 8 小时。

十、社区矫正人员的人身安全、合法财产和辩护、申诉、控告、检举以及其他未被依法剥夺或者限制的权利不受侵犯。社区矫正人员在就学、就业和享受社会保障等方面不受歧视。

被宣告缓刑的罪犯，应当遵守下列规定：

（一）遵守法律、行政法规，服从监督；

（二）按照考察机关的规定报告自己的活动情况；

（三）遵守考察机关关于会客的规定；

（四）离开所居住的市、县或者迁居，应当报经考察机关批准。

under community corrections shall participate in community service, restore social relations, and cultivate a sense of social responsibility, collective awareness and sense of discipline. A convict under community corrections should take no less than eight hours of community service every month.

10. The personal safety, legal property and rights of defense, appeal, accusation, report and other rights that are not been deprived or restricted in accordance with the law shall not be violated. A convict under community corrections shall not be discriminated in areas such as education, employment and social security.

Convicts who have been sentenced to probation must observe the following regulations:

(1) Comply with laws and administrative regulations and obey supervision;

(2) Report their activities to the inspection agency in accordance with regulations;

(3) Comply with the regulations of the inspection agency on meeting guests; or

(4) If they leave the city or county where they live or move, they should report to the inspection agency for approval.

| | |
|---|---|
| 被判处管制的罪犯，在执行期间，应当遵守下列规定： | Convicts who have been sentenced to supervision without incarceration must observe the following regulations： |
| （一）遵守法律、行政法规，服从监督； | （1）Comply with laws and administrative regulations and obey supervision； |
| （二）未经执行机关批准，不得行使言论、出版、集会、结社、游行、示威自由的权利； | （2）Shall not exercise the rights of freedom of speech，publication，assembly，association，marching and demonstration without the approval of the law enforcement agency； |
| （三）按照执行机关规定报告自己的活动情况； | （3）Report their activities to the enforcement agency in accordance withregulations； |
| （四）遵守执行机关关于会客的规定； | （4）Comply with the regulations of the enforcement agency on meeting guests； or |
| （五）离开所居住的市、县或者迁居，应当报经执行机关批准。 | （5）If they leave the city or county where they live or move，they should report to the enforcement agency for approval. |

## 被拘役人员权利义务告知书

| 中文版 | 英文版 |
|---|---|
| **被拘役人员权利义务告知书** | **Notification of Rights and Obligations to A Convict in Limited Incarceration** |
| 基本信息：拘役是对罪犯短期剥夺人身自由，并由公安机关实行就近关押改造的刑罚方法。拘役是介于管制与有期徒刑间的一种较轻的刑罚。 | Basic information：limited incarceration is a criminal penalty in which criminals are deprived of personal freedom and reform for a short period of time at nearby |

拘役的期限，为1个月以上6个月以下，数罪并罚最高不能超过1年。

在执行期间，被判处拘役的罪犯1个月可以回家1天至2天；参加劳动的，可以酌量发给报酬。拘役的刑期，从判决执行之日起计算；判决执行以前先行羁押的，羁押一日折抵刑期一日。

被判拘役的罪犯必须遵守如下规定：

一、拥护中国共产党和社会主义制度，不准散布敌对言论和煽动敌对情绪。

二、遵守社会公德，讲究文明礼貌，严禁阅读、传抄黄色书刊，散布违法犯罪思想，不准在交往中有粗俗、野蛮的行为。

detention by public security organs. Limited incarceration is a relatively lighter penalty between supervision without incarceration and fixed – term imprisonment. The period of detention is no less than one month but no more than six months, and the maximum length for combined punishment for more than one crime shall not exceed one year.

During the period of criminal detention, a convict in criminal detention may go home for one or two days each month; a discretionary amount of payment may be given to those who participate in labor. The term of criminal detention shall be counted from the date of the execution of the judgment; if the criminal is held in custody before the execution of the judgment, one day in custody shall be considered one day of the term sentenced.

Convicts in criminal detention must observe the following regulations:

1. Uphold the Communist Party of China and the socialist system; it is not allowed to spread reactionary speech or incite hostility.

2. Observe social ethics, be respectful to others; it is not allowed to read or copy erotic books, spread illegal and criminal thoughts or behave rude in communication.

三、尊重、服从管教，严禁无理取闹。

四、认罪认错，接受教育，不准消极对抗、自伤自残、图谋报复。

五、遵纪守法，矫正恶习，安心改造，不准进行违法犯罪活动，严禁擅自离开规定的活动范围，不准逃跑或唆使、协助他人逃跑。

六、互相监督，互相帮助，共同进步，不准恃强凌弱、敲诈勒索，严禁损坏、侵占公物和他人财物，严禁欺骗管教、包庇坏人坏事、栽赃陷害他人。

七、加强集体观念，建立正常关系，严禁搞拉帮结派、刺字文身。

八、努力学习政治、科学文化知识，严禁旷课、迟到、早退，严禁违反课堂纪律、损坏教学设施。

九、积极参加劳动，保质保量完成安排的任务，不准旷工、抗工、消

3. Respect and obey management; unruly behavior is not allowed.

4. Admit guilty and mistakes, receive education; passive aggression, self-injury and attempt to revenge are not allowed.

5. Observe laws and disciplines, correct bad habits, reform yourselves peacefully; it's not allowed to engage in any illegal and criminal activities, or to leave prescribed area for activity without authorization, or to escape, instigate or assist others to escape.

6. Supervise and help each other, make progress together; do not bully, blackmail others or damage or encroach public and others' property; do not deceive management personnel, cover up the bad, or frame others.

7. Strengthen the collective spirit, establish normal relationships. it's not allowed to form cliques or tattoo.

8. Work hard on politics, science and culture; absenteeism, lateness, and early leaving are strictly prohibited; it's not allowed to violate the classroom discipline, or damage teaching equipment.

9. Participate in labor actively and finish assigned work task and meet the requirements of quality and quantity; ab-

| | |
|---|---|
| 极怠工，伪造病情逃避劳动，损坏生产设施和劳动工具。 | senteeism, refusal to work, passive resistance to work, malingering or damaging the production equipment orlabor tools are prohibited. |
| 十、遵守作息制度，服从统一安排，不准无故不参加集体活动、扰乱公共秩序。 | 10. Follow the timetable and obey arrangements; it's not allowed to be absent of collective activities or disrupt public order. |

## 监狱服刑人员行为规范[1]

| 中文版 | 英文版 |
|---|---|
| **监狱服刑人员行为规范**<br>基本规范<br>　第一条　拥护宪法，遵守法律法规规章和监规纪律。<br><br>　第二条　服从管理，接受教育，参加劳动，认罪悔罪。<br><br>　第三条　礼貌诚信，互助友善，勤俭自强。<br><br>　第四条　依法行使权利，采用正当方式和程序维护个人合法权益。 | **Rule for Prisoners**<br>Basic Rules<br>　1. Uphold the Constitution of People's Republic of China and observe laws, regulations and the rule and discipline for prisoners.<br>　2. Obey management, receive education, participate in labor and admit guilty.<br>　3. Have good manners and integrity, help each other; be friendly, diligent, thrift and motivated.<br>　4. Exercise rights in accordance with the law and protect individual legal rights and interests in proper methods and due procedures. |

---

　〔1〕　基于 2004 年《监狱服刑人员行为规范》修改而成。

第五条　服刑期间严格遵守下列纪律：

（一）不超越警戒线和规定区域、脱离监管擅自行动；

（二）不私藏现金、刃具等违禁品；

（三）不私自与外界人员接触；不准向外界人员索取、借用、交换、传递钱物；

（四）不准擅自使用绝缘、攀援、挖掘物品；

（五）不准偷窃、赌博；

（六）不打架斗殴、自伤自残；

（七）不拉帮结伙、欺压他人；

（八）不传播犯罪手段、怂恿他人犯罪；

（九）不习练、传播有害气功、邪教。

生活规范

第六条　按时起床，有秩序洗漱、如厕，个人物品摆放整齐。

第七条　按要求穿着囚服，佩戴统一标识。

第八条　按时清扫室内外卫生，保持环境整洁。

5. Strictly observe the following rules while in prison：

（1）Keep away from the cordon and stay in prescribed areas；do not act without supervision or authorization；

（2）Do not hide prohibited items such as cash，cutting tools，etc. ；

（3）Do not contact person outside of the prison without authorization；do not ask for，borrow，exchange or pass any money or goods from person outside of the prison without authorization；

（4）Do not use insulation，climbing，or excavation tools without authorization；

（5）Do not steal or gamble；

（6）No fighting or self-injury；

（7）Do not form cliques or bully others；

（8）Do not spread criminal methods orinstigate crimes；or

（9）Do not practice harmful Qigong or spread heresy.

LivingRules

6. Get up on time，wash up in order and put personal items neatly.

7. Wear prison uniforms and logos as required.

8. Do cleaning regularly，keep indoors and outdoors clean and tidy.

第九条 保持个人卫生，衣服、被褥定期换洗。

第十条 按规定时间、地点就餐，爱惜粮食。

第十一条 集体行进时，听从警官指挥，保持队形整齐。

第十二条 不饮酒，不违反规定吸烟。

第十三条 患病时向管教报告，看病时遵守纪律，配合治疗。不私藏药品。

第十四条 进入管教办公室时，在门外报告，经允许后进入。

第十五条 在野外劳动现场向警官反映情况时，在三米以外报告。

第十六条 遇到问题，主动向警官汇报。与警官交谈时，如实陈述、回答问题。

第十七条 在指定铺位就寝，就寝时保持安静，不影响他人休息。

9. Maintain personal hygiene and regularly change and wash clothes and bedding.

10. Have meal at the prescribed time and place; do not waste food.

11. During marching in groups, follow the order of police of ficer and keep the orderly formation.

12. No alcohol; do not smoke against rules.

13. Report to management when sick, keep discipline and accept treatment when seeing a doctor; do not keep any drugs without authorization.

14. When entering the management office, report outside the door and get permission before entering.

15. When reporting to police officer at field work site, convicts should be three meters away from the officer.

16. When facing problems, convicts should report to the police officer voluntarily. When talking with police officers, convicts should make statement and answer questions truthfully.

17. Sleep in prescribed bunk and keep quiet when sleeping; do not disturb others.

学习规范

第十八条 接受法制、道德、形势、政策等思想教育，认清犯罪危害，矫治恶习。

第十九条 接受心理健康教育，配合心理测试，养成健康心理。

第二十条 尊重教师，遵守学习纪律，爱护教学设施、设备。

第二十一条 接受文化教育，上课认真听讲，按时完成作业，争取良好成绩。

第二十二条 接受技术教育，掌握实用技能，争当劳动能手，增强就业能力。

第二十三条 阅读健康有益书刊，按规定收听、收看广播电视。

第二十四条 参加文娱活动，陶冶情操。

劳动规范

第二十五条 积极参加劳动。因故不参加劳动，须事先经警官批准。

Education Rules

18. Receive education on laws, ethics, trend and policies; be clearly aware the harm of crimes and correct bad habits.

19. Receive education on mental health, cooperate when taking psychological test and develop a healthy mental state.

20. Respect teachers and observe teaching discipline; take good care of the teaching equipment and tools.

21. Receive education on general knowledge, listen to teachers carefully, finish homework on time and work hard for a better score.

22. Receive vocational education and master practical skills; strive to be skillful and more competitive in job market.

23. Read positive and beneficial books and magazines; listen to radio and watch TV program required by rules.

24. Participate in recreational activities to cultivate taste.

Work Rules

25. Participate in labor actively; those who are unable to participate in labor shall be approved by the police officer in advance.

第二十六条 劳动期间，遵守劳动纪律，坚守岗位，服从生产管理和技术指导。

第二十七条 严格遵守操作规程和安全生产规定，不违章作业。

第二十八条 爱护设备、工具。生产时厉行节约，减少损耗，杜绝浪费。

第二十九条 保持劳动现场卫生整洁，工具、材料、产品摆放整齐。

第三十条 不将劳动工具和危险品、违禁品带进监舍。

第三十一条 完成劳动任务，保证劳动质量，珍惜劳动成果。

礼貌规范

第三十二条 不随地吐痰，不乱扔杂物，不损坏监狱花草树木。

第三十三条 言谈举止文明。不讲脏话、粗话。

第三十四条 礼貌称谓他人。对警察称"警官"，服刑人员之间互称姓名，不准用绰号。

26. During work hours, remain in your post, obey labor discipline and follow production management and technical guidance.

27. Strictly observe the operating protocols and safety production rules; do not operate against rules herein.

28. Take good care of equipment and tools; production should be energy – saving and resource – saving and do not waste anything.

29. Keep the work site clean and tidy; place tools, materials and products in order.

30. Do not take labor tools, dangerous or prohibited goods into the prison.

31. Finish assigned work task and meet the requirements of quality and quantity; cherish labor results.

Etiquette Norms

32. No spitting on the ground; No litter; do not damage the plants in the prison.

33. Watch your language; be polite and show good manners all the time; no foul language.

34. Address people politely; use "officers" to address police, and use real names to to address other convicts; no nicknames allowed.

| 第三十五条　与来宾、警官相遇时，文明礼让；来宾、警官进入监舍时，除患病和按规定就寝外，起立致意。 | 35. When meeting guests or police officers, convicts should be polite and show good manners; when guests and police officers enter the cell, convicts shall stand up and greet politely except the situations where they are sick or go to sleep as required. |
|---|---|

# 相关英文表达

| 英文表达 | 中文意思 |
|---|---|
| ensure safety | 保证安全 |
| detention facility | 看守所 |
| national law | 国家法律 |
| CPC policies | 党的政策 |
| comply with the rules and regulations | 遵守规章制度 |
| management personnel | 服从管理人员 |
| keep hygiene | 保持卫生 |
| hide or conceal criminal act | 隐瞒包庇犯罪行为 |
| retaliate against the informant | 打击报复检举人 |
| community service | 社区服务 |
| adverse effect | 不利影响 |
| in a timely manner | 及时 |
| community correction | 社区矫正 |
| submit their health review | 报告病情复查情况 |
| medical parole | 保外就医 |
| prohibition from entering certain areas | 禁止进入特定区域 |
| county-level judicial administrative agency | 县级司法行政机关 |

续表

| 英文表达 | 中文意思 |
|---|---|
| enhance the concept of law | 加强法律意识 |
| cultivate a sense of social responsibility | 培养社会责任感 |
| limited incarceration | 拘役 |
| discretionary amount of payment | 酌量报酬 |
| spread reactionary speech | 散布敌对言论 |
| incite hostility | 煽动敌对情绪 |
| observe social ethics | 遵守社会公德 |
| passive aggression | 消极对抗 |
| self-injury | 自残 |
| attempt to revenge | 图谋报复 |
| prescribed area | 规定的活动范围 |
| instigate or assist others to escape | 唆使或协助他人逃跑 |
| deceive management personnel | 欺骗管教人员 |
| form cliques | 拉帮结派 |
| disrupt public order | 扰乱公共秩序 |
| participate in labor | 参加劳动 |
| excavation tool | 挖掘工具 |
| prison uniform | 囚服 |
| keep discipline | 遵守纪律 |
| keep any drugs without authorization | 私藏药品 |
| mental health | 心理健康 |
| psychological test | 心理测试 |
| vocational education | 技术教育 |
| recreational activity | 文娱活动 |
| cultivate taste | 陶冶情操 |
| remain in post | 坚守岗位 |

续表

| 英文表达 | 中文意思 |
|---|---|
| technical guidance | 技术指导 |
| safety production rule | 安全生产规定 |
| operating protocol | 操作规程 |
| energy-saving | 节能 |
| prohibited good | 违禁品 |
| cherish labor result | 珍惜劳动成果 |
| etiquette norm | 礼貌规范 |
| No litter | 不乱扔杂物、垃圾 |
| foul language | 粗话脏话 |
| good manner | 文明礼仪 |

# 律师办案常用语中英对照

## 侦查阶段

### 面谈（电话）咨询高频问答

| 中文版 | 英文版 |
| --- | --- |
| 客户：你好！<br>律师：你好！<br>客户：我是×××的弟弟。请问推荐人是您的什么人？<br><br>律师：他的好朋友是我的学生，这么介绍来的。 | Client：How do you do！<br>Lawyer：Hello！<br>Client：I am the younger brother of ＊＊＊. What's the relation between you and the middleman？<br>Lawyer：His good friend is a student of mine and he heard that our team are specialized in criminal defense, so he introduced us. |
| 客户：你的律所是不是叫×××？<br>律师：是的。<br>客户：能否简要介绍一下您的律所？<br>律师：我们律所成立于……<br>客户：我查了一下，你们所在中国律所排行榜上都没有。你确定你有足够的经验？我们可不想白花钱。 | Client：Your firm is called ＊＊＊？<br>Lawyer：That's right.<br>Client：Could you briefly introduce your firm？<br>Lawyer：Our firm was found in...<br>Client：I checked the Chinese law firm ranking and your firm is not on the list. Are you sure you have enough experience？ We don't want to spend money for nothing. |

律师：是这样的，我们的所/团队是专门做刑事案件的。那些头部的综合性律所因为业务范围更多样化，其他业务是他们的主要营收来源，所以才排在前面。单从排行榜上看是有差距，但我们所/团队好在专注刑事案件，只做刑事案件，所以接触的案件相对较多，也积累了较丰富的经验。

客户：这些中间人跟我说了。

律师：我们的所训是……意思是……

客户：你们之前做过什么类似的成功案例？

律师：有的。去年，我们有个案子……

客户：那我这个案件也能取保/缓刑吗？

律师：这取决于您案件的具体情况，我之前也只是听说了大概，您能否简要介绍一下关于……

客户：好吧……

律师：就知道这些？你们有拘留通知书吗？

客户：给你/没有拿到过，这有什么重要的？

Lawyer：The fact is that our firm/team focuses on criminal legal service. And those leading law firms are there because they have a bigger variety of legal services as their major source of revenue, which take them to the top of the ranking. If you look at the list alone, we are not ahead; but our firm/team concentrates on the criminal cases and nothing else, so we have dealt with more criminal cases, and are relatively more experienced.

Client：I heard that from the middleman.

Lawyer：Our motto is...which means...

Client：Do you have successful cases which is similar as this one?

Lawyer：Yes. Last year, we had a case...

Client：Do you think we can get bail out/probation for this case?

Lawyer：It depends on the specific circumstance of your case. I only had a broad outline of it, would you briefly tell us about...

Client：All right...

Lawyer：That's all you know? Can you show me the Notice of Detention?

Client：It's here. /No, we haven't received any. What's so important about it?

律师：拘留通知书上可以看出这些信息：（1）罪名，便于预估情节和刑期，即"严不严重"；（2）拘留开始时间，非常关键，便于预估刑事程序性走向，即"何时开展工作"；（3）办案机关，即"和谁说话"，便于后续沟通，依法了解案件信息。

客户：那你们到底能不能把×××取保？

律师：首先您需要了解，在我国，虽然近几年有一些改变，但羁押仍然是常态，取保是例外，这是由另一种很不相同的法律体系和司法实践决定的，两者截然不同。在我国，必须要符合下列条件之一，才可能被取保候审：

（一）可能判处管制、拘役或者独立适用附加刑的；

Lawyer: There are many crucial information we can get from that notice. The first is the crime charged, for us to predict the sentence, which is "how serious"; the second one is the starting time of detention, which is vital, so we can know "when to work" and predict the procedural trend of this case; the third thing we could know is the authority responsible for this case, which is "who to talk to", so we could communicate with them and get some information in accordance with laws.

Client: So can you get * * * bailed out or what?

Lawyer: First thing you need to know is that in our country, despite some changes in recent years, detention is still the norm and bailout is the exception, which is determined by a very different legal system and judicial practices, and I am talking about a world of difference between two systems. In our country, if you want to get bail out after detention, one of the following conditions must be met first:

（1）The criminal suspect or defendant may be sentenced to supervision without incarceration, limited incarceration, or an accessory penalty only;

（二）可能判处有期徒刑以上刑罚，采取取保候审不致发生社会危险性的；

（三）患有严重疾病、生活不能自理，怀孕或者正在哺乳自己婴儿的妇女，采取取保候审不致发生社会危险性的；

（四）羁押期限届满，案件尚未办结，需要采取取保候审的。

具体到你的案子，根据你刚才提供的信息，我们首先要进一步了解……才能预判到底是否构成犯罪，如果构成犯罪，刑罚会有多重。同时，我们还需要和办案机关沟通，尽可能多地了解相关情况，以评估取保的可能性……

客户：别废话了，你们到底有没有关系？我是说能改变局面的那种关系。我跟你们说，在我们国家，我认识好多很厉害的律师和检察官，我只

（2）The criminal suspect or defendant may be sentenced to fixed-term imprisonment or a heavier penalty but will not cause danger to the society if granted bail;

（3）The criminal suspect or defendant suffers a serious illness, cannot take care of himself or herself or is a pregnant woman or a woman who is breastfeeding her own baby, and will not cause danger to the society if granted bail; or

（4）The term of custody of the criminal suspect or defendant has expired but the case has not been closed, and a bail is necessary.

For your case, based on the information you just provided, we still need to know the following information... so we could prejudge whether your act constitutes any crime and if so, how serious the punishment would be. Meanwhile, we need to communicate with the handling authority and learn as much information as we possibly can, in order to assess the odds of bailout afterwards...

Client: No shit! Do you have relationship or not? I mean the game-changing kind of relationship. I will tell you what, in my country, I am familiar

要打个响指，人就能放出来。

律师：那是在您的国家，我国有不同的国情和司法现状。

客户：在我们国家都能那样操作，你们国家肯定可以！你们到底行不行？有没有关系？我付律师费不是为了买一堆法律文书的！

律师：既然您也知道我们两国具有不同的社会体制和司法现状，所以在你们国家可以实现的，我们这里不一定能实现。您的问题很常见，我也能理解，换做是我们遇到您这样的情况也会有同样的想法。所以我们在办案过程中会用尽所有的沟通渠道，全力以赴去争取。

客户：你们怎么收费的？计时收费还是一口价？

律师：对于您的案子而言，一口价对您或者对我们都不公平。所以我们一般是计时收费。您需要先付一笔律师费来启动工作。我们的小时费率是……我们每周都会发给您工作报告，包含工时以及具体完成的工作。

客户：你们用不用北极星计费法？

with many famous lawyers and prosecutors. I just need to snap my finger like this and the guy will be released.

Lawyer：That's only in your country. In China, we have different condition and judicial practice.

Client：It works in my country, surely it will work in yours! Can you do it or not? Do you have relationship? We aren't here paying for a pile of paperwork!

Lawyer：Since you understand we have different social systems and legal practice, so what happened in your country is not necessarily available here. Your question is very common and understandable. We would feel the same if we are in your shoes. So we would try all communication channels and pull out all stops.

Client：How do you charge us for this case? Pay by hour or lump-sum?

Lawyer：Flat rate for your case is not fair for neither you nor us. So we shall take pay-by-hour plan and you need to prepay a certain amount of retaining fee to get the work started. Our hourly rate is... Every week we will send you the work report including the working hours and specific work done.

Client：Do you take Lodestar Rule?

律师：相关因素在报价方案中已考虑，所以我们不需要北极星计费法。

客户：你们不要什么都往费用里算，我知道你们的套路。

律师：我们所有的费用都基于真实和必要的工作，并且我们都有相应的依据。例如我们路上的时间除以三计入工作用时。

客户：说回刚才那个问题。我们过来不是为了一些文书工作的，是为了关系。

律师：我刚才已经跟您解释了，我们两国有不同的社会体制和司法现状……

客户：不要跟我说这些区别！所有的国家都一样的。每个人都有标价，都可以买通的。你们就告诉我，你们搞关系到底要多少钱？

律师：您的心情完全可以理解。但您要考虑到不同情形。在你们国家，检察官一个人可以作是否起诉的决定；但在中国，一个逮捕的决定需要由检察官层层上报到检察长批准后，才能作出。因此我们的司法制度决定了没有办法跟你们国家一样容易。

Lawyer：Relevant factors have already been taken into account in our package price, so we don't need Lodestar Rule.

Client：Don't make everything billable！I know your trick！

Lawyer：All spent fee will be based on real and necessary work, with relevant proof kept. For instance, only one third of the time en route will be counted in the working hours.

Client：Get back to the issue. We are here not for the paperwork；we are here for the relation.

Lawyer：I have explained to you, that my country and yours don't share the same social system and judicial practice...

Client：Cut the difference crap！All countries are same on it. Every one has his price. We can buy them off. Just tell me, how much for the relationship？

Lawyer：Your mindset is absolutely understandable. But you have to think about different scenarios. In you country, the prosecutors can make decision themselves on whether or not to prosecute；while in China, a decision of arrest will not be made until it goes through every level from the prosecutor up to the head of procuratorate whose duty is to approve

客户：那你说说如果关系没用，你们准备怎么做？

律师：如果我们介入，除了正常的事实之辩和法律之辩外，我们还要挖掘法理、社会、情感、经济、当事人个人情况等多重辩点，辅以和相关司法机关及时、有效的沟通，我们会不遗余力去说服。我之前有一个案子……

客户：那我们如何委托？

律师：首先，您需要仔细阅读并签署两份委托协议、案件风险告知书，以及若干份委托书；然后您需要将相应的律师费打入我们所的账户。这样我们能获取必需的手续，第一时间安排去会见×××，这样辩护工作就能正式开始了。

客户：可不可以出结果后付钱？我听说可以看实际结果付钱。

律师：我之前说过，根据我们团队的资深程度，您的案件的复杂性和工作量，本案是按小时计费的。所以

that decision. Therefore, our judicial system, which is so different from yours, makes it not as easy.

Client：What do you suggest if relationship doesn't work？

Lawyer：If we are retained, except normal defense in law and in fact, we would dig deeper into more defense points on theory of law, society, emotion, economic and personal background, etc. Besides, timely and effective communication with the related judicial authority should also be taken. We spare no efforts on persuasion. There was a case in which I...

Client：Then what should we do to retain your team？

Lawyer：Firstly you need to read the *Retaining Agreement*, *Risk Notice for Criminal Legal Service* and several POAs before signing them; then you need to arrange the wiring of the retaining fee, so we could have all necessary documents for defense and arrange the visit to start our defense work.

Client：Can I wire the retaining fee after the result? I heard we can pay based on actual result.

Lawyer：As I said before, based on the our team level, complication and workload of your case, it's a pay-by-hour

你需要预付一部分律师费，启动工作。我们的方式是预付 200 小时的工作时间。在 200 小时即将结束前，我们会及时通知您。为避免案件效果受影响，您需要预先支付下 100 小时的费用，然后我们再做 100 小时的工作，以此类推。

客户：我的意思是，我们可不可以约定等×××取保了，我们付你一部分；×××将来缓刑了，我们再付你一部分。类似常见的网上体验—付款模式，免费试用一段时间，这段时间里我们可以决定是否购买你们的服务。

律师：首先，您说的基本属于风险收费的模式，我国法律和律师行业规范明令禁止刑事案件风险代理；其次，绝大部分市面上的商品和服务都没有这种体验式消费，不可能仅仅因为饭菜没有想象中好吃就不付钱；最后，网购的体验模式是建立在资本和技术保障的前提下的一种吸引客流的促销方式。网购的目的是生活消费，而辩护工作涉及生命自由。因此辩护律师并不需要这样促销，而且也并非我们找的你们，而是你们上门来聘请

plan. So you need to prepay a certain amount of retaining fee to get the work started. Our practice is to prepay 200 hours retainer first. When it's close to the end of these 200 hours, we will notify you in time. In order not to affect your case, you need to prepay the next 100 hours retainer, and we work for another 100 hours, and so on.

Client: I mean, can we have a deal like certain amount will be paid if * * * were bailed out; another amount will be paid if the sentence for him is probation. Something like common online try-and-buy plan that it can be used free for a limited period of time, during which you can decide whether you want to buy it or not.

Lawyer: First of all, what you said is basically a contingent rate. While law and bar regulation clearly prohibited it for criminal service in our country; next, this try-and-buy plan is especially of computer programs and equipment, not common for other service. The food simply is not as tasty as you expect is not the reason not to pay; last, this try-and-buy plan is guaranteed by capital and technology, and is a promotion method in nature to attract customers. Online shopping is

我们。您一定要认清面前的现实。

客户：一定要先付吗？可不可以先付一部分？像首付款一样？

律师：抱歉，我无权这样操作。正如我说过的，这是计时收费，必须预先支付一部分费用。

客户：我想这钱这么贵，肯定要包括关系的费用！

律师：正如我之前说的，律师也要根据法律和事实做工作，你所谓的关系并非律师的职责范围，我们的费用也不会包含这块。

客户：我们能不能见到他？

律师：根据《中华人民共和国刑事诉讼法》，目前只有律师和领馆的相关人员可以会见外籍嫌疑人。但领馆会根据自己的工作安排会见，不由你们。所以意味着只有律师能会见。

for household consumption, but the defense work involves freedom and life. Therefore, counsels don't need such promotion. Moreover, it is not us that come to you; it is you coming to retain us. You have to face it.

Client：Do I have to pay all first? Can I pay part of it instead of all the 200-hour amount? Like a down payment?

Lawyer：Sorry, not in my power to make such a deal. Like I said it's a pay-by-hour plan and a prepaid amount for 200 hours is required.

Client：I guess it must cover the relation since the rate is so high!

Lawyer：As I said before, lawyers have to work on the basis of law and fact. The so-called relation is not part of our duty, so our retainer will not cover anything of such kind.

Client：Can we go and visit him?

Lawyer：According to *Criminal Procedure Law of the People's Republic of China*, only lawyers and related personnel from embassies and consulates have authority to visit a foreigner suspect. However, the embassies and consulates only arrange visit according to their own timetable, not up to you, which means only lawyers can visit him.

客户：你们最快什么时候可以去会见他？

律师：如果您这边现在能定下来，我们最快后天可以会见。

客户：疫情会不会妨碍会见？

律师：有一定影响，例如至少提前一天预约。但所有材料我们都有准备，例如核酸证明。因此我们会把影响最小化。

客户：会见时我们能否跟他视频？

律师：根据我国法律和律师行业的规定，我们是不能使用手机的，而手机在会见前也必须全部寄存。所以你们无法跟他视频。

客户：他这个人比较固执，疑心很重，你们要耐心。跟他说我的名字，他就知道了。

律师：谢谢您的提醒。我们会先介绍自己的来由，建立基本信任。

客户：你们最快什么时候去和公安机关沟通？

律师：在我们会见完他，充分研

Client：What is the earliest time that you can arrange the first meeting with him?

Lawyer：If you could make decision now, we could arrange it the day after tomorrow.

Client：Will the pandemic stand in the way of the visit?

Lawyer：To some degree, yes. For instance, we have to reserve the visit at least one day before. However, we could minimize the impact by having everything ready such as PCR test.

Client：Can we webcam with him during visit?

Lawyer：Law and bar regulation of our country clearly prohibited to use cellphone during the visit, and cellphones must be checked in the locker before visit. So you could not webcam with him.

Client：He is pretty headstrong and suspicious, so you have to be patient when meeting him. Just tell him my name and he will know it.

Lawyer：Thank you for your advice. We will introduce ourselves first to establish trust.

Client：What is the earliest time that you can arrange the first communication with the police?

Lawyer：After the first meeting with

判案情后，会安排与公安机关沟通。但也要取决于公安机关的时间安排，因为肯定要事先预约。总之我们会尽早。

客户：你们能不能见到报案人？和他谈谈？

律师：根据相关法律规定，辩方律师不能随意接触被害人。况且，目前案件情况我们都还没有初步了解，时机还不成熟。

客户：我们呢？我们能不能去见被害人？和他们坐下来谈谈？

律师：虽然法律不禁止你们接触被害人，但是对你们来说也有比较大的法律风险，尤其是在被害人因为你们的接触而改变陈述时，可能涉及刑法的妨碍诉讼相关罪名。

客户：这个案子能不能罚点钱完事了？

律师：目前来看，本案已刑事立案，是国家介入的公诉案件，即便最后只判罚金刑，也需要法院的相关判决才能确定。按照你们的描述，结合我们的办案经验和法律规定，只判罚

him, we will study this case fully and layout necessary points and then arrange communication with the police. It's up to their schedule so we need to make appointment beforehand. We will try to make it happen as possibly early.

Client：Can you meet the accusers and talk to them?

Lawyer：According to relevant laws and regulations, counsels are not allowed to contact the accusers at will. Moreover, we don't even have a preliminary understanding of the case, so we are not there yet.

Client：What about us? Can we meet the accusers and talk to them?

Lawyer：Although there is no clear ban in the law for you to meet them, there is also a relatively obvious legal risk for you, especially when they change their statement due to your meeting, which may involve charges of impairing legal proceedings.

Client：Can we just pay a fine and get this thing over?

Lawyer：So far, the police has filed the criminal case against him, which makes it a case of public prosecution, so it's him vs. the State. Even if there is only a sentence of fine at the end of the day,

金刑的可能性很小。

客户：如果被害人愿意撤销指控，能不能撤案？或者至少先取保候审？

律师：我刚才说了，本案已经是国家介入的公诉案件，不能轻易撤案，更不会因为被害人想撤回报案就随便撤案。至于取保候审，则要看×××在本案中的具体情节以及有无其他法定情况，来判断是否符合取保候审的要求，所以目前信息不足，需要进一步了解情况。

客户：我们可以引渡他回国吗？

律师：我们两国间是没有引渡条约的。

客户：我们可以跟中国政府交涉互换关押人员吗？

律师：你的思路很新颖。但这不属于律师的职责和能力范围。

客户：如果我们委托你们团队，你们有多大把握能赢？

律师：赢的定义如果是无罪，那

it still needs to be judged by the court. Based on your description, our experience and the related law and regulations, the odds are against him.

Client: If the accuser withdraws his accusation, shall the case be dismissed too? Or at least bail him out first?

Lawyer: I said before, this is a case of public prosecution, which is him vs. the State, so it can not be dismissed easily, even if the accuser himself wishes to withdraw his accusation. As for the bailout, it relies on specific situation of this case and whether it meets any legal conditions of bailout for us to assess thepossibility of it. Therefore, information is not enough so far for us to tell, so we have to find more to evaluate current situation.

Client: Can we extradite him back to my country?

Lawyer: There is no extradition treaty between your country and mine.

Client: Can our government talk to yours to exchange prisoners?

Lawyer: It's very creative, while it's not in lawyers' scope of ability and duty.

Client: If we retain your team, what's the odds of winning?

Lawyer: If the definition of winning

| | |
|---|---|
| 么肯定不会容易；如果是想办法让他罪轻，我们可以全力争取。<br><br>　　客户：我跟家人电话商量一下，你等我一会可以吗？<br>　　律师：好。<br>　　…………<br><br>　　客户：我决定委托你们。你一定要把他取保出来！他是无罪的！<br><br>　　律师：我们会深入研究，然后尽快给你反馈。你有什么话要转达给他吗？不能与案件细节相关。<br><br><br>　　客户：我电话问问他家人再告诉你。 | is innocence, it shall not be easy; if it means lesser punishment, we have a fighting chance for it.<br><br>　　Client：Let me discuss with his family, can I have a minute?<br>　　Lawyer：Sure.<br>　　...<br><br>　　Client：I decided to retain you for now. But you have to bail him out because he is innocent!<br><br>　　Lawyer：We will look into this case and give you feedback as soon as possible. Do you have anything to tell him? Something irrelevant to the details of this case.<br><br>　　Client：I will tell you after the phone with his family. |

## 涉外刑事案件委托合同实例（辩护）

| 中文版 | 英文版 |
|---|---|
| **刑事法律服务委托合同**<br><br>　　委托人姓名：＿＿＿＿<br>　　委托人身份证明编号：＿＿＿＿<br><br>　　受托人：＿＿＿＿ 律师事务所<br><br>　　本人＿＿＿＿，根据《中华人民 | **Entrustment Agreement for Criminal Legal Service**<br><br>The Entruster：＿＿＿＿<br>ID Number：＿＿＿＿<br><br>The Entrustee：＿＿＿＿ Law Firm<br><br>I, the undersigned Mr. /Ms. ＿＿＿＿, |

共和国刑事诉讼法》第 34 条的规定，现决定委托_____律师事务所在_____案中提供刑事法律服务。现双方达成如下委托合同：

一、本法律服务包括以下三阶段：

1. 在侦查阶段担任辩护律师；

2. 在审查起诉阶段担任辩护律师；

3. 在审判阶段担任辩护律师。

二、_____律师事务所指派_____律师团队担任本案的辩护人。

三、律师费用按以下方式支付：

委托人应支付_____美元给受托人账户。账户信息如下：_____（律所账户细节信息）

四、委托人应当于合同签订起 2 日内支付上述全部律师费用。

according to the Article 34 of the *Criminal Procedure Law of the People's Republic of China*, hereby decided to entrust _____ Law Firm to provide criminal legal service in the case of _____ and reach an agreement as followed：

1. This legal service includes the following three phases：

1. 1. As the defense lawyer during the period of the investigation；

1. 2. As the defender lawyer during the period of examination of prosecution；

1. 3. As the defense lawyer during the period of the first instance.

2. _____ Law Firm assigns team of _____ as the defender lawyer for this case.

3. The lawyer's fee will be paid in the following way：

The entruster shall pay US ＄_____ into the entrustee's account as follows：

_____（detailed information of the bank account of entrusted law firm）

4. The entruster shall pay all the lawyer's fee to the above－mentioned account within 2 days since signing this agreement.

| | |
|---|---|
| 五、双方均应按照约定履行合同，不得随意解除合同。如案件提前终结，或委托方单方解除合同，律师费均不予退还。 | 5. Both parties shall fulfill this agreement as planned and shall not terminate it casually. The lawyer's fee will not be returned if the case is concluded in advance or the entruster unilaterally terminates the contract. |
| 六、风险警示。详见附件中《刑事案件委托风险告知书》，委托人需签字确认该文件。 | 6. Risk warning. Please refer to the attached *Risk Notice for Criminal Legal Service*, and entruster needs to sign to confirm thereon. |
| 委托人（签字及手印） | The entruster（signature and fingerprints） |
| 日期 | Date |
| 受托人（公章） | The entrustee（stamp） |
| 日期 | Date |

## 涉外刑事案件授权委托书实例（辩护）

| 中文版 | 英文版 |
|---|---|
| **授权委托书**<br><br>本人_____，根据《中华人民共和国刑事诉讼法》第 34 条的规定，现指定_____律师事务所_____律师为涉嫌_____案件的犯罪嫌疑人（被告人）_____的辩护人。 | **Power of Attorney**<br><br>I, the undersigned Mr. /Ms. _____, according to the Article 34 of the *Criminal Procedure Law of the People's Republic of China*, hereby retain _____ from _____ Law Firm as the defense lawyer/lawyers in the case of _____ |

| | （the name of the suspect）alleged of ＿ ＿＿＿＿. |
|---|---|
| 本委托书有效期自即日起至＿＿＿ ＿＿止。 | This letter of authorization is valid until＿＿＿＿. |
| 委托人签字捺印： | Signature and fingerprint： |
| 日期： | Date： |
| 委托律师联系电话： | Mobile Number of the Lawyer： |

## 刑事法律服务风险告知书

| 中文版 | 英文版 |
|---|---|
| **刑事法律服务风险告知书** | **Risk Notice for Criminal Legal Service** |
| 　　您拟委托我所办理＿＿＿＿＿一案，为维护您的合法权益，根据《中华人民共和国律师法》以及相关法律法规的规定，特向您告知以下事项： | 　　Since you intend to entrust our firm to handle the case of ＿＿＿＿＿, in order to protect your lawful rights and interests, in accordance with the *Lawyers Law of the People's Republic of China* and relevant laws and regulations, we hereby inform you of the following items： |
| 　　一、刑事案件具有法律风险，包括但不限于家属在判决生效前无法与嫌疑人/被告人会面、无法获得取保候审、案件周期过长、会见可能需要经司法机关批准或陪同、嫌疑人/被告人被提审时律师无法陪同等。在聘请律师前，请认识到以上风险的存在，并 | 　　1. Criminal cases involve legal risk of many kinds, including but not limited to family members unable to meet the suspect or defendant before the judgment coming into effect, the suspect or defendant unable to get bailed, case handling period too long, meeting by lawyer may |

在身心上做好准备，承受以上风险带来的影响。

二、刑事案件在侦查阶段，律师可以向侦查机关了解犯罪嫌疑人涉嫌的罪名和案件有关情况，提出意见，为犯罪嫌疑人申请变更强制措施等。在案件移送检察机关之前，无法看到案件的证据材料。律师在检察机关或法院获取的案卷材料均不能提供给委托人。

三、律师可以基于案件的证据、事实和适用法律等提出自己的预判，然而基于众多不确定的原因，上述推测仅依据律师专业经验作出，不具有最终决定性，不代表律师对案件结果的承诺，律师对案件的分析只能作为参考，律师只能承诺最大限度地保障嫌疑人或被告人的合法权益。

require consent or escort from judicial organs, lawyer not allowed to be present when the suspect or defendant being arraigned. So please be aware of the above risk and make sure you are mentally and physically prepared for the impact from them before you retain a lawyer.

2. During the period of criminal investigation, a defense lawyer may learn the charges against a criminal suspect and relevant case information from the criminal investigation authority, offer opinions and apply for modifying a compulsory measure. Only when the case is transferred for examination and prosecution, lawyer can obtain evidence of the case. None of those evidence obtained by lawyer from procuratorate or court can be offered to the client.

3. Lawyer may offer his own prediction based on evidence and fact of the case and application of law, but owing to many uncertainties, the above prediction can only be made according to lawyer's experience, which is not conclusive and does not represent any promise of result by lawyer. The analysis by lawyer is for reference only, lawyer can promise but safeguarding the greatest lawful rights and interests of the suspect or defendant.

四、遇有如下情形，律所不予退费：

1. 委托人同时委托其他律师事务所的律师代理的；

2. 签订委托合同后，委托人以结果不理想或收费过高为由要求退费的；

3. 委托人单方终止合同的。

五、委托人向律师提供证据的，请提供复印件或复制品，原件自行保管。律师要求提供原件的，请保留好由事务所或律师出具的原件收据。

六、律师不通过任何违法或违规的方式办理案件，并不提供任何采取非正当方式处理案件的建议，委托人不得要求律师向案件经办人员行贿或者变相贿赂，委托人就案件采取任何不当方式应自行承担全部后果。

七、如遇以下情况，您的合法权益将可能无法得到保障，且律师事务所有权向您追究相关责任：

4. Law firm does not refund fees under following circumstances：

4. 1. The client retains lawyers from other law firms；

4. 2. After the signing of entrustment contract, the client requests a refund for the reason that the result is undesirable or the fee is too high；

4. 3. The client unilaterally terminates the contract.

5. In the case that client provides evidence to lawyer, photocopied version is recommended and original copy shall be well-kept by client himself. In the case that the lawyer requires the original copy, client shall keep well the receipt of original copy from the law firm or lawyer.

6. The lawyer shall not handle the case through any means against law or regulation, nor provide any suggestions for handling the case improperly. Client shall not ask lawyer to bribe or bribe in disguised form case handler. Client who takes any improper measures shall be at his own risk.

7. Your lawful rights and interests may not be fully safeguarded and law firm has the right to hold you accountable under any of the following circumstances：

1. 委托事项违法的；

2. 陈述案情与事实不符或提供虚假证据材料的。

八、委托辩护案件中，如委托人非犯罪嫌疑人、被告人的近亲属，委托人代为委托的，则需取得犯罪嫌疑人、被告人本人的同意。

九、如律师有悖其职业道德、执业纪律等行为，委托人有权向事务所及其主管部门投诉，要求更换律师；因违法、违规造成损失的，有权向承办律师和律师事务所索赔。

承办律师已告知委托人上述事项，委托人已完全知晓该风险告知书中所提示的全部内容。

委托人签名：

时间：年 月 日

7. 1. The matter commissioned by client is illegal；

7. 2. Client's statement is inconsistent with the fact or client provides fake evidence.

8. In the case of defense service, where the client is not the close relatives of the suspect or defendant, he or she needs the consent of the suspect or defendant to retain a lawyer.

9. In the case that lawyer violates his professional ethics and discipline, the client has the right to file a complaint with the law firm and its competent authority to change the lawyer; if there is loss caused by violation of laws or regulations, the client has the right to claim compensation from the responsible lawyer and law firm .

Lawyer has informed the client of the above matters, and the client is fully aware of all the contents in this Risk Notice.

Signature of the client：

Signing date：

# 首次会见高频问答示例

| 中文版 | 英文版 |
|---|---|
| 嫌疑人：你是谁？你们哪里来的？ | Client：Who are you and where are you from？ |
| 辩护人：我们是××律师事务所的，是你儿子聘请的律师。 | Lawyer：We are counsels from ＊＊ Law Firm. Your son retained us to provide legal service to you. |
| 嫌疑人：有意思。我怎么知道你就是他聘请的？ | Client：So funny. How could I know that he retained you？ |
| 律师：首先我这里有他签字的委托书。他还给了我一张你家人的合影（展示打印的照片）。你可以看看。 | Lawyer：One thing, I have a POA signed by him. He also gave me one family photo. Check this out. |
| 嫌疑人：他们花了多少钱请你？ | Client：How much did they spend to retain you？ |
| 律师：本案是你家人的好朋友介绍的，也是我们的同仁，律师费我们已经尽可能给予优惠，你家人也表示接受。 | Lawyer：It is a good friend of your family that introduced us, who is a lawyer too. Therefore, we gave our best price and your family accepted it. |
| 嫌疑人：告诉我真相！多少钱！我想知道。 | Client：Tell me the truth！ How much？ I want to know！ |
| 律师：当务之急是将你的案子处理好，一切以案子优先，别的你先不用多虑。我发誓，你的家人可以负担得起。毕竟这不是在你们国家，那里的律师费用相对较高。 | Lawyer：The priority at the moment is to handle your case and your case only. No need to worry about anything else. I swear your family can afford it. It is not in your country after all, and the retainer is higher there. |
| 嫌疑人：你/你们几岁？ | Client：How old are you？ |
| 律师：我今年××岁。 | Lawyer：＊＊. |

嫌疑人：××岁？我儿子都比你大。你太年轻了，办不好我的案子。换个人来。我喜欢年纪大一点的。你们主任多大？

律师：别看我们岁数不大，其实有很多年办理这类案件的经验了。

嫌疑人：你们办过多少案子了？有什么成功案例？

律师：你是否知道……

嫌疑人：帮我个忙。我想打个电话给我家里人，你现在就帮我拨通电话。

律师：看守所里不能使用手机，我们的都外存了。

嫌疑人：那你这个电脑可以视频吧，我要跟我家里人视频一下。

律师：我理解你的心情，换作我是你，我也想和家里人联系。但这里没有网络，确实不能视频。

嫌疑人：那你们能不能把我保释出去？

律师：在我国的司法制度和实践下，取保候审需要满足以下几个条件之一，才能被取保候审：

（一）可能判处管制、拘役或者独立适用附加刑的；

Client：* *? Even my son is older than you! You are too young for my case. Get someone else. I like someone older. How old is your director?

Lawyer：Although we are not as old, we have many years of experience on dealing with cases like yours.

Client：How many cases have you handled? And any successful cases?

Lawyer：Have you heard. . .

Client：Do me a favor. I want to talk to my family. Make a call now.

Lawyer：It's not allowed to use cellphone here, and we have checked them outside.

Client：Then use your computer. I want to webcam with them.

Lawyer：I can understand how you feel. I want to talk to them too if I were you. But we don't have any network here, so it's impossible for webcam.

Client：Then can you bail me out or not?

Lawyer：Under the law and judicial practice of our country, you must meet at lease one of the following conditions to be bailed out：

（1）The criminal suspect or defendant may be sentenced to supervision without incarceration, limited incarcera-

（二）可能判处有期徒刑以上刑罚，采取取保候审不致发生社会危险性的；

（三）患有严重疾病、生活不能自理，怀孕或者正在哺乳自己婴儿的妇女，采取取保候审不致发生社会危险性的；

（四）羁押期限届满，案件尚未办结，需要采取取保候审的。

嫌疑人：我显然符合其中的第二条！我没有社会危险性，就算我后面坐牢现在也可以先取保！

律师：我们因为案件办理需要，针对社会危险性这点研究过大量相关的论文、案例、法规。简单来说，在实践中，司法机关对于是否会有社会危险性这点考量的主要因素是犯罪嫌疑人是否涉嫌故意杀人、强奸、抢劫、绑架、放火、爆炸、投放危险物质等危害国家安全、公共安全或者社会秩序犯罪，是否参与恐怖活动，黑社会

tion, or an accessory penalty only;

（2）The criminal suspect or defendant may be sentenced to fixed-term imprisonment or a heavier penalty but will not cause danger to the society if granted bail;

（3）The criminal suspect or defendant suffers a serious illness, cannot take care of himself or herself or is a pregnant woman or a woman who is breastfeeding her own baby, and will not cause danger to the society if granted bail; or

（4）The term of custody of the criminal suspect or defendant has expired but the case has not been closed, and a bail is necessary.

Client: Obviously I meet condition No. 2! Even it's a sentence of imprisonment later, you can still bail me out for now because I will cause no danger to the society!

Lawyer: Out of necessity of case-handling, we have done plenty of study of related thesis, cases and laws and regulations on danger to the society. To put it simple, in judicial practice, the top factor for authority to consider danger to society is whether the criminal suspect is involved in crimes endangering national security, public safety or society such as

性质犯罪，严重暴力犯罪和毒品犯罪集团。而你涉嫌的犯罪就在其中。你认为自己没有社会危险性，我们也认为你没有，但司法机关有一套自己的判定标准，并不按你理解的字面意思。

嫌疑人：所以你们到底能不能把我保释？

律师：我们一步步来可以吗？罗马不是一天建成的。取保候审需要我们了解清楚所有情况后再作一个预判。我们现在都还没有谈过案件。

嫌疑人：好吧。你有什么要问的？

律师：你涉嫌的罪名是……按照刑法的相关规定，你的罪名构成是这样的……

嫌疑人：我没有犯罪，因为……

律师：你先别着急，先回忆一下你被提审过几次？分别是什么时候做的？多久？说了什么内容？

嫌疑人：很重要吗？我记不太清了。

intentional homicide, rape, robbery, kidnapping, arson, explosion, dissemination of hazardous substances, or whether to participate in terrorist activities, crimes of gangland nature, serious violence or drug criminal groups. And your crime is among them. You think you are not dangerous to this society, which we agree, but the authority has its own criteria to decide, which is not consistent to the literal meaning as you see it.

Client: So can you bail me out or not?

Lawyer: Can we do it step by step? Rome was not built in a day. We need to acquire all the related details before we can predict. We haven't even talked about the case yet.

Client: Fine. What do you want to know?

Lawyer: Your crime charged is... according to the related provisions of criminal law, the following elements constitutes your crime...

Client: I am not guilty, because...

Lawyer: No hurry, try to recall how many times have you been arraigned? When, how long and how you answered?

Client: Does it even matter? I cannot remember clearly.

律师：当然。你的供述是案件认定的重要证据之一，我们掌握得越详细，对案件的判断就越精准。

嫌疑人：好吧，我第一次笔录是在……我想抽根烟，给我根烟。

律师：抱歉，我们不抽烟，而且会见室也不允许抽烟。

嫌疑人：难以置信。还有，这里的饭菜我吃不惯，能不能跟他们说给我单独准备一份饭？

律师：如果你确实因为信仰，不能吃特定食物，可以申请其他饮食；如果只是因为口味不习惯，可能没法办到，因为里面绝大多数人都吃同一种食物。我可以让你家属为你再多存一些生活费，你可以额外购买食品改善一下。

嫌疑人：我能不能和被害人坐下来谈谈？

律师：首先你现在是羁押状态，被害人无法见到你；即使你可以见到他，对你来说也有比较大的法律风险，尤其是在被害人因为你的接触而改变陈述时，可能涉及刑法规定的妨碍诉

Lawyer：Certainly. Your statement is a vital source of evidence that may be used to ascertain the fact. More detailed of the statement we know, more accurate we can predict.

Client：All right. My first arraignment was on. . . I need to smoke. Do you have one?

Lawyer：Sorry, we don't smoke and it is not allowed to smoke here.

Client：Unbelievable. One thing, I am not happy with the food here. Can you tell them to prepare a meal for me separate from others?

Lawyer：If you cannot eat certain food because of your religion, you may apply for other meals；however, if you want to change food simply for its taste, it's not gonna work because most people eat the same food in here. I can tell your family to deposit more money in your account here, so you can buy extra food to improve your diet.

Client：Can I meet the accusers and talk to them?

Lawyer：First thing is you are under detention, they are not be able to meet you；even if you meet them, there is also a major legal risk for you, especially when they change their statement due to

讼相关罪名。

嫌疑人：如果被害人愿意撤销指控，能不能撤案？或者至少先取保候审？

律师：本案已经是国家介入的公诉案件，不能轻易撤案，更不会因为被害人想撤回报案而随便撤案。至于取保候审，则要看×××在本案中的具体情节以及有无其他法定情况，以判断是否符合取保候审的要求，所以目前信息不足，需要进一步了解情况。

嫌疑人：被害人还欠我 100 万美元，你帮我出去跟他说，如果他撤案，我就不要他还这个钱了。

律师：我刚才说了，本案是国家介入的公诉案件，不能轻易撤案，更不会因为被害人想撤回报案而随便撤案，不像民事案件那样。

嫌疑人：太荒唐了。我出去以后一定要跟我们政府说，你们居然在案子还在侦查时就把我关在这儿！

your meeting, which may involve charges of impairing legal proceedings.

Client: If the accuser withdraws his accusation, shall the case be dismissed too? Or at least bail me out first?

Lawyer: This is a case of public prosecution, which is you vs. the State, so it can not be dismissed easily, even if the accuser himself wishes to withdraw his accusation. As for the bailout, it relies on specific situation of this case and whether it meets any legal conditions of bailout for us to assess the possibility of it. Therefore, information is not enough so far for us to tell, so we have to find more to evaluate current situation.

Client: He still own me 1 million dollars. You go to tell him that if he dismisses the case, I don't want this money back.

Lawyer: I said it before this case is public prosecution, which is you vs. the State, so it can not be dismissed easily, even if the accuser himself wishes to withdraw his accusation, unlike civil cases.

Client: That's ridiculous. When I walk out, I will tell my government that you hold me in custody while you are still investigating!

律师：首先，对你的羁押是依法的，你的罪名本身就是重罪，和你罪名一样的嫌疑人基本都以羁押为主；其次，很多其他罪名在侦查期间，即便是三年以下的轻罪，也有相当一部分要被羁押，这是我国的司法现状，并不是针对你个人；最后，我刚才也说过了，取保候审必须要符合若干法定情形中的一种，而你目前并不符合。

嫌疑人：我这里有一张字条，能不能帮我带出去？

律师：你能直接念一下吗？

嫌疑人：可以。但这是西班牙语的，我念了你也不懂。

律师：那你可以用英语把意思说出来，我记下。

嫌疑人：不行，你要帮我把字条带出去给我家人看。

律师：律师行业规范不允许律师在会见时夹带嫌疑人的信件出去，这是违法违规的，我们也会因此"丢饭碗"。望理解！

嫌疑人：别糊弄我了！我听说里面就有人让律师带纸条出去的。

Lawyer：Firstly, your detention is based on the law here; next, your crime is a felony in nature, suspects with your crime normally will be detained; besides, many with other crimes, whose punishment are under three year imprisonment, are also detained during investigation period. This is the judicial practice in our country, not specifically to you; I have mentioned before that you have to meet one of the several conditions to be bailed out, and you currently meet none of them.

Client：I have a written note. Would you take it out for me?

Lawyer：Can you just read out to me?

Client：OK. But it is in Spanish, even if I read it, you cannot understand.

Lawyer：Then you can paraphrase it in English. I will take note.

Client：Nope. You have to take this note out for me to my family.

Lawyer：Our bar regulation prohibits us from taking any notes from out, which is against the law and rules. We will lose our jobs by doing so. Hope you can understand!

Client：You are bluffing! I heard people here let lawyers take notes out!

律师：其他律师这么做，不等于这是对的；其他律师违法违规，不等于我也必须违法违规。

嫌疑人：我要见总领事，我有话跟他说。

律师：你的领事馆应该已经知道你被羁押了，会安排人员处理的。但我作为你的律师，没法跟他们直接对接。

嫌疑人：你们一定要把我弄出去！马上！

律师：我刚才也已经分析了，你的案子现在还需要弄清楚这几件事……后续我们准备做这些工作……这些工作如果顺利，我们会申请取保候审……

嫌疑人：谁是你们所最资深的？我要请他当我的律师。

律师：虽然你的案子我们主任不直接介入，但对于你这样的重大疑难案件，我们所内部有一个讨论会商机制，相当于医生会诊。讨论一般都会有主任的参与；如果你坚持要更换律师，让我们主任参与主办，恐怕要重新委托，重新签订合同，既耽误时间，花费还会更大。

嫌疑人：算了。里面太无聊，能不能帮我送几本书进来？

Lawyer：Others doing it doesn't make it right；Other lawyers against the law and rules is not the reason for me to breach them.

Client：I want to meet the consul general. I have something to say to him.

Lawyer：Your consul should be aware of your detention and on the way of handling your situation. But as your lawyer, I have no way to contact them.

Client：You have to get me out! Right now!

Lawyer：As I explained, about your case, you have to straighten out a few things first...later we have to work on these issues...if all above matters go well, we will apply for your bail...

Client：Who is the most experienced in your firm? I want him to be my lawyer!

Lawyer：Although our director is not retained for your case, but for a major case like yours, our firm will have a group consultation, so do doctors. The director normally will attend the discussion；if you insist on change of counsel, I am afraid you have to sign POA and agreement again, which is time-consuming and more costly.

Client：Never mind. it's so boring in here, can you bring in some books for me?

律师：送物取决于疫情期间各个看守所的内部规定，我会帮你询问。如果可以，我让你家人送来或寄来。

嫌疑人：我在里面没人听得懂英语，能不能让他们安排一个能说英语的人做我室友？

律师：这个你可以申请一下，只要要求合理，条件允许，相信他们也会考虑。

嫌疑人：你们下一步有什么打算？

律师：我刚才说了，我们现在还需要弄清楚这几件事……后续我们准备做这些工作……这些工作如果顺利，我们会申请取保候审……

嫌疑人：我需要做什么？除了在这里等判决什么都不能做吗？

律师：恰恰相反，你在这里也有很多事可以做。有一件最重要的事，你可以先做，就是你先理清这几样东西……

嫌疑人：我到底有哪些权利？

律师：依据《中华人民共和国刑法》和《中华人民共和国刑事诉讼法》，你享有以下权利：

一、不通晓当地通用的语言文字时有权要求配备翻译人员，有权用本

Lawyer：During pandemic, it depends on whether the jail allows the package from outside to be delivered in. I will help you check with them too. If possible, I will make your family do so.

Client：None of my cellmates here speaks English, can you let them arrange someone who can speak English to be my cellmate?

Lawyer：You may apply for it. I believe as long as it's reasonable andfeasible, they will consider.

Client：What's your next move?

Lawyer：Like I mentioned, currently we have to sort these things out... later we have to work on these issues... if all above matters go well, we will apply for your bail...

Client：What am I supposed to do now? Do nothing but stay here to cop it?

Lawyer：Quite the contrary, there is plenty you can do while you are here. The first and foremost thing you can do is to straighten out a couple of things such as...

Client：What on earth are my rights?

Lawyer：According to the *Criminal Law of the People's Republic of China* and *Criminal Procedure Law of the People's Republic of China*, you enjoy following rights：

1. You have the right to request for an interpreter and use your native langua-

民族语言文字进行诉讼。

二、对于公安机关及其侦查人员侵犯其诉讼权利和人身侮辱的行为，有权提出申诉或者控告。

三、在某些情形下，有权申请侦查人员、鉴定人、记录人、翻译人员回避。

四、在接受传唤、拘传、讯问时，有权要求饮食和必要的休息时间。

五、对于采取强制措施超过法定期限的，有权要求解除强制措施。

六、对于侦查人员的提问，应当如实回答。但是对与本案无关的问题，有拒绝回答的权利。在接受讯问时有权为自己辩解。如实供述自己罪行的，可以从轻处罚；因如实供述自己罪行，避免特别严重后果发生的，可以减轻处罚。

七、你有核对讯问笔录的权利，如

ges in litigation.

2. You have the right to file accusations against public security authority and investigators who infringe upon their procedural rights or inflict personal insult on them.

3. You have the right to demand the withdrawal of a investigator, a appraiser, a clerk or an interpreter under certain circumstances.

4. During the period of interrogation by summons or forced appearance, you have the rights to have the meals and necessary rest time.

5. You have the right to require termination of a compulsory measure taken by public security authority when the term of the compulsory measure expires.

6. You shall truthfully answer the questions of the investigators, but you have the right to refuse to answer questions irrelevant to the case. During interrogation, you have the right to defend yourself. Where you truthfully confesses to the facts of the crime, you may be given a lighter penalty; and you may be given a mitigated penalty if any especially serious consequence is avoided for your truthful confession.

7. You have the right to confirm your

果笔录记载有遗漏或者差错，可以提出补充或者改正。

八、犯罪嫌疑人请求自行书写供述的，应当准许。

九、如果你自愿如实供述自己的罪行，承认指控的犯罪事实，愿意接受处罚的，可以依法从宽处理。

十、你有权知道用作证据的鉴定意见的内容，并可以申请补充鉴定或重新鉴定。

嫌疑人：监规没有英文版，我又看不懂中文，让他们翻译一个英文版贴墙上。

律师：好的，你在里面申请一下。我也帮你说一下。

嫌疑人：那你用这个电脑给我拍张照，我的家人他们肯定很担心。

律师：抱歉，律师行业规范不允许我们在会见时摄录，否则会受暂停执业等处分。你看得到这个房间两头都有监控，我只要一使用摄像头，恐怕你就要委托其他律师了。

interrogation transcripts. If there are any omissions or errors in the transcripts, you may suggest supplements or corrections.

8. You shall be permitted to personally write a confession, if you so request.

9. If you voluntarily and truthfully confess to your crime, admit to the facts of the crime that you are charged with, and are willing to accept punishment, you may be granted leniency in accordance with Chinese law.

10. You have the right to know the expert opinion to be used as evidence. And you may apply for a re-identification or re-evaluation.

Client：There is no English jail rule, and I don't understand Chinese. Can you let them translate it into English and put it on the wall.

Lawyer：OK. You apply for it and I will tell the management too.

Client：Use your computer and take a photo of me. My family should be worrying about me.

Lawyer：Sorry, the bar regulation doesn't allow us to use any camera during the visit, otherwise our licence would be suspended. You can see the CCTV camera in both ends of this room. Once I use mine, I am afraid you have to retain an

嫌疑人：我家里人有什么话要对我说的？

律师：你家人有这些话要转告你……你在里面还有没有什么需要？

嫌疑人：你跟我家人说，让他们给我买……

律师：我刚说了，疫情期间，送物取决于看守所是否允许。肯定不如之前方便。我去帮你打听送物规定，如果实在不行，先给你存足生活费，你可以在里面先行购买满足需要。

嫌疑人：我的罪到底重不重？我要坐几年牢？

律师：你说的是你案件的最终结果，需要法院来判。但是在法院确定刑期之前，结果都是动态变化的，所以我们需要尽可能去努力。

嫌疑人：好吧。那祝你们好运！

律师：如果没有其他问题，请在委托书上签字，确认对我们的委托。

other lawyer.

Client: Is there any message from my family?

Lawyer: The messages are as follows. . . do you need anything in here?

Client: Tell my family to buy. . . for me.

Lawyer: Like I just said, during pandemic, it depends on whether the jail allows the package from outside to be delivered in. it's definitely not as easy as before. I will go and help you check with them too. If not possible, I will tell your family to deposit enough money for you to buy needed things in here for the moment.

Client: Is my crime serious? How many years am I going to stay in prison?

Lawyer: You are talking about the final result of your case, which will be determined by the court. Before any judgement coming into effect, the result is not fixed, so we have to work in our full strength.

Client: All right. Good luck then!

Lawyer: If there is no more questions, please sign on this POA and confirm retaining us.

# 首次会见后向家属反馈高频问答

| 中文版 | 英文版 |
| --- | --- |
| 家属：现在他怎么样？我们全家都在这儿，很关心他。你这次去拍了照片吗？给我们看看。 | Client：How is he now？We have everyone here worrying about him. Have you taken any photo of him？We want to take a look. |
| 律师：他目前身体状况都好，情绪也比较稳定，你们不用担心。上次接待你们的时候，我跟那位男士也说过，我们的法律和行业规范都禁止律师在会见时摄录。并且我们的手机都在会见室外的锁柜里存着，没法使用。因此我们没办法拍照，抱歉。 | Lawyer：He is physically well and mentally stable for now. No worries. During our talk last time, I told that gentleman that law and bar regulation of our country clearly prohibited to use cellphone during the visit, and cellphones must be checked in the locker before visit. So we could not take any photos, sorry. |
| 家属：他在里面一天怎么过的？要干活吗？ | Client：What's his life like in there？Does he have to work？ |
| 律师：他基本的日程安排是每天6点半起床，然后洗漱，整理内务，7点左右吃早饭。结束后学习监规。11点吃中饭，然后休息到下午2点半，起来后有活动时间。17点吃晚饭，结束后看电视到21点。然后就寝。他所在的看守所里，除了打扫监室卫生以外，不用额外干活。 | Lawyer：Here is his daily schedule：get up at 6.30, wash up and clean up. 7.00 for breakfast, and then learn the discipline. 11.00 for lunch. And lunch break till 14.30. After he will have some spare time for workout or something. 17.00 for supper and then watch TV till 21.00 and go to bed. Apart from his own cell cleaning, there is no extra work for him. |
| 家属：他这个罪重不重？能不能取保候审？ | Client：Is his crime serious？Can he get bailed？ |

律师：目前来看，他涉嫌的罪名本身是个重罪，所以取保会比其他罪困难。但后续我们会关注案件发展，分析相关事实，递交材料去沟通，争取取保候审。

家属：为什么关了这么长时间？他们为什么不先把人放出来？

律师：你说的还是取保候审的问题。根据《中华人民共和国刑事诉讼法》，现在他刚被逮捕。接下来还要有至少2个月，公安机关会进行侦查。从他现在的情况来看，不符合取保候审的任何一个条件，所以目前来看没这么快取保候审。

家属：2个月？为什么要侦查这么长时间？如果没有足够证据，要先放人！

律师：首先，从他进来到现在，公安机关的侦查工作开展了1个多月。虽然对你们来说很久，我们能理解，但是根据我们的经验，针对这种涉外的、存在一定争议的案子来说，2个月实属正常。你说的证据问题，目前他们肯定是掌握了一部分能证明他有犯罪行为的证据，才能执行拘留，他才会被批准逮捕。至于是什么证据，还需要我们和公安机关沟通后进一步了解。

Lawyer：So far, his crime is a felony, so bailout for him would be harder than others. But we would keep an eye on the development of the case, analyze relevant facts, present defense material and persuade the authority, and make all-out efforts to bail him out.

Client：Why are they holding him so long? Why don't let him out first?

Lawyer：It is still about bail. According to *Criminal Procedure Law of the People's Republic of China*, he has just been arrested and there are at least another 2 months for the police to carry out investigation. So far his circumstances do not meet any of the conditions of bail, so he will not get bailed this soon.

Client：2 months? What took so long? If they don't have enough evidence, they should release him first!

Lawyer：Since his detention, the investigation by the police went on for more than a month. it's too long for you, which we can understand. But based on our experience, for cases like his, particularly foreigner-related and controversial in nature, two months is common practice. Your second question is on evidence. By now, they must have had certain evidences that can prove his guilt, and that's

家属：就是说不能取保？我们打了这么多律师费给你们，居然不能取保？你们到底干了些什么？

律师：你先不要激动。我们才刚介入不到1周，加上他目前被逮捕不久，这时被取保的可能性本来就不大。就这么几天，我们已经做了大量工作，包括会见，梳理、分析案情，搜集类案数据，撰写法律文书，准备沟通提纲等。工作要一步步开展，我们也不是上帝，不可能一介入人就出来了。

家属：我不想扯这些。你就告诉我什么时候能取保？什么时候能判决？

律师：取保必须要结合案件本身的进展和办案单位的意见。例如，羁押期限届满，经我们的沟通办案单位认为案件仍没有充分证据来起诉，到时必须取保候审。至于判决，关系到案件办理期限，像他这样的重大疑难案件，可能要一年左右的时间才能出结

the reason why he got detained and arrested. As for the evidence, we need to talk to the police to find out.

Client: Are you saying he cannot be bailed? We gave you so much money, and you cannot bail him out?! What have you done on earth?!

Lawyer: Keep your cool. Since we have just been retained for less than a week, plus he has been arrested not long ago, the probability for bailout is unsurprisingly not high for now. During these days, we are into multiple tasks, including visiting, summarizing and analyzing the case, looking for parallel cases, drafting legal documents and preparing outline for communication with the police. The work has been done step by step. We are not god almighty, so it's impossible to retain us today and bail him out tomorrow.

Client: Cut the crap. Just tell me when he can be bailed out? And when can we get a judgement?

Lawyer: The bail must be based on the timeline of the case and opinion of the authority. If the term of custody of him has expired but the case has not been closed, and a bail is necessary. As for the judgement, it has something to do with the case-handling period. For a major

果……

家属：什么？一年？他要在里面待上一年？

律师：你先听我说完，我说一年的时间出结果，不意味着他必须也在看守所待上一年。

家属：他那天到底是怎么回事？你详细跟我们说一下。

律师：根据法律，案件细节属于侦查机密，不能以任何途径外泄。我把大致情况跟你说一下……

家属：你们知不知道证人有谁？

律师：证人具体姓名我目前还不了解，他既不说中文，也不知道那些证人的名字。我们团队在阅卷后会掌握详细情况。

家属：被害人叫什么名字？联系电话和地址是什么？

律师：这些我们都还不清楚，要等将来阅卷后才能确定。

家属：我不信。

and difficult case like his, it might take a year or so to get a result...

Client: What? A year? He has to stay there for a year?

Lawyer: Let me finish. I said a year or so to close this case, not that he has to stay there for a year.

Client: What's on earth happened on that day? Explain to us in detail.

Lawyer: According to the law, details of the case is confidential, which should not be leaked in any means. I will tell you roughly what happened...

Client: Do you know who are the witnesses?

Lawyer: We don't know the specific name of the witnesses. He doesn't speak any Chinese, and have no idea about their names. Our team would know them when it's allowed to consult the case file later.

Client: What's the name of the victim? What's his phone number and address?

Lawyer: We don't know them for sure either, it can only be ascertained after we consult the evidence. And we don't have his phone number and address.

Client: I don't believe it.

律师：不管你信与不信，我们确实不掌握。

家属：那你们去查，找私人侦探，去偷、去借、去求，不择手段都要给我们查出来，毕竟我们委托了你。

律师：不是我不愿意帮忙，私家侦探在我们国家是违法的。而且你为什么非要这些信息呢？

家属：我们要找他好好谈一谈。那你帮我们去问，问到了帮我们去谈，毕竟我们来你们国家也不方便。

律师：虽然法律不禁止你们接触被害人，但是对你们来说也有比较大的法律风险，尤其是在被害人因为你们的接触而改变陈述时，可能涉及刑法规定的妨碍诉讼相关罪名。法律是不准律师随意接触被害人的。

家属：我如果只是想和解行不行？我们国家都可以和解赔钱撤案的。

律师：我之前在接待中说过，本案已经是国家介入的公诉案件，不能轻易撤案，更不会因为被害人想撤回

Lawyer：No matter you believe or not, we don't have those information.

Client：Then you try to find out, to hire private eye, to beg, borrow or steal, whatever you do, since we retain you.

Lawyer：It's not that I don't want to help, private eye is against the law in China. By the way, what do you want to use those information for?

Client：I want to talk with them over. Or you may help us to get those information and talk to them on behalf of us, since it's not easy for us to go to your country.

Lawyer：Although there is no clear ban in the law for you to meet them, there is also a relatively obvious legal risk for you, especially when they change their statement due to your meeting, which may involve charges of impairing legal proceedings. And counsels are not allowed to contact the accusers at will according to the law.

Client：What if I just want to settle with them? In our country, we could settle with the victim, compensate and dismiss the case.

Lawyer：I said in the meeting before, this is a case of public prosecution, which is him vs. the State, so it can

报案而随便撤案。

家属：这个案子到底严不严重？×××要坐几年牢？

律师：你说的是案件的最终结果，需要法院来判。但是在任何刑期生效前，结果都是动态变化的，所以我们需要尽可能去努力。

家属：我们能不能申请取保？

律师：根据《中华人民共和国刑事诉讼法》第97条的规定，犯罪嫌疑人、被告人及其法定代理人、近亲属或者辩护人有权申请变更强制措施。所以近亲属是可以申请取保候审的。但我的建议是目前他刚被逮捕，贸然申请取保候审，结果多半是不通过。

家属：那你们下一步准备怎么办？

律师：下一步我们要分析案情，准备材料，整理沟通提纲，准备与承办人沟通。

家属：我们能做什么？

律师：你们能做很多，首先你们能够给他写信、寄照片等。这是对他

not be dismissed easily, even if the accuser himself wishes to withdraw his accusation.

Client：Is this case serious？How many years is he going to stay in prison？

Lawyer：You are talking about the final result of this case, which will be determined by the court. Before any judgement coming into effect, the result is not fixed, so we have to work in our full strength.

Client：Can we apply for the bail？

Lawyer：According to the *Criminal Procedure Law of the People's Republic of China* Article 97, a criminal suspect or defendant or his or her legal representative, close relative, or defender shall have the right to apply for modifying a compulsory measure. So the answer is yes, you may apply for his bail. But my recommendation is a "no". Because he has just been arrested, if you apply now, probably they won't agree.

Client：Then what's your plan？

Lawyer：Next step is to analyze the case, prepare the material and outlines, in order to communicate with the handling authority.

Client：How can we help？

Lawyer：There is a lot you can do. First you may write to him, and together

有效的鼓励，也是他在里面最想看到的。其次，你们需要配合我们的工作，及时提供相应的证明材料。最后，你们自己也要注意甄别消息，不要相信小道消息。

家属：他在里面缺什么？

律师：他说现在他急需这些东西……

家属：我们能不能见他？我们能不能作为你的助理进去见一下他？

律师：目前家属还不能去见他。你们当然也不能作为助理进去，作为助理至少也需要实习律师证。

家属：我们能不能给他电话？

律师：目前还不行。

家属：我们能不能给他写信？

律师：可以，不要写任何关于案件的内容。可以提一些家常琐事、子女近况，可以附一些家人的照片。主要起到鼓励他的作用。另外，篇幅尽可能短、简洁、字迹清晰。

with family photos, which is huge comfort to him, and it's what he wants to see most in there. Secondly, you need to work with us to provide all the needed material. Last, you need to examine the information carefully and do not believe those through the grapevine.

Client: Is there anything he needs in there?

Lawyer: He said he needs following things. . .

Client: Can we visit him? Or can we go to see him as your assistant?

Lawyer: For now you can not visit him. And also you can not see him as my assistant, because an apprentice lawyerlicense is needed.

Client: Can we talk to him over the phone?

Lawyer: Negative for now.

Client: Can we write to him?

Lawyer: Yes, you can, like I mentioned a moment ago. But make sure it does not contain anything about the case. Just tell him about some household chores, stories about children and attach some family photos, aiming to encourage him. Moreover, the letter should be as brief, concise and clear as possible.

| | |
|---|---|
| 家属：我写的是英文，他也能收到吗？<br><br>律师：里面也有会英文的民警。会审查后转达的。<br><br>家属：他有什么话带给我们吗？<br><br>律师：他有这些话要对你说…… | Client：Can he receive it if it's in English?<br><br>Lawyer：In there some police officers understand English and will examine the letters before relaying to him.<br><br>Client：Any message from him for us?<br><br>Lawyer：He wanted to tell you that... |

## 审查逮捕前会见高频问答

| 中文版 | 英文版 |
|---|---|
| 当事人：今天如何？<br><br>律师：谢谢。我很好。我今天来告知你，公安机关今天已经将你的案子报请检察院批准逮捕。检察院将在 7 日内决定是否逮捕你。<br><br>当事人：公安机关要让检察院逮捕我？简直荒唐！他们凭什么逮捕我？我完全是无罪的！<br><br>律师：你先冷静一下，你情绪稳定了跟我说，我再跟你分析。<br><br>当事人：我好了，你说吧。<br><br>律师：根据《中华人民共和国刑事诉讼法》第 53 条，公安机关提请批准逮捕书、人民检察院起诉书、人民法院判决书，必须忠实于事实真相。故意隐瞒事实真相的，应当追究责任。 | Client：How are you?<br><br>Lawyer：I am doing fine, thank you. I am here to inform you that the police has delivered your case to the procuratorate for approval of arrest, and the procuratorate will decide whether to arrest you within 7 days.<br><br>Client：The police want the prosecutor to arrest me? That's absurd! They arrest me for what? I am completely innocent!<br><br>Lawyer：Take some time and keep cool and then I will explain.<br><br>Client：I am ready. You may start.<br><br>Lawyer：According to the Article 53 of *Criminal Procedure Law of the People's Republic of China*, a written request of a public security authority for approval of an arrest, an indictment of a people's |

因此他们有忠实事实的义务，不能放纵犯罪，更不能冤枉无辜的人。因此即便他们逮捕你，也是一种诉讼保障措施，不代表你就有罪。有罪无罪只能由法院定，但你有准确向司法机关陈述事实的义务，我们也会和他们进行沟通，防止他们在认定事实时产生偏差。

当事人：那我该如何跟他们准确陈述事实呢？

律师：这就需要你仔细梳理案发当时的细节，重点强调这几个问题……这几个问题你如实说清楚了，司法机关才能准确判定。后续检察官也可能会来提审你，他带着看案卷后的问题，会有重点地向你提问，你要如实、准确地回答，慢慢讲没关系，整理好思路再讲，这很重要。

当事人：好的，我会好好再回忆

procuratorate, and a sentence of people's court must be consistent with the truth. Where truth is withheld intentionally, liability shall be investigated. Therefore, they are obliged to respect the truth, not to indulge criminals or wrong innocent people. That means even if they arrest you, it's just a method to ensure the criminal proceedings, not to say that you are guilty, which has to be decided by the court only. However, you are required by law to state the fact accurately to the judicial authority, and we will also communicate with them to avoid any misunderstanding of the fact by them.

Client: Then how can I state the fact accurately?

Lawyer: You need to go through the details of the case when it happened and stress the following points... the judicial authority may make the decision justly only if you expound these points truthfully and clearly. The prosecutor may arraign you later with the interested questions he has after examining the case file. It is important for you to answer questions truthfully and accurately. You may go slow, but remember to clear your head before speaking.

Client: Noted. I will try to jog the

一下当时的细节。要多少时间检察院才会答复？

律师：《中华人民共和国刑事诉讼法》规定，人民检察院应当自接到公安机关提请批准逮捕书后的 7 日以内，作出批准逮捕或者不批准逮捕的决定。人民检察院不批准逮捕的，公安机关应当在接到通知后立即释放，并且将执行情况及时通知人民检察院。对于需要继续侦查，并且符合取保候审、监视居住条件的，依法取保候审或者监视居住。也就是检察院 7 天内就会给出决定，如果不批准逮捕，你会被立即释放。

当事人：太好了。

律师：但请注意，这种情况只是可能性之一。至于到底会不会逮捕你，我们会去和检察官全力沟通，争取最佳结果。

memory of what happened at that time. How long does it take for the prosecutor to make decision?

Lawyer: According to the *Ciriminal Procedure Law of the People's Republic of China*, a people's procuratorate shall make a decision to approve or disapprove an arrest within 7 days after receiving a written request for approval of arrest from a public security authority. If the people's procuratorate disapproves the arrest, the public security authority shall release the detainee immediately after receiving anotice regarding the decision and notify the people's procuratorate regarding execution in a timely manner. If further investigation is necessary and the conditions for bail or residential confinement are met, the criminal suspect shall be released on bail or placed under residential confinement in accordance with the law. That means you will receive a decision within 7 days. If it's not approved, you will be released immediately.

Client: That's great!

Lawyer: Please note that it's just one of the possible scenarios. As for their decision, we will do our utmost and communicate with the prosecutor for the best-possible result.

当事人：他们释放我的可能性大不大？

律师：如果沟通情况良好，我们的意见都被采纳，那么不批捕很有希望。

当事人：你认为他们会采纳你的意见吗？

律师：这个要看我们的沟通，我们会全力以赴的。不沟通是不知道的。

当事人：他们逮捕我会通知我吗？

律师：会的。根据《中华人民共和国刑事诉讼法》第93条的规定，公安机关逮捕人的时候，必须出示逮捕证。逮捕后，应当立即将被逮捕人送看守所羁押。除无法通知的以外，应当在逮捕后24小时以内通知被逮捕人的家属。

当事人：千万不要这样。上帝保佑。

律师：我们已经准备好了所有相关材料，会尽全力跟检察官沟通的。

当事人：谢谢！等你们的好消息！

Client：What is the odds for the disapproval of arrest?

Lawyer：If the communication goes well and our points are adopted, the arrest might well be disapproved.

Client：Do you think they will adopt your points?

Lawyer：It depends on our communication, for which we will go all out. But we won't know their view until we communicate with them.

Client：Will I be notified if I am arrested?

Lawyer：You will be notified. According to the Article 93 of *Criminal Procedure Law of the People's Republic of China*, when arresting a person, a public security authority must produce an arrest warrant. After a person is arrested, the arrestee shall be immediately transferred to a jail for custody. The family of the arrestee shall be notified within 24 hours after arrest, unless such notification is impossible.

Client：For Gods' sake it doesn't happen.

Lawyer：I have all the materialsready, and we will do everything in our power to communicate with them.

Client：Thank you! I am looking forward to some good news from you!

# 与侦查机关沟通后向家属反馈高频问答

| 中文版 | 英文版 |
|---|---|
| 家属：今天见到办案民警了吗？男的女的？ | Client：Have you seen the of ficer that handles the case? Is that he or she? |
| 律师：见到了，我们和民警沟通了1个小时，民警是中年男性。 | Lawyer：He is a middle-aged man and we have talked to him for an hour. |
| 家属：今天他怎么说？ | Client：What did he say? |
| 律师：我们今天获取了一些信息，也按照工作进度提出了本案的全部疑点及争议，民警的意思是嫌疑人不认罪还推说是被害人的责任…… | Lawyer：We have acquired some information and put forward all the doubts and controversies in this case based on our progress. That of ficer said the suspect did not plead guilty and point finger at the victim. . . |
| 家属：这太荒唐了！在我们国家有沉默权，你知道米兰达规则吗？可以拒绝他们的问题！×××是美国人，也应该享有沉默权！ | Client：This is ridiculous! In our country, we have right to remain silent, you know The Miranda Rule? We could refuse to answer their question! * * * is American, so he should have right to keep silent! |
| 律师：如果他在美国，可以享有美国法律里的诉讼权利。但现在他是在中国境内触犯中国法律，按照《中华人民共和国刑法》的明确规定，要按照中国刑事法律追究刑事责任。而中国刑事法律中并没有沉默权一说，只规定了嫌疑人有如实供述的义务。你们在不了解中国法律的前提下，说出这些话可以理解。但他的案子目前 | Lawyer：If he is in the States, he may enjoy that procedural right. But now he is a suspect who breached Chinese criminal law within the territory of China, so he will be charged according to *Criminal Law of the People's Republic of China*, in which there is no such a right to keep silent. There is only obligation to truthfully answer the questions of the in- |

要按照中国法律处理，为了便于你们跟进案情，我们会根据需要跟你们介绍中国刑事法律，你们应当关注。

家属：为什么还不释放他？

律师：警官表示，目前他们正在按照办案程序走，会在期限截止前移送检察院。目前即便我们申请取保候审，也不会批准。

家属：侦查为什么要这么长时间？他怎么解释？

律师：他说首先本案为比较重大的涉外案件，需要很多额外的报告手续；其次我们沟通后公安机关也同意本案存在一定争议，所以他们仍然要进一步取证；最后警官最近手头其他案子比较多，有点忙不过来。

家属：那有关被害人的情况替我们问了吗？名字叫什么？地址和电话？

律师：被害人的信息，公安机关表示暂时不能透露。

家属：凭什么不告诉我们？我们有权利知道！

律师：出于职责，他们考虑的问

vestigators. Without knowing Chinese law, it's understandable for you to say that, but now this case will be handled according to Chinese criminal law. For you to keep up with this case, we will introduce Chinese criminal law according to your needs, which you shall keep an eye on.

Client: Why he is not released yet?

Lawyer: Officer said now they are following the proceedings to transfer this case to the procuratorate before the deadline. Now they are not considering approving the bail, even if we apply.

Client: Why it takes so long to investigate? Any explanation from him?

Lawyer: He said this case is a major case which involves foreigner, so it needs much extra reporting; and after our talk he admits that there is some controversies in this case, that's why additional investigation is required; the last, that officer is a bit swamped with cases recently.

Client: Have you asked about the victim? His name, address and number?

Lawyer: Police said they could not share with us that information for the moment.

Client: Why not? We have rights to know!

Lawyer: Out of their duty, the police

题跟我们不完全相同。我们问了，他们目前认为不能跟我们透露，有串供的风险。

家属：串供？我们不会的，我们就是去问问被害人是怎么回事和他们有什么需要。

律师：我也相信你们不会，但公安机关拒绝透露，目前也没有其他任何途径能获取。

家属：现在他们有什么证据？

律师：我们初步了解，目前有笔录、监控录像和法医鉴定意见等证据。

家属：我们能看一下证据吗？

律师：目前不行。即便是律师也要到审查起诉阶段才能看到。家属在开庭时可以旁听，证据都会展示，你们到时也看得到。

家属：那现在他们还在等什么？

律师：目前他们还在侦查。

家属：这要到什么时候？

律师：按照《中华人民共和国刑事诉讼法》第 156 条的规定，对犯罪嫌疑人逮捕后的侦查羁押期限不得超过 2 个月。案情复杂、期限届满不能终结的案件，可以经上一级人民检察

see a different picture from us. We have argued with them, but they think they are not in the position to disclose that information because of the risk of collusion.

Client：Collusion？We will not！We just want to check out what's going on with them and what they need.

Lawyer：We believe you won't too. But since they don't tell us, there is no other way to acquire it.

Client：What evidence do they currently have?

Lawyer：As far as we know, the evidence include statements, CCTV footage and forensic opinion, etc.

Client：Can we take a look at them?

Lawyer：Not for now. Even defense lawyers have to wait till the examination of prosecution. As his family, you may attend the hearing and all the evidence will be shown, and you can see and hear them.

Client：Then what are they waiting for?

Lawyer：They are still investigating.

Client：Till when?

Lawyer：According to the Article 156 of *Criminal Procedure Law of the People's Republic of China*, the period of custody during criminal investigation after a criminal suspect is arrested shall not exceed

院批准延长 1 个月。所以逮捕后一般情况下 2 个月后移送审查起诉。

家属：为什么不能先把人取保出来再侦查？

律师：我之前说过，目前他并不符合取保候审的任何一个条件。如果羁押期限届满，案件尚未办结，这时会采取取保候审。也有可能办案机关认为他这个罪名有潜在社会危险性。

家属：社会危险性？不可能的，他原来连一只虫子都不敢打。

律师：你们会这么问很正常，源于你们自己对"社会危险性"的理解。我们因为案件办理需要，针对社会危险性这点研究过大量相关的论文、案例、法规。简单来说，在实践中，司法机关对于是否会有社会危险性这点考量的主要因素是犯罪嫌疑人是否涉嫌故意杀人、强奸、抢劫、绑架、放火、爆炸、投放危险物质等危害国家安全、公共安全或者社会秩序犯罪，

two months. If the investigation of a complicated case cannot be closed within the period, the period may be extended for one month with the approval of the people's procuratorate at the next higher level. So normally it takes two months for them to transfer the case to the procuratorate after arrest.

Client: Why don't they bail him out and investigate?

Lawyer: I explained before that he does not meet any of the conditions for bail at the moment. If the term of custody has expired but the case has not been closed, he will be bailed. Or the authority may think his crime has potential danger to the society.

Client: Danger to the society? That's impossible! He does not even want to hit a bug!

Lawyer: Your question is common for my client, which is based on the understanding of danger to the society. Out of needs of case-handling, we have done plenty of study of related thesis, cases and laws and regulations on danger to the society. To put it simple, in judicial practice, the top factor for authority to consider danger to society is whether the criminal suspect is involved in crimes en-

是否参与恐怖活动，黑社会性质犯罪，严重暴力犯罪和毒品犯罪集团。而他涉嫌的犯罪就在其中。你认为他没有社会危险性，我们也认为没有，但司法机关有一套自己的判定标准，并不按你理解的字面意思。

家属：他的案子目前还在侦查，这是好事还是坏事？

律师：这只能说办案单位比较审慎负责，调查和认定都尽可能做到不冤枉当事人，所以才会需要继续侦查。

家属：这个案子到底重不重？×××要坐几年牢？

律师：这是法院决定的，不是公安机关。但是在任何判决生效前，结果都是动态变化的，所以我们需要尽可能去努力。

家属：被害人口供怎么说的？

律师：具体的供述我现在还不清

dangering national security, public safety or society such as intentional homicide, rape, robbery, kidnapping, arson, explosion, dissemination of hazardous substances, or whether to participate in terrorist activities, crimes of gangland nature, serious violence or drug criminal groups. And his crime is among them. You think he is not dangerous to this society, which we agree, but the authority has its own criteria to decide, which is not consistent to the literal meaning as you see it.

Client: His case is still under investigation, which do you think is a good sign or not?

Lawyer: It only means the authority is so prudent and responsible as not to treat him unjustly during investigation and identification, that is why they keep investigating.

Client: Is this case serious? How many years is he going to stay in prison?

Lawyer: It is decided by the court rather than the police. Before any judgement coming into effect, the result is not fixed, so we have to work in our full strength.

Client: What did the victim say?

Lawyer: We don't have the details of

楚，公安机关也不会透露的，要看到时审查起诉阶段阅卷的情况。

家属：我们现在能不能见到他？

律师：目前他还处于逮捕状态，你们还见不到他。

家属：那我们什么时候能见他？

律师：两种情况你们能见到他，一种是他被取保候审；一种是判决生效。

家属：那你们下次什么时候见他？

律师：我们下次根据工作需要，安排在1周后左右见他。

家属：你们什么时候申请取保候审？

律师：我刚才也说了，现在即便申请，公安机关批准的概率也很小。因为他刚被逮捕，根据我们的经验，我们建议最好1个月后再做相关申请工作。

家属：那我等你们的好消息，祝你们好运！

his statement, which the police won't let us know either. It all depends on the analysis of case file during the examination of prosecution.

Client: Can we meet him or not?

Lawyer: Negative, he is under arrest, which means you cannot meet him.

Client: When can we meet him?

Lawyer: There are two circumstances that you may meet him. The first is the time when he gets bailed; the second is when the judgement comes into effect.

Client: Then when are you going to meet him again?

Lawyer: We will arrange next visit a week later or so.

Lawyer: When are you going toapply for his bail?

Client: I said before that even if we apply now, it is unlikely for the police to approve it. Since he was just arrested, according to our experience, we recommend that we work on it one month after his arrest.

Lawyer: Then I am looking forward to good news. Good luck to you!

# 取保后交代事项高频问答

| 中文版 | 英文版 |
|---|---|
| 当事人：律师，我跟你说过我是无辜的吧。你看他们现在取保我了，是不是代表这个案子我已经赢了？<br><br>律师：如果你说的赢的意思是无罪，那我建议你不要过于乐观。因为你的取保候审决定书上的理由是"羁押期限届满，需要继续侦查"，说明你现在取保只是因为关押太长时间，导致超期，为了保障你的人权，不得不先把你取保，并非侦查机关主动将你取保。这两者还是有很大差别的。而且决定书里明确写了将继续侦查。说明你这个案子远没有结束。如果他们认为你无罪，你收到的应该是《终止侦查决定书》。<br><br><br>当事人：律师，你不用说这些了。我今年60岁了，我生活经验丰富，人情世故我都懂，我知道他们把我取保意味着什么。<br><br>律师：总之目前我们建议你不要过于乐观，当他们收集到足够证据时，仍然可能将你移送检察院，甚至报请 | Client：Sir, I told you I was inno-cent. You see they bailed me now. Does that mean I have won this case?<br><br>Lawyer：If that "won" means inno-cence, I suggest you not be over–opti-mistic. Because the reason on your notifi-cation of bail is "the term of custody has expired but the case needs further investi-gation", which means your bail is owing to too much time of detaining and protec-tion of your human rights, not your inno-cence. it's they "have to" bail you, not they "want to" bail you. There is a huge difference between the two. And the noti-fication has it clearly that they will con-tinue investigation, so your case is far from the end. If they think you are clean, you should receive a *Decision of the Close of Criminal Investigation*.<br><br>Client：Sir, no need for this. I am 60 years old and very experienced and worldly, so I know what they mean by bailing me out.<br><br>Lawyer：In a word, my suggestion is not to be over–optimistic on the case, since they may transfer this case to proc- |

逮捕。

当事人：什么？他们还能逮捕我？你是说我出来了还会再进去？

律师：是的，存在这个可能性。

当事人：太荒唐了，我这辈子都不想回去了。

律师：但愿你不用再回去。我们也会尽力去做工作。

当事人：我现在可以回国吗？

律师：目前你的护照被公安机关依法扣押，而且你的身份因本案被边控，无法出境。

当事人：那我的护照什么时候能还我？我的出境限制什么时候能解除？我要回国！

律师：你想归国的心情我完全能理解。你的护照在结案时会归还给你。一般来说，当办案机关归还你护照的时候，你的出境限制不久也会解除。即便你不得不服刑，你也会在刑期结束后取回你的护照。

当事人：上帝啊，我是无辜的，为什么要坐牢？你是我的律师，怎么

uratorate or even request them to approve the arrest of you when theyhave sufficient evidence.

Client：What? They can still arrest me? Are you saying that I may still go back in after I walk out?

Lawyer：That's right. There is a possibility for that.

Client：This is absurd. I don't want to go back there ever again.

Lawyer：I hope so. And we will work on it.

Client：Can I go back to my country?

Lawyer：According to Chinese law, for now your passport is impounded by the police and your ID is under border control for this case, so you are prohibited to travel to other countries.

Client：When can I have my passport back? And when will they lift the ban? I need to go back!

Lawyer：I fully understand your feel. Your passport will be returned when your case is closed. Usually, when they return your passport, the ban will be lift very soon. Even if you have to serve a prison sentence, you will have your passport back when the term is over.

Client：For Chris sake, why I get a prison sentence while I am innocent? You

能让这种事发生？

律师：正因为我是你的律师，才需要将所有的情形告知你，而不是对你有所隐瞒。案件情况多变，谁都不能百分之百保证一定是好结果。我们只有尽我们所能去争取。对了，你的家属有拿到谅解书吗？

当事人：我是无辜的为什么要谅解书？

律师：我跟你家属也讲过，谅解书并不等于认罪；在你的谅解书中，只是对案发当天的事实感到抱歉，并不意味着你就有刑事责任。

当事人：那谅解书有什么用？

律师：如果你有谅解书，对你未来定罪量刑都有帮助，属于法定的从宽情节。

当事人：他们为什么谅解还要收钱？

律师：他们的立场决定了他们的观点。你认为自己无罪，但他们认为自己是被害人，所以你理应赔偿他们，来换取谅解书。

are my lawyer, how could you let this thing happen?

Lawyer：Just because I am your lawyer, so I need to tell you all the scenarios, rather than keep something from you. No one can guarantee a good result, since the case is changeable. What we can do is to put in our full strength. By the way, have your family obtained the forgiveness letter from the victim?

Client：I am innocent. Why do I need it?

Lawyer：I have explained to your family before. The forgiveness letter willnot make you guilty; in that letter, you are only sorry for what happened on that day. Not that you have criminal liability.

Client：Then what's in it for me?

Lawyer：If you have it, it will help on your conviction and sentencing, because it's a provision of law on leniency.

Client：Why they want my money by forgiving me?

Lawyer：Their position determines their opinion. You think you are innocent, but they see themselves as victims, so they think you should compensate in exchange for the forgiveness letter.

当事人：他们狮子大开口！这是敲诈！我要告他们！我能不能告他们？

律师：我认为不可行，因为你要或不要谅解书，完全是你的自主决定，没有任何人强制你必须要。如果你取得，可以酌情从轻。如果你不要，也不是一个从重处罚的情节。最重要的是，他们也没有以任何形式威胁你。因此虽然你觉得他们的做法不舒服，但这不是法律意义上的敲诈。

当事人：那你帮我去谈可不可以？

律师：根据法律，辩护人不能随意接触被害人。但考虑到你的实际情况，所以虽然这并非我的辩护职责，但如果办案单位同意，且最好在办案人员见证下，我愿意以合法形式，尝试和对方谈谈。

当事人：非常感谢！务必帮我跟他们讲价，我现在也没钱。他们这是要榨干我。

律师：如果有机会，我尽可能为你争取。另外，有几个重要事项我再跟你强调一下，如果你要离开居住的

Client: They are asking for a king's ransom! This is blackmailing! I want to sue them! Can I do so?

Lawyer: I don't think it would work, because it's up to you whether you accept the deal or not. No one is forcing you to pay. If you have it, it's a discretionary circumstance of being granted leniency. If you quit, it is not a legal circumstance for heavier punishment. The most important is, they are not threatening you in any way. Uncomfortable you may feel towards what they asked, but it's not blackmail in the sense of law.

Client: Can you go and talk to them on my behalf?

Lawyer: According to relevant laws and regulations, counsels are not allowed to contact the accusers at will. But in light of your circumstance, despite the fact that it's not within our duty, if the authority agrees and better with their witness, we are willing to try it in accordance with the law.

Client: Thank you so much! And do bargain with them for me. I have no money now and they are milking me dry.

Lawyer: If possible, we will shoot our best. Moreover, there are somethingI need to emphasize to you. If you leave the

| 中文版 | 英文版 |
|---|---|
| 市、县，必须要经过办案单位批准；如果住址或联系方式等变动的，一定要 24 小时内跟执行机关报告；另外不得以任何形式干扰证人作证，绝不允许毁灭、伪造证据或者串供。传讯的时候及时到案。<br><br>　　当事人：清楚了。警官跟我讲过了。<br>　　律师：好的。我们保持沟通。 | city or county where you reside, you have to get the approval of the execution authority; you shall report any change of your residence address, or contact information to the execution authority within 24 hours of such change; you shall not interfere in any way with the testimony of witnesses or destroy or forge evidence or make a false confession in collusion; you shall appear in a timely manner when summoned.<br><br>　　Client：Clear. The of ficer already said it.<br>　　Lawyer：Cool. Keep in touch. |

## 与被害方律师沟通后向家属反馈高频问答

| 中文版 | 英文版 |
|---|---|
| 　　家属：他们有几个人来了？<br><br>　　律师：他们总共来了 2 人，他们的代理律师和律师助理。<br>　　家属：你们谈了多久？<br><br>　　律师：因为初次接触，加上有些问题不能达成一致，整整谈了 3 小时。<br><br><br>　　家属：他们的律师说了什么？ | 　　Client：How many of them were there？<br><br>　　Lawyer：That's two of them – their lawyer and his assistant.<br>　　Client：How long have you been discussing？<br><br>　　Lawyer：Because this is our first meeting with them and there are many issues that we cannot come to an agreement, so it lasted for three hours.<br><br>　　Client：What did their lawyer say？ |

律师：他们的律师先说……最后说希望我们合理赔偿，然后考虑给我们谅解书。

家属：什么？他们去报案把我们送进牢房，还要我们付给他们钱去换所谓的谅解书？

律师：他们的立场决定了他们的观点。我们当然认为自己无罪，但他们认为自己是被害人，所以我们理应赔偿他们，来换取谅解书。而且他们要我们提出具体的赔偿方案。

家属：什么？为什么还要我们提出方案？他们怎么不报价？

律师：他们出于风险防范考虑，不想主动说出这个价格，希望我们提出方案，他们再回应。

家属：那好，即便我们愿意付50万美元，他们愿意出谅解书了。然后呢？

律师：对他未来的取保候审或定罪量刑都有帮助，这属于从轻情节。同时司法机关也会考虑到被害人已谅解，社会关系在一定程度上已经修复，尽可能给当事人轻缓处理。

Lawyer：He said. . .and hope us compensate them properly, and they would consider giving us the forgiveness letter.

Client：What? They reported the case to the police and sent us to the jail, and now they want us pay them for the so-called forgiveness letter?

Lawyer：Their position determines their opinion. You think you areinnocent, but they see themselves as victims, so they think you should compensate in exchange for the forgiveness letter. And they want us to present a detailed compensation plan.

Client：What? Why we have to present that plan? Why don't they offer the price?

Lawyer：They are preventing the risk so they refuse to of fer that price and ask us to give that price. After that, they could respond to it.

Client：Fine, even if we pay them like half a million dollars, they are willing to give us that letter, and then what?

Lawyer：It will help on his conviction and sentencing, because it's a provision of law on leniency. And the authority will consider the forgiveness from the victim, so the social relations have been restored, hence a lighter punishment might be given to him.

家属：谅解书能让他取保吗？

律师：我们拿到之后，会准备相关沟通材料，去和办案单位充分沟通，尽可能争取。

家属：我要一个确定的答案，到底谅解书能不能把他放出来？我们只有确定谅解书有用，才能付钱，否则万一我们付了钱，拿了谅解书还不能取保怎么办？对了，我们付钱了他们一定会给我们谅解书吧？

律师：我们毕竟不是办案机关，我们作不了决定，我们能做的是尽全力沟通。另外，在现在已经逮捕的前提下，司法机关内部也要协调、报请、审批通过后才能决定取保候审，也不是某个警官能说了算的。所以我现在没法给你明确的"是"或者"不是"，只能尽可能去说服他们，提高取保的可能性。但是肯定不能"打包票"能取保候审。另外，我们会和他们签订和解协议，想收到和解款项，就必须要出具谅解书。所以不用担心到时候我们拿不到。

Client：Can that letter bail him out?

Lawyer：After we obtain it, we would prepare related materials to communicate with the authority to the best of our ability.

Client：I need a definite answer. Will the forgiveness letter set him free? We will not pay until we are sure it's gonna work. What if we pay them to get that letter and he still cannot get bailed? By the way, we will get the letter when we pay them, right?

Lawyer：We are not the authority so we are not in the position to make that decision. What's in our power is to persuade them. Moreover, given he is already arrested, the bail needs coordination, reporting and approval within the authority. So it's not up to any individual police officer for now. That's why I can not reply you by a simple "yes" or "no", what we can do is to do our utmost to persuade them and increase the likelihood of bail. But no one can say for certain that he can be bailed. Besides, we will sign with them the settlement agreement in which if they want to be compensated they have to provide that letter. So no need to worry about the letter.

家属：那你告诉我，拿到谅解书后，取保的概率是多少？

律师：就这类案件，我们取保和不取保都碰到过，但是个案有所不同，而且办案人员也都不同，申请前真的要去沟通了再看。

家属：那谅解书能让他少坐几年牢？

律师：目前并不明确，但如果他最后要判徒刑，谅解书也能让他从宽处理。

家属：谅解书不是意味着我们认罪了吗？

律师：不是的。谅解书并不等于认罪；在谅解书中，他只是对案发当天的事实感到抱歉，并不意味着他就有刑事责任。

家属：这没道理啊！不做错需要谅解吗？

律师：谅解书里没有承认有"罪"，所以并非认罪的表示。

家属：我无法理解你们的司法操作。既然现在是无罪辩护思路，为什么非要谅解书？

Client：Then you tell me the chance of being bailed after we get the letter？

Lawyer：For this kind of case, we have met clients bailed and not bailed, each are unique in evidence. And their handling officers are also varied, we need to communicate with them first before we apply.

Client：How many years can that letter cut from his sentence？

Lawyer：It's uncertain for now. But in case he is facing imprisonment, he can still get lesser punishment with that letter.

Client：Does that letter prove our guilt？

Lawyer：Not at all. The forgiveness letter will not make him guilty；in that letter, he is only sorry for what happened on that day, not that he has criminal liability.

Client：It doesn't make any sense！If he is not wrong, why he needs forgiveness from others？

Lawyer：No one admits guilt in this letter, so it's not an indication of admission of guilt.

Client：I don't quite follow the legal practice in your country. Since we defend him for his innocence, why do we still need that letter？

律师：无罪思路是基于当事人的辩解，认为当时不存在犯罪事实。但万一随着案件侦查的进展，有更多的证据反映出存在犯罪事实，此时就需要谅解书了。我们既要无罪辩护，又要为可能出现的其他情况做准备。而且我刚才说了，谅解书本身也能减轻司法机关的压力，有助于提升取保概率。

家属：那他们有没有说事发经过？

律师：他们只是说事情我们自己心里很清楚，拒绝跟我们谈事件细节。

家属：我们怎么会清楚？

律师：他们作为代理律师，是来谈和解的，一般不会详细说的。但他们说被害人仍很气愤，对这件事耿耿于怀。

家属：那他不说我们怎么知道我们有没有错？

律师：这次去的重点并非查清事实，查清事实由侦查机关负责。我们

Lawyer：For now, our defending points are mainly based on his own statements and memory. What if there are more evidence coming up with the investigation against him that can prove his guilt? We are gonna need that forgiveness letter by then. So we should not only defend for his innocence, but prepare for other worse scenarios. I also mentioned a short while ago that the forgiveness letter will alleviate some pressure on the authority, so it's gonna help increase the odds of bail.

Client：Have they mentioned what happened on that day?

Lawyer：They said we know it perfectly well and refused to go into details of the event.

Client：How could we possibly know what happened on that day?

Lawyer：As lawyers representing the victims, they were there to talk about the settlement, so obviously they are reluctant to disclose any details. They mentioned that the victim is still in anger and hold the grudge.

Client：If they don't tell us, how could we possibly know if it's our fault?

Lawyer：This meeting is not to find out the fact. The fact-finding is the job of

这次去是谈谅解。如果谅解书可以取得，对我们后续都有帮助。

家属：他们认为我们犯罪了吗？

律师：被害人肯定认为我们是有罪的。

家属：那他有没有证据？

律师：证据现在公安机关还在进一步收集。

家属：被害人做过笔录了吧，他笔录上怎么说的？

律师：我们还不清楚，他们也不说。审查起诉阶段开始时我们会去阅卷，到时候就可以获取。审判阶段也会举证，你们旁听时也都听得到。

家属：那被害人叫什么名字？住址和电话是什么？

律师：我们目前还不知道。

家属：难以置信，简直一问三不知。那你们下一步准备怎么办？

律师：下一步我们的方案是……

家属：还有，和解协议里一定要写上，我们打款之后，他们一定要保证撤销案件，不追究他的刑事责任。

the investigators. We were there to talk about the settlement. If we could obtain it, it would help in the days to come.

Client：Do they think we are guilty?

Lawyer：The victims absolutely think so.

Client：Then do they possess any evidence?

Lawyer：Now police are still collecting the evidence.

Client：The victim has made statement, hasn't him? What did he say in it?

Lawyer：We don't have this information yet and they refuse to tell us. Defense lawyers may obtain it during the examination of prosecution. As his family, you may attend the hearing and all the evidence will be shown, and you can see and hear them.

Client：What's the name of the victim? What's his address and number?

Lawyer：We don't know it yet.

Client：Unbelievable, there is nothing you know. What's your plan next?

Lawyer：Our plan is...

Client：One more thing. You have to put it in the settlement agreement that they guarantee they will withdraw the case and stop holding him criminally liable after we remit the money.

| | |
|---|---|
| 律师：我很明确地告诉您，如果这条也要放在上面，对方肯定不会签。因为撤销案件不是我们两方的任何一方可以决定的，而是由办案机关决定，因为这是公诉案件。这样去谈和解肯定谈不下来…… | Lawyer：I can tell you explicitly that if you want to put this sentence in the agreement, they will never sign it. Because the withdrawal of this case is not decided by any of the two parties, but by the authority. Since it is a case of public prosecution. You will never get this agreement signed by doing so... |

# 和解协议示例

| 中文版 | 英文版 |
|---|---|
| **和解协议书**<br><br>甲方：×××<br>乙方：×××<br><br>　　甲、乙双方为甲方涉嫌犯罪一事的妥善解决，经友好协商，达成如下协议，以资信守：<br><br>　　一、甲方承诺并保证：<br><br>　　（1）自本合同成立之日，即双方签订合同之日即支付＿＿＿＿＿美元（USD）至乙方指定账户……<br><br>　　二、乙方承诺并保证： | **Settlement Agreement**<br><br>Party A：＊＊＊<br>Party B：＊＊＊<br><br>Following friendly consultations between Party A and Party B, the following items relating to Party A as a suspect between two parties have been agreed：<br><br>1. Party A promises and guarantees the following item：<br><br>1. 1. Party A shall, since the establishment of this contract (the date of both parties signing this contract), remit ＿＿＿＿ US dollars to the account assigned by Party B...<br><br>2. Party B promises and guarantees the following item： |

（1）自本合同生效之日即收到第一款第一项下款项后出具谅解书两份……

三、本协议自本合同第 1 条第 1 项货款到账后生效。

四、如本协议无效或被撤销，甲方所承诺内容不视为自认；乙方亦不对甲方涉嫌犯罪行为进行任何形式的谅解。

五、本协议未尽事宜，遵照中华人民共和国有关法律、法规和规章办理。

六、任何因本协议引起的争议，应通过友好协商方式解决。如不能协商解决，则争议任何一方均可将争议事项提交甲、乙两方各自所在地法院起诉。

七、本协议一式 4 份，甲、乙双方各执 1 份，交司法机关 2 份，具同等法律效力。

八、若乙方在本协议生效后未能按约定向甲方提供 2 份谅解书，甲方保留采取法律行动的权利，包括但不限于……

2. 1. Party B shall, since this agreement comes into effect, provide to Party A with two copies of forgiveness letter. . .

3. This agreement shall come into effect since Party B receives the payment mentioned in the Article 1. 1.

4. Where this agreement is invalidated or revoked, the promises and guarantees of party A are not deemed as self-admission and Party B doesn't provide any form of forgiveness to Party A either.

5. Other matters not covered by this agreement shall be solved according to the related laws and regulations of the People's Republic of China.

6. Any disputes caused by this agreement shall be solved through friendly, cooperative negotiations between the two parties. If any party fails to settle the disputes, either party could bring the lawsuit to the court in his area.

7. This agreement is made in quadruplicate with each party having one copy, the other two handed in to the judicial authority. All the four copies of this agreement have equal legal effect.

8. If Party B, since this agreement comes into effect, fails to provide to Party A with two copies of forgiveness letter, Party A reserves the right to take legal

| | |
|---|---|
| 九、本协议生效后，乙方视为自动放弃主张任何形式的索赔权利，其中包括但不限于以下索赔内容：利息损失，汇率损失或停工等。 | action including but not limited to ...<br><br>9. Since this agreement comes into effect, Party B shall give up the right to claim the compensation of any kind including but not limited to the interest, foreign currency rate, suspension of the production. |
| 甲方<br>（签字及手印）：<br>签订时间：　　年　　月　　日<br>签订地点：<br><br>乙方<br>（签字及手印）：<br>签订时间：　　年　　月　　日<br>签订地点： | Party A<br>Signature and fingerprint：<br>Date of signing：<br>Place of signing：<br><br>Party B<br>Signature and fingerprint：<br>Date of signing：<br>Place of signing： |

## 谅解书示例

| 中文版 | 英文版 |
|---|---|
| **谅解书** | **Forgiveness Letter** |
| ×××区人民检察院： | People's Procuratorate of ＊＊＊ district： |
| 本人与×××因……相识多年。针对20××年 X 月 X 日下午发生的事，考虑到×××的真诚道歉及对双方之间 | I have been knowing ＊＊＊ for may years. As for what happened on ＊＊，＊＊，20＊＊，considering his sinc- |

| | |
|---|---|
| 纠纷的妥善处理，本人愿意对×××表示谅解，请求司法机关在法律允许的范围内，对×××做不起诉或免于追究刑事责任等从宽处理。<br><br>谅解人：<br>日期： 年 月 日 | ere apology and proper settlement of the dispute between us, I am willing to forgive him and I plead with the authority, based on Chinese law, to give * * * a lighter judgement such as non-prosecution or exemption from criminal punishment.<br><br>Signature of forgiver：<br>Date of signing： |

## 侦查终结前会见高频问答

| 中文版 | 英文版 |
|---|---|
| 律师：我们收到侦查机关通知，你的案子近期将移送检察院审查起诉。<br><br>嫌疑人：什么时候开庭？<br>律师：开庭还早，刑事案件分三个阶段：侦查阶段、审查起诉阶段、审判阶段。你的案子目前还在第一阶段，即将进入第二阶段，而开庭是在第三阶段。所以还有一段时间。<br><br>嫌疑人：为什么公安机关要把案子移送检察院？<br>律师：因为他们认为你的案子搜集的证据已经达到了起诉标准，因此移送检察院审查起诉。 | Lawyer：We are notified by the investigation authority that your case will be transferred to the procuratorate for examination for prosecution.<br><br>Client：When is the court hearing?<br>Lawyer：It's too early for court hearing. A criminal case usually has three stages：investigation, examination for prosecution and trial. Your case is about to enter the stage two, and the trial is the third one. So there is still some time.<br>Client：Why do they have to transfer the case to the procuratorate?<br>Lawyer：Because they reckon that the evidence they collected has reached the standard for prosecution, that why they transferred the case. |

嫌疑人：什么？你不是说我是无罪的吗？

律师：我们之前是根据你自己的辩解，认为你可能无罪。这也是我们目前能了解的全部信息，但仍然有很多证据是我们无法获取的，例如监控记录、被害人和证人陈述等。这些都有待我们在第二阶段去了解。到时就能知道为什么你的案子会被移送了。

嫌疑人：这是好事还是坏事？

律师：我认为是正常的程序。因为移送检察院后，检察官会审查案件证据，如果检察官认为证据不确实、充分，或不能排除合理怀疑，就会退回公安机关进行补充侦查，回来后再次审查看能否达到起诉标准。这些程序既是履行他们法律监督的职责，又是对你的案子负责的表现。

嫌疑人：我这个案子到底还要多久？

律师：你关押到现在快 97 天了，第一阶段即将结束。在进入审查起诉阶段后，你的案子最少 1 个月，最多 6 个半月，检察官会决定是否将你的

Client：Excuse me? Did you say that I am innocent?

Lawyer：Our point was based on your own defense, in which you believe you are not guilty. However, there are may more evidence that we are not able to acquire, such as CCTV footage, the statements of the victim and the witnesses. All of those are yet to be found during the second stage. By then, we will discover why it's transferred.

Client：Do you think it's good or not?

Lawyer：To me, it's usual procedure of authority. Because when the prosecutors receive the case file, they would examine them; if they think the evidence is not hard and sufficient and the fact is not beyond reasonable doubt, they would initiate an additional investigation; when the new evidence comes back, they examine again for prosecution. This proceeding is not only the performance of their legal supervision duty, but also a sense of responsibility for your case.

Client：How much longer will this case take?

Lawyer：It's almost 97th day since you are detained here, and the stage one is about to close. When it comes to the stage of examination of prosecution, your

案子起诉至法院。到法院后，还需要2个月至6个月。所以你的案子还需要大约1年不到的时间才能一审终结。

嫌疑人：你是说我还要在里面待上1年？

律师：你不要悲观，我说还要一年不到的时间结案，没说你还要在里面待1年。检察官在审查案件后，如果认为本案证据不足或超过羁押期限等，可能先将你取保候审。所以你不要悲观，即便你需要继续待在里面，我们也会定期来会见你，并跟你通报案件情况，让你掌握最新进展。

嫌疑人：他们还会不会过来？

律师：侦查机关前几天来提审过你一次吧，那次就是侦查终结前的例行程序。你回忆一下你说了什么内容？

嫌疑人：我说了这些……
律师：好的，基本跟之前的一致。

嫌疑人：警官不停问我要不要认罪，我到底要不要认罪？

case takes one month least, six and a half months tops, for the prosecutor to decide whether brings your case to the court. When it hits the court, it needs another 2-6 months. So there is about less than a year to close it.

Client：What? A year? I have to stay here for year more?

Lawyer：Do not get pessimistic. I said less than a year to close this case, not that you have to stay here for a year. After examining the case file, if the prosecutor reckon that the evidence is not sufficient or custody is overtime, you may get bailed. So stay strong, even you have to stay in here, we will come to meet you regularly and inform you about the case to keep you posted.

Client：Will they come to question me again?

Lawyer：I remember the police came to arraign you couple of days ago? That's the standard practice before closing of investigation. Could you please recall all your answers?

Client：I said. . .

Lawyer：OK, same statement as before.

Client：The police kept asking me if I want to plead guilty. Shall I do so?

律师：此时认不认罪完全取决于你自己。因为之前根据你自己的陈述，我们认为你的行为是否涉罪存在争议；但公安机关跟我们的看法不同，我们沟通后也不同意我们的取保候审申请。所以我们需要根据第二阶段的案卷材料来进一步判断。如果我们看到案卷后认为你可能构罪，我们会来跟你分析认罪认罚的利弊，仍然由你自己决定；如果我们看案卷后认为是否构成犯罪存在争议，我们会去跟检察官沟通，然后回来跟你通报。

嫌疑人：你们第二阶段就能看到所有案卷吗？

律师：是的，只要是案卷内的，律师依法均可以查阅、复制、摘抄。

嫌疑人：那你们可以给我看吧。

律师：你自己的笔录我们会跟你核对，但是其他的证据材料，只要法律和行业规定允许披露的，我们都会给你展示。

嫌疑人：在我们国家，只要交点钱就能保释。你现在把我保释出去，我再给你们一笔钱！

律师：每个国家都有自己的保释制度。我们司法机关在符合取保候审

Lawyer：It's absolutely up to you. Because based on your statement before, we reckon it's still controversial for your act to be guilty；but the police obviously hold otherwise, and they disagree when we apply for your bail. So we have to base further defense on the case file which we can duplicate in the next stage. If it seems to us after we analyze the case file that your act constitutes the crime, we will come and discuss with you over the plea bargain issue；if otherwise, we will contact the prosecutor and present our opinion and get back to you later.

Client：So you may see all the case file in the next stage？

Lawyer：That's correct. As long as it's in the case file, we may consult, extract, and duplicate them according to law.

Client：Then you will show them to me too, right？

Lawyer：We will verify your own statement with you. But for other materials, as long as it's in compliance with the law and bar rules, we would disclose them to you.

Client：In our country, we could get bailed once we pay a surety bond. If you bail me out now, I will pay you once again！

Lawyer：Each country has it's own bail provisions. Chinese authority will co-

条件的情况下，就可以考虑。但你目前的情况并不符合取保候审的条件，案件也即将移送检察院。但我相信只要你的辩解能够得到其他在案证据的充分印证，检察官可能会考虑我们的取保候审申请。

nsider bail once a suspect or defendant meets the condition of it. However, your condition does not meet any of the conditions of bail in the law, plus your case is about to be transferred to the procuratorate. But we believe if your self‑defense would be sufficiently justified by other evidence of the case, the prosecutor will consider our bail application.

嫌疑人：直说吧，你们到底要多少钱？

律师：我说的是实话，信不信由你。我们不需要除律师费外的任何费用，正如我们签订合同时所承诺的。尤其当你说的钱是去从事行贿等违法犯罪的行为，我们律师没法做到，法律明确禁止，也是我们之间的合同签订时风险告知书上明确禁止的。

嫌疑人：简直不敢相信。你们可以走了。我想一个人冷静一下。你们看到案卷了再来看我。

律师：好的。还有什么需要？

嫌疑人：你跟我家人说，让他们买……

律师：记下了。保重。有急事让管教联系我们。

Client：Let's call a spade a spade, how much money do you want？

Lawyer：I am speaking the truth, believe it or not. As we promised in our agreement, we don't take any extra money besides the retainer, especially the money you referred to is used for illegal act such as bribery. As practice lawyers, it's beyond our ability and against the law, and is prohibited in the *Risk Notice* attached in our agreement.

Client：Unconscionable. You may go. Leave me alone. Come again when you see the evidence.

Lawyer：All right. Do you need anything？

Client：Tell my family that I need them to buy. . .

Lawyer：Noted. Take care. Let officers in here contact me if there is any emergency.

# 相关英文表达

| 英文表达 | 中文意思 |
| --- | --- |
| Lodestar Rule | 北极星计费法［一种律师收费规则，据以确定经合法授权的律师的费用额。其计算方法是以合理花费的小时数乘上社会上同类工作通行的计时报酬比率（hourly rate），然后再根据其他因素，如案件的不确定性、提供代理服务的质量等加以适当调整。］ |
| judicial practice | 司法实践 |
| breastfeed her own baby | 哺乳自己的婴儿 |
| pull out all stops | 全力以赴 |
| pay by hour | 按小时计费 |
| lump-sum | 一口价 |
| relevant factors | 相关因素 |
| relevant proof | 相关依据 |
| en route | 在途 |
| buy off | 收买 |
| spare no efforts | 不遗余力 |
| complication and workload | 复杂性和工作量 |
| try-and-buy | 试用后购买 |
| contingent rate | 风险收费 |
| bar regulation | 律师行业规范 |
| PCR test | 聚合酶链反应检测（新冠核酸检测的一种） |
| preliminary understanding | 初步了解 |
| impair legal proceedings | 妨害诉讼 |
| public prosecution | 公诉 |

续表

| 英文表达 | 中文意思 |
| --- | --- |
| the odds are against someone | 对某人来说胜算不大 |
| extradite someone back | 把某人引渡回国 |
| exchange prisoners | 交换关押人员 |
| legal service | 法律服务 |
| defense lawyer | 辩护律师 |
| period of examination of prosecution | 审查起诉阶段 |
| lawyer's fee | 律师费 |
| above-mentioned | 上述的 |
| Power of Attorney | 授权委托书 |
| Risk Notice | 风险告知书 |
| mentally and physically prepared | 身心上做好准备 |
| at one's own risk | 自行承担后果 |
| competentauthority | 主管部门 |
| claim compensation | 索赔 |
| best price | 最优惠价格 |
| intentional homicide | 故意杀人 |
| hazardous substance | 危险物质 |
| gangland nature | 黑社会性质 |
| drug criminal group | 毒品犯罪集团 |
| step by step | 逐步 |
| Rome was not built in a day | 罗马非一夕建成/冰冻三尺非一日之寒 |
| related provisions | 相关规定 |
| time-consuming | 费时的 |
| cop it | 接受惩罚 |
| straighten out | 理清 |
| file accusation | 提出控告 |

| 英文表达 | 中文意思 |
|---|---|
| infringe upon | 侵犯 |
| procedural rights | 诉讼权利 |
| inflict personal insult | 人身侮辱 |
| demand the withdrawal | 申请回避 |
| under certain circumstances | 在特定情形下 |
| forced appearance | 拘传 |
| defend yourself | 为自己辩解 |
| lighter penalty | 从轻处罚 |
| mitigated penalty | 减轻处罚 |
| serious consequence | 严重后果 |
| interrogation transcripts | 讯问笔录 |
| supplements or corrections | 补充或改正 |
| voluntarily and truthfully confess | 自愿如实供述 |
| be granted leniency | 从宽处理 |
| jail rule | 监规 |
| physically well | 身体健康 |
| mentally stable | 情绪稳定 |
| No worries | 别担心 |
| make all-out efforts | 全力以赴 |
| on earth | 究竟 |
| parallel case | 类案 |
| outline for communication | 沟通提纲 |
| cut the crap | 少说废话 |
| term of custody | 羁押期限 |
| or so | 大约 |
| private eye | 私家侦探 |

| 英文表达 | 中文意思 |
| --- | --- |
| beg, borrow or steal | 不择手段去做某事 |
| on behalf of | 代表某人 |
| in our full strength | 竭尽全力 |
| handling authority | 承办机关 |
| through the grapevine | 小道消息 |
| apprentice lawyer license | 实习律师证 |
| judicial authority | 司法机关 |
| clear your head | 理清思路 |
| jog the memory | 唤起记忆 |
| go all out | 全力以赴 |
| arrest warrant | 逮捕通知书 |
| plead guilty | 认罪 |
| point finger at | 指责 |
| The Miranda Rule | 美国联邦最高法院在 1966 年米兰达诉亚利桑那州一案中确立的规则，要求警察对其拘留或逮捕的犯罪嫌疑人在讯问前必须告知其享有某些宪法性权利，包括：①有权保持沉默；②其所作的任何陈述可能成为对其不利的证据；③有权要求律师在场；④如无力聘请律师但又有此要求时，须在讯问前为其指定律师。如果犯罪嫌疑人未被告知上述权利或犯罪嫌疑人未有效地放弃上述权利，则讯问所得的任何陈述不得在庭审时用作对嫌疑人不利的证据。 |
| keep silent | 保持沉默 |
| keep an eye on | 密切注意 |
| be swamped with | 忙于处理…… |
| next higher level | 上一级 |
| potential danger to the society | 潜在的社会危害性 |

续表

| 英文表达 | 中文意思 |
| --- | --- |
| literal meaning | 字面意思 |
| good sign | 好事 |
| work in our full strength | 全力以赴 |
| over-optimistic | 过于乐观 |
| border control | 边控 |
| keep something from | 对某人隐瞒某事 |
| forgiveness letter | 谅解书 |
| what's in it for me | 对我有什么好处 |
| criminal liability | 刑事责任 |
| conviction and sentencing | 定罪和量刑 |
| king's ransom | 一大笔钱 |
| discretionary circumstance | 酌定情节 |
| milk me dry | 把我榨干 |
| shoot one's best | 尽力而为 |
| execution authority | 执行机关 |
| residence address | 居住地址 |
| false confession | 虚假供述 |
| come to an agreement | 达成一致 |
| detailed compensation plan | 详细的赔偿方案 |
| offer price | 报价 |
| to the best of one's ability | 尽我们全力 |
| definite answer | 明确答复 |
| in the position to do something | 能够做 |
| in our power | 在我们能力范围内 |
| do our utmost | 尽我们全力 |
| increase the likelihood | 增大可能性 |

续表

| 英文表达 | 中文意思 |
|---|---|
| say for certain | 肯定地说 |
| settlement agreement | 和解协议 |
| make sense | 说不通 |
| legal practice | 司法实践 |
| odds of bail | 取保可能性 |
| go into details | 详细说 |
| hold the grudge | 耿耿于怀 |
| fact-finding | 查清事实 |
| in the days to come | 今后 |
| self-admission | 自认 |
| bring the lawsuit to the court | 向法院提起诉讼 |
| in quadruplicate | 一式四份 |
| equal legal effect | 同等法律效力 |
| reserves the right to | 保留权利做某事 |
| including but not limited to | 包括但不限于 |
| suspension of the production | 停工 |
| sincere apology | 真诚的道歉 |
| proper settlement | 妥善处理 |
| plead with | 向……恳请 |
| exemption from | 免于 |
| non-prosecution | 不起诉 |
| by then | 到那时 |
| usual procedure | 常规程序 |
| case file | 卷宗 |
| hard and sufficient | 确实充分 |
| beyond reasonable doubt | 排除合理怀疑 |

续表

| 英文表达 | 中文意思 |
|---|---|
| legal supervision | 法律监督 |
| a sense of responsibility | 责任感 |
| couple of days | 几天 |
| standard practice | 常规做法 |
| constitute a crime | 构成犯罪 |
| plea bargain | 认罪协商 |
| get back to somebody | 回复某人 |
| in compliance with | 符合…… |
| surety bond | 保证金 |
| call a spade a spade | 有话直说 |

# 审查起诉阶段

## 阅卷后会见高频问答

| 中文版 | 英文版 |
|---|---|
| 嫌疑人：你们看到案卷了吗？<br><br>律师：我们团队花了 1 天时间，复制了全部案卷；又花了 3 天时间，浏览了第一遍。<br><br>嫌疑人：给我看一下。<br><br>律师：你自己的笔录我们会跟你核对，但是其他的证据材料，只要法律和行业规定允许披露的，我们都会给你展示。你是不是做过一次笔录…… | Client：Have you seen the evidence?<br><br>Lawyer：Our team spent a whole day on duplicating all the case file; and another three days on scanning them for the first time.<br><br>Client：Let me see it.<br><br>Lawyer：We will verify your own statement with you. But for other materials, as long as it's in compliance with the law and bar rules, we would disclose them to you. Did you make a statement on... |

嫌疑人：我觉得问题有这些……再给我念一下被害人的笔录，一字一句慢慢翻译给我听……

律师：被害人的详细笔录恕我不能念给你，但我可以给你简要介绍一下……

嫌疑人：凭什么我不能知道？我请你来干嘛的？我难道连指控我的证据都不知道就要为此坐牢吗？

律师：你先冷静一下。首先，法律和行业规范禁止律师在第二阶段将全部案件证据透露给当事人。曾经有律师仅因为透露了起诉意见书便受到了律师协会的处罚，被停止执业6个月，也有律师因为泄露了证人的信息而被处罚。因此，如果你不想更换律师，就请理解我们的难处。另外，你在第三阶段庭审时也能听到指控你的详细证据，这只是一个时间问题。

嫌疑人：简直胡说！我出来了一定要投诉你们！

律师：你如果坚持要因为我们合

Client: It has problems such as...And you read the statement of the victim, slowly translate them to me, word by word...

Lawyer: I am afraid I am not allowed to literally translate it to you, but I can brief you...

Client: why I could not know? You think I retain you for what? Do I have to go to jail without knowing the evidence for charging me?

Lawyer: Keep your calm for now. For one thing, the law and bar rules prohibit us from disclosing all the case evidence during the second stage. There was once a lawyer punished by bar association with suspension of licence for six months simply for leaking the written prosecution opinion. There was also lawyer punished for disclosing the information of witnesses. Therefore, ifyou don't want to change lawyer, please don't give us a hard time. Moreover, you will be able to hear all the evidence for the change against you during the trial session. So it's only a matter of time before you know them.

Client: Bullshit! I will make a complaint against you when I am out!

Lawyer: If you insist on making that

法合规的服务而投诉我们，那就请便。你们家属之前在委托时签署的《刑事法律服务风险告知书》明确规定："律师在检察机关或法院获取的案卷材料均不能提供给委托人。"我们同时也理解你想了解案件的心情，所以我们这次准备了关于案卷的大致介绍，并且针对案卷中反映出的、跟你关系最直接的争议问题，重点跟你核实。希望不放过任何一个对你有利的事实。

嫌疑人：不说这个了。那些笔录肯定是假的，因为……

律师：好的。我问你这几个问题……

嫌疑人：证人有哪些人？

律师：证人具体身份就是我刚才说的目前不方便向你透露的内容。

嫌疑人：那你给我念一下证人的笔录。

律师：具体的笔录既不方便详细念，也没有必要这么做，因为跟你有关的核心内容我们已经帮你概括了。本案中证人指认你的核心内容大致有……

嫌疑人：他说得不对，因为……

律师：我记下了。我再问你一下，关于……

complaint for our lawful service, be my guest. Your family signed on the *Risk Notice for Criminal Legal Service* which states that the case file obtained by lawyers from the procuratorate or court shall not be offered to the clients. And we understand your desire of seeing the evidence, so we have prepared to brief you today about the case evidence, and to verify with you about the controversial issues that matter you most.

Client: Never mind. Of those statements, some are not true, because...

Lawyer: Got it. May I ask some questions...

Client: Who are the witnesses?

Lawyer: The specific identities of the witnesses are among the contents that I am not at liberty to share with you.

Client: Then read their statements to me.

Lawyer: I am not at the liberty to read those statements to you in details, plus there is no need for that. Because we have collected all the core issues concerning you. And those issues including...

Client: He is wrong, for that...

Lawyer: Noted. I need to ask you more about...

嫌疑人：监控录像有没有？我要看一下录像。

律师：监控录像是有的，因为文件个数比较多而且长，我们还在看。而且看守所会见中也有硬性规定，不得将手机、电脑屏幕上的内容给嫌疑人观看。所以我们在看完后会再过来跟你通报一下监控的情况。

嫌疑人：那录像上有什么内容？

律师：根据我们初步观看，有些监控也没有直接反映案件事实，所以等我们看完一遍后再来跟你反馈，信息也更全面。

嫌疑人：你们见到检察官了吗？他说我有没有罪？

律师：目前我们只知道检察官是谁，同时在案件刚到达检察院时便将案卷复制，进行分析研判。检察官这边肯定也没有看完所有案卷，所以我们此时跟他沟通，效果也不会太好。我们这边会加班加点，争取比检察官先阅完卷，形成一个初步的意见，然后跟检察官沟通。

Client：Do you have camera recording? I want to see them.

Lawyer：Yes, we have them. There are too many of them and some arereally long, so we haven't finish watching. And the jail rule has it that lawyers shall not show the contents on the screen of cellphone or computer to the suspects. Therefore we will come back to brief you when we finish watching and analyzing them.

Client：What's on that footage?

Lawyer：Among the several videos we have watched, some are not direct reflection of the fact. So please wait here till we have watched everything for the first time, which is closer to the full picture.

Client：Have you met the prosecutor? Does he think I am guilty?

Lawyer：So far we only know his name, and we have duplicated and started analyzing the case file the moment it entered the second stage. The prosecutor definitely hasn't finished reading yet. So if we discuss with him over the case details now, it won't be very promising. We are working overtime to finish reading the case file ahead of the prosecutor and come up with a preliminary written opinion, and then go to communicate with them.

嫌疑人：你认为他会觉得我无罪还是有罪？

律师：目前还不好说，我们只是初步浏览了一遍案卷。我们认为目前案件事实还存在这些不能解释的矛盾……

嫌疑人：他有没有说什么时候把我取保？

律师：还没有。案件刚到检察院，检察官自己甚至都没有开始看案卷。所以你说的取保问题，他肯定要结合案件和你自身情况来综合判断的。不过我们会和他保持密切联系，一旦有取保的法定事由，我们就会全力争取。

嫌疑人：那你们下一步怎么做？

律师：你也对目前的在案证据提出了一些质疑，我们下一步首先要分析这些质疑的合理性以及有无在案证据能够印证你的质疑。然后我们结合你的辩解，形成书面材料，争取和检察官当面沟通，引起他们的重视。

嫌疑人：你们能不能找点关系，走个"后门"？我在我们自己国家请的大律师都可以直接搞定法官、检察官，我以前都是胜诉的。你是我请的律师，你们为什么不去试试？

Client：Do you think he will see me guilty or not?

Lawyer：Hard to say. We just did the first scan of the case file and there are following contradictions between facts without explanation. . .

Client：Did he say when I can be bailed out?

Lawyer：Not yet. The case has just arrived and he hasn't even started looking at the case file. As for your bail, he shall certainly take into account the case file and your own circumstance. Once there appears a condition of bail, we would make all-out efforts for it.

Client：So what to do next?

Lawyer：You have questioned some of the evidence so far, and we have to sort them out and to dig into the case file for more evidence to support your points. Then we would draft a written defense opinion combining your points and discuss, face-to-face if possible, with the prosecutor, in order to bring to his attention.

Client：Can you find some relationship and pull some strings for me? In our country, I always retain attorneys who can take care of the judges and prosecutors, and I always won. You are my lawyer. Why wouldn't you try?

律师：你有这种想法很正常，但是从目前来看，我们的司法体制和你们国家的还是有很大区别的。我们这里一个重要决定的作出需要层层把关，并不是一个人就可以说了算的。所以你的想法在你们国家可能行得通，但在中国不现实。

嫌疑人：那我这个案子还要多久？

律师：目前我们正处于第二阶段，这个案子的第一次审查起诉需要1个月至1个半月的时间；如果检察官认为证据情况不足以起诉，会要求公安机关补充侦查，2次为限；如果检察官认为已经可以起诉，会直接起诉；如果他认为本案符合不起诉条件，则可能直接作相对不起诉处理。总之第二阶段在你被关押的情况下，最多6个半月、最少1个月便会有结论。

嫌疑人：我知道了。希望你们尽快说服检察官，让我无罪，或者至少让我先保释。

律师：我们会尽力的。

Lawyer：It's quite natural for you to feel this way. But for now, the judicial system here is way different from yours. The decision here, especially for major and sensitive cases like yours, which needs to go through level by level, which is not someone's own decision to make. So maybe it works in your country, but not in China.

Client：Then how much longer it's gonna take?

Lawyer：Your case is in phase 2, and normally the first examination of prosecution takes one to one and half months; if the prosecutor reckons that the evidence is not sufficient for prosecution, he will initiate an additional investigation by the police, twice maximum; if he reckons it's ready for prosecution, he will transfer this case to the court; if he thinks this case meets the condition of non-prosecution, he will make such decision. In a word, the time for the second stage is one month least and six and a half months most before a decision.

Client：I got it. Hopefully you can persuade him as soon as possible andmake me innocent, or at least bail me out first.

Lawyer：We will pull out all stops.

## 与检察官沟通后向家属反馈高频问答

| 中文版 | 英文版 |
| --- | --- |
| 家属：检察官说什么了吗？<br><br>律师：这次我们去沟通了解到了很多之前不知道的信息。<br><br>家属：你们怎么一开始不知道？<br><br>律师：之前我们都没能约到检察官，电话也联系不上他。这次的当面沟通很充分，所以我们了解到了更多信息，以及检察官的个人观点。<br><br>家属：哪些？<br><br>律师：……<br><br>家属：这次他有没有说到取保？<br><br>律师：我们在充分陈述我们这方的观点和疑点后，检察官对于其中的一部分表示同意。同时他很坦率地说，虽然还存在疑点，但因为本案还需要补充侦查，加上目前他还不满足取保候审的条件，所以暂不考虑取保候审的申请。<br><br>家属：为什么不考虑？如果证据足够就起诉！如果证据不足就应该把他先放了，为什么还要把人关着？ | Client：What did the prosecutor say?<br><br>Lawyer：We have learned much information that we didn't know before.<br><br>Client：How could you not have those information in the first place?<br><br>Lawyer：We haven't managed to make the appointment of meeting the prosecutor and it's difficult to get him through the phone. Thanks to the effective communication this time, we are able obtain more information and his own opinions.<br><br>Client：What are they?<br><br>Lawyer：. . .<br><br>Client：Did he mention the bail?<br><br>Lawyer：After we stated the our opinions and questions, the prosecutor agreed upon part of them and said it frankly that although there are some doubts but due to need for additional investigation, plus he does not meet any condition for bail, therefore the bail is out of the question for now.<br><br>Client：Why？If they have enough evidence, just prosecute! If not, set him free! Why keeping him so long? |

律师：这个问题我之前也说过，因为他这个罪名属于重罪，本身符合逮捕关押的条件。我国的取保候审是列举式规定，符合条件之一的，可以取保候审。而且在逮捕后取保候审，比起拘留后取保肯定更加严格。因此肯定要看是否符合取保候审的条件。目前他还不符合其中任何一条，因此目前还不能取保候审。但我们至少通过沟通，了解到检察官也同意我们提出的疑点，认为本案确实需要将事实查清楚。这对于他来说是很有利的消息。

家属：什么时候能有结果？

律师：审查起诉期限是 1 个月，可以延长半个月，最长 1 个半月，检察官就要决定是否退回补充侦查，起诉或不起诉。

家属：你觉得 1 个月到了会不会不起诉？

律师：我觉得对于这种重大敏感涉外的案件来看，第一次审查起诉后就不起诉的可能性比较低。很可能至

Lawyer: I have explained it before that because his crime is a felony, and it meets the condition for arrest. In China, the conditions for bail are enumerative, which means the law names explicitly the conditions for bail. Only if one of the conditions is met, the bail might be approved. And the bail after the arrest must be more challenging than the bail after detention, where the conditions for bail must be met. So far he doesn't meet any of the conditions, hence he cannot be bailed. But at least we learned that the prosecutor agrees with us on those doubts because of our opinion and he sees it necessary to find the clear fact, which should be in favor of him.

Client: When can we get a result?

Lawyer: The period for examination of prosecution is one month, or one and a half tops, during which the prosecutor has to decide whether to return the case for additional investigation, to prosecute or to non-prosecute.

Client: Do you think the prosecutor will non-prosecute this case after one month?

Lawyer: Based on my experience, for a major, sensitive and foreigner-related case like yours, non-prosecution

少退回补充侦查一次。

家属：那还要多久？

律师：退回补充侦查以 1 个月为限，回来后检察院还会再有最长 1 个半月的审查起诉期。

家属：退回来以后你们还要去看案卷，对不对？

律师：当然，我们还会去查阅、摘抄、复制以及分析案卷，然后跟你们反馈，就像这次一样。

家属：这个案子，如果大使馆介入调停有用吗？

律师：如果你的意思是外交渠道，作为律师我们只能从法律角度给予服务，具体作用我这边也无法预估。另外我也需要提醒您，根据《维也纳外交关系公约》第 41 条的规定："一、在不妨碍外交特权与豁免之情形下，凡享有此项特权与豁免之人员，均负有尊重接受国法律规章之义务。此等人员并负有不干涉该国内政之义务。"而中国和你们国家都是这个公约的缔约国。根据《中华人民共和国刑法》，凡在中华人民共和国领域内犯罪的，除

right after one month of prosecution is highly unlikely. There will probably be at least one additional investigation.

Client: Then how much longer it's gonna take?

Lawyer: The time length for additional investigation is one month. Then the case file returns to the procuratorate, there will be another one and a half months at most for examination of prosecution.

Client: And you will go to see the case file when it returns, won't you?

Lawyer: Sure. We will go to consult, extract, copy and analyze the case file once again, then we bring you the feedback, like we did this time.

Client: Do you think it will help if the Embassy mediates for this case?

Lawyer: If you mean the diplomatic channel, since we are lawyers who only offer legal service, it's hard for us to evaluate the effects. But one thing I have to remind you of is that according to the Article 41 of the *Vienna Convention on Diplomatic Relations*: without prejudice to their privileges and immunities, it is the the duty of all persons enjoying such privileges and immunities to respect the laws and regulations of the receiving State. They also have a duty not to inter-

法律有特别规定的以外，都适用本法。外国及外交人员不得干涉我国司法。因此所谓的外交渠道您一定要慎重，警惕诈骗。

fere in the internal affairs of that State. And China and your country are both the contracting states of it. *Criminal Law of People's Republic of China* shall be applicable to anyone who commits a crime within the territory and territorial waters and space of the People's republic of China, except as otherwise specifically provided by law. No foreign countries nor foreign diplomatic staff shall intervene the judicial activities in our country. Therefore it's better for you to be aware of the socalled diplomatic channel and alert to any fraud.

家属：那我还认识××的××高官，我让他去说说情可以吗？

Client：I also know the high-ranking officers at..., can I ask him to say something in our favor?

律师：首先我们之前都是明确提示了法律风险的。我们之前给你们看过，你们签字的《刑事法律服务风险告知书》上也明确：委托人就案件采取任何不当方式应自行承担全部后果。如果你们因为去找那个你所谓的高官，产生了违法犯罪的风险，或对本案产生了不利影响，这些风险需要你们自担。

Lawyer：Firstly, we have clearly alerted you of legal risk before our service. The written *Risk Notice* is shown and signed by you, in which it's clearly stated that the client shall bear all the consequences caused by his improper acts towards the case. In the case that you face risk of crime or cause any adverse effect to this case because of your approach to that officer, you do so at your own risk.

家属：按照我们国家的法律规定，他这种行为不算犯罪。你们这儿为什么要定罪？

Client：In our country, his act is not taken as a crime. Why do you have to convict him?

律师：首先，你们国家和我们国家的法律从体系上就不同。你们国家是判例法，我们国家是成文法。我国的刑事诉讼定罪是根据合法的证据所证明的事实，结合我国的刑法和相关法律法规来判断是否符合犯罪的构成要件，有无出罪事由，最后定罪或不定罪的一个过程。依照本案目前的证据，侦查机关认为符合本罪名的构成要件，所以移送审查起诉；但检察院还需要进一步审查，来决定起诉、不起诉或退回补充侦查。最终定罪还是需要法院，所以现在还没有定论。我们也会和检察官保持沟通，第一时间跟进信息。

家属：我们现在能不能见他？

律师：还不可以。目前有两种情况你们能见到他，一种是他被取保候审，一种是判决生效。

家属：你们原来说阅卷以后就能知道证人、被害人的姓名和联系方式等，这些你们现在告诉我们吧。

律师：这些我们在之前的《刑事

Lawyer: Firstly we don't share the same law system. Your country has case law, while we have the statute law. The conviction in our country is based on the fact supported by legal evidence andcriminal law and other related laws, to see if it constitutes the crime and whether there is any impunity fact. According to the case file at present, the investigators reckon it constitutes the crime, that's why the police transferred the case to the procuratorate; while the prosecutor has to examine further to decide whether to prosecute, non-prosecute or return the case for additional investigation, so we have no conclusion so far. We will keep in close touch with the prosecutor and stay posted.

Client: Can we meet him now?

Lawyer: Not yet. There are two circumstances in which you may meet him. The first is the time when he gets bailed; the second is when the judgement comes into effect.

Client: You said before when you have seen the case file you would know the names and numbers of the victims and the witnesses. Now you tell me those information.

Lawyer: The written *Risk Notice*

法律服务风险告知书》中也提过，你们都签了字：律师在检察机关或法院获取的案卷材料均不能提供给委托人。我之前也说过，只要是法律允许我们透露的，我们都会告知你们，正如我之前跟你们介绍的。其他内容，法律和办案单位都不准我们透露，如果泄露被处罚，我们会失业的，到时你们又要重新委托律师了，经济上和时间上都不划算。如果你们真的想了解，在庭审阶段会展示所有的定罪证据，到时你们也能知道。

家属：那你们下一步准备怎么办？

律师：我们下一步要……

signed by you has it that the case file obtained by lawyers from the procuratorate or court shall not be of fered to the clients. As long as it's in compliance with the law and bar rules, we would disclose them to you, as I have briefed you before. But for other materials prohibited by laws and bar regulation, we would lose our jobs by leaking any, and you have to retain other lawyers, which is time - wasting and not cost - efficient. If you really want to know, during the trial session the prosecutor will read all the evidence for conviction and sentencing, you may learn by then.

Client：So what's your next move?

Lawyer：We plan to. . .

## 二退期间高频问答

| 中文版 | 英文版 |
| --- | --- |
| 嫌疑人：今天有什么进展？<br><br>律师：首先我们来是通知你，你的案件昨天开始第二次补充侦查。然后你的第一期律师费对应的工作时间已用尽，你的家属坚持需要你签字同意，才转账给我们，所以我们来这里…… | Client：Anything new?<br><br>Lawyer：Above all, we are here to inform you that your case is about to have the second additional investigation. And the working time of your first payment is all consumed, and your family insist on seeing your written confirmation for payment before they pay, that's why we come here... |

嫌疑人：我被关这么久，还没跟你计较，你居然还敢跟我要律师费？

律师：你先冷静一下。我和你们家人签的合同明确写明是按小时计费，我们也每次都给你看了工时记录清单，上面我们每次工作的时间和内容及凭据都很清楚。我们现在已经把你们预交费用对应的时长全部用完了，甚至已经超出了。再这样我们就等于免费在给你提供服务，这是我们行业规定所不允许的。按照合同我们完全可以在此时停止服务，但你的案子如果因此错过了关键的时间节点，没有做应该做的工作，最终承担后果的人还是你自己。所以我们也是为了辩护工作能继续推动，才跟你提出来的。

嫌疑人：可笑，我看你们这样很好赚钱，也没什么成本，就这么跑跑，最多出了点汽车油钱。

律师：那你可以请个出租车司机给你跑跑，也就出点油费，比我们便宜。

嫌疑人：那你说你们的成本在哪里？

Client：I have stayed here so long and I haven't gotten even with you on this. How dare you have the nerve to ask for money?

Lawyer：Keep cool. The contract between your family and us has it clearly that you pay on hourly basis and we have all the detailed report of work and time spent. Now the working time of your first payment is all consumed, and we are even working overtime. It means we are providing legal service for free, which is not allowed by the bar regulation. According to our contract, we have reason to stop service now. However, if your case misses some crucial time window because of absence of legal service, you are the only person to pay the fiddler at the end of the day. So in order to push the defense work forward, we have to notify you of what's going on with your money.

Client：It's funny. It seems pretty easy for you to make money. What's your cost? The only thing you have to pay for is the gas.

Lawyer：Then you could hire a taxi driver, whose cost is only gas, which is cheaper than us.

Client：Then you tell me where do you spend my money on?

律师：我们做的工作远不止路上，还包括整理案件资料、搜集案例和理论、分析案情、组织讨论案件、撰写材料、面对面沟通等。

嫌疑人：写材料？对你们来说肯定也很快的，你们是吃这碗饭的，用不了多少时间。

律师：别的律师是怎么做的我们不清楚。至少我们是根据每个案件单独制订方案，尽可能查找相关所有案例和理论，挖掘所有该考虑的辩点，再经过多名律师的集体讨论，反复修改才能定稿……

嫌疑人：你上次跟我说半个月以后肯定可以取保，怎么我还在里面？

律师：我们绝对没有说过类似的话。我和另外一名律师都在场，这是很严肃的司法结论，我们没有办案单位的明确消息是不可能跟你说这样的话的。你一定是记错了。

嫌疑人：你们跟我说过可以取保的。公安机关怎么还要侦查？不是已经侦查过这么多次了吗？

Lawyer：Our cost is far more than on the way. It includes the collection of case materials, parallel cases and theories, analysis and discussion over the case, writing opinions and face-to-face persuasion.

Client：Writing materials？It's your job！It won't take up too much of your time.

Lawyer：We don't know how much time other lawyers spend. For us, we customize each case and try our utmost to look for relevant cases and theories, dig all possible defense points and group discuss over the case and finalize the written material after many times of revising...

Client：You told me half a month ago that I could be bailed. Why am I still in here？

Lawyer：We have never said anything like this. My partner and I were both present when we met you. The bail is a serious judicial decision, without clear and definite information from the authority, we would never tell you so. You must have misremembered.

Client：You told me that I could be bailed. Why do the police investigate again？They have investigated so many times！

律师：上次是第一次补充侦查，现在是第二次补充侦查。

嫌疑人：你说最多 2 次侦查，但现在已经 3 次了！上次移送检察院前是第一次，3 个月前你跟我说补充侦查是第二次。这次已经是第三次了！你们到底会不会数数？

律师：我再跟你讲解一下侦查的基本流程和次数。首先你被逮捕前后的侦查都只是侦查程序，还在第一阶段，不是补充侦查，就是侦查；现在你的案件处于第二阶段——审查起诉阶段，在这个阶段，检察院根据查清事实的实际需要，可以发起 2 次补充侦查，这时候相当于退还给公安机关，有目的地进行补充侦查。这时候的补充侦查以 2 次为限，每次的补充侦查时间为 1 个月。这时的补充侦查是由检察院发起，公安机关去做。之前侦查阶段的侦查是公安机关自主进行，检察院很少介入。

Lawyer：Last time is the first additional investigation. Now is the second one.

Client：You said two investigations tops. But now it's already the third! Before transfer, that's the first time; and three months ago, you told me that two investigation tops. And this time is the third one! Can you do the math or not?

Lawyer：Let me explain the process of investigation and how many times for it. In the first place, before and after arrest, all the investigations are only inthe first stage, which is called investigation period, not additional investigation; now your case is at the second stage, which is examination of prosecution. At this stage, based on the needs of finding the fact, the prosecutor may initiate two times of additional investigation, which means the prosecutor returns the case purposefully back to the police for further collection of evidence. And there are only two times of additional investigation at most, each with time length of one month. So the additional investigation is initiated by the prosecutor but carried out by the police; while the investigation of the first stage is an act on police's own, seldom with participation of procuratorate.

嫌疑人：我真是弄不懂你们这一套。

律师：所以你需要多了解这个刑事诉讼制度的运行方式，才可以心中有数，不至于产生刚才的误会。

嫌疑人：那我还要等多久？

律师：你的案子刚开始第二次补充侦查，补充侦查的时间为 1 个月，案件回来后我们还会去补充阅卷和分析，检察官也有最长 1 个半月的时间进行审查起诉，这样加起来就是第二阶段还有 2 个半月的时间。

嫌疑人：上帝啊。结束后呢？我就能被取保吗？

律师：这取决于补充回来的案卷情况以及我们和检察官的沟通，如果检察官可以被说服，认为本案确实存在较大争议，需要将你取保，那你还是有希望先出来的。

嫌疑人：那到法院还要多久？

律师：如果你不被取保，你的案子 2 个半月后会被移送法院；如果你被取保，那时间就以你的取保时长来

Client: This is so over my head.

Lawyer: That's why you need to know how the whole criminal proceeding works in order to have a clear idea about what we are facing and avoid the misunderstanding just now.

Client: Then how much longer do I have to wait?

Lawyer: They just started the second additional investigation, and it lasts for one month. When it returns, we will go and copy all the evidence and analyze them. And the prosecutor will also have another one and half months at most for work. So together it's two and half months before the end of the second stage.

Client: Jesus. What's after? Can I get bailed?

Lawyer: It depends on the case file we obtained after the additional investigation and the communication with the prosecutor. If he can be persuaded that this case is still highly controversial and there is a need to bailyou, then you might be bailed first.

Client: How much longer before it gets to the court?

Lawyer: If you are not bailed, it takes two and half months before transfer; if you are bailed, the time will go with

| 计算。 | your bail period. |
|---|---|
| 嫌疑人：呼叫警官给我拿纸笔，我给家人手写个打款授权信。 | Client：Call the management to get me a pen and paper. I write a payment authorization letter. |
| 律师：好的，你写完管教先要审核。隔着玻璃我拿不到。 | Lawyer：OK. The officer has to exam it when you finish. I cannot get it with the glass between us. |

## 起诉前会见高频问答

| 中文版 | 英文版 |
|---|---|
| 嫌疑人：案子有什么好消息吗？ | Client：Any good news with my case? |
| 律师：我今天来是跟你沟通认罪认罚事宜的。 | Lawyer：Today we are here to discuss with you over the plea bargaining. |
| 嫌疑人：我有点搞不懂，上次公安机关跟我说愿不愿意认罪认罚，还让我让签一个类似认罪书的东西，我说不认罪认罚，最后就没签。那个东西不是认罪认罚吗？怎么又要来问我一次？ | Client：I am confused here. Last time the police asked me if I plead guilty, and they want me to sign something like a document of admission of guilt. I said I didn't admit guilt so I refused to sign. Was that thing the plea bargain? Why are they mentioning it again? |
| 律师：之前警官让你签的是认罪认罚的意向书，只是公安机关了解你们认罪态度的一种方式。现在我们面对的是《认罪认罚具结书》，这是刑事诉讼法里规定的正式认罪认罚程序，需要在你自愿的基础上，并在律师的 | Lawyer：The document that the police showed to you was more like a memo, in order to know your intent of pleading guilty, or to remind you of your right of pleading guilty. Now we are talking about the *Recognizance to Admit* |

见证下，你和检察官白纸黑字确认量刑建议。

嫌疑人：认罪认罚到底对我有什么好处？

律师：首先认罪认罚的好处在于：①可以依法从宽；②提前知道刑期；③减少诉累，缓解焦虑。坏处在于：①直接按有罪认定；②不好反悔，庭审辩护空间小；③一旦接受，不建议上诉。所以你需要慎重决定。

嫌疑人：现在检察官给我什么量刑建议？我如果认罪认罚判几年？不认判几年？

律师：如果你认罪认罚，检察官目前给出的建议是×年。你觉得如何？如果不认，依照我们的经验和类案判例，可能要判×年。

*Guilt and Accept Punishment*, which is an of ficial proceeding in the criminal procedure law. It is on voluntary basis and with the witness of lawyer. We all need to write it down in black and white and sign thereon.

Client：What's in it for me?

Lawyer：The benefits of it including: 1. you may be granted leniency in accordance with the law; 2. know your sentence ahead of time; 3. no need to worry about the trial session and easeyour tension; The downsides are: 1. you accept the plea deal, you have to admit guilt first; 2. difficult to take it back and you don't have much room to defend yourself once you accept it; 3. if you accept it, to appeal is not recommended. Therefore you need to be very careful and prudent.

Client：Now what's the sentence recommendation he gave to me? If I accept it, how long do I have to stay in prison? What if I don't?

Lawyer：If you plead guilty, he gives you the recommendation of * years. What do you think? If not, according to our experience and parallel cases, it might be * years.

嫌疑人：说实话，虽然我不了解你们国家的法律，但是我觉得我做的这件事情的确有错。但我在我的国家都有家人，他们都还在等着我回去，如果我在这里服刑，他们这么远也不可能常来看我。希望你能再跟检察官说说，能不能再少几年？

律师：你目前还没有完全退赃。因为你之前也实际获利了，如果你认罪认罚，你肯定是要退出赃款的。检察官这边也说你如果接受量刑建议，一定要全额退赃。如果你退赃了，我愿意为你再去和检察官沟通。

嫌疑人：你跟他们说，如果不给我判三年以下我就不认罪认罚，一分钱也不退！

律师：你完全弄反了。认罪认罚程序虽然是辩诉双方协商程序，但始终是控方给你量刑建议，并不是相反；走认罪认罚程序或不走，对他们来说

Client：To be honest, little that I understand about the law in your country, I admit that I was wrong for what I did. But you know that I have my family back in my country and that's a big family without any income and they are waiting for me. If I have to serve prison sentence here, it's impossible for them to come and see me very of ten. So I hope you can talk to the prosecutor and cut my years in prison. Would you please?

Lawyer：You haven't surrendered all gains from it. Because you indeed obtained those money, so you ought to surrender them if you admit guilty and accept punishment. And the prosecutor also suggested if you decide to take the sentence recommendation you have to give up all the money you gained. If you make up your mind to give it up, I am willing to try again persuading the prosecutor.

Client：You tell them! If they don't give me a sentence recommendation less than three years, I will not admit guilty, accept punishment nor give up a penny!

Lawyer：You get the wrong end of the stick. Though Plea bargaining in China is based on the negotiation between the accused and prosecutor, but it is al-

都是本职工作，并没有实质差别，但对你来说却可以实实在在地获得相应的从宽处理。如公诉人不给你做认罪认罚他们并不会少拿工资。但你要注意，这并不意味着我们只能听天由命。虽然决定权在他们手里，但我们的工作还是可以更主动，例如凑足全部赃款，在适当的时间全额退赃并充分沟通等。

嫌疑人：那我能不能先退一部分？

律师：退一部分就是没有全额退赃，对于量刑建议的争取角度来讲，肯定是全退比较好。不只和认罪认罚态度一致，而且显得你更有诚意。

嫌疑人：我在里面怎么退？

律师：你如果决定退赃，我会和你家属通报，由他们先行代你退赃。

嫌疑人：就算我认罪，退不退赃到底会相差多少？

律师：我知道你什么意思。你的

ways the prosecutor that gives the sentence recommendation, not the other way around; whether you plead guilty or not makes little difference to them because it's but their duty, which, however, means an opportunity of being granted leniency for you. No matter you plead guilty or not, the prosecutors get the same salary. But one thing worth noting is, it's not saying that you have to resign yourself to your fate. Although they can decide, we could take initiative in our work. For instance, we could collect all the ill-obtained money and let your family surrender it for you at a proper time and persuade them, etc.

Client: May I just give up part of it first?

Lawyer: To give up part of it means you still keep a part. For sake of plea bargaining, it's better to give up all you got from it, which seems more genuine.

Client: How could I give the money while I am in here?

Lawyer: If you make up your mind and give it up, I will notify your family and they would do it on behalf of you.

Client: Even if I plead guilty, what difference does it make?

Lawyer: I see what you mean. The

退赃表现和认罪认罚必须是一致的，退赃本身就是认罪认罚的一部分。如果你在想不退钱的同时享有从宽利益，这样做多半行不通。因为在曾经获利并且在有能力退而不退的情况下，检察官或法官会认为你不积极退赃，而否定你的认罪认罚态度，认为你不真诚。反而会影响你的从宽幅度，甚至导致不从宽。那刑期就不是退不退赃的差距了，而是认不认罪的差距了。我建议你只要有能力筹措，就尽早积极退赃，不要影响从宽幅度。

嫌疑人：我能不能缓刑？

律师：首先根据《中华人民共和国刑法》，缓刑的前提包括认罪。但是并不是你只要认罪了就能缓刑。

嫌疑人：但你刚才不是说我如果不认罪认罚，可能判×年，那我都认罪认罚了，为什么还不能缓刑？

律师：首先认罪认罚是从宽情节，

money you give up must be consistent with your plea, so giving it up is a part of your guilty plea. If you plan to enjoy the leniency of plea bargaining without surrendering what you obtain from it, you are probably not going to make it work. Since you have gained money from it and refuse to give it up while you can, the prosecutor and judge will be under the impression that you are not 100% genuine on plea of guilty, which will affectthe extent of leniency on you, even result in no leniency at all. So the difference is not between you give it up or not, but actually between you plead guilty or not. That is why I suggest you collect as much as you can and give it up as soon as possible（ASAP）, in order not to affect the leniency on you.

Client：Can I get probation sentence recommendation?

Lawyer：According to Chinese criminal law, one of the prerequisites for probation is to admit guilty. But that is not to say you can get probation once you admit guilty.

Client：You just said that if I don't plead guilty it might be ＊ years. Now that I agree with the plea deal, why should I still cannot get the probation?

Lawyer：Firstly the admission of guilt

并非减轻情节。单有认罪认罚，没有其他减轻情节无法从三年以上的基准刑降到三年以下，只能依法从宽；其次，即便你有减轻情节，你的基准刑降到三年以下，也不等同于你一定就能缓刑。因为三年以下有期徒刑与缓刑还是有差异的，三年以下仍可能判实刑。

嫌疑人：我是不是一定会被驱逐出境？

律师：驱逐出境作为一种刑罚，可以单独适用，也可以附加适用。单独适用比较少见。但并非所有涉外籍被告人刑事案件中都会判驱逐出境，还要结合犯罪的恶性和严重程度，决定是否需要附加适用。

嫌疑人：我这个案子会不会直接判驱逐出境？

律师：据我的经验来看，不大可能。如果实施了你这个罪的行为，后果只是被赶回自己国家，那大家都会

and the acceptance of punishment is a circumstance for leniency, not mitigation of criminal liability. Without other mitigation circumstances but plea of guilty can hardly lower the sentence from 3 years plus to less than 3 years; secondly, even if you have a mitigation circumstance and have a sentence less than 3 years, there is no guarantee that you will get probation sentence. Because of an actual difference between less than 3 years and probation, you may still get a imprisonment sentence of less than 3 years.

Client: Am I going to be deported?

Lawyer: Deportation as a means of criminal penalty, can be applied exclusively or together with others, while the former is less of ten to see. However, deportation is not necessary for all criminal cases involving foreigner defendant, the seriousness and the circumstance of the crime will be considered when deciding whether to apply deportation together with otherpenalties.

Client: Will I be deported directly without other penalties?

Lawyer: Based on my experience, less likely. If one will only end up to be deported after doing that, everyone in the

蜂拥来中国做这个行为了。

嫌疑人：你觉得我这个罪会不会被附加驱逐出境？

律师：结合你这个罪名，我认为附加的可能性比较大。

嫌疑人：对了，签订了的具结书他们不会反悔吧？

律师：据我所知不太可能。除非你的案子出现新事实、新证据、新情况，需要重新审查，并重新确定量刑建议。

嫌疑人：这个协议是口头的还是书面的？

律师：会是书面的，白纸黑字，是我、检察官还有你，三方之间的协议。

嫌疑人：刑期能不能再低点？

律师：我刚才说了，如果你全额退赃，而且现在量刑建议也没有正式确定，我愿意为你再争取一下。

嫌疑人：罚金能不能少一点？

律师：罚金我也会去一并沟通，为你减轻负担。

嫌疑人：谢谢！祝你好运！

world will come here to do it.

Client: Do you think I will be penalized and deported?

Lawyer: Giving your crime, it's more likely for the deportation to be applied with other penalties.

Client: By the way, will they go back on their word on the recognizance?

Lawyer: Not that I know. Unless there is any new facts, new evidence or new circumstance, which need reexamination and reconfirmation of the sentence recommendation.

Client: Is the recognizance verbal or in writing?

Lawyer: It shall be in writing, black and white. It's among me, the prosecutor and you.

Client: Can the sentence be any lower?

Lawyer: I said a while ago that if you are will to give up all you gained from it, since the recommendation is not fixed yet, I am willing to give it a shot.

Client: May the fine be less?

Lawyer: I will discuss with them over that too, if it helps to reduce your burden.

Client: Thanks a lot! Best luck!

# 认罪认罚见证程序高频对话

| 中文版 | 英文版 |
|---|---|
| 检察官：×××，今天我们来给你做认罪认罚手续。今天你的律师也在场。认罪认罚的权利义务和法律效果，我们之前已经告诉你了，你的律师应该也跟你说过了。 | Prosecutor：* * *, we are here today for your request to admit guilt and accept punishment and sign the recognizance in the presence of your defender. Both we and your lawyer have informed you the legal rights, obligations and consequences of the admission of guiltand acceptance of punishment. |
| 嫌疑人：没错，你们跟我说过。 | Client：That's right, you have mentioned it to me. |
| 检察官：现在你的量刑建议是×年，罚金人民币×元，你的律师跟我说，已经跟你沟通过的，你同意了。是吧？ | Prosecutor：Your recommended sentence is * years, with fine of * RMB. Your lawyer told me that you agree with this sentence recommendation, right? |
| 嫌疑人：确实，我愿意认罪认罚。只是，尊敬的检察官先生，您知道我这是第一次在中国触犯法律，我以前根本不知道这件事在中国是犯罪，我现在已经认罪了，看在上帝的份上，能不能再轻一点，给我个缓刑，或者直接把我赶出中国？我发誓再也不会回中国了！ | Client：Yes, I am willing to admit guilty and accept punishment. It's just, respectable Mr. Prosecutor, you know that it's my first time that broke the law of China. I absolutely had no knowledge that it's against the law here. Since I have plead guilty, could you give me lesser punishment for God's sake, or a probation, or deportation alone? I swear I will never come back here ever! |
| 检察官：×××，首先这个案子里 | Prosecutor：* * *, firstly, in this |

你本来就可以判十年以上的刑期，现在量刑建议已经减轻到十年以下，相对十年以上肯定是低了；其次，你律师也在场，他跟我说上次你已经同意×年的量刑建议，你现在又嫌高，还想要缓刑，或者直接驱逐出境，那就是不认可量刑建议。如果你坚持如此，我们只能先撤回量刑建议，让法院去裁判。

律师：我在上次的会见中把本案的性质、认罪认罚和不认罪认罚后可能的量刑及后果都做过分析，你明确表示对×年的量刑建议是可以接受的。刚才检察官询问你，你改变想法，认为量刑还是偏重？

嫌疑人：是的，我上次是同意了。但我回去想了很久，觉得还是要问问检察官还能不能再轻一点。

检察官：首先，我给的也只是量刑建议，最后需要法院来判决；其次，我们讨论的结果是×年的量刑建议对于你的犯罪情节来说，是合适的，已经采纳了律师的意见，给予减轻，变为十年以下了。所以量刑建议不能再

case, you could be sentenced more than 10 years of imprisonment. Now your recommended sentence is less than 10 years, which is much lower already; the second one is that your lawyer said you agreed with the recommendation, and now you go back on your word, even wish probation or deportation alone. Are you saying that you are unhappy with the recommendation? If so, we have no choice but take it back and let the court do their job.

Lawyer: I have explained you last time the nature of this case, possible sentences and consequences with and without the plea agreement. You said clearly that you this recommendation is acceptable. So you changed your mind when the prosecutor asked you? Is it still too much for you?

Client: That's right, I said yes last time. But I have thought it over and decided to ask prosecutor myself to see if it can be any lower.

Prosecutor: Firstly, it's just a recommendation for sentence, whichneeds the court to make final decision; secondly, through discussion, we reckon that for your circumstance in this case, * years of imprisonment is appropriate,

少了。你如果不同意，我先走了。如果你反悔，又想认罪认罚，可以在法院阶段做。

律师：我说两句可以吗？认罪认罚必须建立在你自愿的基础上，如果你经过慎重思考，觉得不认罪，或者觉得刑期还是过重，可以不走认罪认罚程序，在法庭上再发表意见。如检察官所说，万一你后悔了，又想做认罪认罚，当庭也可以认罪认罚。

嫌疑人：真的太难决定了，你们能不能给我 10 分钟？让我再想一想。

检察官：可以。

嫌疑人：你们不会反悔吧？

检察官：我们不会反悔的。白纸黑字三方协议。

嫌疑人：尊敬的检察官，我的罪到底是怎么认定的，你能跟我说说吗？

检察官：庭审时我都会详细举证，你到时候注意听就好了。

and we have taken your lawyer's opinions in account. Therefore, it cannot be any lower. If you decide to take your words back for now, you may also reactivate this procedure during the court session.

Lawyer: Can I say something? This process of admission of guilt and acceptance of punishment should be on voluntary basis. If you have thought it over and decided not to, or the recommendation is too much for you, you may not accept it and voice your own opinion. As the prosecutor said, even you reject it now, you may also reactivate this process during trial if you change your mind.

Client: It's so difficult to make decision, can I have ten minutes to think about it again?

Prosecutor: yes, you can.

Client: Are you guys gonna keep your word?

Prosecutor: We will keep our words. it's in black and white and it involves three parties.

Client: Honorable Mr. Prosecutor, can I ask what is the basis for your conviction?

Prosecutor: For that I will adduce them during the court session and all you need to do is to pay attention to them.

律师：我之前在会见时也跟你大致介绍过。这里就不重复讲了。

嫌疑人：除了我，其他的同案犯都认了吗？

检察官：目前多数都已认罪。具体是谁无可奉告。

嫌疑人：我还是签了吧，我做的事我认。量刑建议如果不能再降低，到时我开始服刑了请跟我家人说一下，让他们不要太担心。

律师：这些我们都会做的。法院还没有判决，现在只是量刑建议。法院判决生效后，我会想办法通知你的家人。

嫌疑人：检察官，法院会按照这个量刑建议判吗？会不会更重？

检察官：如果量刑建议合适，法院一般会采纳。

嫌疑人：就是说不会更重？

检察官：这取决于法官，毕竟判决是由法官作出。我这边不能给任何承诺。

Lawyer：I told you about it last time during our meeting, no need to repeat them.

Client：Has other accomplices all confessed to their crimes?

Prosecutor：For now, most of them have confessed. I will not disclose their names.

Client：I might as well sign on it. Iadmit what I did. If the sentence recommendation cannot go any lower, when I started to serve the sentence, please inform my family and let them do not worry too much about me.

Lawyer：We will do this for sure. The court has not decided yet, so it's just a recommended sentence by the procuratorate. After the judgement, I will try to inform your family about it.

Client：Mr. Prosecutor, will the court follow the recommendation? Will it be any higher?

Prosecutor：If the recommendation is appropriate, the court normally will adopt it.

Client：You mean it will not go any higher?

Prosecutor：It's up to the judge. The judgment is made by him after all. We cannot promise you anything.

| 嫌疑人：那会不会更轻？ | Client：Is it possible for it to be any lower？ |
|---|---|
| 检察官：这同样取决于法官。在法院阶段你们可以向法官表达意见。但记住你是签署过《认罪认罚具结书》的，你得遵守自己的承诺。 | Prosecutor：It's also up to the judge. And during the court session you may present your opinions to the judges. But bear in mind that you have signed the *Recognizance to Admit Guilt and Accept Punishment*, so you need to keep your own words. |
| 嫌疑人：我知道了。谢谢。 | Client：Got it. Thank you. |

## 相关英文表达

| 英文表达 | 中文意思 |
|---|---|
| suspension of licence | 吊销执照 |
| written prosecution opinion | 起诉意见书 |
| give somebody a hard time | 为难某人 |
| trial session | 审判阶段 |
| matter of time | 时间问题 |
| make a complaint | 投诉 |
| at liberty to | 有权做某事 |
| core issue | 核心内容 |
| work overtime | 加班加点 |
| preliminary written opinion | 初步的书面意见 |
| make all-out efforts | 全力以赴 |
| sort out | 挑选出来 |
| face-to-face | 当面 |
| bring to attention | 引起注意 |

续表

| 英文表达 | 中文意思 |
|---|---|
| pull some strings | 走后门 |
| hopefully | 但愿 |
| in the first place | 起初 |
| in favor of | 有利于 |
| return the case | 退回案件 |
| contracting state | 缔约国 |
| judicial activity | 司法活动 |
| case law | 判例法 |
| statute law | 成文法 |
| impunity fact | 出罪事由 |
| stay posted | 跟进最新信息 |
| cost-efficient | 划算的 |
| additional investigation | 补充侦查 |
| confirmation for payment | 付款确认 |
| get even | 算账 |
| have the nerve to | 有勇气做某事 |
| pay the fiddler | 承担后果 |
| push forward | 推进 |
| group discuss | 集体讨论 |
| finalize | 最终敲定 |
| do the math | 做算数 |
| at most | 最多 |
| over my head | 难理解 |
| go with | 与……相匹配 |
| with the witness of | 在某人见证下 |
| ease your tension | 缓解你的紧张情绪 |

| 英文表达 | 中文意思 |
|---|---|
| admit guilt | 认罪 |
| surrendered all gains | 退出全部犯罪所得 |
| serve prison sentence | 服刑 |
| get the wrong end of the stick | 弄反了 |
| the other way around | 相反 |
| worth noting | 值得注意 |
| resign oneself to one's fate | 听天由命 |
| take initiative | 主动 |
| ill-obtained money | 违法所得 |
| at a proper time | 在合适的时间 |
| for sake of | 为了 |
| under the impression | 留下……的印象 |
| ASAP = As Soon As Possible | 尽快 |
| probation sentence recommendation | 缓刑的量刑建议 |
| now that | 既然 |
| go back on one's word | 食言 |
| give it a shot | 试试 |
| in the presence of | 某人在场 |
| take words back | 收回说过的话 |
| reactivate this procedure | 激活该程序 |
| might as well | 还是……的好 |

# 一审阶段

## 开庭前会见高频问答

| 中文版 | 英文版 |
| --- | --- |
| 被告人：你好。<br><br>律师：你好。你的案子后天就要开庭了。我今天来给你做一下庭前准备。 | Defendant：Hello.<br><br>Lawyer：Hello. Your case is about to hold a court session the day after tomorrow. I am here today to prepare you for the hearing. |
| 被告人：我们有没有陪审团？<br><br>律师：与英美国家不同，我国实行人民陪审员制度。没有陪审团。 | Defendant：Do we have jury here?<br><br>Lawyer：Different from the UK and US, our country has the people's assessor system rather than jury. |
| 被告人：我的案子是会公开审理？还是不公开审理？<br><br>律师：你的案子会公开审理。 | Defendant：Is my hearing going to be open or closed?<br><br>Lawyer：Your case hearing is going to be open. |
| 被告人：我开庭需要注意什么？<br><br>律师：我跟你详细介绍一下开庭的大致流程，穿插跟你说注意事项。审判长查明当事人是否到庭，宣布案由；宣布合议庭的组成人员、书记员、公诉人、辩护人、诉讼代理人、鉴定人和翻译人员的名单；告知当事人有权对合议庭组成人员、书记员、公诉人、鉴定人和翻译人员申请回避；告知被告人享有辩护权利。被告人认罪 | Defendant：Is there anything I need to pay special attention to during the hearing?<br><br>Lawyer：Now I am expounding you the procedures of hearing, and something you need to pay attention to. The presiding judge shall check whether all parties are in court and announce the cause of action; announce the names of the members of the collegial panel, court clerk, public prosecutor, defenders, litigation representative, identification or evaluation ex- |

认罚的，审判长应当告知被告人享有的诉讼权利和认罪认罚的法律规定，审查认罪认罚的自愿性和《认罪认罚具结书》内容的真实性、合法性。

perts, and interpreters; inform the parties of their right to applyfor disqualification of the members of the collegial panel, court clerk, public prosecutor, identification or evaluation experts, and interpreters; and inform a defendant of his or her defense right. Where a defendant admits guilt and accepts punishment, the presiding judge shall inform the defendant of his or her procedural rights and the provisions of law on the admission of guilt and acceptance of punishment, and examine the voluntariness of the admission of guilt and acceptance of punishment and the authenticity and legality of the recognizance to admit guilt and accept punishment.

被告人：知道了。

律师：然后是法庭调查，公诉人在法庭上宣读起诉书后，被告人、被害人可以就起诉书指控的犯罪进行陈述，公诉人可以讯问被告人。我们辩护人也会发问。审判人员可以讯问被告人。我在庭上会问你这些问题，你需要如实回答……

Defendant: Understood.

Lawyer: Then comes the court investigation, After the public prosecutor reads out the indictment in court, a defendant and a victim may present a statement regarding a crime alleged in the indictment, and the public prosecutor may question the defendant. We defender lawyers will ask you questions too. A judge may question a defendant. And the questions I am going to ask you at that time are as follows, you need to answer them truthfully. . .

被告人：好的。我有意见就可以表达吗？

律师：当法官让你发表对起诉书指控内容的意见时，你就可以回答。此时回答注意针对起诉书具体指控的内容，只要简略表达你对起诉书指控内容认可或对某个指控的事实不认可即可，不用详细展开。

被告人：知道了。

律师：接下来是质证环节，公诉人、辩护人应当向法庭出示物证、书证等证据，让当事人辨认、核对，对未到庭的证人的证言笔录、鉴定人的鉴定意见、勘验笔录和其他作为证据的文书，应当当庭宣读。审判人员应当听取公诉人、当事人和辩护人、诉讼代理人的意见。法庭审理过程中，合议庭对证据有疑问的，可以宣布休庭，对证据进行调查核实。

被告人：他们会出示哪些证据？

律师：除了我之前跟你介绍过的

Defendant：All right. Can I speak whenever I want?

Lawyer：When the judge asks you about your opinions towards the charges in the indictment, you may answer. And please focus on the charges, and present your opinions briefly on whether you approve them or not, no need to expand your points.

Defendant：Noted.

Lawyer：Next is the examination of the evidence. The public prosecutor and a defender shall adduce physical evidence before court for the parties to identify, and a statement of a witness who is not in court, an expert opinion of an identification or evaluation expert who is not in court, transcripts of crime scene investigation, and other documentation serving as evidence shall be read out in court. A judge shall hear the opinions of the public prosecutor, parties, defenders, and litigation representatives. Where, during a court session, a collegial panel has any doubt on evidence, it may announce an adjournment to investigate and verify evidence.

Defendant：What evidence are they going to present to the court?

Lawyer：Apart from the documentary

书证，还有被害人和证人的笔录，这些你需要仔细听，看其中有无与事实不符的地方，在轮到你发言时提出来。要针对证据本身。如果你觉得证据是虚假的，你的依据是什么。如果你觉得证据取得是不合法的，依据是什么。简要表达清楚即可，不要论辩，因为这不是论辩环节。

被告人：知道了。

律师：在质证环节之后，是辩论环节。公诉人会先发表公诉词。法庭审理过程中，对与定罪、量刑有关的事实、证据都应当进行调查、辩论。经审判长许可，公诉人、当事人和辩护人、诉讼代理人可以对证据和案件情况发表意见并且可以互相辩论。一般有两轮辩论。

被告人：知道了，我有发言时间限制吗？

律师：尽可能简洁，之前说过的内容不要重复发表。如果非要说，换

evidence that I have introduced to you, there are still statements of the victims and the witnesses, to which you need to listen and find out whether there is any inconsistency between it and the facts. If you feel the evidence is false, then you have to give your reason. If you think the evidence is illegally obtained, you also need to explain why. Remember do not say more than enough, and do not debate over anything, because this part is not for debating.

Defendant: OK.

Lawyer: After the examination of evidence, comes the debate time. The public prosecutor will make the statement of public prosecution. In a court session, any fact or evidence related to conviction or sentencing shall be investigated and debated. With the permission of the presiding judge, the public prosecutor or a party or the defender or litigation representative thereof may present opinions on the evidence and circumstances of a case and debate with opposing parties. Normally there are two rounds of debate.

Defendant: Got it. Is there a time limit for my speech?

Lawyer: Just be as brief as possible, and do not repeat what you said before,

种说法发表。最后是陈词环节。审判长在宣布辩论终结后，被告人有最后陈述的权利。

被告人：我该怎么说？

律师：你说说自己的心里话，除了你之前说过的话以外。例如你的家庭情况，你之前的工作事业情况，这次对你的教训等。简要跟法庭发表一下自己的想法，之前说过的就不用说了。

被告人：我有没有希望取保候审？

律师：根据我上次跟法官沟通的情况，考虑到你的涉案情节，你取保候审的可能性不大。

被告人：我的家人会不会来旁听？

律师：我已经将开庭的时间、地点告知他们，他们说会尽可能派人到场。

被告人：我能否跟家人说几句？

律师：开庭的时候恐怕不能，有什么你可以现在跟我说，我帮你转达。

or paraphrase it if you have to. The last part is the closing statement. After the presiding judge declares an end of debate, the defendant shall have the right to present a closing statement.

Defendant：What should I say then?

Lawyer：Your innermost thoughts and feelings, besides what you said before, such as your family background and career path related to this case, and the lesson you learn from this crime. Just briefly express your views, no need to repeat what you said before.

Defendant：Is that possible for me to get bailed ?

Lawyer：Based on the communication with the judge last time and the circumstance of your crime, there is only a fat chance of it.

Defendant：Will my family be present to observe the hearing?

Lawyer：I have notify the time and place of the hearing, and they said they will try and send someone.

Defendant：Can I have a word with them?

Lawyer：During the hearing? I am afraid you cannot. If you have anything to say to them, I could relay the message.

| | |
|---|---|
| 被告人：开庭后我的家人能不能来见我？ | Defendant：Can my family come and see me after the hearing? |
| 律师：你如果不取保候审，最早能见到家人的时间是判决生效，你的刑罚开始执行后，你家人可以向监管单位申请会见你。 | Lawyer：If you don't get bailed, the earliest possible time that you may see your family is when the judgment comes into effect, then you family may go to prison and apply for the visit to you. |
| 被告人：我知道了，如果我开始服刑，请通知我的家人我服刑的地点，他们好来看我，我们能相见。 | Defendant：I see. When I start serving my sentence, please inform my family about my place so that they couldcome and we could meet each other. |
| 律师：一定。 | Lawyer：Certainly. |

## 开庭情况向家属反馈高频问答

| 中文版 | 英文版 |
|---|---|
| 家属：现在我们能不能见他？<br>律师：现在你们还见不了他。<br>家属：什么时候能见他？<br>律师：要等判决生效，开始服刑后家属才能申请会见。 | Client：Can we visit him now?<br>Lawyer：Not yet.<br>Client：When can we meet him?<br>Lawyer：You have to wait till the judgment comes into effect, and then you could apply for visiting him. |
| 家属：开庭后你还能见他吗？ | Client：Can you meet him after the hearing? |
| 律师：可以的，我昨天已经预约了，后天见他。 | Lawyer：Yes, yesterday I have made the appointment to meet him the day after tomorrow. |
| 家属：你觉得他庭上表现怎样？ | Client：What do you think of his performance during the court hearing? |

律师：说的内容基本比较中肯、客观，就是翻译有些不行，没有把他的一些意思翻译准确。

家属：哪些地方？

律师：比如……

家属：你觉得对他会有什么影响吗？

律师：不会有实质性影响。

家属：你觉得他大概要判几年？

律师：按照他的情节，位于3年至10年的量刑区间。但现在还不确定到底是几年。

家属：大致是几年？10年和3年相差很多！

律师：按照我们的既往案例，他类似性质的量刑在5年至7年。但你知道，案子之间有很多不同，这个区间仅供参考。

被告人：您能否再跟法官说说，让他给个缓刑，或者直接驱逐出境。

律师：我作为他的辩护人，当然是希望他能够被判轻一些。但就目前

Lawyer：The thing he said was to the point and based on fact, only with some flaws in translation, which are not very accurate.

Client：What are they?

Lawyer：To name just a few...

Client：Do you think it will affect his sentence?

Lawyer：I don't think this will make substantial difference.

Client：How many years is he going to stay in the prison?

Lawyer：According to his circumstance of crime, his sentence is between 3 to 10 years, but it's difficult to predict it accurately.

Client：Do you have a ballpark number? 3 years is way different from 10!

Lawyer：Based on the cases we handled before, cases of his kind and circumstance, the sentence falls between 5 to 7 years. Be that as it may, there could still differences between his case and others, so this prediction is for reference only.

Client：Can you talk to the judge to give him a probation or an exportation alone?

Lawyer：As his counsel, I do hope he can get a sentence as light as possi-

的涉案情节来看，仍然在3年到10年的量刑区间，缓刑和单独适用驱逐出境的可能性很小。我这边会跟法官保持沟通，有什么信息及时跟你们反馈。

家属：开庭以后多久能有结果？

律师：依照《中华人民共和国刑事诉讼法》第208条的规定：人民法院审理公诉案件，应当在受理后2个月以内宣判，至迟不得超过3个月。对于可能判处死刑的案件或者附带民事诉讼的案件，以及有本法第158条规定情形之一的，经上一级人民法院批准，可以延长3个月；因特殊情况还需要延长的，报请最高人民法院批准。按照我们的经验，一审一般在开庭后的1个月左右，法院会有判决结果。但他这个案件人数多、案卷多，定性存在一定争议，多数人未认罪认罚，法院会比较谨慎，可能会审理较长时间。

ble. Giving the circumstance of this case, it's still somewhere between 3 to 10 years, with slight possibility of probation or an exportation alone. I will keep in contact with the judge and keep you posted.

Client: How long does it take for the judgement to be made?

Lawyer: According to the Article 208 of the *Criminal Procedure Law of the People's Republic of China* of our country, a people's court shall announce a sentence for a case of public prosecution within two months, or three months at the latest, after accepting the case. For a case with the possibility of a death penalty or a case with an incidental civil action or under any of the circumstances as set forth in Article 158 of this Law, the period of trial may be extended for three months with the approval of the people's court at the next higher level; and, if more extension is needed under special circumstances, the extension shall be reported to the Supreme People's Court for approval. Based on our experience, the first instance will normally come up with a judgement in one month or so. However, we have to look at the number of defendants and case files, the controversial part

家属：你觉得找使馆出面和你们政府沟通有用吗？

律师：我个人认为没有用，不建议这么做。因为根据《维也纳外交关系公约》第41条的规定："一、在不妨碍外交特权与豁免之情形下，凡享有此项特权与豁免之人员，均负有尊重接受国法律规章之义务。此等人员并负有不干涉该国内政之义务。……"而中国和你们国家都是这个公约的缔约国。根据《中华人民共和国刑法》，凡在中华人民共和国领域内犯罪的，除法律有特别规定的以外，都适用本法。外国及外交人员不得干涉我国司法。因此所谓的外交渠道您一定要慎重，警惕诈骗。

of this case and the fact that most of them haven't pleaded guilty, so the court might be so prudent in making decision as to prolong the time of handling.

Client: Do you think it will work by looking for help from the Embassy to intermediate with your government for this case?

Lawyer: I don't think so. According to the Article 41 of the *Vienna Convention on Diplomatic Relations*: without prejudice to their privileges and immunities, it is the the duty of all persons enjoying such privileges and immunities to respect the laws and regulations of the receiving State. They also have a duty not to interfere in the internal affairs of that State. And China and your country are both the contracting states of it. *Chinese Criminal Law* shall be applicable to anyone who commits a crime within the territory and territorial waters and space of the People's Republic of China, except as otherwise specifically provided by law. No foreign countries nor foreign diplomatic staff shall intervene the judicial activities in our country. Therefore you better be aware of the so-called diplomatic channel and alert to any fraud.

| | |
|---|---|
| 家属：那么他到时候能不能提前假释出来？<br><br>律师：根据《中华人民共和国刑事诉讼法》和相关司法解释，被判处有期徒刑的罪犯，在执行期间确有悔改或者立功表现，应当依法予以减刑、假释的时候，由执行机关提出建议书，报请人民法院审核裁定，并将建议书副本抄送人民检察院。人民检察院可以向人民法院提出书面意见。假释肯定会比减刑严格一些。你们会见他后，有什么问题可以随时问我。 | Client：Then can he get released on parole?<br><br>Lawyer：According to the *Criminal Procedure Law of the People's Republic of China* and related legal explanation, where a convict sentenced to fixed-term imprisonment shows true repentance or has meritorious acts while serving his or her sentence and shall be granted commutation or parole in accordance with the law, the execution authority shall submit a written recommendation to the people's court for examination and decision, and send a copy of it to the people's procuratorate. The people's procuratorate may provide a written opinion to the people's court. Parole shall be stricter than commutation. After you are able to meet him in person, you may ask me should you have any questions. |
| 家属：谢谢你！<br>律师：不客气，本职工作。 | Client：I appreciate it!<br>Lawyer：Not at all. it's my duty. |

## 开庭后会见高频问答

| 中文版 | 英文版 |
|---|---|
| 被告人：你认为我在庭上如何？ | Client：How is my performance at the court? |
| 律师：说的内容基本比较中肯、客 | Lawyer：What you stated was mostly |

观，就是翻译有些不行，没有把你的一些意思翻译准确。

被告人：哪些地方？

律师：比如……

被告人：你觉得这会影响法官对我的印象吗？

律师：不会有实质性影响。

被告人：你觉得法官会接受我的辩解吗？

律师：我认为你说的还是符合案件事实和常理的，主要看法官如何衡量这个案子。

被告人：什么意思？

律师：如果法官认为你的辩解能够说服他，他就会至少作罪轻判决；如果他认为你的辩解站不住脚，恐怕罪轻空间就比较小了。

被告人：可不可能判我无罪？

律师：你的案件证据上确实存在一些缺乏合理解释的矛盾，这些矛盾如果法官认为不能排除的合理怀疑，那可能会要求公安机关进行补充侦查，也是以2次为限。但这种情况发生的概率不大。

impartial and objective, despite the inaccurate translation which didn't convey your meaning accurately.

Client：What specifically?

Lawyer：Like...

Client：Do you think it will affect my impression on the judge?

Lawyer：Not substantially.

Client：From your perspective, will the judge accept my defense?

Lawyer：To me, your defense is consistent with the fact of the case and common sense. So it's largely rely on how the judges evaluate this case.

Client：What do you mean?

Lawyer：If the judge regards your defense persuasive, at least he will give you a lighter sentence；in the case that he sees it groundless, then there is less room for lighter result.

Client：Can I get a sentence of not guilty?

Lawyer：Some evidence on the facts of this case does contradict each other without reasonable explanation. If the judge deems that it's not yet beyond reasonable doubt, he may request the police to carry out additional investigation, twice maximum. But this case does not happen very often.

被告人：这是好事还是坏事？

律师：如果发生这样的事，对你来说不一定是坏的。表明法院相对还是比较中立的，没有被指控思路牵着鼻子走。

被告人：开庭以后多久能有结果？

律师：依照《中华人民共和国刑事诉讼法》第 208 条的规定：人民法院审理公诉案件，应当在受理后 2 个月以内宣判，至迟不得超过 3 个月。对于可能判处死刑的案件或者附带民事诉讼的案件，以及有本法第 158 条规定情形之一的，经上一级人民法院批准，可以延长 3 个月；因特殊情况还需要延长的，报请最高人民法院批准。按照我们的经验，一审一般在开庭后的 1 个月，法院会有判决结果。但你这个案件人数多、案卷多，定性存在一定争议，多数人未认罪认罚，法院会比较谨慎，可能讨论较长时间。

Client：So is this good or not?

Lawyer：If such happens, it's not necessarily a bad thing to you. It represents impartiality of the court, unaffected by the prosecution.

Client：How long does it take for the judgement to be made?

Lawyer：According to the Article 208 of the *Criminal Procedure Law of the People's Republic of China*, a people's court shall announce a sentence for a case of public prosecution within two months, or three months at the latest, after accepting the case. For a case with the possibility of a death penalty or a case with an incidental civil action or under any of the circumstances as set forth in Article 158 of this law, the period of trial may be extended for three months with the approval of the people's court at the next higher level; and, if more extension is needed under special circumstances, the extension shall be reported to the Supreme People's Court for approval. Based on our experience, the first instance will normally come up with a judgement in one month or so. However, we have to look at the number of defendants and case files, the controversy part of this case and the fact that most of them haven't pleaded gui-

被告人：你认为我要坐几年牢？

律师：按照你的情节，你位于 3 年至 10 年的量刑区间。但现在还不确定到底是几年，因为你和你邻近的人都未认罪认罚，且多人犯罪需要对每个被告人的刑罚做慎重的量刑平衡。

被告人：大概是几年？10 年和 3 年相差很大！

律师：按照我们的既往案例，你这样性质的量刑在 5 年至 7 年。但你知道，案子之间有很多不同，这个区间仅供你参考。

被告人：你能否再跟法官说说，让他给我个缓刑，或者直接驱逐出境。

律师：我作为你的辩护人，当然是希望你能够被判轻一些。但以你目前的涉案情节来看，仍然在 3 年到 10 年的量刑区间，缓刑和单独适用驱逐出境的可能性很小。我会跟法官保持

lty, so the court might be so prudent in making decision as to prolong the time of handling.

Client：How many years am I going to stay in the prison?

Lawyer：According to your circumstance of crime, your sentence is between 3 to 10 years. But it's difficult to predict it accurately because you and the defendants next to you haven't pleaded guilty, and case with many defendants needs particularly careful weighing and balancing of the punishment of each.

Client：Do you have a ball‐park number? 3 years is way different from 10!

Lawyer：Based on the cases we handled before, cases of your kind and similar circumstance, the sentence falls between 5 to 7 years. Be that as it may, there could still differences between your case and others, so this prediction is for reference only.

Client：Can you talk to the judge to give me a probation or an exportation alone?

Lawyer：As your counsel, I do hope you can get a sentence as light as possible. Giving the circumstance of this case, it's still somewhere between 3 to 10 years, with slight possibility of probation or an

沟通，有什么信息及时跟你反馈。

被告人：我如果被判 6 年，能不能减刑？

律师：当然可以。你的罪名不属于限制减刑的范畴，可以按照规定提出申请，经过审查批准后，走相关的减刑程序。

被告人：那我能不能假释？

律师：根据《中华人民共和国刑事诉讼法》，被判处有期徒刑罪犯，在执行期间确有悔改或者立功表现，应当依法予以减刑、假释的时候，由执行机关提出建议书，报请人民法院审核裁定，并将建议书副本抄送人民检察院。人民检察院可以向人民法院提出书面意见。但假释肯定会相对严格一些。

被告人：到时候你还能来见我吗？

律师：在本案判决生效后，我就

exportation alone. I will keep in contact with the judge and keep you posted.

Client：Can I get commuted if I were sentenced six-year imprisment?

Lawyer：Sure you can. Your charge is not within the scope of those crimes that may entail restriction of commutation, so you may apply according to rule. Once it's approved, related commutation proceedings will be activated.

Client：Then can I be released on parole?

Lawyer：According to the *Criminal Procedure Law the People's Republic of China*, where a convict sentenced to fixed-term imprisonment shows true repentance or has meritorious acts while serving his or her sentence and shall be granted commutation or parole in accordance with the law, the execution authority shall submit a written recommendation to the people's court for examination and decision, and send a copy of it to the people's procuratorate. The people's procuratorate may provide a written opinion to the people's court. Parole shall be stricter than commutation.

Lawyer：Can you come and visit me then？

Client：After the judgement comes

| | |
|---|---|
| 没有权限见你了。但你的家人可以会见你，如你有疑问，可以让你的家人转达给我。<br><br>被告人：谢谢！<br>律师：不客气。保重。 | into effect, I will be no longer authorized to meet you. But your family can do it. And you may let them relay your questions to me if any.<br><br>Lawyer: Thanks!<br>Client: You are welcome. Take care. |

<h2 align="center">一审宣判后上诉期间会见高频问答</h2>

| 中文版 | 英文版 |
|---|---|
| 　　上诉人：律师，×年虽然比我预计的最坏结果要好一点，但是对我来说还是很重。我不知道为什么法官非要把我判这么重。当时量刑建议不是一个区间吗，最轻只有×年，为什么不是×年？<br><br>　　律师：关于这个问题我也和法官沟通了。法官考虑到你这边虽然有认罪认罚的从宽情节，但除此之外你没有任何其他从轻减轻的情节，而且你至今都未退赃。<br><br><br><br>　　上诉人：这不公平，我都花掉了，我身上一分钱都没有！我家人也不在这里，我怎么拿出这笔钱？<br><br><br>　　律师：也有外籍被告人最终想办 | 　　Client: Sir, * years is better than the worst case scenario, but it's still too much for me too. I have no idea why the judge made it so heavy. Was the sentence recommendation a range? Since the lowest is * years, why cannot I get that?<br><br>　　Lawyer: I have communicated over this with the judge. He regards that there is no circumstance of lighter or mitigated punishment other than your lenient circumstance of admitting guilty and accepting punishment, plus you haven't given up what you obtained in this case.<br><br>　　Client: It's not fair! I have spent all those money and I don't have a penny with me now! Also my family are not here in China, how can I hand over that money?<br><br>　　Lawyer: But you see there are also |

法全退或退了一部分，但你一点都没有退，就比较不利。

上诉人：太不公平了……

律师：你是否要上诉？

上诉人：我想上诉。

律师：本案你已经自愿签署《认罪认罚具结书》，上诉的后果我也必须跟你讲清：一旦检察院知道你在认罪认罚的基础上还上诉，肯定会抗诉，二审人民法院就可以依法加重你的刑罚。所以你要慎重。

上诉人：我再考虑考虑。那我现在能不能见到我家人？

律师：现在是上诉期间。如果上诉期满你不上诉，判决就自动生效，你就开始服刑。虽然你还会在看守所待一段时间，但是这段时间也是你有期徒刑的一部分。根据《中华人民共和国刑法》，有期徒刑的刑期，从判决执行之日起计算；判决执行以前先行羁押的，羁押一日折抵刑期一日。你原先在看守所待的每一天也会在总刑期里扣除；如果你选择上诉，则一

other foreign defendants who have surrendered their part, while you haven't given up any, which is adverse to you.

Client: This is so unfair. . .

Lawyer: Do you choose to appeal?

Client: I do want to appeal.

Lawyer: Since you have already voluntarily signed the *Recognizance to Admit Guilt and Accept Punishment* in this case, so I have to bring home to you the consequences of appealing: Once the procuratorate is aware that you appeal after admitting guilt and accepting punishment, it will certainly file a counterappeal too, and in this case the people's court of second instance may aggravate your criminal punishment. Thus you have to be very careful on that.

Client: I will think it over. Can I meet my family now?

Lawyer: Currently your case is during the period of appeal. If you don't appeal within the period, the verdict will come into effect, and you will begin serving the sentence. Although you still need to stay here for a while, but this time period is part of your term of imprisonment. According to *Criminal Law of the People's Republic of China*, a term of fixed-term imprisonment shall be counted from the

审判决不生效，案件进入二审阶段。《中华人民共和国刑事诉讼法》规定，第二审的判决、裁定和最高人民法院的判决、裁定，都是终审的判决、裁定。所以二审判决后，本案就有了生效判决。只有在你开始服刑后，你的家人才能申请见你。

上诉人：如果我上诉，你还会继续为我辩护吗？

律师：你的委托是到一审终结，不包含二审阶段。如果你的家人愿意委托我，我会为你在二审阶段辩护。

上诉人：你觉得二审给我减刑的希望大不大？

律师：我认为本案存在一定争议，二审会不会改判，取决于二审法官的看法和我们与法院的沟通情况。现在

date the judgment begins to be executed; if the criminal is held in custody before the execution of the judgment, one day in custody shall be considered one day of the term sentenced; if you choose to appeal, then the verdict of first instance will not come into effect and this case will enter the stage of second instance. According to the *Criminal Procedure Law of the People's Republic of China*, a sentence or ruling of a people's court of second instance or a sentence or ruling of the Supreme People's Court shall be final. Therefore, after the second instance, you will have a legally effective judgement for this case and you may start serving the sentence. Only then can your family apply to meet you.

Client: If I appeal, will you continue defending for me later on?

Lawyer: My delegation will end when the first instance concludes, so the second trial is not included. If your family tend to retain me, I will be your counsel of second instance.

Client: What do you think is the odds of mitigation during the second instance?

Lawyer: The way I see it, this case is controversial in some sense. But it's up to the panel of second instance and how

| | |
|---|---|
| 下结论还为时过早。但有一点是肯定的，如果你家人还是选择让我代理，我会跟之前一样全力以赴。<br><br>　　上诉人：我知道了。谢谢你一直为我的案子所做的努力。 | is the communication with them. It's too early to jump to the conclusion. But one thing is certain, if your family choose me, I will spare no pains as before.<br><br>　　Client：Got it. Thank for all your efforts you made for my case. |

# 相关英文表达

| 英文表达 | 中文意思 |
|---|---|
| hold a court session | 开庭 |
| jury | 陪审团 |
| people's assessor system | 人民陪审员制度 |
| presiding judge | 审判长 |
| collegial panel | 合议庭 |
| court clerk | 书记员 |
| public prosecutor | 公诉人 |
| litigation representative | 诉讼代理人 |
| read out | 宣读 |
| innermost thought | 内心想法 |
| career path | 职业道路 |
| fat chance | 希望渺茫 |
| observe the hearing | 旁听庭审 |
| ballpark | 大致的 |
| be that as it may | 尽管如此 |
| for reference only | 仅供参考 |
| at the latest | 至迟 |
| incidental civil action | 附带民事诉讼 |

续表

| 英文表达 | 中文意思 |
|---|---|
| the Supreme People's Court | 最高人民法院 |
| *Vienna Convention on Diplomatic Relations* | 《维也纳外交关系公约》 |
| released on parole | 假释 |
| meritorious act | 立功 |
| be granted commutation | 获得减刑 |
| reasonable explanation | 合理解释 |
| death penalty | 死刑 |
| worst case scenario | 最坏情况 |
| other than | 除了 |
| bring home to | 给某人讲清楚某事 |
| spare no pains | 不遗余力 |

# 二审阶段

## 二审期间会见高频问答

| 中文版 | 英文版 |
|---|---|
| 上诉人：我这个案子还有望改判吗？<br><br>辩护人：我已经和二审法官就这个案子的争议以口头和书面方式进行了充分沟通，他同意我的部分观点，例如……也认为其中一些情况不妥，例如……他后续还会找你提审，在提审中，有这些注意事项…… | Client: Is it possible to modify the original sentence?<br><br>Lawyer: As to the controversy of this case, I have discussed with the judge of the second instance over it, both verbally and in writing. He agrees with me on some points, such as... but there some views he didn't go along with, such as... He will arraign you later, during wh- |

上诉人：为什么一审法官没听我们的意见？

辩护人：我当时跟你说过，一审法官认为……

上诉人：一审都没听，你怎么知道二审会听？

辩护人：二审法官我已经沟通过，他总的来说比较和气，也很理性、耐心，愿意听取我们的意见。我们的意见他已经认真听取了，而且同意我们的部分观点。

上诉人：二审改判概率是多少？

辩护人：如果二审法官采纳我们全部的辩护意见，改判的概率还是很大的。

上诉人：我在里面听说二审没用，一般都会维持一审判决，是吗？

辩护人：二审还是有一定概率会改判的，每个案件都不一样，千差万别。本案改判概率多少，如我之前所说，要看法官是否采纳我们意见里的核心观点。

上诉人：那如果不采纳，岂不是我要坐穿牢底了？

辩护人：也没这么严重，因为毕

ich you need to pay attention to the following issues. . .

Client: Why the judge of the first instance didn't listen to us?

Lawyer: We have been through this already, he believes that. . .

Client: If they didn't listen in the first instance, how do you know they will listen in the second one?

Lawyer: I have talked with the judge of second instance, who is easygoing, reasonable, patient and willing to listen to our opinions. He has heard all our opinions with attention and agreed with some of them.

Client: What's the odds of modification of the original sentence?

Lawyer: If he adopts all our defense opinions, the odds is in our favor.

Client: I heard that the second instance is useless, the norm is upholding the original sentence. Is that right?

Lawyer: There is a chance of modification of the original sentence, which varies greatly from case to case. As for this case, as I said, it really depends on whether the judge accepts our points.

Client: If he doesn't , do I have to stay in here for my life time?

Lawyer: It's not that bad, since he

竟他现在已经认同我们部分观点了。

上诉人：那你帮我想想办法，要不要送点钱给他？

辩护人：这样做不仅违法而且行不通。最稳妥的还是将法律问题技术化，依照法律和事实辩护。

上诉人：会有用吗？

辩护人：如果这样做没有用，其他的办法更没有用。

上诉人：二审法官是什么样的人？他会不会听我们说的？

辩护人：我刚才已经说了，我接触下来发现他还是属于比较善于倾听律师意见的法官，他听取了我们的意见，而且赞同我们的部分观点。接下来如果法官来提审你，就需要你准确陈述事发经过，让法官清楚事件全貌，来判断争议点。当然，后续我们也会和法官保持沟通，让你获知案件进展。

上诉人：你有没有跟他说过我们的观点？

辩护人：当然，我们的观点我已经和他充分沟通了。

上诉人：二审会不会像一审一样开庭？

already accepts some of our points now.

Client: Then you do something about it, how about giving him some money?

Lawyer: It is against the law and will not work out. The safest way is to technicalize a legal problem by defending according to law and fact.

Client: Will it work?

Lawyer: If it's not helping, so is other means.

Client: What kind of person the judge of the second instance is? Will he listen to us?

Lawyer: As I mentioned before, in our first meeting, the judge is a good listener, and he has heard all our opinions with attention and agreed with some of them. If he arraigns you later, you need to state the fact accurately in order to let the judge know the whole picture so as to deal with the controversy. We will surely stay in touch with him to keep you posted.

Client: Have you told him about our opinions?

Lawyer: Certainly. We have communicated with him about it thoroughly.

Client: Will it be heard in a court session like what we did in the first instance?

辩护人：这点我也问过法官了，他目前准备不开庭审理本案……

上诉人：凭什么不开庭？我的案子有很大争议！

辩护人：你先别急，听我把话说完。根据《中华人民共和国刑事诉讼法》第234条规定，第二审人民法院对于下列案件，应当组成合议庭，开庭审理：

（一）被告人、自诉人及其法定代理人对第一审认定的事实、证据提出异议，可能影响定罪量刑的上诉案件；

（二）被告人被判处死刑的上诉案件；

（三）人民检察院抗诉的案件；

（四）其他应当开庭审理的案件。

我们认为，你的案件符合以上四种情形中的第一种，因此有必要开庭审理。我们已经准备好了开庭审理申请书，争取让本案开庭审理。

上诉人：怎么才能让二审开庭？

辩护人：我说了，我们会准备好

Lawyer: I have asked him about it too. His plan is not to hold a court session to hear the case. . .

Client: Why not? My case is very controversial!

Lawyer: Take it easy and let me finish. According to the Article 234 of the *Criminal Procedure Law of the People's Republic of China*, a people's court of second instance shall form a collegial panel to hear the following case in a court session:

（1）An appellate case where a defendant or a private prosecutor or the legal representative thereof has raised any objection to the facts and evidence determined in the trial at first instance, which may affect conviction and sentencing;

（2）An appellate case where the defendant is sentenced to death penalty;

（3）A case appealed by the people's procuratorate; or

（4）Any other case which shall by heard in a court session.

We regards that your case meets the first circumstance and thus it should be heard in a court session. We have the written application for open hearing ready, and we will try everything for it.

Client: How can we make it happen?

Lawyer: Like I said, we will have

申请材料，再跟法官沟通，争取开庭审理。

上诉人：如果不开庭你们准备怎么办？

辩护人：如果不开庭，我们会和法官保持密切沟通，也会适时会见你，尽可能引起法官对本案争议点的重视。

上诉人：根据之前你们做过的案子，不开庭是好还是不好？

辩护人：不开庭也有不开庭的优势；但对于争议较大的案件，开庭相对来说会更有利于上诉人。

上诉人：在之前你们做过的案子里，有没有我这种案子二审改判的？

辩护人：有的。虽然案件与你不可能完全相同，但也类似，比如……因此你也不要过于绝望。

上诉人：二审宣判后我家人能见我吗？

辩护人：第二审的判决、裁定和最高人民法院的判决、裁定，都是终审的判决、裁定，一经裁判，立即生效。因此，在二审裁判后，除法院裁定撤销原判并发回原审人民法院重新审判这种情形外，你会开始服刑，你的家属可以跟执行机关申请会见。但

the application ready and try to talk him into it.

Client：What if there is no open hearing? What you gonna do about it?

Lawyer：If it's not happening, we will keep in close contact with the judge and meet you timely, in order to bring to the attention of him.

Client：Based on your experience, not hearing in a court session means good or not to the case?

Lawyer：Not hearing has its own advantages；but for cases with big controversy, open hearing is more favorable to appellant.

Client：Among cases you handled before, any modification happened on cases like mine?

Lawyer：Yes. Not exactly like your case, but case of similar circumstance. For example. . . so don't lose hope.

Client：Can I meet my family after the verdict of the second trial?

Lawyer：A sentence or ruling of a people's court of second instance or a sentence or ruling of the Supreme People's Court shall be final, which means it comes into effect when it's pronounced. Therefore, unless the court revokes the original sentence and remands the case to the ori-

具体时间和方式需要后续跟执行机关确定。

上诉人：二审要多久才能出结果？

辩护人：根据《中华人民共和国刑事诉讼法》，第二审人民法院受理上诉、抗诉案件，应当在 2 个月以内审结。对于可能判处死刑的案件或者附带民事诉讼的案件，以及有本法第 158 条规定情形之一的，经省、自治区、直辖市高级人民法院批准或者决定，可以延长 2 个月；因特殊情况还需要延长的，报请最高人民法院批准。因此在通常情况下，2 个月至 4 个月出结果。

上诉人：我知道了，谢谢你。祝你好运。请一定要帮帮我。

辩护人：我尽全力。

ginal trial court for retrial, you will start serving sentence after the verdict of second instance, and your family could apply to the jail for visiting you. As for the time and way of visit, they need to confirm with the jail later.

Client: How long do I have to wait for the result?

Lawyer: According to the *Criminal Procedure Law of the People's Republic of China*, After accepting an appellate case, a people's court of second instance shall close the trial of the case within two months. For a case with the possibility of a death penalty or a case with an incidental civil action or under any of the circumstances as set forth in Article 158 of this law, the period of trial may be extended for two months with the approval or decision of the higher people's court of a province, autonomous region, or municipality directly under the Central Government; and, if more extension is needed under special circumstances, the extension shall be reported to the Supreme People's Court for approval. So normally, you need to wait two to four months for the verdict to be made.

Client: I got it. Thank you! Good luck to you! Please do help me!

Lawyer: I will do my utmost.

# 相关英文表达

| 英文表达 | 中文意思 |
|---|---|
| modify the original sentence | 改判 |
| go along with | 赞同 |
| uphold the original sentence | 维持原判 |
| life time | 一辈子 |
| raise an objection | 提出异议 |
| appellate case | 上诉案件 |
| lose hope | 绝望 |
| autonomous region | 自治区 |
| municipality directly under the central government | 直辖市 |

# 工时记录清单示例

| 中文版 | | | |
|---|---|---|---|
| 日期 | 工作简述 | 工作时长 | 证明材料 |
| 20××年××月××日 | 11：00-13：00 法律咨询及委托协议签订<br>14：10-15：30 赶往市看守所会见（途中用时）<br>15：35-19：00 会见当事人。展示推荐信，自我介绍，刑事风险提示，法律咨询，获取案件信息，提供相关分析和解决方案，安抚当事人<br>19：01-20：01 从市看守所返回（途中用时）<br>21：00-00：00 整理所有案件信息<br>0：00：00-02：00 形成初步辩护方案 | 法律咨询 2 小时<br>会见 3 小时 25 分钟<br>路途时间 2 小时 20 分钟<br>整理案件信息 3 小时<br>制定初步辩护方案 2 小时<br>共 12 小时 45 分钟 | 电子邮件和微信聊天记录<br>收费站缴费单据<br>会见记录<br>法律服务方案<br>案发经过描述 |

续表

| 中文版 | | | |
|---|---|---|---|
| 20××年××月××日 | 10：00-11：00 细化并翻译会见记录 | 细化并翻译会见报告1小时 | 会见报告 |
| 20××年××月××日 | 9：00-9：30 赶往公安局沟通（途中用时）<br>9：30-10：30 与承办民警沟通<br>10：30-11：00 从公安局返回（途中用时） | 路途时间1小时<br>与民警沟通用时1小时<br>共2小时 | 沟通记录 |
| 20××年××月××日 | 9：40-10：40 赶往市看守所会见（途中用时）<br>11：35-16：35 第二次会见当事人。更新案件进展，核实案情，记录当事人自我辩护观点，法律咨询，介绍工作方案，传递家事及商务事项<br>16：35-18：05 从市看守所返回（途中用时）<br>20：00-22：00 整理所有案件信息 | 路途时间2.5小时<br>会见用时5小时<br>整理案件信息2小时<br>共9.5小时 | 会见记录<br>收费站缴费单据<br>法律服务方案 |
| 20××年××月××日 | 8：00-11：00 根据会见情况调整辩护策略<br>16：00-18：00 细化并翻译会见记录 | 调整辩护策略3小时<br>细化并翻译会见报告2小时<br>共5小时 | 会见记录<br>调整后的辩护策略 |

| 英文版 | | | |
|---|---|---|---|
| Date | Abstract of work | Length of time | Proof |
| * * * *<br>20 * * | 11：00-13：00 Legal advice& sign the agreement<br>14：10-15：30 Visit to the jail (en route)；<br>15：35-19：00 (showing the recommendation letter and self-introducing, informing the risk, detailed counseling, acquiring the circumstance of the case, fully ana- | Legal advice 2h<br>Visit 3h 25min<br>Time en route 2h 20min<br>Arrange all the case file 3h Form initial defending plan 2h<br>12h 45min in total | Email and Wechat history<br>Tollgate invoice (two)<br>The report<br>Legal solution<br>Storyline of the case |

续表

| | 英文版 | | |
|---|---|---|---|
| **Date** | **Abstract of work** | **Length of time** | **Proof** |
| | lyzing, solution providing, communication between the client and the suspect) <br> 19: 01–20: 01 Way back <br> 21: 00–00: 00 Sort out all the case file and information <br> 0: 00: 00–02: 00 Form initial defending plan | | |
| ＊ ＊ ＊ ＊ <br> 20＊＊ | 10: 00–11: 00 Elaborate and translate the report | Elaborate the visit report 1h | The visit report |
| ＊ ＊ ＊ ＊ <br> 20＊＊ | 9: 00–9: 30 en route to the police station <br> 9: 30–10: 30 discussion with the police of ficer responsible <br> 10: 30–11: 00 way back | En route 1 hour <br> Discussion 1 hour <br> 2 hours in total | The discussion report |
| ＊ ＊ ＊ ＊ <br> 20＊＊ | 9: 40–10: 40 Visit to the jail ( en route) ; <br> 11: 35–16: 35 2nd visit ( up-to-date work report, verification of the circumstance, collection of the self-defense, legal counseling, introduction of the work plan, relay family/business matters) <br> 16: 35–18: 05 Way back <br> 20: 00–22: 00 Sort out all the case file and information | En route 2. 5 hour <br> Visit 5 hours <br> The case file 2 hours <br> 9. 5 hours in total | The relayed information <br> Tollgate invoice <br> Legal solution |
| ＊ ＊ ＊ ＊ <br> 20＊＊ | 8: 00–11: 00 Update defense strategy based on the information from the visit <br> 16: 00–18: 00 Elaborate and translate the report | Strategy 3 hours <br> The report 2 hours <br> 5 hours in total | The visit report <br> Updated defense strategy |

# 相关英文表达

| 英文表达 | 中文意思 |
| --- | --- |
| abstract of work | 工作简述 |
| length of time | 工作时长 |
| en route | 在途 |
| defense strategy | 辩护策略 |
| recommendation letter | 介绍信 |

# 附　录

## 《中华人民共和国刑事诉讼法》（2018 年）词汇表

| 单词 | 国际音标 | 词性及中文意思 |
| --- | --- | --- |
| abide | əˈbaɪd | vt. 忍受，容忍；停留；遵守 |
| absent | ˈæbsənt | adj. 缺席的；缺少的；不在场的 |
| accede | əkˈsiːd | vi. 加入；同意，接受；就任 |
| acceptance | əkˈseptəns | n. 接受；赞同；容纳 |
| accessory | əkˈsesəri | n. 从犯<br>adj. 副的；同谋的；附属的 |
| accomplice | əˈkɑːmplɪs | n. 从犯，共犯 |
| accordance | əˈkɔːrdns | n. 依据；一致，给予；同意 |
| according | əˈkɔrdɪŋ | adv. 根据<br>adj. 相应的；一致的 |
| account | əˈkaʊnt | n. 原因，理由，详细报告，账目（户），利润（益） |
| accurate | ˈækjərət | adj. 精确的，准确的，正确无误的 |
| accuse | əˈkjuːz | vt. 控诉，控告；指责，谴责 |
| acknowledgment | əkˈnɑːlɪdʒmənt | n. 承认，承认书，感谢 |
| acquire | əˈkwaɪər | vt. 获得，取得，调用；收购（公司等） |
| acquittal | əˈkwɪtl | n. 无罪裁定，清偿债务，履行职责 |
| activity | ækˈtɪvəti | n. 活动；行动；活跃 |
| actual | ˈæktʃuəl | adj. 实际的，现实的；目前的，现行的；事实上的 |

| 单词 | 国际音标 | 词性及中文意思 |
|---|---|---|
| addition | əˈdɪʃn | n. 追加，附加（物）；头衔，称号；附录，增补，补充，附件 |
| addressee | ˌædreˈsiː | n. 收件人，（信用证的）收信人 |
| adduce | əˈduːs | v. 援引，引证，提出（理由，证据等），引出 |
| adjournment | əˈdʒɜːrnmənt | n. 休庭，休会，延期，押后 |
| administration | ədˌmɪnɪˈstreɪʃn | n. 经营，管理，（法院指定的管理人进行的）遗产管理；行政，行政机关，局，处；执行，实施 |
| administrative | ədˈmɪnɪstreɪtɪv | adj. 行政的，管理的 |
| admonished | ədˈmɑːnɪʃ | v.（对不当行为、犯罪等的）告诫，警告 |
| adopted | əˈdɑːptɪd | adj. 被收养的；被采纳的 |
| adult | ˈædʌlt | n. 成年人<br>adj. 成年人的，已成人的 |
| advantage | ədˈvæntɪdʒ | n. 有利条件，有利因素，优势，益处，利益<br>vt. 有利于；使处于优势<br>vi. 获利 |
| advice | ədˈvaɪs | n. 通知（书），报单，汇票票根，消息，劝告，意见，咨询，顾问，（法律援助中的）咨询服务 |
| affect | əˈfekt | vt. 影响；假装；感染<br>vi. 倾向；喜欢 |
| affixed | əˈfɪkst | v. 粘上，附上，（使）附于；可固定（affix 的过去式及过去分词）<br>adj. 附着的，黏着的 |
| against | əˈgenst | prep. 违反，反对，对抗，对比，防备 |
| agency | ˈeɪdʒənsi | n. 代理，中介，经销处，代理处，代理机构，代理权 |
| agent | ˈeɪdʒənt | n. 行为者，代理人，代理商；原因，动因；间谍，特务<br>adj. 代理的 |
| aggravate | ˈægrəveɪt | vt. 加重；使恶化；激怒 |

续表

| 单词 | 国际音标 | 词性及中文意思 |
|------|---------|----------------|
| alibi | ˈæləbaɪ | n. 不在场证明或辩解；托辞<br>v. 辩解；找托辞开脱 |
| alitigation | ˌlɪtɪˈɡeɪʃn | n. 诉讼，打官司，诉讼程序 |
| alleged | əˈledʒd | adj. 提出而尚未证实的，诉称的，宣称的，被指称的 |
| amnesty | ˈæmnəsti | n. 大赦，赦免<br>v. 实行大赦 |
| anew | əˈnuː | adv. 再，重新 |
| announcement | əˈnaʊnsmənt | n. 公告；宣告；发表；通告 |
| anonymously | əˈnɑːnɪməsli | adv. 不具名地；化名地 |
| apology | əˈpɑːlədʒi | n. 辩解，道歉 |
| appeal | əˈpiːl | n. 上诉（状），请求，（行政）复议<br>v. 上诉，控告，（行政）复议，诉诸，请求，求助，呼吁 |
| appearance | əˈpɪrəns | n. 出庭，应诉，举止 |
| appellate | əˈpelət | adj. 受理上诉的，上诉权限的，复议的 |
| applicant | ˈæplɪkənt | n. 投保人，申请人，请求者，候补人，原告 |
| appropriate | əˈproʊpriət | adj. 适当的，相关的<br>v. 拨款，侵吞，窃取，占用 |
| approval | əˈpruːvl | n. 认可，赞同，核准，批准，许可 |
| arise | əˈraɪz | vt. 呈现；出现；发生<br>vi. 起身，起来，起立 |
| arraign | əˈreɪn | v. 堂讯，审讯，控告，指责 |
| arrange | əˈreɪndʒ | v. 调解，调停，安排，整理 |
| arrest | əˈrest | n. 刑事扣押，逮捕，扣留，拘押，阻止，抵制<br>v. 逮捕，拘留，扣押 |
| arrestee | əˌresˈti | n. 被捕者 |
| ascertain | ˌæsərˈteɪn | v. 查明，弄清，确定 |

| 单词 | 国际音标 | 词性及中文意思 |
|------|----------|----------------|
| aspect | ˈæspekt | n. 方面；方向；形势；外貌 |
| assemble | əˈsembl | v. 集合（会），调集，汇编 |
| assess | əˈses | v. 估价，按税率征收，确定数额 |
| assessor | əˈsesər | n. 保险损失估价人，财产估价人，奉估定人，税额审查员，专家陪审员 |
| assign | əˈsaɪn | v. 让与，动产转让，拨款，过户；指派；归属；提出，指定 |
| assistance | əˈsɪstəns | n. 援助，帮助，（法律援助中的）法律协助 |
| association | əˌsoʊsiˈeɪʃn | n. 社团，协会，合伙，交际，联合 |
| attached | əˈtætʃt | adj. 附加的，隶属的，查封的，扣押的 |
| attained | əˈteɪnd | vt. 取得，得到，获得（attain 的过去式） |
| attempt | əˈtempt | n. 图谋（或企图）犯罪，企图<br>v. 企图，谋略 |
| attorney | əˈtɜːrni | n. 法律代理人，律师，受任（权）人，代办人，检察官 |
| audio | ˈɔːdioʊ | adj. 听觉的，声音的 |
| audio-visual | ˌɔːdioʊˈvɪʒuəl | adj. 视听的，音像的 |
| authority | əˈθɔːrəti | n. 权力，管辖权，代理权，当局，官方，委托书 |
| autonomous | ɔːˈtɑːnəməs | adj. 自治（主）的，自治权的 |
| autopsy | ˈɔːtɑːpsi | n. 尸体解剖（检验），亲自勘察，实地观察，（对意见等的）分析 |
| awareness | əˈwernəs | n. 察觉；觉悟；意识 |
| bail | beɪl | n. 保释（人、金），（动产的）寄托，保证服从，担保（金）<br>v. 准许保释，为某人作保释人，将（动产）寄托于人 |
| base | beɪs | adj. 基本（础）的，初（低）级的，劣等的<br>v. 以为基础的<br>n. 基础 |

续表

| 单词 | 国际音标 | 词性及中文意思 |
|---|---|---|
| batter | ˈbætər | v. 殴打，重击，虐待 |
| beat | biːt | v. 打，战胜，杀价，欺诈<br>n. 敲打，（警察等的）巡逻区域 |
| behalf | bɪˈhæf | n. 方面，利益，赞同 |
| behavior | bɪˈheɪvjər | n. 行为，品行，举止，态度 |
| believing | bɪˈliːvɪŋ | adj. 有信仰的 |
| belong | bɪˈlɔːŋ | v. 属于，作为成员，应归入，适应 |
| bend | ˈbend | v. 弯曲 |
| between | bɪˈtwiːn | prep. 在…之间<br>adv. 在中间 |
| beyond | bɪˈjɑːnd | prep. 超出，超越 |
| biological | ˌbaɪəˈlɑːdʒɪkl | adj. 生物学上（的），生态学的 |
| blood | blʌd | n. 血统，血亲，家族 |
| board | bɔːrd | n. 委员会，局，机构，（公司）董事会 |
| bond | bɑːnd | n. 债券，契约，同盟，盟约，公债，保单，镣铐，监禁，约束<br>v. 充当保释人，抵押 |
| bonus | ˈboʊnəs | n. 红利，奖金，额外津贴，退职（伍）金，免费赠品 |
| breastfeeding | ˈbrestfiːdɪŋ | n. 母乳哺育<br>v. 用母乳喂养（breastfeed 的现在分词） |
| bribery | ˈbraɪbəri | n. 行贿（罪），受贿（罪），贿赂 |
| burden | ˈbɜːrdn | n. 负担，义务，（举证）责任，载重，障碍，限制，负荷，制造费用，间接费用<br>v. 负担 |
| capacity | kəˈpæsəti | n. 行为能力，资格，身份，容积，能力 |
| capture | ˈkæptʃər | n. 掳掠占领，拘捕，捕获，战利品，俘获物，扣押财产<br>v. 俘（捕）获，攻占，夺取 |

| 单词 | 国际音标 | 词性及中文意思 |
|---|---|---|
| case-handling | keɪs ˈhændlɪŋ | adj. 办案的 |
| cause | kɔːz | n. 成因, 案件, 诉讼, 事业, 目标<br>v. 造成, 引起, 导致 |
| certificate | sərˈtɪfɪkət | n. 证书, 执照, 证券, 股票, 单据, 凭单 |
| channels | ˈtʃænls | n. 方法, 途径, 航道, 海峡, 调拨（基金）（channel 的复数） |
| chapter | ˈtʃæptər | n.（社团等的）分部；分支机构；分会；（法律、法规的）章、节 |
| characteristics | ˌkærəktəˈrɪstɪks | n. 特性（征）（characteristic 的复数） |
| chief | tʃiːf | n. 领袖, 首领, 头, 重要部分<br>adj. 主（首）要的, 第一位的, 首席的 |
| circumstance | ˈsɜːrkəmstænsiz | n. 环境, 条件, 情况 |
| circumvention | ˌsɜːkəmˈvenʃn | n.（用欺骗手段进行的）陷害, 计谋, 欺诈,（法律）规避 |
| claimed | kleɪmd | v. 声称；宣称；断言（claim 的过去式） |
| clarify | ˈklærəfaɪ | vt. 澄清；阐明<br>vi. 得到澄清；变得明晰；得到净化 |
| clerk | klɜːrk | n. 秘书, 书记员（官）, 职员, 办事员, 文书, 记账员, 实习法学院学生<br>v. 做秘书工作, 干书记员工作 |
| client | ˈklaɪənt | n. 当事人,（诉讼）委托人, 顾客 |
| clue | kluː | n. 线索<br>v. 暗示；提示 |
| collection | kəˈlekʃn | n. 收款（账）,（票据的）托收, 代收, 收入款项, 募捐, 捐款, 收藏品（物）, 征收, 收集, 采集 |
| collective | kəˈlektɪv | adj. 总的, 集体的, 共同的<br>n. 集体企业, 团体, 集团, 集体 |

续表

| 单词 | 国际音标 | 词性及中文意思 |
|------|----------|----------------|
| collegial | kəˈliːdʒɪəl | n. 合议庭的 |
| collusion | kəˈluːʒn | n. 共谋欺诈，勾结，串通，（离婚双方为达到离婚目的对法庭的）共谋欺骗 |
| combating | ˈkɑːmbætɪŋ | vi. 战斗；搏斗；反对（combat 的现在分词） |
| combination | ˌkɑːmbɪˈneɪʃn | n. 结合；组合；联合 |
| comments | ˈkɑːments | n. 评论（comment 的复数）；注解<br>v. 评论（comment 的第三人称单数形式）；解释 |
| commit | kəˈmɪt | v. 犯（罪），做（错事、坏事），授权，委托，承担，监禁，判处，押交 |
| committee | kəˈmɪti | n. 委员会，促进会，监护人，受托人 |
| commonly | ˈkɑːmənli | adv. 一般地；通常地；普通地 |
| communicate | kəˈmjuːnɪkeɪt | vi. 通讯，传达；相通；交流；感染<br>vt. 传达；感染；显露 |
| community | kəˈmjuːnəti | n. 社区，居民区，聚居区，镇，乡，公社，团体，（政治）共同体，同一社区居民，公众，共有，共同性，一致 |
| commute | kəˈmjuːt | v. 兑换，补偿，减刑，改变付款方式，经常来往于（某两地间） |
| compel | kəmˈpel | vt. 强迫，逼迫，迫使屈服 |
| compensation | ˌkɑːmpenˈseɪʃn | n. 补偿，赔偿（物、金），工资，报酬，（债等的）抵消 |
| competent | ˈkɑːmpɪtənt | adj. 有能力的，有法定资格的，主管的，能胜任的 |
| complaint | kəmˈpleɪnt | n. 民事诉状，刑事自诉状，起诉，申诉 |
| complete | kəmˈpliːt | v. 完成；填写（表格）；（使）完整 |
| completion | kəmˈpliːʃn | n. 完成，结束；实现，竣工 |
| compliance | kəmˈplaɪəns | n. 顺从，服从；符合；屈从；可塑性 |
| complicated | ˈkɑːmplɪkeɪtɪd | adj. 难懂的，复杂的 |
| comply | kəmˈplaɪ | vi. 遵守；顺从，遵从；答应 |

| 单词 | 国际音标 | 词性及中文意思 |
|------|---------|--------------|
| composition | ˌkɑːmpəˈzɪʃn | n. 作文；构成；合成物；成分 |
| comprehensive | ˌkɑːmprɪˈhensɪv | adj. 综合的；广泛的；有理解力的<br>n. 综合学校 |
| compromise | ˈkɑːmprəmaɪz | n. 妥协，和解；妥协（或折中）方案；达成妥协<br>v. 妥协，折中；违背（原则），达不到（标准）；（因行为不当）使陷入危险，名誉受损 |
| compulsory | kəmˈpʌlsəri | adj. 强制的，强迫的，义务的 |
| conceal | kənˈsiːl | v. 隐瞒，隐匿，保守秘密 |
| concentrates | kɑnsenˌtrets | n. 浓缩液（concentrate 的复数） |
| concluded | kənˈkluːdɪd | v. 结束；推断；作结论（conclude 的过去分词）<br>adj. 推论的 |
| concurrently | kənˈkɜːrəntli | adv. 同时发生地，并存地 |
| condition | kənˈdɪʃn | n.（生活或工作等的）条件；（影响某事发生的）物质环境；（天气、地面等的）情况<br>n. 疾病；条款；先决条件<br>v. 制约；（使）接受；（使）达到所要求的状态 |
| conditional | kənˈdɪʃənl | adj. 有条件的；假定的<br>n. 条件句；条件语 |
| conduct | ˈkɑːndʌkt | n. 行为，品格，操守，行径，指导，引导，经营（权），处理（方式），运作，举办<br>v. 实施，处理，引导，指导，经营，进行 |
| confession | kənˈfeʃn | n. 供认，供状，（坦白）书，声明，自白 |
| confidential | ˌkɑːnfɪˈdenʃl | adj. 机密的；表示信任的；获信任的 |
| confinement | kənˈfaɪnmənt | n. 限制；监禁；分娩 |
| confirm | kənˈfɜːm | vt. 确认；确定；证实；批准；使巩固 |
| confiscate | ˈkɑːnfɪskeɪt | vt. 没收；充公；查抄<br>adj. 被没收的 |
| congress | ˈkɑːŋɡrəs | n.（正式的）代表大会，大会，[美]国会，议会，委员会，（国会或议会的）会议（期），聚会，社交 |

续表

| 单词 | 国际音标 | 词性及中文意思 |
|------|---------|----------------|
| consent | kənˈsent | n. 同意，批准，赞同，协议，承诺<br>v. 同意，批准，赞同 |
| consequence | ˈkɑːnsɪkwens | n. 后果，结果，推断，论断，重要性 |
| consistent | kənˈsɪstənt | adj. 始终如一的，一致的；坚持的 |
| consisting | kənˈsɪstɪŋ | v. 组成；存在；一致（consist 的现在分词） |
| constitute | ˈkɑːnstɪtuːt | v. 组成，构成，任命，选定，制定（法律等），设立，使（文件等）通过法律手续 |
| constitution | ˌkɑːnstɪˈtuːʃn | n. 宪法（制、章），章程，法规，构造，组成（方式），设立，建立，制定，任命，政体，体质，性格，素质 |
| construction | kənˈstrʌkʃn | n. 解释（尤指制定法的解释），解释过程，法律释义，建筑（物），建设，结构，构成，意义 |
| consultation | | |
| contact | ˈkɑːntækt | n. 接触，联系<br>vt. 使接触 |
| contents | ˈkɑːntents | n. 内容；目录；要旨（content 的复数）<br>v. 使满意（content 的第三人称单数） |
| continue | kənˈtɪnjuː | v. 继续，延续（伸、长），停留，使（诉讼）延期 |
| contraband | ˈkɑːntrəbænd | n. 走私；走私货；战时禁运品（等于 contraband of war）<br>adj. 禁运的；非法买卖的 |
| contradict | ˌkɑːntrəˈdɪkt | vt. 反驳；否定；与…矛盾；与…抵触<br>vi. 反驳；否认；发生矛盾 |
| control | kənˈtroʊl | n/v. 支配，控制（权），掌管，抑制，管制（控、辖），监督，调节 |
| convey | kənˈveɪ | vt. 传达；运输；让与 |
| conviction | kənˈvɪkʃn | n. 定罪；确信；证明有罪；确信，坚定的信仰 |
| cooperation | koʊˌɑːpəˈreɪʃn | n. 合作，协作，[劳经] 协力 |

| 单词 | 国际音标 | 词性及中文意思 |
|------|----------|----------------|
| coordinate | koʊˈɔːrdɪneɪt | v. 调节，配合；使动作协调<br>adj. 同等的，并列的；配位的；坐标的<br>n. 坐标；配套服装；同等的人或物 |
| copy | ˈkɑːpi | n. 文本，副本，抄本，制成本，复制件，范本<br>v. 复写（印、制），誊抄，模仿，临摹，抄袭 |
| corpse | kɔːrps | n. 尸体 |
| correction | kəˈrekʃn | n. 改正，修改，（对罪犯的）矫正，纠正机关，责备，惩罚，制止，（证券等交易中价格上涨后的）回落 |
| correctly | kəˈrektli | adv. 正确地；得体地 |
| corrupt | kəˈrʌpt | adj. 腐败的，贪污的；堕落的<br>vt. 使腐烂；使堕落，使恶化<br>vi. 堕落，腐化；腐烂 |
| count | kaʊnt | vt. 计算；认为<br>vi. 计数；有价值<br>n. 计数；计算 |
| counterclaim | ˈkaʊntərkleɪm | n. 反诉，反对要求<br>vt. 反诉<br>vi. 提起反诉 |
| course | kɔːrs | n. 航线，路线，路（进、过）程，程序，行进方向，路线，河流，行动方针，方法，行为，做法，课程，教程，学科，科目 |
| court | kɔːrt | n. 法院（庭），审判庭，法官，[美] 立法机关，法院建筑物，议会，宫廷，朝廷，（公司等的）委员会，董事会，理事会，讨好 |
| courtroom | ˈkɔːrtrʊm | n. 法庭，审判室 |
| cover | ˈkʌvər | v. 担保，给（货物等）保险，投保，含，包括，覆盖，隐匿，掩盖（饰），包庇，购进，供给，补进，足数，足以抵补，补（抵）偿，负担支付（开支等），弥补（损失等），购进，补进，适合于<br>n. 担保，保证金，购买替代物权，覆盖物，庇护，（信函等）封袋，包（装）皮，封皮，隐匿（处），（支票的）保证金，覆盖 |

| 单词 | 国际音标 | 词性及中文意思 |
|---|---|---|
| credence | ˈkriːdns | n. 信任；凭证 |
| credential | krəˈdenʃl | n. 证书；凭据；国书 |
| crime | kraɪm | n. 罪行，犯罪；罪恶；犯罪活动<br>vt. 控告……违反纪律 |
| criminal | ˈkrɪmɪnl | n. 罪犯，犯人<br>adj. 刑事的，罪犯的，犯罪的，非法的 |
| cross-examined | ˌkrɔːs ɪɡˈzæmɪn | v. （尤指在法庭上对证人的）盘问，反诘，仔细询问 |
| custody | ˈkʌstədi | n. （对未成年人的）监护权，监管（督、视），保管（护），管理，拘留（押），羁押，扶养权 |
| danger | ˈdeɪndʒər | n. 危险，风险，危险原因，威胁 |
| deadline | ˈdedlaɪn | n. 最终期限；（监狱范围的）死线 |
| deal | diːl | n. 交易，买卖，互利协议，[美] 密约，秘密妥协，待遇，特定政策，实行特定政策的时期，局面，情况<br>v. 处理，待遇，分配，应付，论述，讨论，对付，打交道，经营，交易，做买卖，卖，出售，[俚] 卖毒品 |
| debate | dɪˈbeɪt | n. 辩论；（正式的）讨论<br>v. （尤指正式）讨论，辩论；仔细考虑 |
| deceased | dɪˈsiːst | adj. 已故的<br>n. 死者；[法] 被继承人<br>vi. 死亡（decease 的过去式） |
| deceit | dɪˈsiːt | n. 欺骗；谎言；欺诈手段 |
| decision | dɪˈsɪʒn | n. 决定（议、断），判决，裁定（决），坚定，结果 |
| declare | dɪˈkler | v. 宣言（布、告、称），声明，断言，供述，陈述，申报 |
| decrease | dɪˈkriːs | v. 减少，减小，降低<br>n. 减少，减小，减少量；减少过程 |
| decree | dɪˈkriː | n. 判决，裁判（决、定），法（政、命）令，布告<br>v. 判（裁）决，颁布，规定 |

| 单词 | 国际音标 | 词性及中文意思 |
|---|---|---|
| deduct | dɪˈdʌkt | vt. 扣除，减去；演绎 |
| deem | diːm | v. 视为，认定，相信 |
| defame | dɪˈfeɪm | v. 侵犯名誉，毁誉 |
| defendant | dɪˈfendənts | n. 被告代理人 |
| defender | dɪˈfendər | n. 辩护人，保护人，[苏] 被告 |
| defense | dɪˈfens | n. 防卫，防护；防御措施；防守 |
| definite | ˈdefɪnət | adj. 一定的；确切的 |
| delay | dɪˈleɪ | n. 耽搁，迟滞 |
| deliberation | dɪˌlɪbəˈreɪʃn | n. 审议；考虑；从容；熟思 |
| delinquent | dɪˈlɪŋkwənt | adj. 有过失的；怠忽的；拖欠债务的<br>n. 流氓；行为不良的人；失职者 |
| deliver | dɪˈlɪvər | v. 释放，解脱（救），移交，引渡，交付（货），放弃，投递，传送，提供，宣布，供给，发表，陈述，拉（票），给予（打击），运载，排放 |
| democratic | ˌdeməˈkrætɪk | adj. 民主的，民主政体的，平民的，[美] 民主党的（大写） |
| deny | dɪˈnaɪ | vt. 否定，否认；拒绝给予；拒绝…的要求<br>vi. 否认；拒绝 |
| deposit | dɪˈpɑːzɪt | n. （储蓄）存款，存放，寄存，委托款项，保证（释）金，定金，公积金，寄存物（处），仓库，[罗] 无偿保管货物的寄托<br>v. 交付，存放，寄存，储蓄，付（保证金、保释金等） |
| deprivation | ˌdeprɪˈveɪʃn | n. 剥夺（被告的产权），丧失，宗教上的剥夺 |
| deprived | dɪˈpraɪvd | adj. 贫困的，穷苦的，严重匮乏的；（人）丧失的，被剥夺的 |
| designate | ˈdezɪgneɪt | vt. 指定；指派；标出；把…定名为<br>adj. 指定的；选定的 |
| desistance | dɪˈzɪstəns | n. 断念 |

续表

| 单词 | 国际音标 | 词性及中文意思 |
| --- | --- | --- |
| destroy | dɪˈstrɔɪ | v. 破（毁）坏，摧毁，毁灭，打破（计划，希望），消（歼）灭，减损，使无效 |
| detainee | ˌdiːteɪˈniː | n. 未判决囚犯；被扣押者 |
| detention | dɪˈtenʃn | n. 拘留，扣押（留），羁押，拘役，监禁，禁闭，阻止，滞留 |
| determine | dɪˈtɜːrmɪn | v.（使）下决心，（使）作出决定<br>vt. 决定，确定；判定，判决；限定<br>vi. 确定；决定；判决，终止；［主用于法律］了结，终止，结束 |
| diagnosis | ˌdaɪəɡˈnoʊsɪs | n. 诊断 |
| diplomatic | ˌdɪpləˈmætɪk | adj. 外交的，外交上的，文献上的 |
| directly | dəˈrektli | adv. 直接地；立即；马上；坦率地；正好地 |
| disability | ˌdɪsəˈbɪləti | n.（法律上的）无行为能力，无资格，病残，残废，劳动能力丧失，无能 |
| disagree | ˌdɪsəˈɡriː | vi. 不同意；不一致；争执；不适宜 |
| disappear | ˌdɪsəˈpɪr | vi. 消失；失踪；不复存在<br>vt. 使…不存在；使…消失 |
| disapproval | ˌdɪsəˈpruːvl | n. 不赞成；不喜欢 |
| disaster | dɪˈzæstər | n. 灾难，大祸，祸患，大不幸，灾害 |
| disciplinary | ˈdɪsəpləneri | adj. 规律的；训练的；训诫的 |
| disclose | dɪsˈkloʊz | v. 使显露，揭发，批（揭、透、泄）露，公开（秘密） |
| discovery | dɪˈskʌvəri | n. 发现，发觉 |
| discussion | dɪˈskʌʃn | n. 讨论，议论 |
| dismiss | dɪsˈmɪs | v. 解（遣）散，打发，解雇，免职，开（消）除，驳回，不考虑 |
| disposal | dɪˈspozl | n. 处理；支配；清理；安排 |
| dispute | dɪˈspjuːt | n. 辩论；争吵；意见不同<br>v. 辩论；对……进行质疑；争夺；抵抗 |

| 单词 | 国际音标 | 词性及中文意思 |
|---|---|---|
| disqualification | dɪsˌkwɑːlɪfɪˈkeɪʃn | n. 不合格；取消资格 |
| disqualify | dɪsˈkwɑːlɪfaɪ | vt. 取消…的资格 |
| dissent | dɪˈsent | v. 不同意；对国教（或东正教教义）不遵循<br>n.（意见的）不一致；不服从裁判；异议声明 |
| distinguish | dɪˈstɪŋgwɪʃ | vt. 区分；辨别；使杰出，使表现突出<br>vi. 区别，区分；辨别 |
| distribute | dɪˈstrɪbjuːt | v. 分配（发、布），散布，区分，分类，在特定的市场销售商品，把货物运送至个别顾客 |
| districted | ˈdɪstrɪktɪd | adj. 分区的，被分区的 |
| disturbing | dɪˈstɜːrbɪŋ | adj. 令人不安的；烦扰的<br>v. 干扰；打断（disturb 的现在分词） |
| division | dəˈvɪʒən | n. 部门；分配 |
| document | ˈdɑːkjumənt | n. 文件，公文<br>vt. 记录，记载 |
| documentary | ˈdɑːkjumənt | n. 公文，证（文）件，单据（证），凭证，记录，资料，证券（书），诉讼案卷，文据（献），（证据法中的）书证<br>v. 提供文件（或证书），用文件（或证书）证明，为船舶提供船证后附装运单据于汇票 |
| drug | drʌg | n. 毒品，麻醉剂（如鸦片、吗啡等），制药公司股票或证券等，滞销品 |
| duplicate | ˈduːplɪkeɪt | n. 复本，复制正本，当票<br>adj. 复本的，成对的，二倍的<br>v. 复制（写、印），加倍，重复 |
| duration | djuˈreɪʃn | n. 时长，持续时间，持续，存续期间 |
| education | ˌedʒuˈkeɪʃn | n. 教育，教育程度，教育学 |
| effective | iˈfektiv | adj. 有效的；有力的；印象深刻的；实在的；备战的<br>n. 兵员；实际可作战的部队 |

| 单词 | 国际音标 | 词性及中文意思 |
|---|---|---|
| electronic | ɪˌlekˈtrɑːnɪk | adj. 电子的 |
| embezzlement | ɪmˈbezlmənt | n. 侵吞，挪用 |
| emergency | iˈməːdʒənsi | n. 紧急情况，非常时期 |
| employee | ɪmˈplɔɪiː | n. 雇员；从业员工 |
| endanger | ɪnˈdeɪndʒə | v. 使危险，危及 |
| enforcement | ɪnˈfɔːrsmənt | n. 执行，实施；强制 |
| engaging | ɪnˈgeɪdʒɪŋ | v. 参与<br>adj. 动人的 |
| ensure | ɪnˈʃʊr | vt. 保证，确保；使安全 |
| entail | ɪnˈteɪl | vt. 使需要，必需；承担；遗传给；蕴含<br>n. 引起；需要；继承 |
| enticement | ɪnˈtaɪsmənt | n. 诱惑；怂恿；引诱物；吸引力 |
| entire | ɪnˈtaɪər | adj. 全部的，整个的；全体的 |
| entity | entɪtɪ | n. 法律实体，统一体，存在物，个体，本质，单位 |
| equally | ˈiːkwəli | adv. 同样地；相等地，平等地；公平地 |
| erroneous | ɪˈroʊniəs | adj. 错误的；不正确的 |
| error | ˈerər | n. 误差；错误；过失 |
| escape | ɪˈskeɪp | n. 罪犯脱逃，私放拘押人员罪，逃避，忘记，免除 v. 罪犯脱逃，逃避，避免 |
| established | ɪˈstæblɪʃt | v. 建立，设立；制定；（使）立足；得到认可；证实<br>adj. 已确立的，确定的；著名的；得到承认的；早已投入使用的；资深的 |
| ethnic | eθnɪk | adj. 种族的；人种的 |
| evaluation | ɪˌvæljʊˈeɪʃən | n. 估计，评审，评价 |
| evidence | evɪdəns | n. 证据，凭证，证据法，人证 v. 作证，证明，以证据支持 |
| evidential | ˌevɪˈdenʃl | adj. 证据的；基于证据的；提供证据的；可作证据的 |

| 单词 | 国际音标 | 词性及中文意思 |
|------|---------|---------------|
| evidentiary | ˌevəˈdenʃəri | adj. 证据的 |
| examination | ɪɡˌzæmɪˈneɪʃn | n. 考试；检查；查问 |
| examine | ɪɡˈzæmɪn | v. 审讯，诘问，查问，考试，验尸，研究，调查 |
| exceed | ɪkˈsiːd | v. 超过，越出 |
| excessive | ɪkˈsesɪv | adj. 过度的，额外的，超额的，分外的 |
| excluded | ɪkˈskluːdɪd | adj. 排除的<br>v. 排除（exclude 的过去式和过去分词）；驱逐；拒绝接纳 |
| exclusion | ɪkˈskluːʒn | n. 排除；排斥；驱逐；被排除在外的事物 |
| execution | ˌeksɪˈkjuːʃən | n. 实行，执行，使生效，处死刑，签名盖章，执行令状 |
| exemption | ɪɡˈzempʃn | n. 免除，豁免；免税 |
| expenditure | ɪkˈspendɪtʃə | n. 支出，花费，消费，开销，经费，费用，支出额，消费额 |
| expense | ɪkˈspens | n. 费用，开支，消费，支出 v. 收取费用，记入费用账，作为开支勾销 |
| expertise | ˌekspɜːrˈtiːz | n. 专门知识；专门技术；专家的意见 |
| expiration | ˌekspɪˈreɪʃən | n. 期满，届满，终止，截止 |
| expiry | ɪkˈspaɪəri | n. 满期，到期；终结；呼气；死亡 |
| expose | ɪkˈspəʊz | v. 故意置人于危险境地，揭露，陈列，暴露，披露，使面临 |
| extension | ɪkˈstenʃn | n. 拓展；延伸；接发 |
| extent | ɪkˈstent | n. 程度，限度，范围，广度，宽度，长度，一大片，收回债款执行令，收回债款执行令或扣押令 |
| extortion | ɪkˈstɔːʃən | n. 敲诈，勒索，勒索财产罪，勒索财物 |
| extract | ɪkˈstrækt | n. 诉状，起诉书，摘录，引用 v. 提取，推断 |
| extraordinarily | iksˈtrɔːdnrili | adv. 极其，极端地；奇怪地 |

续表

| 单词 | 国际音标 | 词性及中文意思 |
|------|---------|----------------|
| eyewitness | aɪwɪtnəs | n. 目击者；见证人 |
| fabrication | ˌfæbrɪˈkeɪʃn | n. 制造，建造；装配；伪造物 |
| facility | fəˈsɪləti | n. 设施，设备；（机器等的）特别装置，特殊功能；（特定用途的）场所；才能，天赋 |
| fact | fækt | n. 事实；实际；真相 |
| filing | ˈfaɪlɪŋ | n. 文件归档 |
| financial | faɪˈnænʃəl | adj. 财政的，金融的 |
| fingerprint | ˈfɪŋgərprɪnt | n. 指纹；手印<br>vt. 采指纹 |
| fixed-term | fɪkst-tɜːm | n. 固定的期限 |
| focus | ˈfoʊkəs | n. 焦点；中心；清晰<br>vt. 使集中<br>vi. 集中 |
| following | ˈfɑːloʊɪŋ | adj. 其次的，接着的；下面的<br>n. 拥护者，追随者；下列；如下<br>prep. 在（某事）以后<br>v. 跟随；沿行；（时间、顺序）排在……之后；按照……执行；密切注意；从事（职业）（follow 的现在分词） |
| foreigner | fɒrɪnə | n. 外地人，外国人 |
| forensic | fəˈrenzɪk | adj. 法医的；法院的；辩论的；适于法庭的<br>n. 司法鉴定手段；司法鉴定部门 |
| forfeited | ˈfɔːrfɪtɪd | v. 丧失；被迫放弃；被剥夺（forfeit 的过去分词） |
| forgery | ˈfɔːrdʒəri | n. 伪造；伪造罪；伪造物 |
| forgiveness | fərˈgɪvnəs | n. 宽恕；宽仁之心 |
| formalities | fɔrˈmælətis | n. 手续；礼节（formality 的复数） |
| foster | ˈfɑːstər | v. 促进；抚育（他人子女一段时间）；收养；把（孩子）交托给养父母<br>adj. 代养的，寄养的 |

| 单词 | 国际音标 | 词性及中文意思 |
|---|---|---|
| fraud | frɔːd | n. 欺诈，欺诈罪，因应付欺诈之缘故，诡计 |
| freedom | friːdəm | n. 自由，自主，免除，解脱，放肆，自由权，特权 |
| frozen | frəʊzn | adj. 冰冻的，冻伤的，冻结的 |
| fugitive | ˈfjuːdʒətɪv | adj. 逃亡的；无常的；易变的<br>n. 逃亡者 |
| function | ˈfʌŋkʃn | n. 功能；职责；盛大的集会<br>vi. 运行；活动；行使职责 |
| future | fjuːtʃə | adj. 前途的，未来的，期货的，远期的 |
| gain | geɪn | n. 收益，营利，利得，盈余，夫妻共同财产增益，额外盈余，增加，获得物，选票份额的增加 v. 赢得，获得 |
| gang | gæŋ | n. 群；一伙；一组<br>vt. 使成群结队；结伙伤害或恐吓某人<br>vi. 成群结队 |
| gangland | gæŋlænd | n. 犯罪集团圈子，黑社会 |
| gathering | gæðərɪŋ | n. 捐款，结集，凝集，集会，聚集，收集 |
| genuine | ˈdʒenjuɪn | adj. 真实的，真正的；诚恳的 |
| governing | ˈgʌvərnɪŋ | adj. 统治的；控制的；管理的；治理的<br>v. 统治；支配；控制；影响；抑制（情绪）；成为……的法律（govern 的现在分词） |
| government | gʌvənˌmənt | n. 政府，内阁统治，政体，政治学，治理，行政管理，管理机构，统辖，统治权，行政区，政府债券 |
| granted | grɑːntid | conj. 算是如此，但是 |
| gravely | ˈgreɪvli | adv. 严重地；严肃地；严峻地；沉重地 |
| gravity | ˈgrævəti | n. 重力，地心引力；严重性；庄严 |
| gross | groʊs | adj. 总共的；粗野的；恶劣的；显而易见的；恶心的<br>vt. 总共收入<br>n. 总额，总数 |
| guardian | gɑːdɪən | n. 监护人 |

| 单词 | 国际音标 | 词性及中文意思 |
|---|---|---|
| guardianship | gɑrdɪənˈʃɪp | n. 监护权，监护人的职责，保护 |
| guilt | gɪlt | n. 犯罪，过失；内疚 |
| guilty | gɪltɪ | adj. 有罪的，犯罪的，内疚的 n. 犯人，陪审团的有罪裁决，被告的认罪供述 |
| handicapped | ˈhændikæpt | adj. 残疾的；有生理缺陷的 n. 残疾人；缺陷者 |
| handle | hændəl | v. 处理，管理，经营，搬运，买卖，操纵 |
| harbor | ˈhɑːbə | n. 港口，避风港 v. 使船在港内停泊，船入港停泊，窝藏 |
| hardship | ˈhɑːrdʃɪp | n. 困苦；苦难；艰难险阻 |
| hereof | ˌhɪrˈʌv | adv. 关于这个，就此；在本文件中 |
| identification | aɪˌdɛntɪfɪˈkeɪʃən | n. 鉴定，识别，确认，查明，验明，证件，身份证明，贷款等项目选定 |
| identify | aɪˈdentɪfaɪ | vt. 确定；鉴定；识别，辨认出；使参与；把……看成一样 vi. 确定；认同；一致 |
| identity | aɪˈdentɪtɪ | n. 身份，本人，一致，同一人，相同，正身，个性，特征 |
| illegal | ɪˈliːgəl | adj. 不合法的，违法的，非法的，违例的 |
| immediately | ɪˈmiːdɪətli | adv. 立即，立刻；直接地 conj. 一……就 |
| immunity | ɪˈmjuːnəti | n. 豁免权，侵权豁免权，证人豁免权，免除，免疫，安全性 |
| impact | ˈɪmpækt | n. 冲击，司法影响，影响力，效力，碰撞，撞击力 |
| impairment | ɪmˈpeɪmənt | n. （身体或智力方面的）缺陷；（身体机能的）损伤，削弱 |
| impede | ɪmˈpiːd | vt. 阻碍；妨碍；阻止 |

续表

| 单词 | 国际音标 | 词性及中文意思 |
|---|---|---|
| impose | ɪmˈpəʊz | v. 征税，强加，欺骗，使他人买受，施加负担，利用，欺骗 |
| impossible | ɪmˈpɑːsəbl | adj. 不可能的；不可能存在的；难以忍受的；不真实的<br>n. 不可能；不可能的事 |
| impoundment | ɪmˈpaʊndmənt | n. 扣留 |
| imprisonment | ɪmˈprɪznmənt | n. 监禁，关押；坐牢；下狱 |
| improper | ɪmˈprɑːpər | adj. 不正确的，错误的；不适当的；不合礼仪的 |
| inappropriate | ˌɪnəˈproʊpriət | adj. 不适当的；不相称的 |
| incarceration | ɪnˌkɑːrsəˈreɪʃn | n. 监禁；下狱；禁闭 |
| incidental | ˌɪnsɪˈdentl | adj. 附带的；偶然的；容易发生的<br>n. 附带事件；偶然事件 |
| inconsistent | ˌɪnkənˈsɪstənt | adj. 不一致的；前后矛盾的 |
| incorrect | ˌɪnkəˈrekt | adj. 错误的，不正确的；不适当的；不真实的 |
| incriminated | ɪnˈkrɪmɪneɪtɪd | vt. 控告；暗示 ... 有罪（incriminate 的过去式、过去分词） |
| independently | ˌɪndɪˈpendəntli | adv. 独立地；自立地 |
| indicate | ˈɪndɪkeɪt | vt. 表明；指出；预示；象征 |
| indictment | ɪnˈdaɪtmənt | n. 起诉书；控告 |
| indirectly | ˌɪndaɪˈrektli | adv. 间接地；不诚实；迂回地 |
| individual | ˌɪndɪˈvɪdʒuəl | n. 个人，个体，独立单位，自然 adj. 单独的，自然人的，个别的，特别的，有特性的 |
| induce | ɪnˈdjuːs | v. 引诱，劝诱，诱发，诱致 |
| inflict | ɪnˈflɪkt | v. 惩处，处罚，加刑，予以打击，使遭受损害 |
| informant | ɪnˈfɔːmənt | n. 举报人，告密者，线人，报告人，通知人，提供消息的人，被征询人 |
| informed | ɪnˈfɔːrmd | adj. 见多识广的；消息灵通的；有根据的；明智的（猜测或决定）<br>v. 通知；使了解；提供资料（inform 的过去式和过去分词） |

| 单词 | 国际音标 | 词性及中文意思 |
|---|---|---|
| infringe | ɪnˈfrɪndʒ | v. 破坏，侵犯，违背 |
| initiate | ɪˈnɪʃieɪt | vt. 开始，创始；发起；使初步了解<br>n. 开始；新加入者，接受初步知识者<br>adj. 新加入的；接受初步知识的 |
| injury | ˈɪndʒəri | n. 损害，冤屈，受伤处 |
| innocence | ˈɪnəsns | n. 清白，无罪；天真无邪 |
| inquiry | ɪnˈkwaɪəri | n. 探究；调查；质询；询盘，询价 |
| inspection | ɪnˈspekʃn | n. 检查，调查，监察，验尸 |
| instance | ˈɪnstəns | n. 实例；情况；建议<br>vt. 举…为例 |
| institution | ˌɪnstɪˈtjuːʃn | n. 提起，指定，机构，学会，制度，建立，惯例，条例，协会，学校，事业单位，团体，风俗，习惯，会址，所址，精神病院，授予圣职 |
| instrument | ˈɪnstrəmənt | n. 票据，文据，正式文件，证券，手段，工具 |
| insufficient | ˌɪnsəˈfɪʃnt | adj. 不足的；不能胜任的，缺乏能力的 |
| insult | ɪnˈsʌlt | n. 侮辱；凌辱；损害名誉 |
| integrity | ɪnˈtegrəti | n. 完整性，完善，正直，廉正 |
| intentional | ɪnˈtenʃənl | adj. 故意的，有意的 |
| interference | ˌɪntərˈfɪrəns | n. 干扰，冲突；干涉 |
| interim | ˈɪntərɪm | adj. 临时的，暂时的；中间的；间歇的<br>n. 过渡时期，中间时期；暂定 |
| intermediate | ˌɪntəˈmiːdiət | v. 起媒介作用，起调解作用 adj. 中间的，媒介的<br>n. 中间人，媒介，中转港，半成品 |
| interpreter | ɪnˈtɜːrprətər | n. 解释者；口译者 |
| interrogate | ɪnˈterəgeɪt | vt. 审问；质问 |
| interrupt | ˌɪntəˈrʌpt | vt. 中断；打断；插嘴；妨碍<br>vi. 打断；打扰<br>n. 中断 |

续表

| 单词 | 国际音标 | 词性及中文意思 |
|---|---|---|
| interview | ˈɪntərvjuː | n. 接见，采访；面试，面谈<br>vt. 采访；接见；对…进行面谈；对某人进行面试 |
| intimidate | ɪnˈtɪmɪdeɪt | vt. 恐吓，威胁；胁迫 |
| investigation | ɪnˌvestɪˈgeɪʃn | n. 调查；调查研究 |
| investigator | ɪnˈvestɪgeɪtər | n. 研究者；调查者；侦查员 |
| involuntary | ɪnˈvɑləntɛri | adj. 无意识的；自然而然的；不知不觉的 |
| involvement | ɪnˈvɑːlvmənt | n. 参与；牵连；包含；混乱；财政困难 |
| irrelevant | ɪˈreləvənt | adj. 不相干的；不切题的 |
| irresistible | ˌɪrɪˈzɪstəbl | adj. 不准保释的，不能发还的 |
| judge | dʒʌdʒ | n. 法官；裁判员；鉴定人<br>v. 判断；猜测（大小、数量等）；裁判；评价；审判，判决 |
| judgment | ˈdʒʌdʒmənt | n. 审判，裁判，判决，判断，鉴定，评价，法官判案的理由，意见，看法，批评，指责 |
| judicial | dʒuˈdɪʃl | adj. 司法的，审判的，法院判决的，公正的，明断的，周密考虑的 |
| jurisdiction | ˌdʒʊərɪsˈdɪkʃn | n. 司法权，审判权，管辖权；权限，权力 |
| just | dʒʌst | adv. 只是，仅仅；刚才，刚刚；正好，恰好；实在；刚要<br>adj. 公正的，合理的；正直的，正义的；正确的；公平的；应得的 |
| justice | ˈdʒʌstɪs | n. 正义，公正执法，公正原则，司法，审判，法律制裁，正当理由，合法，正确，确实，公平处理，公平待遇，应得 |
| justifiable | ˈdʒʌstɪfaɪəbl | adj. 可辩解的，有道理的；可证明为正当的 |
| justification | ˌdʒʌstɪfɪˈkeɪʃn | n. 理由；辩护；认为有理，认为正当；释罪 |
| juvenile | ˈdʒuːvənaɪl | adj. 青少年的；幼稚的<br>n. 青少年；少年读物 |

续表

| 单词 | 国际音标 | 词性及中文意思 |
|---|---|---|
| lawful | ˈlɔːfl | adj. 合法的，法定的，守法的，法律许可的，依法的 |
| legality | lɪˈɡæləti | n. 合法；合法性 |
| legally | ˈliːɡəli | adv. 合法地；法律上 |
| leniency | ˈliːniənsi | n. 宽大，仁慈；温和 |
| lenient | ˈliːniənt | adj. 宽大的；仁慈的 |
| liability | ˌlaɪəˈbɪləti | n. 责任，义务，债务，负债，缺点，赔偿责任，不利条件 |
| license | ˈlaɪsns | n. 特许证，特许权，许可证，执牌照，放纵，准许 v. 发许可证 |
| limitation | ˌlɪmɪˈteɪʃn | n. 法定的提起诉讼的限期，诉讼时效，法律规定的有效期，限度制，局限，限制因素 |
| litigation | ˌlɪtɪˈɡeɪʃn | n. 诉讼；起诉 |
| lodging | ˈlɑːdʒɪŋ | n. 寄宿；寄宿处；出租的房间、住房 |
| maintain | meɪnˈteɪn | v. 宣称，断言，维护，继续，坚持，经办，协助诉讼，唆讼，介入他人诉讼 |
| majority | məˈdʒɔːrəti | n. 多数；成年 |
| malfeasance | ˌmælˈfiːzns | n. 渎职，违法行为；不正当，坏事 |
| management | ˈmænɪdʒmənt | n. 管理部门，经营才能，安排，支配，处理，厂资方，经理 |
| manner | ˈmænər | n. 方式，方法，举止，态度，习惯，风俗 |
| material | məˈtɪriəl | adj. 物质的，身体上的，有形的，实体的，重要的，必需的，决定性影响的，实质性的 n. 材料，题材，证据，必需品，设备 |
| means | miːnz | n. 方法，手段，工具，原因，财产，收入 |
| mediation | ˌmiːdiˈeɪʃn | n. 调解；仲裁；调停 |
| member | ˈmembər | n. 成员；会员 |
| merely | ˈmɪrli | adv. 仅仅，不过，只不过 |

| 单词 | 国际音标 | 词性及中文意思 |
|------|----------|----------------|
| meritorious | ˌmerɪˈtɔːriəs | adj. 有功的，值得称赞的，善意的，有法律价值的，法律上可能胜诉的 |
| merit | ˈmerɪt | n. 优点，价值；功绩；功过<br>vt. 值得<br>vi. 应受报答 |
| method | ˈmeθəd | n. 方法，做事的条理，秩序，计划 |
| minor | ˈmaɪnər | adj. 未成年的；次要的；较小的<br>n. 未成年人 |
| minority | maɪˈnɒrəti | n. 少数，未达法定年龄者，未成年，不到法定年龄的状态 |
| misappropriate | ˌmɪsəˈprəʊprieɪt | v. 非法侵占 |
| mitigation | ˌmɪtɪˈgeɪʃn | n. 减刑，减轻，缓和，安慰 |
| modification | ˌmɑːdɪfɪˈkeɪʃn | n. 修改，修正；改变 |
| modify | ˈmɑːdɪfaɪ | vt. 修改，修饰；更改<br>vi. 修改 |
| monitor | ˈmɑːnɪtər | n. 监视器；监听器；监控器；显示屏；班长<br>vt. 监控 |
| morals | ˈmɒrəlz | n.（尤指性关系方面的）品行，道德<br>n. 道德教训；格言，箴言（moral 的复数） |
| more | mɔr | adv. 更多；此外；更大程度地<br>adj. 更多的；附加的<br>pron. 更多的数量<br>n. 更多 |
| multiple | ˈmʌltɪpl | adj. 多重的；多样的；许多的 |
| municipality | mjuːˌnɪsɪˈpæləti | n. 市政当局；自治市或区 |
| nationality | ˌnæʃəˈnæləti | n. 国籍，国家；民族；部落 |
| necessity | nəˈsesəti | n. 需要；必然性；必需品 |
| negligent | ˈneglɪdʒənt | adj. 玩忽的，粗心大意的，因疏忽造成损害的，依民法应负赔偿责任的，过失的 |

| 单词 | 国际音标 | 词性及中文意思 |
|---|---|---|
| non-disclosure | nanˌdɪsˈkləʊʒə | n. 不披露，保密 |
| non-prosecution | nan ˌprɑːsɪˈkjuːʃn | n. 不起诉 |
| notice | ˈnəʊtɪs | n. 声明，通知书，短评，广告，招贴，标记，招牌，注意，知悉，开审通知书，报告书，传单，启事<br>v. 通知 |
| notification | ˌnəʊtɪfɪˈkeɪʃn | n. 公告，通告，通报，告示，通知，通知书 |
| notify | ˈnoʊtɪfaɪ | vt. 通告，通知；公布 |
| obey | əˈbeɪ | v. 服从，顺从，遵奉，执行，按照……行动 |
| objection | əbˈdʒɛkʃən | n. 异议，反对；缺陷，缺点；妨碍；拒绝的理由 |
| objective | əbˈdʒɛktɪv | n. 目的；目标；（军事行动的）攻击目标<br>adj. 客观的；客观存在的 |
| obligation | ˌɒblɪˈɡeɪʃn | n. 法律义务，道德上的义务，责任，职责，债，债务，债权关系，合同，证券，待付保留额，承付款项，束缚，偿付债务的款项，恩惠 |
| observer | əbˈzɜːrvər | n. 观察者；［天］观测者；遵守者 |
| obstacle | ˈɑːbstəkl | n. 障碍，干扰，妨碍；障碍物 |
| obstruct | əbˈstrʌkt | v. 阻碍，妨碍，阻挠，设置障碍 |
| obtainment | əbˈteinmənt | n. 获得 |
| obviously | ˈɒbviəsli | adv. 明显地 |
| occur | əˈkɜːr | v. 事件发生，出现，存在，被想到，想起 |
| occurrence | əˈkʌrəns | n. 出现，发生，偶发事件，事变 |
| of fer | ˈɒfər | n. 要约，出售，供应，出价，提议，企图 v. 出价，开价，提出，出售，出卖，提供，提议 |
| of ficial | əˈfɪʃl | adj. 官方的；正式的；公务的<br>n. 官员；公务员；高级职员 |
| omission | əˈmɪʃn | n. 疏忽，遗漏，省略；冗长 |

| 单词 | 国际音标 | 词性及中文意思 |
|------|----------|----------------|
| operating | ɑpəretɪŋ | adj. 操作的；（外科）手术的；营业收支的<br>v. 操作；动手术（operate 的现在分词） |
| ordinary | ˈɔːrdneri | adj. 普通的；平凡的；平常的<br>n. 普通；平常的人（或事） |
| original | əˈrɪdʒənl | adj. 原来的；开始的；首创的，新颖的，创新的；原作的<br>n. 原件，原版，古怪的人 |
| outlying | ˈaʊtlaɪɪŋ | adj. 边远的；无关的<br>v. 放在…外面；在撒谎上胜过（outlie 的现在分词） |
| oversee | ˌoʊvərˈsiː | vt. 监督；审查；俯瞰；偷看到，无意中看到 |
| panel | ˈpænl | n. 陪审团名单，一组陪审团员，合议庭，（选定的）专门小组<br>v. 选定（陪审团） |
| paragraph | ˈpærəɡræf | n. （法律条文和制定法，诉讼档条文中的）项，段落，节 |
| parole | pəˈroʊl | n. 假释（指在刑事判决执行结束前释放被监禁者），宣誓，战俘所作暗号（号令）<br>v. 假释，使（俘虏）宣誓后释放 |
| participant | pɑːrˈtɪsɪpənt | n. 参与者（多指非正式成员或无正式资格者） |
| participate | pɑːrˈtɪsɪpeɪt | vt. & vi. 参加，参与 |
| particular | pərˈtɪkjələr | adj. 单独的，具体的，个别的，特殊的，特别（定、指、有）的，指定的，各个的，分项的<br>n. 详细的单独事项，具体部分，详细说明（pl.）细目，要点，摘要 |
| party | ˈpɑːrti | n. （诉讼）当事人，关系人，参与者，团体，政党，（社交、游戏等的）集会，宴会 |
| penalty | ˈpenəlti | n. 刑罚（尤指罚金和监禁），处罚，惩罚性赔偿金，（凭标准买卖的商品）低质减价 |

| 单词 | 国际音标 | 词性及中文意思 |
|------|---------|----------------|
| pending | ˈpendɪŋ | adj. 未决的，待决的<br>prep. 在持续期间，在某期间之内，直到 |
| perform | pərˈfɔːrm | v. 履行，执行，完成，进行 |
| period | ˈpɪriəd | n. 期间，时期，期限 |
| perishable | ˈperɪʃəbl | n. 易腐货物，易腐物品<br>adj. 会毁坏的 |
| perjury | ˈpɜːrdʒəri | n. 伪证，伪誓<br>v. 仔细巡视，彻底调查 |
| permission | pərˈmɪʃn | n. 允许（行为），许可（证书），批准，同意，授权 |
| permitted | pərˈmɪtid | v. 允许；（使）有可能；批准；可能有；允许有（permit 的过去式及过去分词） |
| personnel | ˌpɜːrsəˈnel | n. 人员，人事部门，人事科（处） |
| petition | pəˈtɪʃn | n. 请求，申请（书），诉状，上诉状，请愿（书）<br>v. 提出申请，呈送申请（或诉状） |
| pettiness | ˈpetinəs | n. 琐碎，小气，卑鄙 |
| physical | ˈfɪzɪkl | adj. 肉体的，身体的，有形的，物质的，自然的<br>n.（pl.）实际货物，现货 |
| physiological | ˌfɪziəˈlɑːdʒɪkl | adj. 生理学的 |
| pilot | ˈpaɪlət | n. 领港员，领航员，引水员，向导，机师，飞行员，驾驶船者<br>adj. 实验性的，示范的，用于实验的，引导的，领航的，示范的，总的 |
| plaintiff | ˈpleɪntɪf | n. 原告 |
| plead | pliːd | vi. 恳求，请求<br>vt. 提出…为借口［理由］<br>vt. & vi. 申诉；答辩；为…辩护 |
| political | pəˈlɪtɪkl | adj. 政治的，与政府行为有关的，党派政治的 |

| 单词 | 国际音标 | 词性及中文意思 |
|---|---|---|
| portion | ˈpɔːrʃn | n.（财产等的）一份，部分，份额，嫁奁，分与遗赠财产 |
| postpone | poʊˈspoʊn | v. 延搁，延期，迟误 |
| preceding | prɪˈsiːdɪŋ | adj. 在前的，在先的，前面的 |
| pregnant | ˈpregnənt | adj. 怀孕的，含蓄的，有意义的 |
| prescribed | prɪˈskraɪbd | adj. 法定的，规定的 |
| preservation | ˌprezərˈveɪʃn | n. 保存，保留 |
| preservative | prɪˈzɜːrvətɪv | n. 防腐剂；预防法；防护层<br>adj. 防腐的；有保存力的；有保护性的 |
| preserve | prɪˈzɜːrv | v. 保护（存、藏），维护（持），使流传，禁猎 |
| preside | prɪˈzaɪd | v. 主持，负责，指挥，管理，控制 |
| president | ˈprezɪdənt | n.（美国等）总统，总裁，大臣，议长，会长，（国家）主席，（联合国大会）主席，院长，庭长，（银行等）行长（总裁），社长，大学校长，董事长总经理 |
| presiding | prɪˈzaɪdɪŋ | v. 主持（会议等）；担任（会议）主席；负责（preside 的现在分词）<br>adj. 主持会议的，指挥的 |
| pretext | ˈpriːtekst | n. 借口，托词 |
| principal | ˈprɪnsəpl | n. 委托人，主犯，主要责任人（或义务人），财产主体，信托主体事务，（债务、投资或基金的）本金，第一被告，主债务人，祖传动产<br>adj. 主要的，最重要的，为首的，第一位的 |
| principle | ˈprɪnsəpl | n. 原则，方针，政策，要素，主义 |
| prior | ˈpraɪər | adj. 在先的，在前的，优先的，更重要的<br>n. [俚] 前科罪 |
| privacy | ˈpraɪvəsi | n.（个人）秘密，隐私，隐退，隐居 |
| private | ˈpraɪvət | adj. 私（个）人的，（公司）股份不上市的，私营的，私设的，秘密的，不公开的，平民的 |

| 单词 | 国际音标 | 词性及中文意思 |
|------|---------|---------------|
| privilege | ˈprɪvəlɪdʒ | n. 特权（指特殊的法律权利），特惠，特殊利益，免责特权，以法律授权为由的抗辩，保密特权，债权人的优先偿付权，支付给船长的货物照料津贴<br>v. 授予特权，特许 |
| probation | prouˈbeɪʃn | n. 缓刑，遗嘱检验，试用，见习期，试用期，察看（以观后效），感化犯人 |
| procedural | prəˈsiːdʒərəl | adj. 诉讼程序（上）的，有关程序的 |
| procedure | prəˈsiːdʒər | n. 程序，手续，司法程序规则 |
| proceed | prəˈsiːd | v. 进行，继续进行，发生，起诉，进行诉讼程序 |
| process | prəˈses | n. 传票，诉讼的进行，刑事检控的进行程序，诉讼过程中的各种命令，诉讼程序，手续，处理<br>v. 对……起诉，向……发出传票，处理，办理，加工，（专利法中的）方法 |
| procurator | ˈprɑkjəˌretər | n. 检察官；代理人；行政长官 |
| procuratorate | ˈprɒkjʊəreɪtərɪt | n. 代理人（代诉人、检察员、检察官等）的职业，检察机关，检察院 |
| procuratorial | ˌprɒkjʊərəˈtɔːrɪəl | adj. 代诉人的，代理人的，检察的 |
| prohibit | prəˈhɪbɪt | vt. 阻止，禁止 |
| promote | prəˈmoʊt | v. 创立（公司或企业），唆使，煽动，推销（商品），设法通过（法律，议案等），（用不正当手段）获得 |
| promptly | ˈprɑːmptli | adv. 敏捷地；迅速地；立即地 |
| proof | pruːf | n. 以证据证明事实，（法院判决的）证据，书证，[苏]法官单独审理证据，校稿，校样，标准 |
| properly | ˈprɑːpərli | adv. 适当地；正确地；恰当地 |
| property | ˈprɑːpərti | n. 产权，财产 |
| proposal | prəˈpoʊzl | n. 申请，方案，提议，求婚，投标，保险申请书 |
| proposed | prəˈpoʊzd | adj. 被提议的；所推荐的<br>v. 提议；计划（propose 的过去式和过去分词） |

| 单词 | 国际音标 | 词性及中文意思 |
|------|----------|----------------|
| prosecuted | prɔsikjuːtid | adj. 被起诉的<br>v. 起诉（prosecute 的过去分词） |
| prosecution | ˌprɑːsɪˈkjuːʃn | n. 起诉，（刑事）检控，（总称）原告及其律师，控方，检察官，进行，实施，从事，经营 |
| prosecutor | ˈprɑːsɪkjuːtər | n. 公诉人，检察官，刑事自诉人 |
| protective | prəˈtektɪv | adj. 保护（贸易）的 |
| prove | pruːv | vt. 证明 |
| provincial | prəˈvɪnʃl | adj. 省的；地方性的；偏狭的<br>n. 粗野的人；乡下人；外地人 |
| provision | prəˈvɪʒn | n. 供应，提供，供给 |
| psychological | ˌsaɪkəˈlɑːdʒɪkl | adj. 心理的；心理学的；精神上的 |
| punishable | ˈpʌnɪʃəbl | adj.（人或罪行）该处罚的；可惩罚的 |
| punishment | ˈpʌnɪʃmənt | n. 处罚，受罚 |
| pursue | pərˈsu | vt. 从事；追赶；继续；纠缠<br>vi. 追赶；继续进行 |
| quantities | kwɑntətiz | n. 数量，工程量（quantity 的复数） |
| random | ˈrændəm | adj. 任意的；胡乱的；随机的 |
| readily | ˈredɪli | adv. 随意地，随时地 |
| reasonable | ˈriːznəbl | adj. 合理的，公平的，正当的，适当的，有道理的，理智的 |
| receipt | rɪˈsiːt | v. 出具收据，开收条，<br>n. 接受行为，收条（据），（pl.）接收物品（或款项），收入 |
| recipient | rɪˈsɪpiənt | n. 受领人，接受者（人），领受者，受援者（国）<br>adj. 接受的，容纳的，感受性强的 |
| reciprocity | ˌresɪˈprɑːsəti | n. 互惠（性），（因商贸或外交关系）相互特许 |
| recommendation | ˌrekəmenˈdeɪʃn | n. 建议，推荐，保举，介绍 |

| 单词 | 国际音标 | 词性及中文意思 |
|---|---|---|
| reconsideration | ˌriːkənˌsɪdəˈreɪʃn | n.（行政）复议，（议会）重新审议，重新考虑 |
| recounted | rɪˈkaʊnt | v. 重算（数、计），重新点数，详细讲述，列举 |
| recovered | rɪˈkʌvərd | v./n. 重获，重新找到，完全收回，恢复，获得，胜诉，追缴，挽回，使清醒，使复活，痊愈，使复原，回收，赔偿 |
| redemption | rɪˈdempʃn | n. 赎回，回赎权，回购，偿付（拖欠的按揭款项），偿还，还清，补偿，补救，可取之处，履行，变卖成现金，改善，修复 |
| reenactment | ˌriːɪnˈæktmənt | n. 重新制定（再次扮演） |
| re-evaluation | ˌriː ɪˌvæljuˈeɪʃn | v. 再评价，重新评价 |
| reexamination | ˌriːɪɡˌzæmɪˈneɪʃn | n. 再检查，再调查；重考 |
| reference | ˈrefrəns | n. 提交，提交案件令，引证，提及，参考，涉及，委托，职权范围，证明书，（品行、能力等的）证明人，保证人 |
| reformation | ˌrefərˈmeɪʃn | n. 改革，修订协议，重新形成，改过自新 |
| reformatory | rɪˈfɔːrmətɔːri | n. 青少年感化院<br>adj. 意在改变的，意在感化的，起改良作用的 |
| refusal | rɪˈfjuːzl | n. 拒绝（要约或要求），谢绝，取舍权，先行决定机会 |
| regard | rɪˈɡɑːrd | n. 注意；尊重；凝视；问候<br>vt. 把…看作；注重，考虑；看待；尊敬；与……有关<br>vi. 注意，注重；注视 |
| re-identification | rɪ aɪˌdentɪfɪˈkeɪʃn | n. 重新鉴定，重新识别 |
| relationship | rɪˈleɪʃnʃɪp | n. 关系，亲属关系 |
| relocating | rɪˈloketɪŋ | n. 重新安置；迁移<br>v. 重新安置；迁移（relocate 的 ing 形式） |
| reluctant | rɪˈlʌktənt | adj. 不愿的，勉强的，难驾驭的，顽抗的 |
| rely | rɪˈlaɪ | v. 依赖，依靠，信赖 |

| 单词 | 国际音标 | 词性及中文意思 |
|------|---------|---------------|
| remand | rɪˈmænd | n. 发回重审，案件发回令<br>v. 还押，押候（指预审之后将被告送交拘押），发回重审 |
| remittance | rɪˈmɪtns | n. 汇付（指支付货价或服务款的一种方式），汇票，汇寄，汇款（额） |
| remuneration | rɪˌmjuːnəˈreɪʃn | n. 报酬，酬金，支付酬金，补偿，赔偿 |
| render | ˈrendər | n. 竞争，战斗，斗殴 |
| repentance | rɪˈpentəns | n. 悔改，悔悟，懊（后）悔 |
| representative | ˌreprɪˈzentətɪv | n. 代表，（代位）继承人，诉讼代理人<br>adj. 代理的，代表的，表现的，表示的，代议制的，典型的 |
| residential | ˌrezɪˈdenʃl | adj. 有关居住的，居所的，适于居住的 |
| resolve | rɪˈzɑːlv | v. 解决（答），消除，决定（议），转为，变为<br>n. 决议（定） |
| respectively | rɪˈspektɪvli | adv. 各自地，各个地，分别地 |
| respondent | rɪˈspɑːndənt | n. 答辩人，被申诉人，被上诉人，被告人 |
| responsibility | rɪˌspɑːnsəˈbɪləti | n. 责任，刑事责任能力，义务履行能力，负担，职责，任务，（财力方面的）可靠性，响应性 |
| responsible | rɪˈspɑːnsəbl | adj. 应负责任的，有责任的，能履行责任的，可靠的 |
| restraint | rɪˈstreɪnt | n. 限（遏、抑）制，贸易限制，（军事）禁闭，羁押，约束力，管束 |
| restricted | rɪˈstrɪktɪd | adj. 受限制的；保密的<br>v. 限制（restrict 的过去式和过去分词） |
| retain | rɪˈteɪn | v. 保持；保留；聘用（顾问、律师） |
| retaliation | rɪˌtæliˈeɪʃn | n. 报仇，[国] 报复，回敬 |
| retrial | ˈriːtraɪəl | n. 复审，再审<br>v. 再审，复审 |

| 单词 | 国际音标 | 词性及中文意思 |
|---|---|---|
| retry | ˌriːˈtraɪ | v. 再审，重新审讯（理），复算 |
| revoke | rɪˈvəʊk | v. 收回，撤回，撤销，废除，取消（法律，允诺等），宣告无效 |
| ruling | ˈruːlɪŋ | n.（尤指法庭的）裁定；统治，支配<br>adj. 统治的，支配的；主导的；流行的，普遍的 |
| safeguard | ˈseɪfɡɑːrd | n. 保护措施，保证条款，安全装置，防护设施，（战时）安全通行证，护照，保护者，护送者，警卫员 保护，维护，捍卫 |
| sample | ˈsæmpl | n. 样品，典型，抽样，货样，实例，标本<br>v. 取样，抽样 |
| scene | siːn | n. 出事地点，（犯罪）现场，情景，(pl.) 实况，吵闹 |
| scheduled | ˈskedʒuːld | adj. 规定价格的；预定的，排定的，严格按时间表生活的 |
| scope | skoʊp | n. 界限，领域，范围，视野，机会 |
| seal | siːl | n. 封条（印），印图，火漆，封条，封铅，密封，保证，〔美〕伪币 v. 批准，保证，确证，盖章于，盖印，密封，禁止接触 |
| section | ˈsekʃn | n.（条文中的）条、款（指制定法中经常分章、条、段、项等的条），地区（段），类，科，处，股，组，部门，工段，节，[美] 1 平方英里面积，640 英亩土地 |
| seizure | ˈsiːʒər | n. 依法占有，充公，没收（物），占领，夺取，捕获，强取，扣留，扣押物 |
| self-incrimination | selfɪnˌkrimiˈneɪʃən | n. 自证其罪 |
| self-inflicted | ˌself ɪnˈflɪktɪd | adj. 自己造成的；加于自身的 |
| sentence | ˈsentəns | n. 刑事判决，判刑，量刑<br>v. 判刑，量刑 |
| separately | ˈseprətli | adv. 分离地；个别地，分别地 |

| 单词 | 国际音标 | 词性及中文意思 |
|------|----------|----------------|
| serious | ˈsɪrɪəs | adj. 严肃的，严重的；认真的；庄重的；危急的 |
| server | ˈsɜːrvər | n. 服务员，（传票、令状等法律文件的）送达员（人、者），送交者 |
| settlement | ˈsetlmənt | n.（家庭）财产让与，和解，（庭外）协议调解，解决，决定，了结，清偿（算、理），支付，决算，（不动产交易等的）成交会，（遗嘱执行人）处置所有遗产，整理，安排，安置，定居，汇款方式 |
| siblings | ˈsɪblɪŋz | n. 兄弟姐妹；同科 |
| signature | ˈsɪɡnətʃər | n. 签名（署），署名，画押，赦令，诏书 |
| socialist | ˈsoʊʃəlɪst | n. 社会主义者，社会党党员 |
| solve | sɑːlv | vt. 解决；解答；溶解<br>vi. 作解答 |
| specialized | ˈspeʃəlaɪzd | adj. 专业的；专门的<br>v. 专攻（specialize 的过去分词）；使…专门化；详细说明 |
| specially | ˈspeʃəli | adv. 特别地；专门地 |
| specific | spəˈsɪfɪk | adj. 特定（有）的，与特定事物相关的，遵守具体要件要求的，从量的，具体的，明确的<br>n. 特性，细节，(pl.)（计划、建议等）详细说明书，特定用途物品 |
| speech-impaired | spiːtʃ ɪmˈperd | n. 语言障碍 |
| spouse | spaʊz | n. 配偶（指夫或妻），已婚者 |
| standing | ˈstændɪŋ | n. 诉权，诉讼资格，持续，期间，地位，身份，名望<br>adj. 已为法律（或习惯）所确定的，固定的，经常的 |
| statement | ˈsteɪtmənt | n. 声明（书），主张，（事实）陈述，（警方对疑犯招供所作的）供述记录 |
| statutory | ˈstætʃətɔːri | adj. 法令的，与法规相关的，制定法创制的，依照制定法的，依法应惩处的 |
| strengthen | ˈstreŋθn | v.（股票）价格上涨，加强，强化 |

| 单词 | 国际音标 | 词性及中文意思 |
|---|---|---|
| subsidization | ˌsʌbsɪdəˈzeɪʃn | n. 补助，津贴 |
| successive | səkˈsesɪv | adj. 连续的，相继的；依次的；接替的 |
| suffering | ˈsʌfərɪŋ | n. 痛苦，苦难，折磨<br>adj. 受苦的；患病的<br>v. 受苦；蒙受（suffer 的现在分词） |
| suffice | səˈfaɪs | vt. 使满足；足够…用；合格<br>vi. 足够；有能力 |
| sufficient | səˈfɪʃnt | adj. 充分（足）的，足够的 |
| suicide | ˈsuːɪsaɪd | n. 自杀；自杀者；自杀行为 |
| summary | ˈsʌməri | n. 概要，一览，总结，摘要，结局<br>adj. 概括的，扼要的，总结性的 |
| summon | ˈsʌmən | v. 传唤（出庭作证），请求 |
| supervise | ˈsuːpərvaɪz | vt. & vi. 监督，管理 |
| supplementary | ˌsʌplɪˈmentri | adj. 增补的，补充的，追加的<br>n. 增补者（物），补充者（物） |
| supreme | suːˈpriːm | adj. 最高的，最重要的 |
| surety | ˈʃʊrəti | n. 保证人，担保，保证，履约保证 |
| surrender | səˈrendər | n. 屈从（权力等），让步，放弃（权利、主张），解约，退保，缴还（保险单），投降，屈服<br>v. 解约，退保，投降，自首，引渡，（要塞）陷落，放弃，让与 |
| surveillance | sɜːrˈveɪləns | n. 监视，看守，监督，管理 |
| suspect | səˈspekt | n. 犯罪嫌疑人，疑犯<br>v. 嫌疑，怀疑 |
| suspend | səˈspend | v. 中止，推迟，延期，打扰，临时中止，暂时停办，无力支付，宣布破产 |
| system | ˈsɪstəm | n. 制度，体系，体制，系统 |
| tackle | ˈtækl | vt. 解决；应付 |

| 单词 | 国际音标 | 词性及中文意思 |
|---|---|---|
| telecommunicat-ions | ˌtelikəˌmjuːnɪˈkeɪʃnz | n. 电信，电讯，通讯 |
| terminate | ˈtɜːrmIneIt | v. 终止，结束，完成，期满，了结 |
| terrorist | ˈterərIst | n. 恐怖分子，恐怖主义者 |
| testify | ˈtestIfaI | v. 证明（实），作证，提供证据，确言，宣称 |
| testimony | ˈtestImoʊni | n. 言辞证据，证言，（刻在两块石碑上的）摩西十诫 |
| thereafter | ˌðerˈæftər | adv. 此后；在那之后 |
| torture | ˈtɔːrtʃər | n. 拷问，刑讯，痛苦，折磨，歪曲 |
| transcript | ˈtrænskrIpt | n. 证言记录，记录副本，抄本，誊本，正本，正式文本 |
| transfer | trænsˈfɜːr | n.（所有权的）让与，（物权、产权等的）转让，过户，汇兑，（会计）转账，调动，转移，<br>v. 转移，让渡，交付，变换，过户，调职 |
| treasury | treʒəri | n. 国库，金库，资金，（国家或机关）所拥有的款项，（大写）财政部 |
| treatment | ˈtriːtmənt | n. 处置，处理，待遇，治疗 |
| treaty | ˈtriːti | n. 条约，谈判，协商，合同，合约，转保协议 |
| trial | ˈtraIəl | n. 审判 |
| truthfully | ˈtruːθflli | adv. 诚实地；深信不疑地 |
| undergoing | ˌʌndərˈgoʊIŋ | vt. 经历，经受；忍受（undergo 的现在分词） |
| unfounded | ʌnˈfaʊndId | adj. 无根据的，无事实依据的，无理由的 |
| unknown | ˌʌnˈnoʊn | adj. 未知的，不确知的，不详的，无名的 |
| uphold | ʌpˈhoʊld | vt. 支撑；鼓励；赞成；举起 |
| urine | ˈjʊrIn | n. 尿 |
| validity | vəˈlIdəti | n. 有效；效力；合法性 |
| verbal | ˈvɜːrbl | adj. 词语的，言语的，字句的，口头的 |
| verify | ˈverIfaI | vt. 核实；查证 |

| 单词 | 国际音标 | 词性及中文意思 |
|---|---|---|
| victim | ˈvɪktɪm | n. 牺牲者；受害人；牺牲品 |
| violence | ˈvaɪələns | n. 激烈；暴力；侵犯；歪曲 |
| vision | ˈvɪʒn | n. 视力；眼力；幻象；美景；想象力 |
| visual | ˈvɪʒuəl | adj. 视觉的，看得见的 |
| voluntarily | ˌvɑːlənˈterəli | adv. 志愿地 |
| waive | weɪv | vt. 放弃；搁置 |
| warrant | ˈwɔːrənt | n. 授权证；许可证 |
| welfare | ˈwelfer | n. 福利；福利事业；幸福；安宁<br>adj. 福利的；接受社会救济的 |
| withdraw | wɪθˈdrɔː | v. 取回 |
| withhold | wɪθˈhoʊld | v. 保留；扣留；抑制 |

# 《中华人民共和国刑法》（2017 年）词汇表

| 单词 | 国际音标 | 词性及中文意思 |
|---|---|---|
| ability | əˈbɪləti | n. 能力，能耐；才能 |
| abandon | əˈbændən | v. 遗弃；离开；放弃；终止；陷入<br>n. 放任，狂热 |
| abduct | æbˈdʌkt | vt. 绑架；诱拐；使外展 |
| abide | əˈbaɪd | vt. 忍受，容忍；停留；遵守<br>vi. 持续；忍受；停留 |
| abet | əˈbet | vt. 煽动，教唆；支持 |
| abnormal | æbˈnɔːml | adj. 反常的，异常的；变态的 |
| aboard | əˈbɔːrd | adv. 在（飞机、火车、船）上<br>prep. 在（船或飞机）上 |
| above-mentioned | əˌbʌv ˈmenʃnd | adj. 上述的，上面提到的 |
| abroad | əˈbrɔːd | adv. 国外（尤指在法院所在地国外）<br>adj. 往国外的 |
| abuse | əˈbjuːs | n. 滥用；虐待（儿童）；非礼或强奸（妇女）<br>v. 滥用；辱骂；虐待；强奸幼女 |
| accept | əkˈsept | vt. & vi. 接受；承担责任<br>vt. 承认（兑、揽），同意；认付（汇票等）；认为，相信 |
| acceptance | əkˈseptəns | n. 接受；赞同；容纳 |
| access | ˈækses | n. 接近（或取得）……的权利 |
| accessory | əkˈsesəri | n. 从犯<br>adj. 副的；同谋的；附属的 |
| accident | ˈæksɪdənt | n. 事故，意外事件，灾害，不幸 |
| accompanying | əˈkʌmpəniɪŋ | v. 陪同；与……同时发生<br>adj. 陪伴的；和……一起发生的；附随的 |

| 单词 | 国际音标 | 词性及中文意思 |
|---|---|---|
| accomplice | əˈkɑːmplɪs | n. 从犯，共犯 |
| accord | əˈkɔːrd | vt. 使一致，符合，调和，同意<br>n. 一致，符合，协议（定），和解，和解性协议 |
| accordance | əˈkɔːrdns | n. 依据；一致，给予；同意 |
| according | əˈkɔrdɪŋ | adv. 根据<br>adj. 相应的；一致的 |
| accordingly | əˈkɔːrdɪŋli | adv. 相应地；因此，于是 |
| account | əˈkaʊnt | n. 原因，理由；详细报告；账目（户）；利润（益） |
| accountant | əˈkaʊntənt | n. 会计；出纳 |
| accounting | əˈkaʊntɪŋ | n. 借贷对照表；账单；清算账目，记账，结算；会计（学） |
| accreditation | əˌkredɪˈteɪʃn | n. 立（备）案；任命；鉴定，认证 |
| accumulated | əˈkjuːmjəleɪtɪd | adj. 累计的 |
| accumulation | əˌkjuːmjəˈleɪʃn | n. 积累，累积（利息）；（利润、息金带来的）资本增益；本利滚计 |
| accumulative | əˈkjuːmjələtɪv | adj. 积累的，累进的 |
| accusation | ækjuˈzeɪʃn | n. 控告，起诉，告发；（被告发、控告的）罪名，罪状；谴责 |
| accuse | əˈkjuːz | vt. 控诉，控告；指责，谴责 |
| accused | əˈkjuːzd | adj. 被指控的，被起诉的 |
| accuser | əˈkjuːzər | n. 原告，指控人，控告者，起诉人 |
| acetic | əˈsiːtɪk | adj. 醋的，乙酸的 |
| acquire | əˈkwaɪər | vt. 获得，取得；调用；收购（公司等） |
| acquired | əˈkwaɪrd | adj. 后天的；已获得的；已成习惯的 |
| acquisition | ˌækwɪˈzɪʃn | n. 征用；取得；买受（进）；招揽；（公司之间的）购并 |

| 单词 | 国际音标 | 词性及中文意思 |
|---|---|---|
| across | əˈkrɔːs | adv. 穿过，越过；横过<br>prep. 穿过；在…对面，另一边；遍及；在…里 |
| act | ækt | n. 行为（动），法（令）；法例，条例，决议（书）；作为，作用；效力<br>v. 代理；采取行为；起作用 |
| acting | ˈæktɪŋ | n. 代理，代理行为；行动；常务 |
| action | ˈækʃn | n. 诉讼，起诉；行动，行为 |
| active | ˈæktɪv | adj. 现行的，实际的，主动的，积极的，活动的，自动的，有意的 |
| actively | ˈæktɪvli | adv. 积极地；活跃地 |
| activity | ækˈtɪvəti | n. 活动；行动；活跃 |
| actor | ˈæktər | n. 起诉者；诉讼代理人；行为人；演员 |
| actual | ˈæktʃuəl | adj. 实际的，现实的；目前的，现行的；事实上的 |
| actually | ˈæktʃuəli | adv. 实际上；事实上 |
| added | ˈædɪd | adj. 额外的；更多的 |
| addictive | əˈdɪktɪv | adj. 上瘾的，使成瘾的，成溺的 |
| addition | əˈdɪʃn | n. 追加，附加（物）；头衔，称号；附录，增补，补充，附件 |
| additionally | əˈdɪʃənəli | adv. 此外；又，加之 |
| adds | ædz | vi. 加；增加；加起来；做加法<br>vt. 增加，添加，补充说；计算……总和（add 的第三人称单数）<br>abbr. 高级数据显示系统（Advanced Data Display System）；美国陆军数据分发系统；应用数字数据系统（Applied Digital Data System） |
| adjudicating | əˈdʒuːdɪkeɪtɪŋ | v. 判决，宣判，裁定；裁判，评判（adjudicate 的现在分词） |
| adjudication | əˌdʒuːdɪˈkeɪʃn | n. 宣布（裁决、法令等），裁决，判决，判案，裁定，宣告 |

| 单词 | 国际音标 | 词性及中文意思 |
|---|---|---|
| administer | əd'mɪnɪstər | v. 管理，掌管，管制，支配，施行，实施，管理遗产，使发誓 |
| administration | əd‚mɪnɪ'streɪʃn | n. 经营，管理，（法院指定的管理人进行的）遗产管理；行政，行政机关，局，处；执行，实施 |
| administrative | əd'mɪnɪstreɪtɪv | adj. 行政的，管理的 |
| administratively | əd'mɪnɪstretɪvli | adv. 行政地；管理地 |
| admit | əd'mɪt | v. 承认；供述；允许 |
| adopt | ə'dɑːpt | v. 收养，领养；正式通过；采用（取、纳） |
| adopted | ə'dɑːptɪd | adj. 被收养的；被采纳的 |
| adulterate | ə'dʌltəreɪt | vt. 掺假，掺杂，假冒<br>adj. 掺假的，通奸的 |
| advance | əd'væns | n. 前进，进行；建议，预付（款），贷款；涨价<br>v. 预付，预支，垫付 |
| advantage | əd'væntɪdʒ | n. 有利条件，有利因素，优势，益处，利益<br>vt. 有利于；使处于优势<br>vi. 获利 |
| adverse | əd'vɜːrs | adj. 相反的，敌对的，逆反的，非法的，不利的，有害的，负面的 |
| adversely | əd'vɜːrsli | adv. 不利地；逆地；反对地 |
| advertisement | ‚ædvər'taɪzmənt | n. 广告，公告，告示，通知 |
| advertising | 'ædvərtaɪzɪŋ | n. 广告业，刊登广告 |
| advise | əd'vaɪz | v. 劝告，通知，告知；提出意见，作顾问，商量 |
| advocate | 'ædvəkeɪt | n. （出庭）辩护人，律师<br>v. 辩护，拥护，提倡，鼓吹 |
| advocating | 'ædvəkeɪtɪŋ | adj. 崇高的 |
| affair | ə'fer | n. 私通事件，事件，事情，事务，事态；公司与股东、董事或职员的关系 |

| 单词 | 国际音标 | 词性及中文意思 |
|------|---------|----------------|
| affect | əˈfekt | vt. 影响；假装；感染<br>vi. 倾向；喜欢 |
| affected | əˈfektɪd | adj. 假装的；受到影响的<br>vt. 影响 |
| aforementioned | əˈfɔːrmenʃənd | adj. 前面提到的，上述的 |
| aforesaid | əˈfɔːrˌsed | adj. 上述的，前述的 |
| against | əˈgenst | prep. 违反，反对，对抗，对比，防备 |
| aged | eɪdʒd | adj. 年老的，年迈的 |
| agency | ˈeɪdʒənsi | n. 代理，中介，经销处，代理处，代理机构，代理权 |
| agent | ˈeɪdʒənt | n. 行为者，代理人，代理商；原因，动因；间谍，特务<br>adj. 代理的 |
| agreed | əˈgriːd | adj. 同意的，赞成的；双方协议的，通过协议的 |
| agreement | əˈgriːmənt | n. 协同行为，协议，合约，合同，契约 |
| agriculture | ˈægrɪkʌltʃər | n. 农业 |
| aid | eɪd | n. 帮助，援助金，救护，辅助（手段、设备），助手<br>v. 协助 |
| aiding | ˈeɪdɪŋ | n. 帮助 |
| aim | eɪm | v. 瞄准，针对 |
| aiming | ˈeɪmɪŋ | v. 瞄准；力求；针对<br>n. 目标 |
| aircraft | ˈerkræft | n. 飞机（艇），航空器 |
| airplane | ˈerpleɪn | n. 飞机，班机 |
| airport | ˈerpɔːrt | n. 飞机场，航空港 |
| allocated | ˈæləkeɪtɪd | adj. 调拨的，分配的，指派的 |
| allocation | ˌæləˈkeɪʃn | n. 拨款，分配，配给，分派，配额，配给量 |
| allow | əˈlaʊ | v. 允许，承认，批准 |

| 单词 | 国际音标 | 词性及中文意思 |
|---|---|---|
| allowance | əˈlaʊəns | n. 允许，准许；津贴，补助，抚养费，手续费，（法院判给受信托人的）信托费用 |
| along | əˈlɔːŋ | adv. 向前；一起<br>prep. 沿着；顺着 |
| already | ɔːlˈredi | adv. 已经，早已；先前 |
| alter | ˈɔːltər | v. 变造（票据、文件等），更改，修正，变动 |
| alternative | ɔːlˈtɜːrnətɪv | adj. 在两者中任择其一的，选择性的，替代的，非传统的<br>n. 取舍，抉择，选择物（者），替代者（物），替代方式 |
| although | ɔːlˈðoʊ | conj. 虽然，尽管 |
| amended | əˈmendɪd | adj. 修正的 |
| amendment | əˈmendmənt | n. （对法律等的）修正案（条款） |
| ammunition | ˌæmjuˈnɪʃn | n. 弹药，军火 |
| among | əˈmʌŋ | prep. 在……中间；在……之中；（群体内部）相互间 |
| amount | əˈmaʊnt | n. 金额，数量 |
| accident | ˈæksɪdənt | n. 飞行事故；飞行失事 |
| ancient | ˈeɪnʃənt | adj. 远古的，古代的，旧的 |
| anhydride | ænˈhaɪdraɪd | n. 酸酐；脱水物 |
| animal | ˈænɪml | n. 动物 |
| announce | əˈnaʊns | v. 宣布，宣告 |
| annual | ˈænjuəl | adj. 年度的，每年的 |
| another | əˈnʌðər | adj. 不同的；另一个 |
| anthem | ˈænθəm | n. 赞美诗；圣歌 |
| anti-drug | ˈænti drʌg | adj. 反麻醉品的 |
| apology | əˈpɑːlədʒi | n. 辩解，道歉 |
| apparatus | ˌæpəˈrætəs | n. 器械，设备 |

| 单词 | 国际音标 | 词性及中文意思 |
|------|---------|---------------|
| apparently | əˈpærəntli | adv. 显然地；似乎，表面上 |
| appendix | əˈpendɪks | n. 上诉状附件，附录，附属物 |
| appliance | əˈplaɪəns | n. 器具，器械，装置 |
| applicable | ˈæplɪkəbl | adj. 适用的，适当的 |
| application | ˌæplɪˈkeɪʃn | n. 适用，投保，分配支付款，请求，申请（书），诉状 |
| apply | əˈplaɪ | v. 提出申请，适用，实施 |
| applying | əˈplaɪɪŋ | n. 应用；阶段；申请 |
| appraiser | əˈpreɪzər | n. 估价人，鉴定人，税收查证人 |
| approval | əˈpruːvl | n. 认可，赞同，核准，批准，许可 |
| approve | əˈpruːv | v. 批准，核准，许可，赞成，同意 |
| aquatic | əˈkwɑːtɪk | adj. 水产的，水域的 |
| arbitrarily | ˌɑːrbɪˈtrerəli | adv. 任意地，擅自地 |
| arbitration | ˌɑːrbɪˈtreɪʃn | n. 仲裁，公断，解决争端 |
| archive | ˈɑːrkaɪv | n. 公文档案，案卷<br>v. 存档 |
| arise | əˈraɪz | vt. 呈现；出现；发生<br>vi. 起身，起来，起立 |
| army | ˈɑːrmi | n. 陆军，军队 |
| arrange | əˈreɪndʒ | v. 调解，调停，安排，整理 |
| arrest | əˈrest | n. 刑事扣押，逮捕，扣留，拘押，阻止，抵制<br>v. 逮捕，拘留，扣押 |
| arson | ˈɑːrsn | n. 纵火罪 |
| article | ˈɑːrtɪkl | n. 章程，法规，条款，规章，条例<br>v. 订条款（或合同），列举（罪状等） |
| artistic | ɑːrˈtɪstɪk | adj. 艺术的 |

| 单词 | 国际音标 | 词性及中文意思 |
|---|---|---|
| aside | əˈsaɪd | adv. 离开，撇开；在旁边<br>n. 私语，悄悄话；离题的话<br>prep. 在……旁边 |
| asking | æskɪŋ | v. 询问；请求；要求 |
| assault | æskɪŋ | n. 企图伤害，暴力胁迫，殴打，强奸<br>v. 暴力胁迫，企图伤害，攻击，强奸 |
| assemble | əˈsembl | v. 集合（会），调集，汇编 |
| assembly | əˈsembli | n. 集合，大会，议会 |
| assessment | əˈsesmənt | n. 估价，确定数额（损害赔偿金、公司征地时的赔偿金等），分摊，摊派额，征税，诉讼费额的评估 |
| asset | ˈæset | n. 资产（指任何不动产和动产及其有关的利息以及可用作偿债的遗产等），财富 |
| assign | əˈsaɪn | v. 让与，动产转让，拨款，过户；指派；归属；提出，指定 |
| assignment | əˈsaɪnmənt | n. 转让（权利、财产、证书等），分配，委派，指定，指派，陈述（理由、动机等），说明 |
| assist | əˈsɪst | v. 支持，援助，帮助 |
| assistance | əˈsɪstəns | n. 援助，帮助，（法律援助中的）法律协助 |
| association | əˌsoʊsiˈeɪʃn | n. 社团，协会，合伙，交际，联合 |
| assume | əˈsuːm | v. 承担（债务、责任等），接受，设想，假定 |
| attach | əˈtætʃ | v. 拘捕，扣押，查封，附加 |
| attack | əˈtæk | v. 攻击<br>n. 攻击，袭击，抨击，辱骂 |
| attain | əˈteɪn | vt. 达到，实现；获得；到达 |
| attempt | əˈtempt | n. 图谋（或企图）犯罪，企图<br>v. 企图，谋略 |
| audio | ˈɔːdioʊ | adj. 听觉的，声音的 |

| 单词 | 国际音标 | 词性及中文意思 |
|---|---|---|
| audiovisual | ˌɔːdiəʊˈvɪʒuəl | adj. 视听的，音像的 |
| audition | ɔːˈdɪʃn | v. 试音，试听 |
| august | ɔːˈɡʌst | adj. 威严的；令人敬畏的 |
| authority | əˈθɒrəti | n. 权力，管辖权，代理权，当局，官方，委托书 |
| authorization | ˌɔːθəraɪˈzeɪʃn | n. 授权书，委托，批准，许可 |
| authorizing | ˈɔːθəraɪzɪŋ | adj. 授权的 |
| autonomous | ɔːˈtɒnəməs | adj. 自治（主）的，自治权的 |
| auxiliary | ɔːɡˈzɪliəri | adj. 附加（属）的，辅助的 |
| avert | əˈvɜːrt | vt. 避免，防止 |
| aviation | ˌeɪviˈeɪʃn | n. 航空，民航 |
| avoid | əˈvɔɪd | v. 使无效，避免，回避，废止，撤销 |
| aware | əˈwer | adj. 知道的；意识到的；有……方面知识的 |
| bacterial | bækˈtɪriəl | adj. 细菌的 |
| balance | ˈbæləns | n. 平衡，（收支）差额，结存，均势，余额，尾数<br>v. 使平衡，平衡 |
| ballot | ˈbælət | n. 无记名投票，投票权<br>v. 投票选举 |
| banking | ˈbæŋkɪŋ | n. 金融，银行业，银行学 |
| bankruptcy | ˈbæŋkrʌptsi | n. 破产，无偿债能力，（名誉、智力等）完全丧失 |
| banned | bænd | adj. 被禁的 |
| banning | ˈbænɪŋ | n. 禁止；禁令 |
| based | beɪst | adj. 有根基的；有基地的 |
| basic | ˈbeɪsɪk | n. 基本原理，基础，根据<br>adj. 基本的，根本的，主要的，首要的 |
| basically | ˈbeɪsɪkli | adv. 基本上，根本上，本质上 |
| basis | ˈbeɪsɪs | n. 基础，根据，准则，基本原理，标准，基本成分 |

| 单词 | 国际音标 | 词性及中文意思 |
|---|---|---|
| battle | ˈbætl | n. 战斗，战役；交战 |
| battlefield | ˈbætlfiːld | n. 战场，战地 |
| battleground | ˈbæt(ə)lɡraʊnd | n. 战场 |
| bear | ber | adj. 卖空者的，价格下跌的<br>v. 负担，担任，忍受；支持，提供，持有 |
| bearing | ˈberɪŋ | n. 方位；举止；关系 |
| beat | biːt | v. 打，战胜，杀价，欺诈<br>n. 敲打，（警察等的）巡逻区域 |
| beating | ˈbiːtɪŋ | n. 殴打，施暴 |
| beauty | ˈbjuːti | n. 美；美丽；美人；美好的东西 |
| beg | beg | v. 乞讨，乞求，请求，恳求 |
| beginning | bɪˈɡɪnɪŋ | n. 开始，起点；根源 |
| begun | bɪˈɡʌn | v. 开始（begin 的过去分词） |
| behalf | bɪˈhæf | n. 方面，利益，赞同 |
| belief | bɪˈliːf | n. （对事实等的）相信；教义；信仰 |
| belong | bɪˈlɔːŋ | v. 属于，作为成员，应归入，适应 |
| belonging | bɪˈlɔːŋɪŋ | n. 附属品，附件；属性 |
| ben | ben | n. 内室，起居室 |
| bending | ˈbendɪŋ | v. 弯曲（bend 的现在分词） |
| beneficiary | ˌbenɪˈfɪʃieri | n. （信托、遗嘱、保险等的）受益人，（国际汇兑的）收款人<br>adj. 受益人的 |
| benefit | ˈbenɪfɪt | n. 利益，权益（利），效益，福利，补助费，救济金，抚恤金 |
| beyond | bɪˈjɑːnd | prep. 超出，超越 |
| bidder | ˈbɪdər | n. 竞投人，投标人，应价人，报价人 |
| bidding | ˈbɪdɪŋ | n. 应价，报价，竞投，投标 |

| 单词 | 国际音标 | 词性及中文意思 |
|---|---|---|
| bill | bɪl | n. 起诉书，诉状，申请，法案，颁布的成文法，票据，发（汇、支、钞）票，账单，证券，纸币，广告，张贴，通知单<br>v. 开账单，要求支付，登账，张贴宣布 |
| bing | bɪŋ | n. 堆；材料堆；微软公司的搜索引擎产品 |
| biochemical | ˌbaɪoʊˈkemɪkl | adj. 生物化学的 |
| birth | bɜːrθ | n. 出生，血统，起源 |
| blank | blæŋk | adj. 空白的，完全的<br>n. 空白表格 |
| blind | blaɪnd | adj. 失明的，盲目的，未填写的 |
| block | blɑːk | n. 街区，地段，大厦，集团，封锁，阻塞物<br>v. 冻结（资金等），封锁，阻塞 |
| blood | blʌd | n. 血统，血亲，家族 |
| bluff | blʌf | n. 哄骗，吓唬 |
| board | bɔːrd | n. 委员会，局，机构，（公司）董事会 |
| bogus | ˈboʊɡəs | adj. 伪造的，假的 |
| bombing | ˈbɑːmɪŋ | n. 轰炸，投弹 |
| bond | bɑːnd | n. 债券，契约，同盟，盟约，公债，保单，镣铐，监禁，约束<br>v. 充当保释人，抵押 |
| booty | ˈbuːti | n. 赃物，劫掠物，战利品 |
| border | ˈbɔːrdər | n. 边界（境），国界（境） |
| borne | bɔːrn | v. 忍受；负荷；结果实；生子女（bear 的过去分词） |
| boundary | ˈbaʊndri | n. 疆界，边界，（地产）分界线 |
| boycott | ˈbɔɪkɑːt | n/v. 联合抵制，拒买或拒经售，抵制外货，拒绝往来 |
| brawl | brɔːl | n. 吵架，打架 |
| breach | briːtʃ | n. 违反（法律、义务等），不履行，侵犯，不和<br>v. 破坏，违反 |

续表

| 单词 | 国际音标 | 词性及中文意思 |
|---|---|---|
| bribe | braɪb | n. 贿赂；行贿物<br>v. 行贿；给予或承诺给予贿赂 |
| briber | ˈbraɪbər | n. 行贿者 |
| bribery | ˈbraɪbəri | n. 行贿（罪），受贿（罪），贿赂 |
| broadcasting | ˈbrɔːdkæstɪŋ | n. （电台、电视台的）广播；播放<br>v. 广播（broadcast 的现在分词） |
| brokerage | ˈbroʊkərɪdʒ | n. 经纪业，经纪费，手续费，佣金，回扣 |
| brokering | ˈbroʊkərɪŋ | n. 中介<br>v. 作为中间人来安排（broker 的现在分词） |
| bully | ˈbʊli | n. 暴徒，恶霸，妓院，拉客者 |
| burglary | ˈbɜːrgləri | n. 夜闯民宅罪，入户行窃，入户盗窃罪 |
| buried | ˈberid | adj. 埋葬的；埋藏的 |
| burning | ˈbɜːrnɪŋ | adj. 燃烧的；强烈的；发热的 |
| cadet | kəˈdet | n. 警官生，警官实习生 |
| cadre | kædrɪ | n. 干部；基础结构；骨骼 |
| cajole | kəˈdʒoʊl | v. 诱供，哄骗，勾引 |
| calamity | kəˈlæməti | n. 不幸事件，灾难，祸患 |
| calculation | ˌkælkjuˈleɪʃn | n. 计算，考虑，推定 |
| cancellation | ˌkænsəˈleɪʃn | n. 退保注销，取消，删除，废除，撤销，作废 |
| capable | ˈkeɪpəbl | adj. 有能力的，有资格的，有才能的 |
| capital | ˈkæpɪtl | n. 资本，股本，首都，省会<br>adj. 资本的，基本的 |
| care | ker | n. 注意，照管，管理，监督 |
| carelessness | ˈkerləsnəs | n. 粗心，疏忽 |
| carriage | ˈkærɪdʒ | n. 运输；运费；举止 |
| carrier | ˈkæriər | n. 承运人，运输行业，搬运工人 |

| 单词 | 国际音标 | 词性及中文意思 |
|------|----------|----------------|
| cash | kæʃ | n. 现金，货币，金钱<br>v. 兑现，付现款 |
| cashier | kæˈʃɪr | n. 出纳员，司库<br>v. 撤职，开除，解雇，拒用，处理，抛弃 |
| casino | kəˈsiːnoʊ | n. 赌场；娱乐场 |
| casualty | ˈkæʒuəlti | n.（严重伤亡）事故，事故伤亡人员（或损害物品），受害者，横祸 |
| category | ˈkætəgɔːri | n. 类型 |
| cause | kɔːz | n. 成因，案件，诉讼，事业，目标<br>v. 造成，引起，导致 |
| certain | ˈsɜːrtn | adj. 确凿的，无疑的，可靠的 |
| certificate | sərˈtɪfɪkət | n. 证书，执照，证券，股票，单据，凭单 |
| certification | ˌsɜːrtɪfɪˈkeɪʃn | n. 保证，证明，鉴定；证书 |
| certify | ˈsɜːrtɪfaɪ | v.（用书面形式）证明，[美] 担保付款 |
| channel | ˈtʃænl | n. 方法，途径，航道，海峡，调拨（基金） |
| chaotic | keɪˈɑːtɪk | adj. 混乱的，无秩序的 |
| chapter | ˈtʃæptər | n.（社团等的）分部；分支机构；分会；（法律、法规的）章、节 |
| characteristic | ˌkærəktəˈrɪstɪk | n. 特性（征）<br>adj. 特有的，典型的 |
| charge | tʃɑːrdʒ | n. 负担，起诉，指控，控告，委托，费用，指令，负责<br>v. 控告，指控，索价，指示，委托，负责，收费 |
| chase | tʃeɪs | n. 追逐；追赶；追击 |
| cheat | tʃiːt | n. 欺骗（行为），骗子<br>v. 欺骗，诈取，逃脱 |

续表

| 单词 | 国际音标 | 词性及中文意思 |
|------|---------|----------------|
| check | tʃek | n. ［美］支票，账单，检查，制止<br>v. 核对，检查，制止 |
| chemical | ˈkemɪkl | adj. 化学的<br>n. 化学制品，化学药品 |
| China | ˈtʃaɪnə | n. 中国 |
| chinas | ˈtʃaɪnəz | adj. 中国的 |
| chinese | ˌtʃaɪˈniːz | adj. 中国的<br>n. 中国人 |
| chlorof orm | ˈklɔːrəfɔːrm | n. 麻醉剂，迷药 |
| circumstance | ˈsɜːrkəmstænsiz | n. 环境，条件，情况 |
| circumstances | ˈsɜːrkəmstæns | n. 情况（circumstance 的复数）；环境；情形 |
| citizen | ˈsɪtɪzn | n. 公民；市民；老百姓 |
| citizens | ˈsɪtəznz | n. 市民；公民（citizen 的复数） |
| city | ˈsɪti | n. 城市，都市，市，全市居民 |
| civil | ˈsɪvl | adj. 公民的，民事的，国内的，民法的 |
| civilian | səˈvɪliən | n. 公民，文职人员，民法<br>adj. 公民的，民政的 |
| claim | kleɪm | n. 主张，索赔，认领，索取，诉讼<br>v. 要求，主张，索取，声称，认领 |
| claimed | kleɪmd | v. 声称；宣称；断言（claim 的过去式） |
| claims | kleɪmz | n. 要求，请求权；索赔（claim 的复数）；债权<br>v. 要求；主张（claim 的第三人称单数） |
| clamor | ˈklæmər | n. 喧闹，叫嚷；大声的要求 |
| clap | klæp | vi. 鼓掌，拍手 |
| classified | ˈklæsɪfaɪd | adj. （信息）归入密级的，保密的 |
| clause | klɔːz | n. 条款，项目，款项，诉状<br>v. 附加条款的 |

| 单词 | 国际音标 | 词性及中文意思 |
|------|----------|----------------|
| clear | klɪr | v. 澄清，宣布无罪，付清，清理，驱逐，交换（票据），卸货<br>adj. 无罪的，清白的，无疑的，确实的 |
| clearly | ˈklɪrli | adv. 清晰地；明显地 |
| client | ˈklaɪənt | n. 当事人，（诉讼）委托人，顾客 |
| clients | ˈklaɪənts | n. 客户端；顾客；救济对象；应受账款；委托方（client 的复数） |
| close | kloʊz | n. 结束，诉讼的终结，结案<br>v. 终结，结束，结案<br>adj. 严格的，密切的，秘密的 |
| clues | kluːz | n. 线索（clue 的复数）<br>v. 暗示；提示（clue 的第三人称单数） |
| cocaine | koʊˈkeɪn | n. 可卡因 |
| codes | koʊdz | n. 道德准则；法典（code 的复数） |
| coerced | koʊˈɜːrsd | v. 强制；强迫；胁迫；压制（coerce 的过去式和过去分词） |
| coerces | kəʊˈɜːrsɪz | vt. 强制；迫使（coerce 的第三人称单数） |
| coercion | koʊˈɜːrʒn | n. 胁迫，强迫（制），压制（迫），威逼 |
| collaborate | kəˈlæbəreɪt | v. 合作，协作（调），勾结，通（资）敌 |
| collect | kəˈlekt | v. 收集，搜集，采集，收（租、税、账等），领取（信件等），聚集，收集募捐（款）<br>adj./adv. 由收到者付款的（地） |
| collected | kəˈlektɪd | adj. 收集成的；（作品等）成集的 |
| collection | kəˈlekʃn | n. 收款（账），（票据的）托收，代收，收入款项，募捐，捐款，收藏品（物），征收，收集，采集 |
| collective | kəˈlektɪv | adj. 总的，集体的，共同的<br>n. 集体企业，团体，集团，集体 |
| collectively | kəˈlektɪvli | adv. 全体地；共同地 |

续表

| 单词 | 国际音标 | 词性及中文意思 |
|---|---|---|
| collectives | kəˈlektɪvz | n. 集团；集合体；集合名词（collective 的复数） |
| collects | kəˈlekts | v. 收集，收藏；使聚集（collect 的第三人称单数） |
| collegial | kəˈliːdʒɪəl | n. 合议庭的 |
| collides | kəˈlaɪdz | vi. 碰撞；抵触，冲突 |
| colluded | kəˈluːdɪd | vi. 勾结；串通；共谋（collud 的过去式） |
| colludes | kəˈluːdz | vi. 勾结；串通；共谋（collud 的第三人称单数） |
| colluding | kəˈluːdɪŋ | vi. 勾结；串通；共谋（collud 的现在分词） |
| collusion | kəˈluːʒn | n. 共谋欺诈，勾结，串通 |
| combat | ˈkɑːmbæt | n. 战斗；争论 |
| combating | ˈkɑːmbætɪŋ | vi. 战斗；搏斗；反对（combat 的现在分词） |
| combined | kəmˈbaɪnd | adj. 联合的，合并的，集团的 |
| combustible | kəmˈbʌstəbl | adj. 易燃的，燃烧性的<br>n. 易燃物 |
| comes | kʌmz | v. 来自；从…来（come 的第三人称单数） |
| coming | ˈkʌmɪŋ | adj. 接着的；即将到来的<br>n. 来到；到达<br>v. 来（come 的现在分词） |
| commander | kəˈmændər | n. 司令官，指挥官 |
| commanders | kəˈmændərts | n. 指挥官（commander 的复数） |
| commencing | kəˈmensɪŋ | v. 开始，着手（commence 的现在分词） |
| commensurate | kəˈmenʃərət | adj.（在时间和空间上）相等的 |
| commercial | kəˈmɜːrʃl | adj. 商业的；营利的；靠广告收入的<br>n. 商业广告 |
| commission | kəˈmɪʃn | n. 委任，委托（书），授权，委员会，署，佣金，（犯罪）行为，作为<br>v. 委任，委托，授权 |
| commissions | kəˈmɪʃnz | n. [会计] 佣金，[会计] 手续费；现金奖励情况（commission 的复数） |

| 单词 | 国际音标 | 词性及中文意思 |
|------|---------|---------------|
| commit | kəˈmɪt | v. 犯（罪），做（错事、坏事），授权，委托，承担，监禁，判处，押交 |
| commits | kəˈmɪts | v. 犯（罪），做（错事、坏事），授权，委托，承担，监禁，判处，押交（commit 的第三人称单数） |
| committed | kəˈmɪtɪd | v. 犯（罪），做（错事、坏事），授权，委托，承担，监禁，判处，押交（commit 的过去式、过去分词） |
| committee | kəˈmɪti | n. 委员会，促进会，监护人，受托人 |
| committing | kəˈmɪtɪŋ | v. 犯（错误）；[计] 提交；答应负责（commit 的现在分词） |
| commodities | kəˈmɑdətis | n. 商品（commodity 的复数）；日用品；商品期货 |
| commodity | kəˈmɑːdəti | n. 商品，货物；日用品 |
| communication | kəˌmjuːnɪˈkeɪʃn | n. 通信（讯），传达，交换（流、往、通），交通工具，（疾病的）传染 |
| community | kəˈmjuːnəti | n. 社区，居民区，聚居区，镇，乡，公社，团体，（政治）共同体，同一社区居民，公众，共有，共同性，一致 |
| commutation | ˌkɑːmjuˈteɪʃn | n. 减刑；交换；经常来往；代偿 |
| commute | kəˈmjuːt | v. 兑换，补偿，减刑，改变付款方式，经常来往于（某两地间） |
| commuted | kəˈmjuːtɪd | v. 兑换，补偿，减刑，改变付款方式，经常来往于（某两地间）（commute 的过去式和过去分词） |
| companies | ˈkʌmpəniz | n. 公司，企业；伙伴（company 的复数形式）；公司财产<br>v. 陪伴，伴随（company 的第三人称单数） |
| company | ˈkʌmpəni | n. 公司，商行，交往，交际<br>vt. 陪伴 |
| comparison | kəmˈpærɪsn | n. 比较，对比 |
| compelled | kəmˈpeld | adj. 被强制的 |

| 单词 | 国际音标 | 词性及中文意思 |
|---|---|---|
| compensated | ˈkɒmpənˌset | v. 赔偿，补偿，（服务等的）酬报 |
| compensation | ˌkɑːmpenˈseɪʃn | n. 补偿，赔偿（物、金），工资，报酬，（债等的）抵消 |
| compensatory | kəmˈpensətɔːri | adj. 赔偿的，补偿的，报酬的 |
| competent | ˈkɑːmpɪtənt | adj. 有能力的，有法定资格的，主管的，能胜任的 |
| complaint | kəmˈpleɪnt | n. 民事诉状，刑事自诉状，起诉，申诉 |
| completed | kəmˈpliːtɪd | v. 完成；填写（表格）；（使）完整（complete 的过去式及过去分词）<br>adj. 完成的；初次同房的；完整的 |
| completely | kəmˈpliːtli | adv. 完全地，彻底地；完整地 |
| composed | kəmˈpoʊzd | adj. 镇静的；沉着的<br>v. 组成；作曲（compose 的过去分词） |
| compromising | ˈkɑːmprəmaɪzɪŋ | adj. 有失体面的；不宜泄露的；使处于难堪境地的<br>v. 妥协，让步；损害（名声）；违背（原则）；达不到（标准）；使陷入危险（compromise 的现在分词） |
| compulsory | kəmˈpʌlsəri | adj. 强制的，强迫的，义务的 |
| computer | kəmˈpjuːtər | n. 计算机；电脑；电子计算机 |
| conceal | kənˈsiːl | v. 隐瞒，隐匿，保守秘密 |
| concealing | kənˈsiːlɪŋ | v. 隐藏（conceal 的现在分词）；掩饰<br>n. 隐藏；掩饰<br>adj. 隐藏的；遮掩的 |
| concealment | kənˈsiːlmənt | n. 隐匿，隐蔽处（或物） |
| conceals | kənˈsiːls | vt. 隐藏；隐瞒（conceal 的第三人称单数） |
| concentrating | ˈkɑːnsenˌtretɪŋ | n. 浓缩；精选<br>v. 浓缩（concentrate 的现在分词）；专心 |
| concerned | kənˈsɜːrnd | adj. 担心的，烦恼的，忧虑的 |
| concerning | kənˈsɜːrnɪŋ | prep. 关于；就…而言<br>v. 涉及；使关心（concern 的现在分词）；忧虑 |

| 单词 | 国际音标 | 词性及中文意思 |
|---|---|---|
| concrete | ˈkɑːnkriːt | adj. 实在的，具体的；有形的 |
| concurrently | kənˈkɜːrəntli | adv. 同时发生地，并存地 |
| conditions | kənˈdɪʃnz | n.（生活或工作等的）条件；（影响某事发生的）物质环境；（天气、地面等的）情况<br>n. 疾病；条款；先决条件（condition 的复数）<br>v. 制约；（使）接受；（使）达到所要求的状态 |
| conduct | ˈkɑːndʌkt | n. 行为，品格，操守，行径，指导，引导，经营（权），处理（方式），运作，举办<br>v. 实施，处理，引导，指导，经营，进行 |
| conducted | kənˈdʌktɪd | v. 管理（conduct 的过去分词）；引导；指挥 |
| conducting | kənˈdʌktɪŋ | v. 指挥；行为；传导（conduct 的现在分词）；指导<br>n. 指挥；执行；传导 |
| confess | kənˈfes | v. 自白，供认，坦白，承认，忏悔 |
| confession | kənˈfeʃn | n. 供认，供状，（坦白）书，声明，自白 |
| confidence | ˈkɑːnfɪdəns | n. 保密（关系），信任（心、赖），自（确、置）信，可信度，大胆，狂妄 |
| confiscation | ˌkɑːnfɪˈskeɪʃn | n. 没收，查抄，征用，充公 |
| conform | kənˈfɔːrm | v. 使一致，符合，遵照，遵奉 |
| congress | ˈkɑːŋɡrəs | n.（正式的）代表大会，大会，[美] 国会，议会，委员会，（国会或议会的）会议（期），聚会，社交 |
| connivance | kəˈnaɪvəns | n. 纵容，默许 |
| connive | kəˈnaɪvəns | v. 默许，纵容，共谋，取得默契 |
| conscription | kənˈskrɪpʃn | n. 征兵；征兵制度；征用 |
| consent | kənˈsent | n. 同意，批准，赞同，协议，承诺<br>v. 同意，批准，赞同 |
| consequence | ˈkɑːnsɪkwens | n. 后果，结果，推断，论断，重要性 |
| considerably | kənˈsɪdərəbli | adv. 相当地；非常 |

| 单词 | 国际音标 | 词性及中文意思 |
| --- | --- | --- |
| consideration | kənˌsɪdəˈreɪʃn | n. 考虑，思考，审议，报酬，补偿，对价，代价，约因，总值，体谅，关心，尊敬 |
| consolidated | kənˈsɑːlɪdeɪtɪd | adj. 巩固的，合并处理的，综合的，统一债券 |
| conspire | kənˈspaɪər | v. 共谋，串谋，密谋策划，图谋，协力促成 |
| constitute | ˈkɑːnstɪtuːt | v. 组成，构成，任命，选定，制定（法律等），设立，使（文件等）通过法律手续 |
| constitution | ˌkɑːnstɪˈtuːʃn | n. 宪法（制、章），章程，法规，构造，组成（方式），设立，建立，制定，任命，政体，体质，性格，素质 |
| construction | kənˈstrʌkʃn | n. 解释（尤指制定法的解释），解释过程，法律释义，建筑（物），建设，结构，构成，意义 |
| consummate | ˈkɑːnsəˌmeɪt | v. 完成，使完善，完婚<br>adj. 完整无缺的，圆满的，极为精通的，尽善尽美的 |
| contact | ˈkɑːntækt | n. 接触，联系<br>vt. 使接触 |
| contagious | kənˈteɪdʒəs | adj. （病）有传染性的 |
| contain | kənˈteɪn | v. 包括（含），等于，相当于，控（遏、抑）制 |
| container | kənˈteɪnər | n. 集装箱，货柜，容器 |
| contaminated | kənˈtæmɪneɪtɪd | adj. 受污染的，弄脏的<br>v. 污染；玷污，毒害（contaminate 的过去式和过去分词） |
| contents | ˈkɑːntents | n. 内容；目录；要旨（content 的复数）<br>v. 使满意（content 的第三人称单数） |
| continue | kənˈtɪnjuː | v. 继续，延续（伸、长），停留，使（诉讼）延期 |
| continuous | kənˈtɪnjuəs | adj. 继续的，连续的，延长的 |
| contraband | ˈkɑːntrəbænd | n. 走私，走私货；战时禁运品（等于 contraband of war）<br>adj. 禁运的；非法买卖的 |

| 单词 | 国际音标 | 词性及中文意思 |
|------|----------|----------------|
| contract | ˈkɑːntrækt | n. 合同，契约，定约规定，承包，承办<br>v. 签约，立约，承办（建、包、揽），订婚，许配 |
| contravene | ˌkɑːntrəˈviːn | v，触犯（法律等），违反，否认，反驳，破坏，侵犯 |
| contribution | ˌkɑːntrɪˈbjuːʃn | n. 贡献，捐款（献），补助品，分摊权，分担金额，（侵权人之间的）分担赔偿份额 |
| control | kənˈtroʊl | n/v. 支配，控制（权），掌管，抑制，管制（控、辖），监督，调节 |
| controller | kənˈtroʊlər | n. 会计主任，总会计师，主计长，审计长（师），主管，检验员，监察员，检查员，调度员，控制人 |
| convenience | kənˈviːniəns | n. 便利，方便，适当的机会，便利设施 |
| convert | kənˈvɜːrt | vt. 使转变；转换……；使……改变信仰<br>vi. 转变，变换；皈依；改变信仰<br>n. 皈依者；改变宗教信仰者 |
| convict | ˈkɑnvɪkt | n. （服刑中的）囚犯，已决犯<br>v. 将某人定罪，证明或宣判有罪 |
| copy | ˈkɑːpi | n. 文本，副本，抄本，制成本，复制件，范本<br>v. 复写（印、制），誊抄，模仿，临摹，抄袭 |
| copyright | ˈkɑːpiraɪt | n. 版权，著作权<br>adj. 具有版权的，著作权的<br>v. 为（书）取得版权 |
| copyrighter | ˈkɑːpiraɪtər | n. 版权所有人 |
| core | kɔːr | n. 核心；要点；果心<br>vt. 挖...的核 |
| corporal | ˈkɔːrpərəl | adj. 肉体的，身体的，有形的（指动产），有体的，具体的，物质的<br>n. （军队中的）最低级军士，下士 |
| corporation | ˌkɔːrpəˈreɪʃn | n. 公司法人，社团，公司，企业，[美] 股份有限公司，公会，协会 |

| 单词 | 国际音标 | 词性及中文意思 |
| --- | --- | --- |
| corpse | kɔːrps | n. 尸体 |
| correction | kəˈrekʃn | n. 改正，修改，（对罪犯的）矫正，纠正机关，责备，惩罚，制止，（证券等交易中价格上涨后的）回落 |
| corrective | kəˈrektɪv | adj. 矫（改、纠、校）正的，惩治的，抑制的，补救的，中和的 |
| corresponding | ˌkɔːrəˈspɑːndɪŋ | adj. 相应的，对应的，一致的，通讯的，符合的 |
| corrosive | kəˈroʊsɪv | adj. 腐蚀性的，侵蚀的<br>n. 腐蚀物（品） |
| corruption | kəˈrʌpʃn | n. 贪污，贿赂 |
| cosmetics | kɑːzˈmetɪks | n. [化工] 化妆品（cosmetic 的复数）；装饰品<br>v. 用化妆品打扮（cosmetic 的第三人称单数） |
| costume | ˈkɑːstuːm | n. 服装，服装式样 |
| council | ˈkaʊnsl | n. 政务会，市政会，理事会，公会，委员会，商议会，（地方）议会，地方自治会，会议，顾问班子，立法班子，议事机构，计议，协商，商讨，讨论，董事会，校董会 |
| counter | ˈkaʊntər | n. 专业辩护人，计算器（员、人），筹码，伪币（指硬币），柜台，反对（面、物），本钱，<br>adj. 相反的，反对的，敌对的，收回成命的，副的<br>prep. 反对，反，逆，防，对应 |
| counterfeit | ˈkaʊntərfɪt | adj. 伪（仿）造的，假冒的，冒牌的，虚假的<br>n. 伪币，假（仿）冒品，冒牌货，伪造品<br>v. 伪造（货币、文件等），仿造 |
| country | ˈkʌntri | n. 国家，祖国，本国，乡邻陪审团，地方（区），家（故）乡，农村<br>adj. 祖国的，家乡的，地方的，乡村的，故乡的 |
| county | ˈkaʊnti | n. [英] 郡，[美] 县 |
| coupon | ˈkuːpɑːn | n. 息票；赠券；联票；配给券 |

续表

| 单词 | 国际音标 | 词性及中文意思 |
|------|----------|----------------|
| course | kɔːrs | n. 航线，路线，路（进、过）程，程序，行进方向，路线，河流，行动方针，方法，行为，做法，课程，教程，学科，科目 |
| court | kɔːrt | n. 法院（庭），审判庭，法官，[美] 立法机关，法院建筑物，议会，宫廷，朝廷，（公司等的）委员会，董事会，理事会，讨好 |
| courtroom | ˈkɔːrtrʊm | n. 法庭，审判室 |
| cover | ˈkʌvər | v. 担保，给（货物等）保险，投保，含，包括，覆盖，隐匿，掩盖（饰），包庇，购进，供给，补进，足数，足以抵补，补（抵）偿，负担支付（开支等），弥补（损失等），购进，补进，适合于<br>n. 担保，保证金，购买替代物权，覆盖物，庇护，（信函等）封袋，包（装）皮，封皮，隐匿（处），（支票的）保证金，覆盖 |
| crack | kræk | v. 兑开（钞票），破（案），解决，辨认（暗号），裂开，打破，砸开，打、击，揭开（秘密），解开（难题），宣布（价格），破门而入（出），闯进，毁损，撞毁<br>n. 快克（也称冰毒，化学名称甲基苯丙胺） |
| crash | kræʃ | n. 冲（碰）撞，毁坏，（飞机等的）坠毁，失事，（行情）大跌，（市场）崩溃，破产，倒闭，失败，垮台 |
| create | kriˈeɪt | v. 创立（制、造、作），设（建）立，设定，产生，引起，造成，封授 |
| creation | kriˈeɪʃn | n. 创造（作、制），产生，形成，设置，作品，创造物，任命，产生，授予 |
| credit | ˈkredɪt | n. 信用，信用贷款，赊销，贷（项、方、款、入），贷方金额，信用证，称赞，荣誉，缓付款的期限，（银行）存款，债权，（税收等的）抵免，减除<br>v. 相信，抵免（税等），归于，记入贷方 |

续表

| 单词 | 国际音标 | 词性及中文意思 |
|---|---|---|
| creditor | ˈkredɪtər | n. 债权人，贷方，债主，贷项 |
| cremains | krəˈmeɪnz | n. 骨灰 |
| crime | kraɪm | n. 犯罪，罪行<br>v. ［英］指控违反军纪，宣告违反军纪罪 |
| criminal | ˈkrɪmɪnl | n. 罪犯，犯人<br>adj. 刑事的，罪犯的，犯罪的，非法的 |
| criminally | ˈkrɪmɪnəli | adv. 刑法上地，与犯罪有关地 |
| critically | ˈkrɪtɪkli | adv. 精密地；危急地；严重地；批评性地；很大程度上；极为重要地 |
| criticizer | krɪtəˈsaɪzr | n. 批评者 |
| crop | krɑːp | n. 农作物，庄稼，收成（获），一批（群），大量 |
| cross | krɔːs | n. 十字（形、物、装饰、花押、架）<br>v. 交叉，相交，横越，翻越，打叉勾销，杂交<br>adj. 交叉的，相互的，交替的，横斜的，反对的 |
| crowd | kraʊd | n. 人群，（在场）交易伙伴 |
| crucial | ˈkruːʃl | adj. 决定性的，紧要关头的，严酷的，困难的 |
| cruel | ˈkruːəl | adj. 残忍（酷）的，令人痛苦的 |
| cruelly | ˈkruːəli | adv. 残酷地；非常 |
| cult | kʌlt | n. 狂热；异教团体；宗教信仰<br>adj. 受特定群体欢迎的 |
| cultivated | ˈkʌltɪveɪtɪd | adj. 耕种的，培育的 |
| culture | ˈkʌltʃər | n. 文化，精神文明，教养，栽培，耕作，养殖 |
| cure | kjʊr | v./n. 矫正，消除（法律瑕疵），纠正（审判过程之错误等） |
| currency | ˈkɜːrənsi | n. 货币；通货 |
| custody | ˈkʌstədi | n. （对未成年人的）监护权，监管（督、视），保管（护），管理，拘留（押），羁押，扶养权 |

| 单词 | 国际音标 | 词性及中文意思 |
|------|----------|----------------|
| custom | ˈkʌstəm | n. 风俗, 习惯, 惯例（法）, 常规, 顾客, 主顾, (pl.) 海关, (pl.) 关税, 进口税<br>adj. 依习惯的, 惯有的, 惯例法的, 习惯法的 |
| damage | ˈdæmɪdʒ | n. 损害（失、坏）<br>v. （受到）损坏, （被）损害<br>adj. （财产或人身）遭到损害的, 与损害相关的（单数和复数形式均可） |
| danger | ˈdeɪndʒər | n. 危险, 风险, 危险原因, 威胁 |
| dangerous | ˈdeɪndʒərəs | adj. （情况、场景）危险的, 不安全的, 有害的, 容易导致严重身体伤害的 |
| data | ˈdeɪtə | n. 资料, 数据, 作为论据的事实 |
| deaf-mute | ˌdef ˈmjuːt | n. 聋哑者 |
| deal | diːl | n. 交易, 买卖, 互利协议, [美] 密约, 秘密妥协, 待遇, 特定政策, 实行特定政策的时期, 局面, 情况<br>v. 处理, 待遇, 分配, 应付, 论述, 讨论, 对付, 打交道, 经营, 交易, 做买卖, 卖, 出售, [俚] 卖毒品 |
| dealt | delt | v. 处理（deal 的过去式和过去分词） |
| death | deθ | n. 死亡, 死亡原因, 剥夺政治权利, 灭亡, 毁灭, 终止, 结束, 杀死, 谋杀 |
| debt | det | n. 债（务）, 欠款, 借款, 非金钱债务, 罪（过）, （普通法上的）偿债令 |
| deceive | dɪˈsiːv | v. 欺骗 |
| deception | dɪˈsepʃn | n. 诈骗 |
| deceptively | dɪˈseptɪvli | adv. 迷惑地 |
| decision | dɪˈsɪʒn | n. 决定（议、断）, 判决, 裁定（决）, 坚定, 结果 |
| declaration | ˌdekləˈreɪʃn | n. 宣布（告、称、言）, 公布, 申报, 声明, 诉状, （证人的）陈述, 供述, （纳税的）申报单, （缔约当事人的）意思表示, 宣告式判决, 事实陈述书 |
| declare | dɪˈkler | v. 宣言（布、告、称）, 声明, 断言, 供述, 陈述, 申报 |

| 单词 | 国际音标 | 词性及中文意思 |
|------|---------|---------------|
| decree | dɪˈkriː | n. 判决，裁判（决、定），法（政、命）令，布告<br>v. 判（裁）决，颁布，规定 |
| deem | diːm | v. 视为，认定，相信 |
| defame | dɪˈfeɪm | v. 侵犯名誉，毁誉 |
| default | dɪˈfɔːlt | n./v. 不履行义务（尤指偿还债务之义务），不作为 |
| defect | ˈdiːfekt | n. 瑕疵（尤指产品瑕疵），缺陷，缺乏，过失<br>v. 开小差，逃跑，背叛，变节 |
| defend | dɪˈfend | v. 作辩护律师，辩护，答辩，防御，保卫 |
| defendants | dɪˈfendənts | n. 被告代理人 |
| defender | dɪˈfendər | n. 辩护人，保护人，[苏] 被告 |
| defense | dɪˈfens | n. 防卫，防护；防御措施；防守 |
| defensive | dɪˈfensɪv | adj. 防御性的，保卫的，消费者必需的，受市场变化影响小的 |
| defiance | dɪˈfaɪəns | n. 挑衅，藐视，违抗 |
| defiling | dɪˈfaɪlɪŋ | v. 亵渎；弄脏；污损（defile 的现在分词） |
| deformity | dɪˈfɔːrməti | n. 残废，智力缺陷，畸形 |
| defraud | dɪˈfrɔːd | v. 欺诈 |
| degree | dɪˈgriː | n. 等级，程度，亲等，（罪行的）轻重，学位，地位，身份，阶层，学位 |
| delay | dɪˈleɪ | n. 耽搁，迟滞 |
| delegated | ˈdelɪgeɪtɪd | adj. 委托的，委任的，授权的 |
| delete | dɪˈliːt | vt. 删除 |
| deliberately | dɪˈlɪbərətli | adv. 慎重地；谨慎地 |
| deliver | dɪˈlɪvər | v. 释放，解脱（救），移交，引渡，交付（货），放弃，投递，传送，提供，宣布，供给，发表，陈述，拉（票），给予（打击），运载，排放 |

| 单词 | 国际音标 | 词性及中文意思 |
|------|---------|----------------|
| demand | dɪˈmænd | n. 请（需）求，要求支付（债务等），征收<br>v. （法院）传唤，请（要）求，查问，追究，需要 |
| democratic | ˌdeməˈkrætɪk | adj. 民主的，民主政体的，平民的，［美］民主党的（大写） |
| demonstrate | ˈdemənstreɪt | n. 表演，表明，示威者<br>v. 示范，示威 |
| demonstration | ˌdemənˈstreɪʃn | n. 示威（游行、集会），显示，实证，确证，（商品的）宣传，示范 |
| denigration | ˌdenɪˈgreɪʃn | vt. <正>诋毁，诽谤 |
| department | dɪˈpɑːrtmənt | n. 部门，部 |
| departure | dɪˈpɑːtʃə(r) | n. 辩护偏离事实，前后辩护相互背离，离境，违背，背离，变更，出发，开始，偏差 |
| dependent | dɪˈpendənt | n. 受赡（扶、抚）养者，家属，依附者，从属物<br>adj. 受赡（扶、抚）养的，从属的，依附的 |
| deportation | ˌdiːpɔːrˈteɪʃn | n. 驱逐出境（尤指驱逐外国人） |
| deposit | dɪˈpɑːzɪt | n. （储蓄）存款，存放，寄存，委托款项，保证（释）金，定金，公积金，寄存物（处），仓库，［罗］无偿保管货物的寄托<br>v. 交付，存放，寄存，储蓄，付（保证金、保释金等） |
| deprivation | ˌdeprɪˈveɪʃn | n. 剥夺（被告的产权），丧失，宗教上的剥夺 |
| deprive | dɪˈpraɪv | v. 剥夺，夺去，使丧失，免职（尤指圣职） |
| deputy | ˈdepjuti | n. 代表，代理人，（众议院的）议员<br>adj. 代理的，副的，助理的 |
| dereliction | ˌderəˈlɪkʃn | n. 抛（遗、废、放）弃，玩忽职守，不负责任，弃产，海（河）边新生地 |
| describe | dɪˈskraɪb | v. 说明，叙述，解释，提出，阐述，说明土地尺寸大小 |

| 单词 | 国际音标 | 词性及中文意思 |
|---|---|---|
| desecrate | ˈdesɪkreɪt | v. 亵渎 |
| desert | dɪˈzɜːrt | n. 功过，应得赏罚的事实（行为、品质），（pl.）应得的赏罚<br>v. 遗（抛）弃，离异，擅离（职守等） |
| desertion | dɪˈzɜːrʃn | n. 遗弃配偶，抛弃 |
| design | dɪˈzaɪn | n. 设计，计谋，企图，外观设计 |
| designated | ˈdezɪgneɪtɪd | adj. 委任的，选派的，指定的，具体写明的 |
| despite | dɪˈspaɪt | prep. 不管，尽管 |
| destroy | dɪˈstrɔɪ | v. 破（毁）坏，摧毁，毁灭，打破（计划，希望），消（歼）灭，减损，使无效 |
| destruction | dɪˈstrʌkʃn | n. 破坏（物、原因），毁坏，消灭 |
| destructive | dɪˈstrʌktɪv | adj. 破坏的 |
| detain | dɪˈteɪn | n. 拘留，扣押，阻止，耽误<br>v. 扣押，扣留，羁押，拘留，阻止，耽误 |
| detaining | dɪˈteɪnɪŋ | vt. 拘留；留住；耽搁（detain 的现在分词） |
| detect | dɪˈtekt | v. 侦查，当场发现，查明，觉察 |
| detection | dɪˈtekʃn | n. 侦查（破），发现（觉），探测 |
| detention | dɪˈtenʃn | n. 拘留，扣押（留），羁押，拘役，监禁，禁闭，阻止，滞留 |
| determined | dɪˈtɜːrmɪnd | adj. 坚定的，坚决的，决意的 |
| device | dɪˈvaɪs | n. 手段，设计，计策（划），策略，方法（式），意志，装置，设备，器具，机件，商标图案，图样 |
| dictatorship | ˌdɪkˈteɪtərʃɪp | n. 专政，独裁（国家、政府），独裁者的职位 |
| dike | daɪk | n. 堤防，堤坝；障碍物；（英）壕沟 |
| diplomatic | ˌdɪpləˈmætɪk | adj. 外交的，外交上的，文献上的 |
| direct | dəˈrekt | adj. 直接的，直系的<br>v. 指示，指导，给予，对某人陈述<br>n. 直诘 |

| 单词 | 国际音标 | 词性及中文意思 |
|------|----------|----------------|
| directing | dəˈrektɪŋ | v. 导演（direct 的现在分词）；指引<br>adj. 指导的；指向的 |
| directly | dəˈrektli | adv. 直接地；立即；马上；坦率地；正好地 |
| director | dəˈrektər | n. 董（理）事，主任，总裁（监），处（局、署）长，指导者，（pl.）[公] 董事会 |
| disability | ˌdɪsəˈbɪləti | n. （法律上的）无行为能力，无资格，病残，残废，劳动能力丧失，无能 |
| disable | dɪsˈeɪbl | v. 使丧失能力，使无资格，使伤残 |
| disablement | dɪsˈeɪblmənt | n. 残废，（法律上）无行为能力 |
| disaster | dɪˈzæstər | n. 灾难，大祸，祸患，大不幸，灾害 |
| discharge | dɪsˈtʃɑːrdʒ | n. 撤销（法院命令），开除，解雇（除、职），（士兵被）勒令退役，免除，释放，履行，清偿，完成（执行）任务，证明书，卸货（载），发射<br>v. 撤销，释放，解雇（除、职），免除，履行，清偿，卸（货），发射 |
| discipline | ˈdɪsəplɪn | n. 纪律，行为准则，规章制度，风纪，惩（处）罚，教规，戒律，训练<br>v. 训练（导），惩（处）罚，约束，控制 |
| disclose | dɪsˈkloʊz | v. 使显露，揭发，批（揭、透、泄）露，公开（秘密） |
| discontinuation | ˌdɪskənˌtɪnjuˈeɪʃən | n. 停止，废止，中止 |
| discovered | dɪˈskʌvɜːrd | adj. 已经发现的 |
| discriminate | dɪˈskrɪmɪneɪt | v. 区别，差别对待，歧视 |
| disease | dɪˈziːz | n. 疾病，伤害，（社会制度等）弊病 |
| disfigurement | dɪsˈfɪgəmənt | n. 毁外形，毁容，破相 |
| disguise | dɪsˈgaɪz | n. &v. 假装（佯、伪）装，托辞 |
| dismiss | dɪsˈmɪs | v. 解（遣）散，打发，解雇，免职，开（消）除，驳回，不考虑 |

| 单词 | 国际音标 | 词性及中文意思 |
|---|---|---|
| disorder | dɪsˈɔːrdər | n. 骚（动、紊）乱，失常，不正当行为<br>v. 使紊乱，使失常 |
| dispose | dɪˈspoʊz | v. 安排，处理（置、分），支配，转让，让与，卖掉，解决，除掉，干掉 |
| disrupt | dɪsˈrʌpt | vt. 使混乱，扰乱 |
| disseminate | dɪˈsemɪneɪt | v. 散布，传播，集装箱分散卸货 |
| distortion | dɪˈstɔːrʃn | n. 畸变，失真，歪曲，曲解 |
| distribute | dɪˈstrɪbjuːt | v. 分配（发、布），散布，区分，分类，在特定的市场销售商品，把货物运送至个别顾客 |
| disturb | dɪˈstɜːrb | v. 滋扰，扰乱，使骚动，妨碍妨害，打断 |
| divert | daɪˈvɜːrt | v. 挪用（资金等），对被告进行审前疏诉处理 |
| divide | dɪˈvaɪd | v. 划分，分配（担、享、开），分歧（意见），隔离 |
| divulge | daɪˈvʌldʒ | vt. 泄露；暴露 |
| document | ˈdɑːkjumənt | n. 公文，证（文）件，单据（证），凭证，记录，资料，证券（书），诉讼案卷，文据（献），（证据法中的）书证<br>v. 提供文件（或证书），用文件（或证书）证明，为船舶提供船证后附装运单据于汇票 |
| domestic | dəˈmestɪk | adj. 本国的，国内的，家庭的，国产的，本州的<br>n. 家庭仆人 |
| dominate | ˈdɑːmɪneɪt | n. （古罗马的）君主制时期<br>v. 支配，统治，控制，施加决定性影响，处于支配地位 |
| donate | ˈdoʊneɪt | vt. 捐赠；捐献 |
| draft | dræft | n. 汇票，法案，草案，付款通知，设计，图样，草图，征兵，征集，挑选，选拔，船舶吃水<br>v. 起草，征召入伍，挑选，迫使做候选人 |
| drug | drʌg | n. 毒品，麻醉剂（如鸦片、吗啡等），制药公司股票或证券等，滞销品 |

| 单词 | 国际音标 | 词性及中文意思 |
|---|---|---|
| dud | dʌd | n. 个人所有物，伪造物<br>adj. 无价值的，假的 |
| dump | dʌmp | v. 倾销，抛售，倒掉，扔掉，丢弃，大量放（发）出，临时堆放，堆集<br>n. 倾销，抛售，倾销或抛售的货物，垃圾堆 |
| duplicate | ˈduːplɪkeɪt | n. 复本，复制正本，当票<br>adj. 复本的，成对的，二倍的<br>v. 复制（写、印），加倍，重复 |
| during | ˈdʊrɪŋ | prep. 在……期间 |
| duty | ˈduːti | n. （法律）责任，义务，职责（务），任务，（侵权法上的）注意，关心，(pl.) 税（尤指关税），税款 |
| earnestly | ˈɜːnɪstli | adv. 认真地；诚挚地；热切地 |
| earning | ˈɜːnɪŋ | n. 收益，(pl.) 赚得的收益（入），营业收入 |
| economic | ˌiːkəˈnɑːmɪk | adj. 经济（学）上的，实用（际）的，节俭的，经济的 |
| education | ˌedʒuˈkeɪʃn | n. 教育，教育程度，教育学 |
| effect | iˈfekt | n. 结果；影响；效果；作用<br>vt. 实现 |
| effective | iˈfektiv | adj. 有效的；有力的；印象深刻的；实在的；备战的<br>n. 兵员；实际可作战的部队 |
| either | ˈaiðə | pron. 两者之一，任一<br>adv. 也不<br>conj. 或；或者 |
| elapse | iˈlæps | vi. 时间过去；消逝<br>n. 时间的过去；流逝 |
| elect | iˈlekt | vt. 选举；选择，决定做某事；上帝挑选某人<br>adj. 卓越的 n. 被选的人；上帝的选民；特权集体 |
| election | ɪˈlekʃən | n. 选举，当选，择一原则，选举程序 |
| electric | ɪˈlektrɪk | adj. 电的；电动的；发电的；导电的；令人震惊的. |

| 单词 | 国际音标 | 词性及中文意思 |
|------|---------|---------------|
| electrical | ɪˈlektrɪkəl | adj. 有关电的；电气科学的 |
| element | elɪmənt | n. 要素，专利因素，成分，零件，自然力，天灾，恶劣天气 |
| elimination | iˌlimiˈneiʃən | n. 消除，排除，抵消，驱除 |
| else | els | adv. 其他；否则；另外<br>adj. 别的；其他的 |
| embezzlement | ɪmˈbezlmənt | n. 侵吞，挪用 |
| emblem | embləm | n. 标志，象征，纹章，徽章 |
| emergency | iˈməːdʒənsi | n. 紧急情况，非常时期 |
| employ | ɪmˈplɒi | v. 利用，聘用，雇用，使用，采用 |
| employee | ɪmˈplɔɪiː | n. 雇员；从业员工 |
| employer | ɪmˈplɒiə | n. 雇主 |
| employment | ɪmˈplɒɪmənt | n. 就业，使用，雇佣关系，雇佣工作，使用，运用，有益的活动 |
| enable | ɪnˈeɪbəl | v. 使实现，使成为可能，授权 |
| encroach | ɪnˈkrəʊtʃ | v. 蚕食，逐渐或悄悄地侵占 |
| endanger | ɪnˈdeɪndʒə | v. 使危险，危及 |
| enemy | enəmɪ | n. 敌人，交战国，敌国，敌国公民，有害物 |
| enforced | ɪnˈfɔːst | adj. 强制执行的；实施的<br>v. 执行 |
| engage | ɪnˈgeɪdʒ | v. 从事，参加，保证，约束，束缚，雇用，聘请，预定，允诺，约定，订婚 |
| engineering | endʒɪˈnɪərɪŋ | n. 工程学，工程师行业 |
| enlist | ɪnˈlɪst | v. 自愿入伍，应募，加入，赞助，支持，偏袒，利用，竞选 |
| enormous | ɪˈnɔːməs | adj. 有加重情节的，特别严重的 |
| enterprise | entəpraɪz | n. 企业，事业，公司，艰难或危险的工作，企图，计划 |

| 单词 | 国际音标 | 词性及中文意思 |
|------|---------|---------------|
| entertainment | entəˈteɪnmənt | n. 交际，娱乐，招待 |
| entity | entɪtɪ | n. 法律实体，统一体，存在物，个体，本质，单位 |
| entrust | ɪnˈtrʌst | v. 委托，信任，托管 |
| entry | entri | n. 登记，记载，分录记录，申报单，海关报关手续，入场权，入城关，项目，条目，不动产的进入权，刑法中的非法进入建筑物 |
| environment | ɪnˈvaɪrənmənt | n. 环境，外界 |
| epidemic | epɪˈdemɪk | n. 流行病，传染病，流行 adj. 传染的，流行性的 |
| equal | ˈiːkwəl | adj. 相等同的，均等的，同平等的，合适的 |
| equipment | ɪˈkwɪpmənt | n. 设备，器材，装置，配备，除房地产外的固定资 |
| erotic | ɪˈrɒtɪk | adj. 色情的；性爱的；性欲的 n. 好色之徒 |
| escape | ɪˈskeɪp | n. 罪犯脱逃，私放拘押人员罪，逃避，忘记，免除 v. 罪犯脱逃，逃避，避免 |
| eschew | ɪsˈtʃuː | vt. 避免；避开；远避 |
| escort | ɪˈskɔt | n. 护送，陪同，护卫者，警卫队，护航舰 v. 护送 |
| especially | ɪˈspeʃəlɪ | adv. 特别；尤其；格外 |
| espionage | espɪənɑːʒ | n. 间谍行为，刺探，侦察 |
| essential | ɪˈsenʃəl | adj. 本质上的，根本的，必需的，主要的 n. 本实质，要点，必需品 |
| establish | ɪˈstæblɪʃ | v. 建立，开设，创办，颁布，制定，委任，安置，证实，认可，使开业，定为国教 |
| estate | ɪˈsteɪt | n. 土地或其他财产之权益，个人或实体拥有的所有财产，全部资产，遗产，产业，不动产所有权，等级，社会阶层，集团，土地 |
| ether | iːθə | n. 乙醚；以太；苍天；天空醚 |
| ethnic | eθnɪk | adj. 种族的；人种的 |

续表

| 单词 | 国际音标 | 词性及中文意思 |
|------|----------|----------------|
| ethyl | eθaɪl | n. 乙烷基；含四乙铅的汽车燃料 |
| evade | ɪˈveɪd | v. 逃躲、回避 |
| evaluation | ɪˌvæljʊˈeɪʃən | n. 估计，评审，评价 |
| even | iːvən | adv. 甚至，即使；愈加，还；实际上<br>adj. 平坦的；平稳的；相等的；均衡的；偶数的；同样大小的；平分的；平局的；镇静的<br>v. 使平坦；使相等 |
| event | ɪˈvent | n. 事件，业务活动，经历，诉讼结果 |
| evidence | evɪdəns | n. 证据，凭证，证据法，人证 v. 作证，证明，以证据支持 |
| evil | iːvəl | n. 邪恶，弊病，不幸，灾难，痛苦，中伤，诽谤<br>adj. 邪恶的，罪恶的，有害的，中伤的 |
| exact | ɪgˈzækt | adj. 确切的，正确的，精确的，严厉的 v. 强求，需要，急需 |
| examine | ɪgˈzæmɪn | v. 审讯，诘问，查问，考试，验尸，研究，调查 |
| excavation | ekskəˈveɪʃən | n. 挖掘；开凿；开凿的洞穴；发掘出来的古迹；出土的文物 |
| exceed | ɪkˈsiːd | v. 超过，越出 |
| except | ɪkˈsept | prep. 除外，不在计算之列<br>v. 反对，抗议 |
| exception | ɪkˈsepʃən | n. 例外，抗辩，对裁决的异议，不服，反对意见，诉讼障碍，查账附注，权益的保留 |
| exceptionally | ɪkˈsepʃənəli | adv. 异常地；特殊地；例外地 |
| excessive | ɪkˈsesɪv | adj. 过度的，额外的，超额的，分外的 |
| exchange | ɪksˈtʃeɪndʒ | n. 汇兑，汇票，外币的兑换，交换，交流，调换，交易所；票据交换所，职业介绍所，讯问 v. 兑换，汇兑，调换，交流 |
| exclusively | ɪksˈkluːsɪvlɪ | adv. 唯一地，专有地，排外地；作为唯一的来源 |

| 单词 | 国际音标 | 词性及中文意思 |
|------|---------|---------------|
| excrement | ekskrɪmənt | n. 粪便，排泄物 |
| execrable | eksɪkrəbəl | adj. 恶劣的；可憎恨的 |
| executable | eksikjuːtəbl | adj. 可执行的，可实施的 |
| execution | ˌeksɪˈkjuːʃən | n. 实行，执行，使生效，处死刑，签名盖章，执行令状 |
| executive | ɪgˈzekjʊtɪv | n. 行政机关，行管人员，执行官，董事，社长<br>adj. 执行的，实施的，行政上的，有执行权力的，行政官的，总经理的 |
| exempt | ɪgˈzempt | n. 免税者，被免除者，特权者 v. 免除，豁免<br>adj. 被免除的，豁免的 |
| exercise | eksəsaɪz | n. 行使，运用，实行，履行，训练，仪式，传统做法，实施 v. 行使，实施，履行，运用，施加，练习，训练 |
| exert | ɪgˈzɜːt | v. 施加，产生，行使，发挥，运用 |
| exhibition | eksɪˈbɪʃən | n. 展览，陈列，出示证件，提出，提示 |
| exit | eksɪt | n. 出境，出口，太平门，退出，死亡，退场，离去，发行，签发 v. 离开，退场，死亡 |
| expenditure | ɪkˈspendɪtʃə | n. 支出，花费，消费，开销，经费，费用，支出额，消费额 |
| expense | ɪkˈspens | n. 费用，开支，消费，支出 v. 收取费用，记入费用账，作为开支勾销 |
| experience | ɪkˈspɪərɪəns | n. 经验，经历，阅历 |
| expert | ekspɜːt | n. 鉴定人，专家证人 adj. 熟练的，老练的，内行的 |
| expiration | ˌekspɪˈreɪʃən | n. 期满，届满，终止，截止 |
| expire | ɪkˈspaɪə | v. 满期，期满 |
| explain | ɪkˈspleɪn | v. 说明；解释 |
| explicitly | ikˈsplisitli | adv. 明白地，明确地 |

续表

| 单词 | 国际音标 | 词性及中文意思 |
|------|----------|----------------|
| explosion | ɪkˈspləʊʒən | n. 爆破 |
| explosive | ɪkˈspləʊsɪv | adj. 易爆炸的，爆炸性的，爆发性的，极易引起争论的 n. 爆炸物，炸药，爆破器材 |
| explosives | ɪkˈsplosɪvz | n. 爆炸物，［化工］炸药；爆炸品（explosive 的复数） |
| export | ˈekspɔːt | n. 出口，出口商品，输出 v. 出口，输出 |
| expose | ɪkˈspəʊz | v. 故意置人于危险境地，揭露，陈列，暴露，披露，使面临 |
| expropriation | eksˌprəʊpriˈeiʃən | n. 征用，没收，所有权的剥夺，让渡，转移，侵占，非法占有 |
| extent | ɪkˈstent | n. 程度，限度，范围，广度，宽度，长度，一大片，收回债款执行令，收回债款执行令或扣押令 |
| extort | ɪkˈstɔːt | v. 敲诈，勒索，逼供，强取 |
| extortion | ɪkˈstɔːʃən | n. 敲诈，勒索，勒索财产罪，勒索财物 |
| extract | ɪkˈstrækt | n. 诉状，起诉书，摘录，引用 v. 提取，推断 |
| extraordinarily | iksˈtrɔːdnrili | adv. 极其，极端地；奇怪地 |
| extremely | iksˈtriːmli | adv. 非常，极其；极端地 |
| extremism | ɪkˈstriːmɪzəm | n. 极端主义 |
| fabricate | ˈfæbrɪkeɪt | v. 伪造，制作，装配 |
| facility | fəˈsɪləti | n. 容易，方便，设施，设备，银行提供服务项目的透支额、贷款额等，生产资料，贷款 |
| fact | fækt | n. 事实；实际；真相 |
| factor | ˈfæktər | n. 代销商；行纪人；保理商；次债务人；案外债务人；地产管理人 v. 代销经营；保理经营；代管产业 |
| factually | fæktʃuəli | adv. 真实地；确实地 |
| fail | feɪl | v. 破产，失败，犯错误，失去支付能力，歉收，缺乏，落价，减价，缺少，不足 n. 不及格，无力交割，交割失信 |

| 单词 | 国际音标 | 词性及中文意思 |
|---|---|---|
| failure | feɪljə | n. 失败；故障；失败者；破产 |
| fairly | feəlɪ | adv. 相当地；公平地；简直 |
| fake | feɪk | n. 伪装，伪造品，赝品，假货，冒牌货，欺骗，捏造的报道，骗子，冒充者 adj. 伪的，假的，冒充的 v. 假装，伪造 |
| falsehood | fɔːlshʊd | n. 虚伪陈述，谎言，谬误，不真实 |
| falsely | fɔːlslɪ | adv. 错误地；虚伪地；不实地 |
| falsified | fɔːlsləd | adj. 弄虚作假的，不真实的 |
| fashion | fæʃn | n. 流行，时尚，风气，样子，方式，制法，构造，红人，上流社会 |
| favor | ˈfeivə | n. 偏袒，优惠，庇护，赠与，赞同，喜爱，礼物，纪念品，徽章，特别的权利 v. 偏袒，庇护，赠与，赞成 |
| favoritism | ˈfeivəritizəm | n. 偏袒，偏爱 |
| fee | fiː | n. 给律师、医生、私人教师等专业人员的报酬，以及入场费、入会费、学费，酬金，小费，税，永赁地权 |
| fertilizer | fɜːtɪlaɪzə | n. 肥料；受精媒介物；促进发展者 |
| fiduciary | fɪˈdjuːʃərɪ | n. 托付事务，受托人 adj. 托付的，信用的，信托的，受托人的 |
| fight | faɪt | v. 与……打仗，与……斗争；打架；竞争；极力反对；努力争取；争辩；参加；反对……提案；指挥作战；奋力灭火；奋力赢得选举；克制情感表露；双方失和；打官司<br>n. 打架；斗争；竞赛；拳击赛；争论；战斗；斗志 |
| figure | fɪgə | n. 图形；数字；人的体形；人物；画像；价格<br>vi. 出现；计算；扮演角色<br>vt. 描绘；计算；认为；象征 |
| filed | faɪld | v. 申请；存档 |
| files | faɪls | n. 文件<br>v. 提出；发送；汇订 |

续表

| 单词 | 国际音标 | 词性及中文意思 |
|------|---------|----------------|
| final | faɪnəl | adj. 确定的，最后的，最终的，决定性的 |
| financial | faɪˈnænʃəl | adj. 财政的，金融的 |
| fine | faɪn | n. 罚款，罚金 v. 处以 adj. 信誉良好的，优等的 |
| firearms | faɪrˌɑrmz | n. 火器，枪炮，轻武器，枪械 |
| fixed | fɪkst | adj. 固定的，确定的，不变的，固执的 |
| fixed – term imprisonment | fɪkst-tɜːm ɪmˈprɪznmənt | n. 有期徒刑 |
| fixed-termed | fɪkst-tɜːmd | adj. 固定期限的 |
| flag | flæg | n. 旗帜，船籍，标志 v. 授予悬挂船旗权，登记船籍，在文件上标着重点符号 |
| flammable radioactive | ˈflæməbl ˌreɪdioʊˈæktɪv | 易燃的放射性 |
| flee | fliː | v. 逃走，进出，损失，消散，抛弃，脱离 |
| flood | flʌd | n. 洪水，水灾，淹没，潮水最高点 v. 使淹没，使泛滥 |
| follow | fɒləʊ | v. 跟随，按照，遵守循，从事职业等，贯彻，仿效，经营，执行，说明，归结，继续 n. 跟随，追随 |
| food-borne | fuːd-bɔːn | adj. 食物传染的 |
| forbidden | fəˈbɪdən | adj. 被禁止的，禁用的 |
| forcible | fɔːsɪbəl | adj. 强制的，有势力的，用暴力的，有说服力的，强有力的 |
| foreigner | fɒrɪnə | n. 外地人，外国人 |
| foreseen | fɔːˈsiːn | v. 预见；预知 |
| forest | fɒrɪst | n. 森林 |
| forestland | fɔːrɪstlənd | n. 林地 |
| forestry | fɒrɪstrɪ | n. 林业学，森林 |
| forfeiture | fɔːfɪtʃər | n. 丧失，没收财产，没收物，罚金，权利的丧失，剥夺权益，取消 |

| 单词 | 国际音标 | 词性及中文意思 |
|---|---|---|
| forge | fɔ:dʒ | v. 伪造，犯伪造罪，编造谎言等 |
| formal | fɔ:məl | adj. 正式的，形式上的，合乎格式的，有效的 |
| formation | fɔ:'meɪʃən | n. 形成，构成物，结构，形式 |
| former | fɔ:mə | adj. 以前的，原先的，从前的 |
| formulate | fɔ:mjʊleɪt | v. 系统阐述，用公式表达，制定 |
| forth | fɔ:θ | adv. 向前，向外；自……以后 |
| fossil | fɒsəl | n. 化石；僵化的事物；顽固不化的人 adj. 化石的；陈腐的，守旧的 |
| founding | faʊndɪŋ | adj. 创办的，发起的<br>n. 创办，发起；铸造；溶解<br>v. 创办组织；建立国家；以……为基础； |
| frame | freɪm | v. 建造，设想，拟定，诬害，捏造证据诬陷无辜者，讲出 n. 框架，机构，组织，体系 |
| fraud | frɔ:d | n. 欺诈，欺诈罪，因应付欺诈之缘故，诡计 |
| fraudulence | fɔ:djʊləns | n. 欺诈；欺骗性 |
| fraudulent | frɔ:djʊlent | adj. 欺诈的 |
| freedom | fri:dəm | n. 自由，自主，免除，解脱，放肆，自由权，特权 |
| frequency | fri:kwənsɪ | n. 某事发生可重复的频率；声波或无线电波的振动频率；波段 |
| frontier | frʌntɪə | n. 国境，边境，科技等的新领域 |
| frozen | frəʊzn | adj. 冰冻的，冻伤的，冻结的 |
| fulfill | fʊl'fil | v. 履行诺言、责任，实现，完成计划、任务等，达到目的，满足愿望、要求等，执行命令、法律，期满 |
| functional | fʌŋkʃənəl | adj. 职能的，功能的，职务上的，职责的，实用的，有作用的，起作用的 |
| functionary | fʌnkʃənərɪ | n. 政府官员，雇员 |

续表

| 单词 | 国际音标 | 词性及中文意思 |
|------|---------|----------------|
| fund | fʌnd | n. 基金，专款，经费，资产，资金，奖金，存款，物资或资源的储备，特别基金管理机构，运用资本净额 v. 提供经费，投资生息，转为长期计息债务 |
| further | fɜːðə | adj. 进一步的，深一层的，另外的，添加的 |
| future | fjuːtʃə | adj. 前途的，未来的，期货的，远期的 |
| gain | geɪn | n. 收益，营利，利得，盈余，夫妻共同财产增益，额外盈余，增加，获得物，选票份额的增加 v. 赢得，获得 |
| gambling | ˈgæmblɪŋ | n. 赌博，投机，冒险 |
| gang | gæŋ | n. 团伙，集团，帮派，班组 v. 伙同行动，成群结队 |
| gangland | ˈgæŋlænd | n. 犯罪集团圈子，黑社会 |
| gas | gæs | n. 天然气，煤气，毒气 |
| gaseous | ˈgæsɪəs | adj. 气体的 |
| gathering | ˈgæðərɪŋ | n. 捐款，结集，凝集，集会，聚集，收集 |
| general | ˈdʒenərəl | adj. 一般的，普通的，全体的，综合的，总的，大众的，首席的 |
| generated | ˈdʒenəˌreɪtəd | adj. 发电的 |
| genuine | ˈdʒenjʊɪn | adj. 真正的，非伪造的 |
| gifts | gɪfts | n. 礼品，赠品；礼物；天赋 v. 赐予；给予 |
| gold | gəʊld | n. 黄金，金币，财宝，大宗款项 adj. 黄金的，金本位的，可以兑换黄金的，用黄金作储备的 |
| governed | ˈgʌvənd | v. 管理（govern 的过去式和过去分词）；统治；支配 |
| government | ˈgʌvənˌmənt | n. 政府，内阁统治，政体，政治学，治理，行政管理，管理机构，统辖，统治权，行政区，政府债券 |
| grab | græb | n./v. 攫取，强夺，不法取得，逮捕，掠夺 |
| graft | grɑːft | v. 贪污公款，受贿 n. 贪污公款，贪污之钱财 |
| gram | græm | n. 克 |

续表

| 单词 | 国际音标 | 词性及中文意思 |
|------|---------|--------------|
| granted | graːntid | conj. 算是如此，但是 |
| graphically | græfikəli | adv. 以书画形式；形象地，逼真地；清晰详细地 |
| gratuitously | grə'tjuːitəs | adj. 无偿的，免费的，没有理由的 |
| grave | greɪv | adj. 严重的，严肃的，重大的，沉重的 n. 坟墓 |
| graveness | greivnis | n. 重大，严重；认真 |
| ground | graʊnd | n. 地面，场所，问题涉及的范围，领域，研究的课题，根据，理由，论据，原因，基础 |
| group | gruːp | n. 集团，团体，小组，群体，派，小分类，分组 |
| guarantee | gærən'tiː | n. 保证人、书，担保 v. 保证，担保，抵押 |
| guaranty | gærəntI | n. 保证书、人，担保品、人，抵押物 |
| guard | gaːd | n. 守卫，保护，监狱看守，狱卒，监视，戒备，哨兵，卫兵 v. 警卫，防守，保护，看守，监视，谨慎使用 |
| guardian | gaːdɪən | n. 监护人 |
| guardianship | gardɪən'ʃɪp | n. 监护权，监护人的职责，保护 |
| guilty | gɪltI | adj. 有罪的，犯罪的，内疚的 n. 犯人，陪审团的有罪裁决，被告的认罪供述 |
| gun | gʌn | n. 枪支，手枪，持枪暴徒，扒手 v. 枪击，枪杀 |
| hamper | hæmpə | vt. 妨碍；束缚；使困累 . n. 食盒，食篮；阻碍物 |
| handle | hændəl | v. 处理，管理，经营，搬运，买卖，操纵 |
| harbor | 'haːbə | n. 港口，避风港 v. 使船在港内停泊，船入港停泊，窝藏 |
| harmful | haːmfʊl | adj. 有害的 |
| hatred | 'heɪtrɪd | n. 敌意，憎恨，憎恶，仇恨 |
| hazardous | hæzədəs | adj. 危险的，冒险的，碰运气的，担风险的 |
| heinous | heɪnəs | adj. 厌恶的，凶残的 |
| herein | hɪər'ɪn | adv. 在此，于此 |

| 单词 | 国际音标 | 词性及中文意思 |
|---|---|---|
| heroin | ˈherəʊɪn | n. 海洛因 |
| hide | haɪd | n. 供养一家人的土地，房屋，居室 v. 躲藏 |
| highway | ˈhaɪweɪ | n. 公路，公共通行权，水路、航空线路 |
| hijack | ˈhaɪdʒæk | v. 劫持 n. 劫持 |
| hire | ˈhaɪə | v. 租用，租借，雇用，受雇，购买临时使用财产 n. 租用，受雇，租金，工钱，劳务费，雇工 |
| historical | hɪˈstɒrɪkəl | adj. 历史性的 |
| holder | ˈhəʊldə | n. 股票、票据、提单等的持有人，财产的占有人或使用人，股东，承租人 |
| hostage | ˈhɒstɪdʒ | n. 人质，质押物品 |
| huge | hjuːdʒ | adj. 巨大的；庞大的；无限的 |
| humiliation | hjuːˌmɪliːˈeɪʃən | n. 耻辱；蒙羞；谦卑 |
| hunt | hʌnt | v. 搜索，追寻，打猎 |
| hurt | hɜːt | n. 危害、伤害，精神、感情上的创伤 v. 危害、伤害，使感情受到创伤 |
| hygiene | ˈhaɪdʒiːn | n. 卫生，卫生学，保健法 |
| hygienic | haɪˈdʒiːnɪk | adj. 卫生的，保健的 |
| identical | aɪˈdentɪkəl | adj. 相同的，外交文件同文的，外交行动方式相同的 |
| identification | aɪˌdɛntɪfɪˈkeɪʃən | n. 鉴定，识别，确认，查明，验明，证件，身份证明，贷款等项目选定 |
| identity | aɪˈdentɪtɪ | n. 身份，本人，一致，同一人，相同，正身，个性，特征 |
| illegal | ɪˈliːgəl | adj. 不合法的，违法的，非法的，违例的 |
| illegitimate | ˌɪləˈdʒɪtəmət | adj. 非法的，非婚生的，不当的，不正确推论的 n. 非婚生子女，无合法身份者 v. 宣布为违法，宣布为非婚生子 |
| illicit | ɪˈlɪsɪt | adj. 违法的，违禁的，被禁止的，不正当的，私的 |

| 单词 | 国际音标 | 词性及中文意思 |
|---|---|---|
| illness | ˈɪlnəs | n. 疾病；病 |
| imitation | ˌɪmɪˈteɪʃn | n. 模仿，商标法上的仿造品，仿制品，赝品 |
| immediate | ɪˈmiːdiət | adj. 直接的，有直接效果的，即时的，最接近的，立即的 |
| imminent | ˈɪmɪnənt | adj. 即将来临的；迫近的 |
| immunity | ɪˈmjuːnəti | n. 豁免权，侵权豁免权，证人豁免权，免除，免疫，安全性 |
| impact | ˈɪmpækt | n. 冲击，司法影响，影响力，效力，碰撞，撞击力 |
| impair | ɪmˈpeər | v. 受损害，削弱，减少财产价值或权利 |
| implement | ˈɪmplɪment | n. 用具，完全履行，执行，实施 v. 履行合同，贯彻，完成，实现，生效，实施，执行 |
| implementation | ˌɪmplɪmenˈteɪʃn | n. 履行，执行，实现 |
| implicitly | ɪmˈplɪsɪtli | adv. 含蓄地；暗中地 |
| import | ˈɪmpɔːt | v. 输入，商品的进口 n. 输入，进口，意义，含义，重要性 |
| import-export | ˈɪmpɔːrtˈekspɔːrt | adj. 进出口的 |
| impose | ɪmˈpəʊz | v. 征税，强加，欺骗，使他人买受，施加负担，利用，欺骗 |
| imprisonment | imˈprizənmənt | n. 监禁，坐牢 |
| improper | ɪmˈprɑːpər | adj. 不正确的，错误的；不适当的；不合礼仪的 |
| incarceration | ɪnˌkɑːsəˈreɪʃn | n. 监禁，禁闭 |
| incident | ˈɪnsɪdənt | n. 事变，附属于财产的权利，附带条件，附属事件 adj. 附属的 |
| include | ɪnˈkluːd | vt. 包含，包括 |
| income | ˈɪnkəm | n. 收入，收益，收款，所得 |
| inconsistent | ˌɪnkənˈsɪstənt | adj. 矛盾的，不一致的，不协调的，多变的 |

| 单词 | 国际音标 | 词性及中文意思 |
|------|----------|----------------|
| incorporation | ɪnˌkɔːpəˈreɪʃn | n. 设立公司，结合，合并 |
| incur | ɪnˈkɜːr | v. 招致，承担 |
| indeed | ɪnˈdiːd | adv. 的确；实在；真正地；甚至 |
| indemnity | ɪnˈdemnəti | n. 赔偿责任，主张赔偿权，补偿，赔偿，免罚，赦免，保护，对于损害或损失的保险 |
| independent | ˌɪndɪˈpendənt | adj. 独立的，自主的，单独的，无党派的 n. 独立的公司，独立经营者 |
| indicator | ˈɪndɪkeɪtər | n. 指标，经济指标 |
| indifference | ɪnˈdɪfrəns | n. 中立，不偏袒，不重视，无足轻重 |
| indirectly | ˌɪndaɪˈrektli | adv. 间接地；不诚实；迂回地 |
| indiscriminately | ˌɪndɪˈskrɪmɪnətli | adj. 不辨善恶的，不分青红皂白的，不加选择的 |
| individual | ˌɪndɪˈvɪdʒuəl | n. 个人，个体，独立单位，自然 adj. 单独的，自然人的，个别的，特别的，有特性的 |
| induce | ɪnˈdjuːs | v. 引诱，劝诱，诱发，诱致 |
| industrial | ɪnˈdʌstriəl | adj. 工业的，产业工人的，劳资争议的，从事工业的，供工业用的，工业高度发达的 n. 工业工人，工业股票，公司雇员 |
| infant | ˈɪnfənt | adj. 婴儿的，初期的，未成年的，新生的 n. 未成年人 |
| infectious | ɪnˈfekʃəs | adj. 有坏影响的，能使成为非法的，能导致全部货物充公的，传染的 |
| inferior | ɪnˈfɪəriər | adj. 差的，次的，劣质的，低品质的，下级的，劣等的，初等的 |
| inflate | ɪnˈfleɪt | v. 使通货膨胀，使物价上涨 |
| inflict | ɪnˈflɪkt | v. 惩处，处罚，加刑，予以打击，使遭受损害 |
| influence | ˈɪnfluəns | n. 影响，势力，权势，感化 |
| inform | ɪnˈfɔːm | v. 告发，诉冤，通知 |

| 单词 | 国际音标 | 词性及中文意思 |
|---|---|---|
| informant | ɪnˈfɔːmənt | n. 举报人，告密者，线人，报告人，通知人，提供消息的人，被征询人 |
| information | ˌɪnfəˈmeɪʃn | n. 通知，报告，情报，资料，消息，信息，知识 |
| infringe | ɪnˈfrɪndʒ | v. 破坏，侵犯，违背 |
| inhabited | ɪnˈhæbitid | adj. 有人居住的 |
| initiative | ɪˈnɪʃətɪv | n. 创制权，动议权，优先权，创始，开创，主动性，首创精神，积极性，进取精神 |
| injecting | ɪnˈdʒektɪŋ | v. 注射（inject 的现在分词） |
| injure | ˈɪndʒər | v. 伤害，毁坏，使受冤屈 |
| injury | ˈɪndʒəri | n. 损害，冤屈，受伤处 |
| inland | ˈɪnlənd ɪnˈlænd | n. 内地，国内，内陆 adj. 内地的，国内的，内陆的 |
| inmates | ˈɪnmeɪts | n. 监狱，囚犯，同房病人 |
| innocent | ˈɪnəsnt | n. 无罪者，无辜者 adj. 无罪的，清白的 |
| insecticide | ɪnˈsektɪsaɪd | n. 杀虫剂 |
| insider | ɪnˈsaɪdər | n. 知情人，知内情的人，局中人，了解内幕者，内部人员 |
| inspect | ɪnˈspekt | v. 检查，监察 |
| inspection | ɪnˈspekʃn | n. 检查，调查，监察，验尸 |
| install | ɪnˈstɔːl | v. 就任，就职 |
| installation | ˌɪnstəˈleɪʃn | n. 就任，就职，安装，设备 |
| installments | ɪnˈstɔːlmənts | n. 分期付款，分期，就职，安顿 |
| instead | ɪnˈsted | adv. 代替；反而；相反 |
| instigate | ˈɪnstɪgeɪt | v. 教唆，主使，煽动，怂恿 |
| instituted | ˈɪnstɪtjuːtɪd | v. 创立；设置 |
| institution | ˌɪnstɪˈtjuːʃn | n. 提起，指定，机构，学会，制度，建立，惯例，条例，协会，学校，事业单位，团体，风俗，习惯，会址，所址，精神病院，授予圣职 |

续表

| 单词 | 国际音标 | 词性及中文意思 |
|------|----------|----------------|
| instructing | ɪnˈstrʌktɪŋ | vt. 指导；教（instruct 的现在分词）；指示<br>adj. 指令型 |
| instrument | ˈɪnstrəmənt | n. 票据，文据，正式文件，证券，手段，工具 |
| insult | ɪnˈsʌlt | n. 侮辱；凌辱；损害名誉 |
| insurance | ɪnˈʃɔːrəns | n. 保险，保险金，安全保障，保证 |
| insured | ɪnˈʃɔːd | adj. 保险过的，投保的 |
| integrity | ɪnˈtegrəti | n. 完整性，完善，正直，廉正 |
| intellectual | ˌɪntəˈlektʃuəl | n. 知识分子 adj. 智力的，需智力的，用脑力的，理智的 |
| intelligence | ɪnˈtelɪdʒəns | n. 情报人员，消息，智力，理解力，才智 |
| intended | ɪnˈtendɪd | adj. 故意的，打算的，预期的，未来的，未婚的 |
| intensive | ɪnˈtensɪv | adj. 集约经营的，精耕细作的，集中的，深入的，细致的 |
| intent | ɪnˈtent | n. 故意，法律的起草目的，计划，意义，打算 |
| intention | ɪnˈtenʃn | n. 故意，文件等的含义，意图，目的 |
| intentional | ɪnˈtenʃənl | adj. 故意的，有意的 |
| intercept | ˌɪntəˈsept | v. 窃听，截取，阻止 |
| intercourse | ˈɪntəkɔːs | n. 交往，交流，性交 |
| interest | ˈɪntrəst | n. 利息，权益，权利，股利，产权，利害关系，重要性，影响，行业，势力，先前的协议，许可证，附属物，关心，兴趣 v. 付利息 |
| interfere | ˌɪntəˈfɪə | v. 干预，对专利权提出争议，发生冲突，抵触，妨害，仲裁，调停 |
| intermediary | ˌɪntəˈmiːdiəri | adj. 中间的，媒介的，调解人的 n. 中间人，调解人，媒介物，手段，工具，媒人 |
| intermediate | ˌɪntəˈmiːdiət | v. 起媒介作用，起调解作用 adj. 中间的，媒介的<br>n. 中间人，媒介，中转港，半成品 |

| 单词 | 国际音标 | 词性及中文意思 |
|---|---|---|
| intermittent | ˌɪntə'mɪtənt | adj. 断续的，间歇的，周期性的 |
| international | ˌɪntə'næʃnəl | adj. 国际的，世界的 n. 外国侨居者，共产国际，国际主义，国际法学家，国际派，国际企业，国际集团，国际股票，国际储存 |
| intimidation | ɪnˌtɪmɪ'deɪʃn | n. 恐吓，威胁 |
| intoxicated | ɪn'tɒksɪkeɪtɪd | adj. 醉酒的 |
| introduce | ˌɪntrə'djuːs | v. 引进，输入，介绍，推荐，采用，提出议案，在法庭上举证 |
| intrude | ɪn'truːd | v. 侵入，侵扰，非法占领，强使采纳 |
| invalid | ɪn'vælɪd | adj. 无效力的，作废的，有病的，伤残的 v. 使生病，使伤残，因伤病而退伍 n. 病人，伤残者 |
| invalidate | ɪn'vælɪdeɪt | v. 使无效，使作废，使无价值 |
| inveigle | ɪn'veɪgl | v. 诱惑，骗取，勾引 |
| invention | ɪn'venʃn | n. 发明，发明物，创造，虚构，捏造 |
| investigate | ɪn'vestɪgeɪt | v. 调查，侦查，审查 |
| investment | ɪn'vestmənt | n. 投资，授权 |
| investor | ɪn'vestər | n. 投资者，客商，授权者 |
| inviting | ɪn'vaɪtɪŋ | adj. 诱惑人的，动人的，吸引人的 |
| invoice | invoice | v. 开发票，开清单 n. 发票，运单，发货单，收货清单 |
| involve | ɪn'vɒlv | v. 包括，使卷入，使陷入，影响，牵连，拖累 |
| irregularity | ɪˌregjə'lærəti | n. 误差，谬误，违章，不规则，不规律，不正当行为，形式上瑕疵，不符合司法程序，妨碍宗教职务 |
| irresistible | ˌɪrɪ'zɪstəbl | adj. 不准保释的，不能发还的 |
| irresponsibility | ˌɪrɪˌspɒnsə'bɪləti | n. 不负责任，无责任，不承担责任 |
| irresponsible | ˌɪrɪ'spɒnsəbl | adj. 不承担责任的，不负责任的，无责任感的 n. 不承担责任的人，无责任感的人，不负责任的人 |

| 单词 | 国际音标 | 词性及中文意思 |
|---|---|---|
| issuance | ˈɪʃuəns | n. 发布，发行 |
| issue | ˈɪʃuː | n. 问题；流出；期号；发行物<br>vt. 发行，发布；发给；放出，排出<br>vi. 发行；流出；造成……结果；传下 |
| jeopardize | ˈdʒepədaɪz | vt. 危害；使陷危地；使受危困 |
| join | dʒɔɪn | v. 结合，参加，使缔交，使联姻，伴同，毗连，接近 |
| joinder | ˈdʒɔɪndər | n. 共同诉讼，合并诉讼或诉讼主张，对他方提出的诉争意见的接受 |
| joint | dʒɔɪnt | adj. 联合的，共同的 |
| jointly | ˈdʒɔɪntli | adv. 共同地；连带地 |
| journal | ˈdʒɜːnl | n. 立法机关的议事录，日志，航海日记，杂志，公报，日记账 |
| judgment | ˈdʒʌdʒmənt | n. 审判，裁判，判决，判断，鉴定，评价，法官判案的理由，意见，看法，批评，指责 |
| judicial | dʒuˈdɪʃl | adj. 司法的，审判的，法院判决的，公正的，明断的，周密考虑的 |
| jurisdiction | ˌdʒʊərɪsˈdɪkʃn | n. 司法权，审判权，管辖权；权限，权力 |
| justice | ˈdʒʌstɪs | n. 正义，公正执法，公正原则，司法，审判，法律制裁，正当理由，合法，正确，确实，公平处理，公平待遇，应得 |
| justifiable | ˈdʒʌstɪfaɪəbl | adj. 可辩解的，有道理的；可证明为正当的 |
| juvenile | ˈdʒuːvənaɪl | adj. 青少年的；幼稚的<br>n. 青少年；少年读物 |
| kickback | ˈkɪkbæk | n. 回扣，佣金；强烈反应；退回赃物 |
| kidnap | ˈkɪdnæp | vt. 绑架；诱拐；拐骗 |
| knowingly | ˈnəʊɪŋli | adv. 故意地；机警地，狡黠地 |
| known | nəʊn | adj. 已知的；知名的；大家知道的 |

| 单词 | 国际音标 | 词性及中文意思 |
|---|---|---|
| labor | ˈleɪbər | n. 劳动；工作；劳工；分娩<br>vi. 劳动；努力；苦干<br>vt. 详细分析；使厌烦 |
| large-scale | ˌlɑːdʒ ˈskeɪl | adj. 大规模的，大范围的；大比例尺的 |
| latter | ˈlætər | adj. 后者的；近来的；后面的；较后的 |
| laundered | ˈlɔːndər | v. 洗钱 |
| lawful | ˈlɔːfl | adj. 合法的，法定的，守法的，法律许可的，依法的 |
| lawsuit | ˈlɔːsjuːt | n. 诉讼，诉讼案件 v. 提起诉讼，起诉 |
| leading | ˈliːdɪŋ | adj. 领导的；主要的<br>n. 领导；铅板；行距 |
| leak | liːk | v. 使渗漏，泄露；漏，渗；泄漏出去；透露<br>n. 泄漏，漏洞，裂缝；泄漏出的液体；秘密信息的透露；撒尿；漏电 |
| leakage | ˈliːkɪdʒ | n. 商业上许可的漏损率，漏出量，渗漏 |
| lease | liːs | n. 租约；租期；租赁物；租赁权<br>vt. 出租；租得<br>vi. 出租 |
| legal | ˈliːgl | adj. 法律的；合法的；法定的；依照法律的 |
| legally | ˈliːgəli | adv. 合法地；法律上 |
| legally-held | ˈliːgəli held | adj. 合法持有的 |
| legally-pres cribed | ˈliːgəliprɪˈskraɪbd | adj. 法定的 |
| legitimate | lɪˈdʒɪtɪmət | adj. 合法的，正统的，真正的，有效的，婚生的，正当的 v. 使合法，宣布为合法，给予合法地位，确立婚生地位 |
| lend | lend | v. 借出，提供，贷款，出租 |
| lesser | ˈlesər | adj. 较轻的 |
| lethal | ˈliːθl | adj. 致命的，毁灭性的 |
| liability | ˌlaɪəˈbɪləti | n. 责任，义务，债务，负债，缺点，赔偿责任，不利条件 |

续表

| 单词 | 国际音标 | 词性及中文意思 |
|------|---------|----------------|
| liberation | ˌlɪbəˈreɪʃn | n. 解放 |
| license | ˈlaɪsns | n. 特许证，特许权，许可证，执牌照，放纵，准许 v. 发许可证 |
| life – imprison-ment | laɪf ɪmˈprɪznmənt | n. 无期徒刑；终身监禁 |
| limbs | lɪmz | n. 四肢 |
| limit | ˈlɪmɪt | n. 界限线，范围，区域，限定，极限，投保年龄限制 v. 限定，确切指派 |
| limitation | ˌlɪmɪˈteɪʃn | n. 法定的提起诉讼的限期，诉讼时效，法律规定的有效期，限度制，局限，限制因素 |
| liquid | ˈlɪkwɪd | adj. 资产流动的，持有流动资产的，容易转换成现金的，不稳定的 n. 液体 |
| liquidation | ˌlɪkwɪˈdeɪʃn | n. 清理，清偿，债务清算，对破产者的清算 |
| listed | ˈlɪstɪd | adj. 挂牌的，已列表的，股票上市的，已登记的 |
| literary | ˈlɪtərəri | adj. 文学的；精通文学的；书面的 |
| litigation | ˌlɪtɪˈgeɪʃn | n. 诉讼，诉讼程序 |
| livelihood | ˈlaɪvlihʊd | n. 生活，生计 |
| loading | ˈləʊdɪŋ | n. 附加人寿保险费，附加费用 |
| loan | ləʊn | n. 借贷，出借，贷款，公债，放款，借出物，贷款公债 v. 借出 |
| local | ˈləʊkl | adj. 地方的，当地的，局部的 n. 当地居民 |
| logging | ˈlɒgɪŋ | n. 木材采运作业 |
| looting | ˈluːtɪŋ | n. 掠夺行为 |
| lower | ˈləʊər | adj. 较低的，较低级的，低级的，下层的 v. 放下，减低，贬低 |
| low-value | ləʊ ˈvæljuː | adj. 低位值 |

| 单词 | 国际音标 | 词性及中文意思 |
|---|---|---|
| lump | lʌmp | n. 整体，许多 v. 总括，一起处理 |
| lure | luər | n. 诱惑物；诱惑；饵<br>vt. 引诱；诱惑 |
| luring | luərɪŋ | vt. 引诱；诱惑（lure 的现在分词） |
| lyric | ˈlɪrɪk | adj. 抒情的；写抒情诗的；歌声柔美的；吟唱的<br>n. 抒情诗；抒情诗体；歌词 |
| machinery | məˈʃiːnəri | n. 机器，体系，机构 |
| made-up | ˈmeɪd ʌp | adj. 捏造的；制成的；化妆过的 |
| magazine | ˌmægəˈziːn | n. 杂志；弹药库；胶卷盒 |
| mail | meɪl | n. 邮件，邮递，租金 v. 邮寄，交承运人转 |
| maintain | meɪnˈteɪn | v. 宣称，断言，维护，继续，坚持，经办，协助诉讼，唆讼，介入他人诉讼 |
| major | ˈmeɪdʒər | adj. 主要的，重要的 . n. 国际石油大公司，大公司，成年人 |
| malpractice | ˌmælˈpræktɪs | n. 职业过失 |
| maltreat | ˌmælˈtriːt | v. 粗暴对待，虐待，滥用 |
| manage | ˈmænɪdʒ | v. 管理，经营，安排，运用，操纵，驾驭，控制 |
| management | ˈmænɪdʒmənt | n. 管理部门，经营才能，安排，支配，处理，厂资方，经理 |
| manager | ˈmænɪdʒər | n. 经理，干事，业务管理人 |
| mandatory | ˈmændətəri | adj. 命令的，强迫的，训令的，委任的，受委托统治的，无选择自由的 n. 受托人，委托统治国，受命者 |
| manipulate | məˈnɪpjuleɪt | v. 操纵股市市价，篡改 |
| manner | ˈmænər | n. 方式，方法，举止，态度，习惯，风俗 |
| manufacture | ˌmænjuˈfæktʃər | v. 制造 n. 制造品，制造业 |

| 单词 | 国际音标 | 词性及中文意思 |
|---|---|---|
| march | mɑːtʃ | vi. 前进；行军，进军；游行示威；进展，进行<br>vt. 使前进；使行军<br>n. 行进，前进；行军；游行示威；进行曲 |
| marijuana | ˌmærəˈwɑːnə | n. 大麻；大麻毒品 |
| mark | mɑːk | n. 标志；符号；痕迹；分数<br>vt. 做标记于；打分数；使有污点；标明方位；庆贺；赋予特征；表明；注意；盯人防守<br>vi. 做记号；打分数；使有污点 |
| marker | ˈmɑːkər | n. 出票人，墓碑 |
| market | ˈmɑːkɪt | n. 市场；行情；股票市场；市面；集市；销路；商店<br>vt. 在市场上出售<br>vi. 做买卖 |
| marriage | ˈmærɪdʒ | n. 结婚，婚礼，联合 |
| marry | ˈmæri | v. 结婚，婚嫁，娶，结合 |
| marshal | ˈmɑːʃl | n. 法院的执行官，市执法官，市警察局长，消防队，典礼官，随从官，元帅，最高级指挥官，法警 v. 安排，排列，整理，调度，决定破产财分割顺序，集合 |
| martyr | ˈmɑːtər | n. 烈士，殉道者；乞怜者；因疾病或困难长期受折磨者；假圣人<br>v. 殉难；折磨；杀害 |
| mass | mæs | n. 大量，群众，团体，总体，主体，质量 adj. 大批的，大量的，大规模的，群众的，民众的，群众性的，总的 v. 使成一团，集中 |
| material | məˈtɪəriəl | adj. 物质的，身体上的，有形的，实体的，重要的，必需的，决定性影响的，实质性的 n. 材料，题材，证据，必需品，设备 |
| materiel | məˌtɪəriˈel | n. 物资；军备 |
| maximum | ˈmæksɪməm | n. 极点，最高限额，最大限度 adj. 最大的，顶点的 |
| mean | miːn | n. 平均数，中等体积，均数，中数 adj. 中间的，价值平均的 |

续表

| 单词 | 国际音标 | 词性及中文意思 |
|------|---------|---------------|
| means | miːnz | n. 方法，手段，工具，原因，财产，收入 |
| measure | ˈmeʒər | n. 手段，办法，措施，法律，立法，测量，标准，计量制度，度量法，程度，范围，分寸，估计 v 量，权衡，调节，配给，分派 |
| media | ˈmiːdiə | n. 媒体；传播媒介 泛指各种出版物、广播、影视 |
| medical | ˈmedɪkl | adj. 医学的，内科的 n. 医疗费用，拖欠医疗费用 |
| medicine | ˈmedsn | n. 药，医学，内科，医生行业 |
| members | ˈmembəz | n. 成员；会员 |
| mendacious | menˈdeɪʃəs | adj. 虚假的；说谎的 |
| mental | ˈmentl | adj. 精神病的，智力的 |
| mentioned | ˈmenʃnd | v. 提到，说起 |
| merchandise | ˈmɜːtʃəndaɪs | n. 商品，存货 |
| meritorious | ˌmerɪˈtɔːriəs | adj. 有功的，值得称赞的，善意的，有法律价值的，法律上可能胜诉的 |
| metal | ˈmetl | n. 金属；合金<br>vt. 以金属覆盖<br>adj. 金属制的 |
| method | ˈmeθəd | n. 方法，做事的条理，秩序，计划 |
| methylaniline | ˈmeθɪˌlanɪˈlaɪn | n. 甲基苯胺 |
| military | ˈmɪlətri | adj. 军事的，战争的 |
| militia | məˈlɪʃə | n. 民兵组织 |
| million | ˈmɪljən | n. 百万；无数<br>adj. 百万的；无数的 |
| mineral | ˈmɪnərəl | n. 矿石 adj. 矿石的 |
| minimum | ˈmɪnɪməm | n. 最低额，最小量，最低限度 adj. 最少的，最低限度的，最低的 |
| mining | ˈmaɪnɪŋ | n. 采矿，矿业 |

| 单词 | 国际音标 | 词性及中文意思 |
|---|---|---|
| minor | ˈmaɪnər | adj. 未成年的；次要的；较小的；小调的；二流的<br>n. 未成年人；小调；辅修科目<br>vi. 辅修 |
| minority | maɪˈnɒrəti | n. 少数，未达法定年龄者，未成年，不到法定年龄的状态 |
| misappropriate | ˌmɪsəˈprəʊprieɪt | v. 非法侵占 |
| misappropriation | ˌmɪsəˌprəʊpriˈeɪʃn | n. 侵吞；滥用 |
| mislead | ˌmɪsˈliːd | vt. 误导；带错 |
| mission | ˈmɪʃn | n. 使命，任务，使节团，负有特殊任务的团体 |
| mistake | mɪˈsteɪk | v. 错误，失策，误解 n. 错误，失策，误解 |
| mistreating | ˌmɪsˈtriːt | vt. 虐待 |
| mitigation | ˌmɪtɪˈgeɪʃn | n. 减刑，减轻，缓和，安慰 |
| mixed | mɪkst | adj. 混合的 |
| molests | məˈlest | v. 性骚扰 |
| monetary | ˈmʌnɪtri | adj. 货币的，币制的，金钱，财政的 |
| money | ˈmʌni | n. 货币，金钱，款项，财富，金融界 |
| monitoring | ˈmɒnɪtərɪŋ | n. 监视，监控；检验，检查 |
| monopolized | məˈnɒpəlaɪz | v. 垄断，独占，专利，专营 |
| monopoly | məˈnɒpəli | n. 垄断，独占权，专利，专卖权，专卖公司 |
| morale | məˈrɑːl | n. 士气，斗志 |
| moreover | mɔːrˈəʊvər | adv. 而且；此外 |
| morphine | ˈmɔːfiːn | n. 吗啡 |
| mortgaged | ˈmɔːgɪdʒ | adj. 按揭的，抵押的，作抵押的 |
| motherlands | ˈmʌðəlænd | n. 祖国；母国 |
| motion | ˈməʊʃn | n. 动机，意向，动议，附带请求，申请，运动，移动，动作 |

| 单词 | 国际音标 | 词性及中文意思 |
| --- | --- | --- |
| motive | ˈməʊtɪv | n. 动机 |
| motor | ˈməʊtər | n. 汽车，机动车 |
| movie | ˈmuːvi | n. 电影；电影院；电影业<br>adj. 电影的 |
| murder | ˈmɜːdər | n. 谋杀罪 v. 谋杀，犯谋杀罪 |
| museum | mjuˈziːəm | n. 博物馆 |
| mutilating | ˈmjuːtɪleɪtɪŋ | v. 使断肢，使残废，使文件残缺 |
| narcotics | narˈkɑtɪks | n. 麻醉剂；麻醉毒品 |
| national | ˈnæʃnəl | adj. 国家的；国民的；民族的<br>n. 国民 |
| nationalities | ˌnæʃəˈnælɪtiz | n. 国籍，国家；民族；部落（nationality 的复数） |
| naturally | ˈnætʃrəli | adv. 自然地，轻而易举地 |
| necessary | ˈnesəseri | adj. 强制的，被迫的，必须的，必需的，必要的 n 必需品，生活必需品 |
| neglect | nɪˈglekt | n. 疏忽，忽略，疏于照顾，过失 v. 忽略，弃置不顾 |
| negligent | ˈneglɪdʒənt | adj. 玩忽的，粗心大意的，因疏忽造成损害的，依民法应负赔偿责任的，过失的 |
| negotiable | nɪˈgəʊʃiəbl | adj. 可转让的，可流通的，可谈判的，可协商的，道路可通行的 |
| network | ˈnetwɜːk | n. 网络；广播网；网状物 |
| newly – commit-ted | ˈnuːli kəˈmɪtɪd | adj. 最新犯下的 |
| newly – discov-ered | ˈnuːli dɪˈskʌvərd | adj. 新发现的 |
| noble | ˈnəʊbl | n. 贵族 |

| 单词 | 国际音标 | 词性及中文意思 |
|---|---|---|
| none | nʌn | pron. 没有人，一个也没有，没有任何东西<br>adj. 没有的，一点没有的<br>adv. 一点也不；决不，不怎么，绝不 |
| non-existing | nɑn ɪɡˈzɪstɪŋ | adj. 不存在的 |
| non-food | nɑn fʊd | adj. 非食物的 |
| non - state -owned | nɑn stet ond | adj. 非国有的 |
| non-sterilized | nɑnˈsterəlaɪzd | adj. 未灭菌的 |
| normal | ˈnɔːml | adj. 正常规的，标准的 |
| normality | nɔːrˈmæləti | n. 规定浓度，正态性 |
| noted | ˈnəʊtɪd | v. 注意；特别提出；记录 |
| notice | ˈnəʊtɪs | n. 声明，通知书，短评，广告，招贴，标记，招牌，注意，知悉，开审通知书，报告书，传单，启事 v. 通知， |
| noticeably | ˈnəʊtɪsəbli | adv. 显著地，明显地；引人注目地 |
| notification | ˌnəʊtɪfɪˈkeɪʃn | n. 公告，通告，通报，告示，通知，通知书 |
| nuclear | ˈnjuːkliər | n. 核武器，核国家 adj. 核子的，原子能的，核动力的，基本 |
| nullified | ˈnʌlɪfaɪd | v. 使无效，使无拘束力，废除，作废，取消，注销 |
| number | ˈnʌmbər | n. 数字，号码 |
| nursing | ˈnɜːsɪŋ | n. 护理；看护；养育<br>v. 看护；养 |
| obey | əˈbeɪ | v. 服从，顺从，遵奉，执行，按照……行动 |
| object | ˈɒbdʒɪkt | n. 目标，物体，实物，原始支出用途，客体，目的，对象 v. 反对，抗议，拒绝，提出作为反对理由 |
| objectively | əbˈdʒektɪvli | adv. 客观地 |

| 单词 | 国际音标 | 词性及中文意思 |
|---|---|---|
| obligation | ˌɒblɪˈgeɪʃn | n. 法律义务，道德上的义务，责任，职责，债，债务，债权关系，合同，证券，待付保留额，承付款项，束缚，偿付债务的款项，恩惠 |
| obscene | əbˈsiːn | adj 淫秽的；下流的；猥亵的；讨厌的；可憎的 |
| observe | əbˈzɜːv | v. 奉行，遵守，观察，监视，陈述意见，评述，庆祝，纪念 |
| obstruct | əbˈstrʌkt | v. 阻碍，妨碍，阻挠，设置障碍 |
| obtain | əbˈteɪn | v. 通过努力获得；取得；占有；持有；拥有 |
| obviously | ˈɒbviəsli | adv. 明显地 |
| occasion | əˈkeɪʒn | n. 时机，场合，机会，近因，偶因，原因，诱因，特殊事件 v. 引起，惹起 |
| occupation | ˌɒkjuˈpeɪʃn | n. 职业，工作 |
| occur | əˈkɜːr | v. 事件发生，出现，存在，被想到，想起 |
| occurrence | əˈkʌrəns | n. 出现，发生，偶发事件，事变 |
| odious | ˈəʊdiəs | adj. 可憎的；讨厌的 |
| offence | əˈfens | n. 犯罪；违反；过错；攻击 |
| offender | əˈfendər | n. 违法者；罪犯 通常指触犯刑律的人，含轻刑犯和违反交通法规 |
| offense | əˈfens | n. 犯罪，过错；进攻；触怒；引起反感的事物 |
| offer | ˈɒfər | n. 要约，出售，供应，出价，提议，企图 v. 出价，开价，提出，出售，出卖，提供，提议 |
| officer | ˈɒfɪsər | n. 军官，警官；公务员，政府官员；船长 vt. 指挥 |
| official | əˈfɪʃl | adj. 官方的；正式的；公务的 n. 官员；公务员；高级职员 |
| official-use | əˈfɪʃl juːs | n. 正式使用权；公务用途 |

| 单词 | 国际音标 | 词性及中文意思 |
|---|---|---|
| offsetting | ˈɒfsetɪŋ | n. 相抵，抵消 adj. 相抵的，抵消的 |
| ongoing | ˈɒngəʊɪŋ | adj. 仍在进行的；不断前进的；持续存在的 |
| openly | ˈoʊpənli | adv. 公开地，公然地 |
| operate | ˈɑːpəreɪt | v. 操作，工作，施行手术，作战，经营，管理，完成，运行，营运 |
| operation | ˌɑːpəˈreɪʃn | n. 运用，作用，实施，生效，经营，管理，交易，买卖 |
| opium | ˈoʊpiəm | n. 鸦片 |
| opportunity | ˌɑːpərˈtuːnəti | n. 机会，良机 |
| opposite | ˈɑːpəzɪt | adj. 反对的，对立的，相反的，相对的 |
| ordinance | ˈɔːrdɪnəns | n. [英]（自治市）条例，传统风俗习惯 |
| organ | ˈɔːrgən | n. 机关，机构，器官，喉舌，报刊 |
| organization | ˌɔːrgənəˈzeɪʃn | n. 体制，编制，组织，团体，机构，设置，设立 |
| organizational | ˌɔːrgənəˈzeɪʃənl | adj. 组织的，编制的，机构的 |
| organize | ˈɔːrgənaɪz | vt. 组织，使有系统化，给予生机，组织成立工会等 |
| organizer | ˈɔːrgənaɪzər | n. 组织者 |
| origin | ˈɔːrɪdʒɪn | n. 缘由，起因，起源，血统，出身，商品原产地（证明书） |
| outstanding | aʊtˈstændɪŋ | adj. 著名的，显著的，突出的，未付的，未解决的，未完成的，（证券等）公开上市的 n. 未偿清的贷款，未清算的账目 |
| overdrawing | ˌəʊvərˈdrɔːɪŋ | v. 透支（银行账户），（夸张地）描述，张拉过度 |
| overlapped | ˌəʊvərˈlæpt | adj. 重叠的 |
| overseas | ˌoʊvərˈsiːz | adv. 在海外，海外 |
| overthrow | ˌoʊvərˈθroʊ | vt. 打倒；推翻 |
| overturning | ˌoʊvərˈtɜːrnɪŋ | v. 打翻，掀翻；推翻，使无效（overturn 的现在分词） |
| owner | ˈoʊnər | n. 所有人，物主，业主 |

| 单词 | 国际音标 | 词性及中文意思 |
| --- | --- | --- |
| ownership | ˈoʊnərʃɪp | n. 所有权，拥有权，所有制，所有者权益（指业主的资本或投资），所有权人身份，合法资产 |
| panel | ˈpænl | n. 陪审团名单，一组陪审团员，合议庭，（选定的）专门小组<br>v. 选定（陪审团） |
| parade | pəˈreɪd | n. 游行；阅兵；行进；炫耀；阅兵场 |
| paragraph | ˈpærəɡræf | n. （法律条文和制定法，诉讼档条文中的）项，段落，节 |
| pardoned | ˈpɑːrdnd | n. &vt. 原谅；赦免；宽恕（pardon 的过去式、过去分词） |
| parole | pəˈroʊl | n. 假释（指在刑事判决执行结束前释放被监禁者），宣誓，战俘所作暗号（号令）<br>v. 假释，使（俘虏）宣誓后释放 |
| partially | ˈpɑːrʃəli | adv. 部分地 |
| participant | pɑːrˈtɪsɪpənt | n. 参与者（多指非正式成员或无正式资格者） |
| participate | pɑːrˈtɪsɪpeɪt | vt. & vi. 参加，参与 |
| particularly | pərˈtɪkjələrli | adv. 特别；尤其 |
| party | ˈpɑːrti | n. （诉讼）当事人，关系人，参与者，团体，政党，（社交、游戏等的）集会，宴会 |
| passenger | ˈpæsɪndʒər | n. 乘客，旅客，过路人 |
| passively | ˈpæsɪvli | adv. 被动地，顺从地 |
| passport | ˈpæspɔːrt | n. 护照 |
| patents | ˈpeɪtnts | n. 专利权；专利（patent 的复数） |
| pathogen | ˈpæθədʒən | n. 病菌，病原体 |
| payable | ˈpeɪəbl | adj. 可支付的，应付的，到期的，可获利的<br>n. （pl.）应付款项，应付项目 |
| payer | ˈpeɪər | n. 付款人；支付者 |

| 单词 | 国际音标 | 词性及中文意思 |
|---|---|---|
| payment | ˈpeɪmənt | n. 支付，付款，支付的款项，报偿，惩罚 |
| penalized | ˈpiːnəlaɪzd | v. 处罚，处以刑罚 |
| penalty | ˈpenəlti | n. 刑罚（尤指罚金和监禁），处罚，惩罚性赔偿金，（凭标准买卖的商品）低质减价 |
| percent | pərˈsent | n. 百分比 |
| perform | pərˈfɔːrm | v. 履行，执行，完成，进行 |
| performance | pərˈfɔːrməns | n. 履行（合同、义务、责任等），执行，完成，清偿（债务等）行为，行动，表现，表演 |
| period | ˈpɪriəd | n. 期间，时期，期限 |
| permanent | ˈpɜːrmənənt | adj. 永远的，长期的，不变的，常设的 |
| permission | pərˈmɪʃn | n. 允许（行为），许可（证书），批准，同意，授权 |
| permit | pərˈmɪt | n. 执照，许可证<br>v. 允许，正式许可，给予机会，准许 |
| persecute | ˈpɜːrsɪkjuːt | v. 迫害，虐待，烦扰，为难 |
| person | ˈpɜːrsn | n. 人，法人，人身，身体 |
| personal | ˈpɜːrsənl | adj. 个人的，私人的，本人的，亲自的，人身的，有关个人的，攻击人的，属于个人的，可动的 |
| personnel | ˌpɜːrsəˈnel | n. 人员，人事部门，人事科（处） |
| persons – in –charge | ˈpɜːrsns ɪn tʃɑːrdʒ | n. 主管 |
| petitioner | pəˈtɪʃənər | n. 请求人，上诉人，原告 |
| pharmaceutical | ˌfɑːrməˈsuːtɪkl | adj. 制药的；配药的 |
| photographing | fotəˌɡræfɪŋ | v. 摄影；照相；摄影自拍（photograph 的现在分词） |
| phrase | freɪz | n. 短语，词组；成语 |
| physical | ˈfɪzɪkl | adj. 肉体的，身体的，有形的，物质的，自然的<br>n. （pl.）实际货物，现货 |

续表

| 单词 | 国际音标 | 词性及中文意思 |
|------|---------|--------------|
| physically | ˈfɪzɪkli | adv. 体格上，身体上 |
| physiological | ˌfɪziəˈlɑːdʒɪkl | adj. 生理学的 |
| plates | pleɪts | n. 盘子（plate 的复数）；板材 |
| plot | plɑːt | n. 小块土地，地区，秘密计划，阴谋<br>v. 阴谋，策划 |
| plotting | ˈplɑːtɪŋ | n. 测绘；标图 |
| plural | ˈplʊrəl | adj. 复数的，多重的 |
| plus | plʌs | n. 客人账单上的附加税收，小费的缩号，附加额 |
| pocket | ˈpɑːkɪt | n. 钱袋，衣袋，钱 |
| pointing | ˈpɔɪntɪŋ | n. 弄尖，指示 |
| poison | ˈpɔɪzn | n. 毒药（物），败坏道德的事<br>v. 投毒，毒害，使中毒，摧毁，败坏 |
| poisonous | ˈpɔɪzənəs | adj. 有毒的，有害的，有恶意的，败坏道德的 |
| police | pəˈliːs | n. 警察，警方，警察当局，警务人员，治安<br>v. 侦破（案件等），维持治安，整顿，警备，设置警察，实施警察制度，管理，管治 |
| policy | ˈpɑːləsi | n. 政策，方针，保险单，数字彩票，法律的总目的 |
| political | pəˈlɪtɪkl | adj. 政治的，与政府行为有关的，党派政治的 |
| pollutant | pəˈluːtənt | n. 污染物（质） |
| pollution | pəˈluːʃn | n. 污染，败坏 |
| poor | pʊrˌpɔːr | adj. 贫民的，贫穷的，需要救济的 |
| poppy | ˈpɑːpi | n. [植] 罂粟属植物；罂粟花；深红色 |
| pornography | pɔːrˈnɑːɡrəfi | n. 色情画，色情文学 |
| pose | poʊz | v. 摆姿势；装模作样；提出…讨论；造成，形成 |
| position | pəˈzɪʃn | n. 位置，方位，地位，身份，职位（务），形势，状况，姿态，见解，立场，阵地，头寸，财务状况，（期货）进货，活期账务的余额，成交量 |

续表

| 单词 | 国际音标 | 词性及中文意思 |
|---|---|---|
| possess | pəˈzes | v. 占有，实际控制 |
| postal | ˈpoʊstl | adj. 邮寄的，邮政的，邮局的 |
| postpone | poʊˈspoʊn | v. 延搁，延期，迟误 |
| post | poʊst | n. 邮件（政、寄），职位（守），哨兵（站），岗位，（交易所的）交易台，（会计）过账<br>v. 交纳，贴（布告等），公布，提示，使列入公布名单内，公告不得侵入 |
| power | ˈpaʊər | n. 权力（范围），权限，政权，势力，能力，（pl.）职权，强国，大国，有权力的人，有影响的机构，授权证书 |
| practical | ˈpræktɪkl | adj. 实际（用、践）的，接近的 |
| practice | ˈpræktɪs | n. 实际（践、行、用），惯例，（律师、医生等）开业，诉讼手续，法院的程序和规则，常规<br>v. 实行，实践，开业，办理手续，习惯于 |
| practitioner | prækˈtɪʃənər | n. 执业者，从业人员（尤指律师、医生等） |
| preceding | prɪˈsiːdɪŋ | adj. 在前的，在先的，前面的 |
| precious | ˈpreʃəs | adj. 宝贵的；珍贵的；矫揉造作的 |
| preferential | ˌprefəˈrenʃl | n. 优先权，特惠，特惠关税率<br>adj. 优先的，特惠的，先取的 |
| pregnant | ˈpregnənt | adj. 怀孕的，含蓄的，有意义的 |
| preparation | ˌprepəˈreɪʃn | n. 犯罪预备，准备 |
| prescribed | prɪˈskraɪbd | adj. 法定的，规定的 |
| present | ˈpreznt | adj. 目前的，现在的，即将发生的，手边的，在场的，出席的，正在审议（研究）的<br>n. 现在，目前 |
| press | pres | n. 出版（界），新闻（界），印刷，通讯社 |
| pressure | ˈpreʃər | n. 压力，强制，紧迫（急），艰难，困苦，电压 |
| pretext | ˈpriːtekst | n. 借口，托词 |
| prevail | prɪˈveɪl | v. 胜诉，普遍被接受，取胜，流行，普遍，劝服 |

| 单词 | 国际音标 | 词性及中文意思 |
|---|---|---|
| previous | ˈpriːviəs | adj. 以前的，生前的，前述的，上面提及的 |
| price | praɪs | n. 价格（值），代价，货价，（悬赏缉拿或追杀的）赏金，（贿赂的）金额 |
| primary | praɪmɛri | n.〔美〕（政党的）预选，初选（制），候选人选拔会，最主要者，居首地位<br>adj. 主要的，首要的，直接的，基本的，初步（级）的 |
| principal | ˈprɪnsəpl | n. 委托人，主犯，主要责任人（或义务人），财产主体，信托主体事务，（债务、投资或基金的）本金，第一被告，主债务人，祖传动产<br>adj. 主要的，最重要的，为首的，第一位的 |
| principles | ˈprɪnsəplz | n. 原则，方针，政策，要素，主义 |
| prior | ˈpraɪər | adj. 在先的，在前的，优先的，更重要的<br>n.〔俚〕前科罪 |
| prison | ˈprɪzn | n.（州或联邦的）监狱 |
| prisoner | ˈprɪznər | n. 犯人，囚犯，羁押犯，罪犯，俘虏，刑事被告 |
| private | ˈpraɪvət | adj. 私（个）人的，（公司）股份不上市的，私营的，私设的，秘密的，不公开的，平民的 |
| privilege | ˈprɪvəlɪdʒ | n. 特权（指特殊的法律权利），特惠，特殊利益，免责特权，以法律授权为由的抗辩，保密特权，债权人的优先偿付权，支付给船长的货物照料津贴<br>v. 授予特权，特许 |
| probation | proʊˈbeɪʃn | n. 缓刑，遗嘱检验，试用，见习期，试用期，察看（以观后效），感化犯人 |
| problem | ˈprɑːbləm | n. 问题，难题 |
| procedure | prəˈsiːdʒər | n. 程序，手续，司法程序规则 |
| proceeding | prəˈsiːdɪŋ | n. 行动，经过，处置，（诉讼）程序，（pl.）诉讼，听证会，（案件中的）具体争议，纪录，会议录，事项 |

续表

| 单词 | 国际音标 | 词性及中文意思 |
|------|---------|----------------|
| process | prəˈses | n. 传票，诉讼的进行，刑事检控的进行程序，诉讼过程中的各种命令，诉讼程序，手续，处理<br>v. 对……起诉，向……发出传票，处理，办理，加工，（专利法中的）方法 |
| procession | prəˈseʃn | n. 队伍，行列 |
| procuratorate | ˈprɒkjʊəreɪtərɪt | n. 代理人（代诉人、检察员、检察官等）的职业，检察机关，检察院 |
| produce | prəˈduːs | v. 产生，创制，提供（档、证据等），出示，产生（利益等），开采（原油）（指将原油开采出地面），制造，引起<br>n. 土产品，农产品 |
| producer | prəˈduːsər | n. 保险推销人 |
| product | ˈprɑːdʌkt | n.（商业销售的供使用或消费的）产品 |
| profession | prəˈfeʃn | n. 专业性职业，专业人员 |
| profit | ˈprɑːfɪt | n. 税前利润，除税前的毛利 |
| profitable | ˈprɑːfɪtəbl | adj. 有益（用、利）的，有利可图的 |
| profiteer | ˌprɑːfɪˈtɪr | n. 奸商（尤指发国难财者），投机商人，牟取暴利者，牟取暴利 |
| profit-making | ˈprɑːfɪt meɪkɪŋ | adj. 营利的，盈利的，赚钱的；有利可图的 |
| program | ˈprəʊɡræm | n. 课程（表），程序（表），计划，节目，节目单，（较大专案的）计划，方案 |
| progress | ˈprɑːɡres | n. 进步，进度 |
| prohibit | prəˈhɪbɪt | vt. 阻止，禁止 |
| prohibitive | prəˈhɪbətɪv | adj. 禁止使用或购买的，禁止性的 |
| project | ˈprɑːdʒekt | n. 方案，计划，规划，工程，（工程、科研等）项目 |
| promiscuous | prəˈmɪskjuəs | adj. 男女乱交的 |
| promise | ˈprɑːmɪs | n. 允诺，许诺 v. 许诺，允诺，作保证 |
| promoter | prəˈmoʊtər | n.（企业）发起人，创办人，推销商，（恶意的）煽动者，带头者（人） |

| 单词 | 国际音标 | 词性及中文意思 |
|---|---|---|
| promptly | ˈprɑːmptli | adv. 敏捷地；迅速地；立即地 |
| promulgate | ˈprɑːmlgeɪt | v.（政府正式）颁布（法律、法令），宣布，传播（信仰，知识等），使之生效 |
| pronounce | prəˈnaʊns | v.（正式）宣布 |
| proof | pruːf | n. 以证据证明事实，（法院判决的）证据，书证，[苏] 法官单独审理证据，校稿，校样，标准 |
| propagate | ˈprɑːpəgeɪt | vt. & vi. 繁衍，增殖 |
| proper | ˈprɑːpər | adj. 适当的；本身的；特有的；正派的<br>adv. 完全地 |
| property | ˈprɑːpərti | n. 产权，财产 |
| proposal | prəˈpoʊzl | n. 申请，方案，提议，求婚，投标，保险申请书 |
| prosecution | ˌprɑːsɪˈkjuːʃn | n. 起诉，（刑事）检控，（总称）原告及其律师，控方，检察官，进行，实施，从事，经营 |
| prospectus | prəˈspektəs | n. 招股（商）章程，（募股）说明书，意见书，计划书，发起书 |
| prostitute | ˈprɑːstɪtuːt | n. 妓女，娼妓，贪墨者<br>v. 沦为妓女，卖淫，滥用（才能等），出卖（名誉），降低，贬低 |
| prostitution | ˌprɑːstɪˈtuːʃn | n. 卖淫罪，卖淫，滥用 |
| protect | prəˈtekt | v. 庇护，保护，警戒，防护，备款（以备期票的）支付 |
| protective | prəˈtektɪv | adj. 保护（贸易）的 |
| prove | pruːv | vt. 证明 |
| provide | prəˈvaɪd | vt. 规定；提供；准备；装备 |
| provider | prəˈvaɪdər | n. 供应者；提供者；（尤指）维持家庭生计者 |
| province | ˈprɑːvɪns | n. 省；领域；职权 |
| provincial-level | prəˈvɪnʃl ˈlevl | adj. 省级的 |

续表

| 单词 | 国际音标 | 词性及中文意思 |
|------|---------|---------------|
| provision | prə'vɪʒn | n. 供应，提供，供给 |
| provisional | prə'vɪʒənl | adj. 暂时的；临时的 |
| provocative | prə'vɑːkətɪv | adj. 煽动性的，刺激性的，挑衅的 |
| public | 'pʌblɪk | adj. 公用的；公众的；公立的；政府的 |
| publication | ˌpʌblɪ'keɪʃn | n. 发表，公布 |
| publicity | pʌb'lɪsəti | n. 公众的注意，众所周知 |
| publicize | 'pʌblɪsaɪz | vt. 宣传 |
| publish | 'pʌblɪʃ | vt. 发表；出版；公布 |
| punishable | 'pʌnɪʃəbl | adj.（人或罪行）该处罚的；可惩罚的 |
| punish | 'pʌnɪʃ | vt. 严厉对待；惩罚 |
| punishment | 'pʌnɪʃmənt | n. 处罚，受罚 |
| purchase | 'pɜːrtʃəs | n. 购买；紧握；起重装置 |
| pureness | pjʊrnɪs | n. 纯粹；清洁；清净 |
| purpose | 'pɜːrpəs | n. 目的；意图 |
| pursuant | pər'suːənt | adj. 依据的；追赶的；随后的 |
| pyramid | 'pɪrəmɪd | n. 金字塔；角锥体 |
| qualification | ˌkwɑːlɪfɪ'keɪʃn | n. 合格证书 |
| quality | 'kwɑːləti | n. 质量，品质；特性；才能 |
| quantify | 'kwɑːntɪfaɪ | vt. 量化；为……定量；确定数量 |
| quantity | 'kwɑːntəti | n. 量，数量；总量；大量 |
| quarantine | 'kwɔːrəntiːn | n.（人或动物生病之后被隔离的）检疫期 |
| quota | 'kwoʊtə | n. 定额，配额，（最高或最低）限额，分摊 |
| radioactive | ˌreɪdioʊ'æktɪv | adj. 放射性的，具有放射性的 |
| railroad | 'reɪlroʊd | v. 铁路运输，草率立法，（对某人）匆忙定罪（尤指虚构罪名或证据不足）<br>n. [美] 铁路，轨道设备，铁路设施，铁路公司，铁路系统 |

| 单词 | 国际音标 | 词性及中文意思 |
|------|---------|---------------|
| railway | ˈreɪlweɪ | n. ［英］铁路；轨道；铁道部门 |
| rape | reɪp | n. 普通法上的强奸罪，制定法上的强奸罪<br>v. 强奸 |
| raw | rɔː | adj. 原始的 |
| readily | ˈredɪli | adv. 随意地，随时地 |
| reality | riˈæləti | n. 现实，实际存在物，实在性，实体，实物 |
| reaping | ˈriːpɪŋ | v. 收割（reap 的现在分词） |
| rebate | ˈriːbeɪt | n. 费用返还（作为折扣或减让），折扣 |
| rebellion | rɪˈbeljən | n. 叛乱，反叛（指公开对抗权威或习惯等），反抗，对抗 |
| recalculated | riːˈkælkjʊleɪtɪd | vt. 重新计算 |
| receive | rɪˈsiːv | v. 接到，收到，接受，承认，受理，听取 |
| recidivist | rɪˈsɪdɪvɪst | n. 累犯，惯犯<br>adj. 惯犯的，再犯的 |
| reclaim | rɪˈkleɪm | v. 开拓，开垦，改造，纠正，使悔改，教化，感化（指对犯错误或犯罪者而言），提出要求，要求归还，利用 |
| recognize | ˈrekəgnaɪz | v. 具结，备案，提交保证金，确认，说明，承认，认可，准许 |
| recordation | ˌrekərˈdeɪʃən | n. （契据或按揭等的）注册登记（行为或程序） |
| recorder | rɪˈkɔːrdər | n. 都市法院法官，档案官员，掌卷官 |
| recovery | rɪˈkʌvəri | n. 追偿，财产收回，取得追索权，（判决或命令中的）救济金额，（经济上的）复苏，痊愈，复原 |
| recruited | rɪˈkruːtɪd | vt. 招聘，雇佣（recruit 过去时）；招募 |
| redeem | rɪˈdiːm | v. 买回，赎回，偿还，偿清，履行（诺言，契约），尽（义务），补偿，弥补（过失），补救，恢复（权利，地位等），挽回荣誉 |

| 单词 | 国际音标 | 词性及中文意思 |
|---|---|---|
| reduce | rɪˈduːs | v. 减少（轻），降低，转换（指将诉讼上的物转换为实际占有的物，变成，改变（状况等），使沦为，降级（职） |
| refer | rɪˈfɜːr | v. 归诸，提交，委托，涉及，提及，有关，查询，参考 |
| reform | rɪˈfɔːrm | n. （法官）修订协议（为衡平法上的救济措施），改革（良、造），革新，改过自新，感化 |
| refund | rɪˈfʌnd | v. （多支付款额的）退还，返还款，（用销售债券收入）偿还债务，发新债券取代旧债券<br>n. 退（返）还，退款（指退回多交税款，或卖方退还多收的货款） |
| refuse | rɪˈfjuːz | v. 拒绝，拒受（给）<br>n. 废料，废物，垃圾<br>adj. 无用的，无价值的，废料，垃圾的 |
| regardless | rɪˈɡɑːrdləs | adv. 不顾后果地 |
| region | ˈriːdʒən | n. 地区，范围，领域，行政区 |
| register | ˈredʒɪstər | n. 登记官员（指负责官方档案登记的政府官员），遗嘱检验法官，（法院的）未决案件登记簿，警方案情登记簿，登记簿（如股东登记簿等），注册，登记，船舶登记簿，海关证明书，记录器，寄存器，自动记录器，记存装置，记录册，登记为选民<br>v. 登记，注册，记录，（律师、当事人、证人在书记员处）签到，挂号（邮寄） |
| regulation | ˌreɡjuˈleɪʃn | n. （行政）规则（章），地方性法规，条例 |
| regulatory | ˈreɡjələtɔːri | adj. 规范（章）的，制定规章的 |
| rehabilitation | ˌriːəˌbɪlɪˈteɪʃn | n. 复权（职、位），（证人）恢复名誉，（破产法中债务人经济状况的）复兴，康复（指犯罪者等经矫正改造恢复社会正常生活） |
| related | rɪˈleɪtɪd | adj. 讲述的，叙述的；有关系的，有关联的 |
| relationship | rɪˈleɪʃnʃɪp | n. 关系，亲属关系 |

| 单词 | 国际音标 | 词性及中文意思 |
|------|----------|----------------|
| relative | ˈrelətɪv | n. 亲属，亲戚<br>adj. 有关系的，相应的，有关的 |
| relay | ˈriːleɪ | vi. 转播；接替 |
| release | rɪˈliːs | n. 免除（义务、责任等），解除（合同），放弃（权利、要求等），弃权书，收据，出版（发行）授权（许可）书，（财产或权益的）转让或处置，财产转让书，解脱束缚，（罪犯等的）释放令<br>v. 解放（除），开释，免除，准予发表，转让（财产等），放弃（权利等） |
| relend | riˈlend | vt. 再借 |
| relevant | ˈreləvənt | adj. 相关的，贴切的，中肯的，成比例的，相应的，有重大意义（作用）的，实质性的 |
| relic | ˈrelɪk | n. 遗物，遗迹，遗产 |
| relief | rɪˈliːf | n. 土地继承费（指土地继承人为获得继承权而供奉给封建领主的费用），协助或援助（尤指国家提供的经济援助），司法救济（尤指衡平法上的救济） |
| relieving | rɪˈliːvɪŋ | adj. 救助的，救援的 |
| religious | rɪˈlɪdʒəs | adj. 宗教的，宗教上的，宗教信仰的 |
| remaining | rɪˈmeɪnɪŋ | adj. 剩余的，保留的 |
| remit | rɪˈmɪt | n. 宽恕，赦免，减轻，缓和，呈送当局（予以裁定），（案件的）发还（高级法院将案件送回原审法院），回复（原状、原位），汇寄（款项等） |
| remittance | rɪˈmɪtns | n. 汇付（指支付货价或服务款的一种方式），汇票，汇寄，汇款（额） |
| remove | rɪˈmuːv | v. 移动，搬开，消除，免职，移送（案件），杀掉，暗杀 |
| remuneration | rɪˌmjuːnəˈreɪʃn | n. 报酬，酬金，支付酬金，补偿，赔偿 |
| render | ˈrendər | n. 竞争，战斗，斗殴 |
| renovation | ˌrenəˈveɪʃn | n. 翻新；修复；整修 |

| 单词 | 国际音标 | 词性及中文意思 |
|------|---------|---------------|
| repay | rɪˈpeɪ | v. 偿还，偿付，补偿，报答，报复 |
| repeatedly | rɪˈpiːtɪdli | adv. 重复地，再三地 |
| repentance | rɪˈpentəns | n. 悔改，悔悟，懊（后）悔 |
| repent | rɪˈpent | v. 悔悟，懊（后）悔，悔改 |
| report | rɪˈpɔːrt | n. 报告（指书面或口头正式陈述事实），（法院的）司法审判笔录，汇报<br>v. 报告（道），汇报，记录，告发，揭发 |
| representative | ˌreprɪˈzentətɪv | n. 代表，（代位）继承人，诉讼代理人<br>adj. 代理的，代表的，表现的，表示的，代议制的，典型的 |
| reprieve | rɪˈpriːv | n. 暂缓行刑，暂缓<br>v. 暂缓行刑 |
| reprimand | ˈreprɪmænd | n. 警告处分，惩戒，申斥 |
| reproduced | ˌriːprəˈdjuːst | v. 再生产，再现，复制，仿造，生育，生殖 |
| republic | rɪˈpʌblɪk | n. 共和国，共和政体，（其成员享有平等权利的）社团 |
| reputation | ˌrepjuˈteɪʃn | n. 名声，名誉，[英] 公认证据（指英证据法准许的在涉及公共利害的案件中采用旧文件或提起诉讼时已死人物的陈述作为证据） |
| request | rɪˈkwest | n. 要求，请求（书），请求之事物<br>v. 请求，要求 |
| require | rɪˈkwaɪər | v. 需要，要求，命令 |
| requirements | rɪˈkwaɪərmənts | n. 所需的东西 |
| requisition | ˌrekwɪˈzɪʃn | n. 正式要求（请求、申请），征用（财产），需要，请购单，调拨单，申请单，必备条件<br>v. 要求，征用（财产） |
| rescinded | rɪˈsɪndɪd | v. （合同等的）废除，取消，撤销，解除，宣告无效 |

| 单词 | 国际音标 | 词性及中文意思 |
|---|---|---|
| rescue | ˈreskjuː | n. 营救，援救，劫夺犯人（指非法武力使罪犯越狱或脱逃），夺回扣押物［国］夺回捕获品<br>v. 援救，营救，夺回（扣押物），劫夺（被拒捕或囚禁者），［国］夺回（被捕获物） |
| research | rɪˈsɜːrtʃ | v. 调查，工作<br>n. 研究 |
| resells | ˌriːˈsel | v. 转售（商品），再出售 |
| reserve | rɪˈzɜːrv | n. 保留，保存（物），储备，保险费净余（指除去支出后所剩下的净值），准备金，公积金，外汇储备，保留地，秘密，限度<br>v. 储备，保存（留），推（延）迟，预订 |
| resettlement | ˌriːˈsetlmənt | n. 重新定居，重予安置，重新处置 |
| residence | ˈrezɪdəns | n. 居所，居住，居留期，公司业务注册地 |
| resist | rɪˈzɪst | vt. & vi. 使用武力阻止（某事）发生；抵抗；对抗 |
| resolve | rɪˈzɑːlv | v. 解决（答），消除，决定（议），转为，变为<br>n. 决议（定） |
| resort | rɪˈzɔːrt | n. 凭借的方法，手段，娱乐场<br>v. 求助，诉诸，采取（某种手段等），常去 |
| resources | rɪˈsɔːrsɪz | 资源 |
| respectively | rɪˈspektɪvli | adv. 各自地，各个地，分别地 |
| responsibility | rɪˌspɑːnsəˈbɪləti | n. 责任，刑事责任能力，义务履行能力，负担，职责，任务，（财力方面的）可靠性，响应性 |
| responsible | rɪˈspɑːnsəbl | adj. 应负责任的，有责任的，能履行责任的，可靠的 |
| restitution | ˌrestɪˈtuːʃn | n. 归还，恢复原状，要求恢复原状之诉，赔偿，赔偿金，恢复，复原 |
| restraint | rɪˈstreɪnt | n. 限（遏、抑）制，贸易限制，（军事）禁闭，羁押，约束力，管束 |

| 单词 | 国际音标 | 词性及中文意思 |
|---|---|---|
| restriction | rɪˈstrɪkʃn | n. 限制，管制，财产受益或使用限制，限制自由（指军法中在道德或法律上对自由的限制，见下列比较），带有限制性的条件或规则 |
| restrictive | rɪˈstrɪktɪv | adj. 限制性的，约束性的 |
| result | rɪˈzʌlt | n. 结果，效果，效验，成效，成绩，（立法机构或议院等的）决议，决定，答案<br>v. 造成，产生，导致，归结为 |
| retained | rɪˈteɪnd | adj. 保留的 |
| retaliate | rɪˈtælieɪt | v. 报复，反击，倒算，征收报复性关税 |
| retaliation | rɪˌtæliˈeɪʃn | n. 报仇，[国] 报复，回敬 |
| reveal | rɪˈviːl | v. 显（揭、透）露，揭发，剖析，泄露（秘密等），启示 |
| revenge | rɪˈvendʒ | n. 报仇雪恨，仇恨，报仇心，复仇心 v. 报复，报仇 |
| revenue | ˈrevənuː | n. （国家的）岁入，税收，收入，收益，总收入，收入项，税署（或局） |
| reversal | rɪˈvɜːrsl | n. 撤销原判（指上级法院撤销下级法院之判决），价格逆变（指证券近期市场价格的变化），颠倒，倒退，反转，推翻，变更 |
| reviling | rɪˈvaɪlɪŋ | vt. 辱骂；斥责（revil 的现在分词） |
| revoked | rɪˈvəʊkt | adj. 取消的 |
| revolutionary | ˌrevəˈluːʃəneri | adj. 革命的 |
| rightful | ˈraɪtfl | adj. 正当的，合法的，公正的，有权取得地位的，有权获得财产的 |
| ringleader | ˈrɪŋliːdər | n. 头目，叛国头子，叛党首领，元凶，首要分子 |
| riot | ˈraɪət | n. 聚众骚乱罪，暴乱罪（指三人或多人非法集会以暴力威胁或恐吓公众的方式破坏治安） |
| risk | rɪsk | n. 危险，风险，风险责任，[险] 保险责任，风险概率，风险程度，保险损失数额，保险对象（人或物），(pl.) 险种，险别<br>v. 冒险，做赌注 |

| 单词 | 国际音标 | 词性及中文意思 |
|---|---|---|
| robbers | ˈrɔbəz | n. 盗贼（robber 的复数） |
| robbery | ˈrɑːbəri | n. 抢劫，劫掠，抢劫案 v. 抢劫，强夺，夺取，剥夺 |
| role | roʊl | n. 角色，任务，作用 |
| ruins | ˈruːɪnz | n. 虚墟；遗迹（ruin 的复数） |
| rules | ruːlz | n.（对某一案件的）裁决，裁定，规则，细则，章程，（确定性的）命令，法规，规律，习惯，通例，统治，管辖 |
| rumors | ˈruːmərs | n. 谣传，流言（rumor 的复数） |
| ruthless | ˈruːθləs | adj. 无情的，残忍的 |
| sabotage | ˈsæbətɑːʒ | n. 破坏行动<br>v. 进行破坏，从事破坏活动，怠工，怠业 |
| safeguard | ˈseɪfgɑːrd | n. 保护措施，保证条款，安全装置，防护设施，（战时）安全通行证，护照，保护者，护送者，警卫员 保护，维护，捍卫 |
| sale | seɪl | n. 卖，出售，销售 |
| sanctions | ˈsæŋkʃnz | n. 制裁；处罚（sanction 的复数）；制发<br>v. 批准；对…实行制裁；赞许（sanction 的第三人称单数） |
| sanitation | ˌsænɪˈteɪʃn | n. 环境卫生，公共卫生，公共卫生设施，卫生状况改善 |
| saplings | ˈsæplɪŋz | n. 树苗，幼树 |
| scene | siːn | n. 出事地点，（犯罪）现场，情景，（pl.）实况，吵闹 |
| scenic | ˈsiːnɪk | adj. 舞台的；风景优美的；戏剧的 |
| school | skuːl | n. 学派，流派，理论，学院，书院，经院，（pl.）学术界，学校，专科学校，校舍，获得知识的方式或活动，环境以及场所等<br>v. 教育，使学会，培养，训练，使接受学校教育，控制，指导 |

续表

| 单词 | 国际音标 | 词性及中文意思 |
|------|----------|----------------|
| science | ˈsaɪəns | n. 科学（研究），学科，自然科学，真理探索，技术，技巧，知识，学问 |
| scientific | ˌsaɪənˈtɪfɪk | adj. 科学的，学术的，精通学理的，有系统的 |
| scope | skoʊp | n. 界限，领域，范围，视野，机会 |
| scrawling | skrɔːlɪŋ | v. 马马虎虎（或潦草）地写（scrawl 的现在分词） |
| seal | siːl | n. 封条（印），印图，火漆，封条，封铅，密封，保证，［美］伪币 v. 批准，保证，确证，盖章于，盖印，密封，禁止接触 |
| searching | ˈsɜːrtʃɪŋ | adj. 锐利的，穿透的；急于发现真情的 |
| secondary | ˈsekənderi | adj. 第二的，从属的，次级（要）的，间接的，附属的，非原始的 n. 副手，次要人物，代理人 |
| secret | ˈsiːkrət | adj. 秘（机）密的，隐蔽的，暗藏的，暗中进行的 |
| secretly | ˈsiːkrətli | adv. 秘密地；背地里 |
| sect | sekt | n. 宗派 |
| section | ˈsekʃn | n.（条文中的）条、款（指制定法中经常分章、条、段、项等的条），地区（段），类，科，处，股，组，部门，工段，节，［美］1 平方英里面积，640 英亩土地 |
| sector | ˈsektər | n. 部门，（国家经济的）部门，扇形，扇形面，部分，成分 |
| security | sɪˈkjʊrəti | n. 保证（人、金），担保（品），抵押（物），安全，安稳，保护，守护，保人，（pl.）产权证明，治安保卫（措施） |
| seduce | sɪˈduːs | v. 勾引，诱惑，诱奸，诱使堕落（或犯罪） |
| seeds | siːdz | n. 种子，籽，萌芽，开端，起因，家系，子孙，后裔 |
| seek | siːk | v. 寻找，搜索（查），追（寻、探、请、征）求 |
| seize | siːz | v. 捉住，逮捕，俘获，占有，夺取，查封，扣押，没收，抓住（时机），掌握 |

| 单词 | 国际音标 | 词性及中文意思 |
|------|---------|--------------|
| seizure | ˈsiːʒər | n. 依法占有，充公，没收（物），占领，夺取，捕获，强取，扣留，扣押物 |
| selectively | sɪˈlektɪvli | adv. 不普遍地 |
| selfish | ˈselfɪʃ | adj. 自私的，出于自私的 |
| senior | ˈsiːniər | adj. 年长的，已届退休年龄的，年事高的，地位（等级等）较高的，资深的，高级的，有优先权的，主要的 |
| sentence | ˈsentəns | n. 刑事判决，判刑，量刑<br>v. 判刑，量刑 |
| separately | ˈseprətli | adv. 分离地；个别地，分别地 |
| seriously | ˈsɪriəsli | adv. 严重地；危险地 |
| server | ˈsɜːrvər | n. 服务员，（传票、令状等法律文件的）送达员（人、者），送交者 |
| serviceman | ˈsɜːrvɪsmən | n. 军人 |
| session | ˈseʃn | n. （法院的）开庭（期）），（立法机关等的）开会（期），一场（场）交易，（交易所等市场的）市（如前市，后市），盘（如前盘，中盘），届 |
| settlement | ˈsetlmənt | n. （家庭）财产让与，和解，（庭外）协议调解，解决，决定，了结，清偿（算、理），支付，决算，（不动产交易等的）成交会，（遗嘱执行人）处置所有遗产，整理，安排，安置，定居，汇款方式 |
| severely | sɪˈvɪrli | adv. 严格地 |
| severity | sɪˈverəti | n. 严重性 |
| sewage | ˈsuːɪdʒ | n. 污水，污物 |
| shake | ʃeɪk | v. 解雇，撵走，敲诈，摇动，减弱<br>n. 解雇，敲诈，勒索，贿金，摇动，挥动，使震动，[俚] 抛弃，摆脱，握手 |
| shareholder | ˈʃerhoʊldər | n. 股东，股票持有人（pl.）[公] 股东大会 |
| share-soliciting | ʃer səˈlɪsɪtɪŋ | n. 募股 |

续表

| 单词 | 国际音标 | 词性及中文意思 |
|------|----------|----------------|
| share-subscrip-tion | ʃer səbˈskrɪpʃn | n. 认购股份 |
| shelter | ˈʃeltər | n. 避税手段，掩（庇、保）护，隐匿，提供住宿<br>v. 庇护（所、物），保护，避难所 |
| shield | ʃiːld | n. 盾，保护者，庇护者，[美] 警察徽章 |
| shipping | ˈʃɪpɪŋ | n. 装运，发货，海运，航运（业），船运，运输（送），船舶（总称），船舶总吨数 |
| shoddy | ˈʃɑːdi | adj. 劣等的，冒牌的<br>n. 劣等品，次货，冒牌货，粗制滥造或虚饰外观的劣等货 |
| shortened | ˈʃɔːrtnd | adj. 被缩短了的 |
| sickness | ˈsɪknəs | n. 疾病 |
| signatory | ˈsɪɡnətɔːri | n. （协议，条约等的）签署者（国、方、者）adj. 签过字的，署名的 |
| signature | ˈsɪɡnətʃər | n. 签名（署），署名，画押，赦令，诏书 |
| significant | sɪɡˈnɪfɪkənt | adj. 重要的，有效的 |
| silver | ˈsɪlvər | n. 银（币），白银<br>adj. 银（质、制）的 |
| similar | ˈsɪmələr | n. 类似物，类似者<br>adj. 相似的，类似的 |
| sincere | sɪnˈsɪr | adj. 真诚的；诚挚的；真实的 |
| site | saɪt | n. 地点，场所，位置（尤指专项财产所在地），（市政）条例，遗址 |
| situation | ˌsɪtʃuˈeɪʃn | n. 形势，政局，位置，地位，处境，境遇 |
| skeleton | ˈskelɪtn | n. 梗概，轮廓 |
| slander | ˈslændər | n. 诽谤（尤指言词），言辞诽谤行为 v. 诽谤 |
| slaughters | ˈslɔːtərs | n. 屠宰；大屠杀；（非正式）彻底击败 |

| 单词 | 国际音标 | 词性及中文意思 |
|------|---------|---------------|
| small-amount | smɔːl əˈmaʊnt | n. 小额；小批量 |
| smashing | ˈsmæʃɪŋ | adj. 粉碎性的，猛烈的；了不起的，极好的 |
| smooth | smuːð | adj. 光滑的；顺利的；平稳的 |
| smuggle | ˈsmʌgl | v. 走私，偷运，偷漏税 |
| snatch | snætʃ | n. 攫取，绑架 |
| social | ˈsoʊʃl | adj. 社会（性）的，有关社会的，社交的 |
| society | səˈsaɪəti | n. 社会（团），团体，会，社，交际界，社交，交往（活动），相处 |
| software | ˈsɔːftwer | n. （计算机）软件，程序设计 |
| soldiers | soldʒərs | n. 士兵；战士数量（soldier 的复数） |
| solicitation | səˌlɪsɪˈteɪʃn | n. 请求（行为），教唆罪 |
| solid | ˈsɑːlɪd | adj. 坚固的，资本（金）雄厚的，纯质的，有根据的，可靠的，确实的 |
| sophisticated | səˈfɪstɪkeɪtɪd | adj. 尖端的，高级的，非常有经验的，老练的，掺假的 |
| source | sɔːrs | n. 渊源，根源，根据，原始资料，提供消息者 |
| sovereignty | ˈsɑːvrənti | n. 主权（国家），统治权，君权，独立国 |
| spawn | spɔːn | n. 菌丝；卵；产物 |
| specific | spəˈsɪfɪk | adj. 特定（有）的，与特定事物相关的，遵守具体要件要求的，从量的，具体的，明确的<br>n. 特性，细节，（pl.）（计划、建议等）详细说明书，特定用途物品 |
| specifications | ˌspesɪfɪˈkeɪʃnz | n. 详述（行为），（性能、使用等）说明书，指控书，范围，规格，明细表，技术条件 |
| specify | spɛsɪfaɪ | vt. 指定；列举；详细说明；把……列入说明书 |
| specimen | ˈspesɪmən | n. 样本（品），实例，（贬义）怪人，怪事 |
| spite | spaɪt | n. 恶意，怨恨<br>v. 轻蔑，恶意对待，刁难，敌意，仇视 |

续表

| 单词 | 国际音标 | 词性及中文意思 |
|------|---------|----------------|
| split | splɪt | n. 告密（者），便衣警察，分裂，派别，派系<br>v. 分离，断绝关系，均分，告密，拆股，分担 |
| spouse | spaʊz | n. 配偶（指夫或妻），已婚者 |
| spread | spred | n. 差价，差额 v. 延伸，分期 |
| spy | spaɪ | n. 间谍，特务 |
| stable | ˈsteɪbl | adj. 稳定的，牢固的，持久的，不动摇的，坚定的 |
| staff | stæf | n. 全体人员，参谋机构，职工，工作人员，参谋部门，指挥棒，警棍<br>v. 配备职员，担任职员，雇佣 |
| staging | ˈsteɪdʒɪŋ | n. 分段运输；脚手架；上演 |
| stamp | stæmp | n. 图章，检验章，邮戳，奖券，标记，标志<br>v. 盖印，打上标记，贴印花税票，标出，压制，镇压，扑灭，消灭 |
| standard | ˈstændərd | n. 本位，官本位，示范，（pl.）道德（伦理，习惯等的）标准，准则 |
| statement | ˈsteɪtmənt | n. 声明（书），主张，（事实）陈述，（警方对疑犯招供所作的）供述记录 |
| state-owned | stet ond | adj. 国有的；国营的；州立的 |
| state-protected | steɪt prəˈtektɪd | adj. 受国家保护的 |
| state-run | steɪt rʌn | adj. ［经］国营的；州立的 |
| states-owned | steɪts oʊnd | adj. 国有的；国营的 |
| statistician | ˌstætɪˈstɪʃn | n. 统计学家，统计员 |
| statutory | ˈstætʃətɔːri | adj. 法令的，与法规相关的，制定法创制的，依照制定法的，依法应惩处的 |
| stealing | ˈstiːlɪŋ | n. 窃取，偷窃行为，（pl.）赃物<br>adj. 有偷盗行为的，偷盗的 |
| stealthily | ˈstelθɪli | adv. 暗地里，偷偷摸摸地 |

| 单词 | 国际音标 | 词性及中文意思 |
|------|---------|---------------|
| stem | stem | n.（花草的）茎，（树木的）干 |
| sterilization | ˌsterələˈzeɪʃn | n. 消除，（黄金等的）查封，冻结，清查，土地的贫瘠化，绝育手术 |
| stiff | stɪf | n.〔美〕普通工人，流动工人，流通（可转让的）票据，钞票，金钱，不肯给小账的<br>adj.（价格）坚挺的，昂贵的，艰难的，费劲的，硬的，硬邦邦的，生硬的，僵化的 |
| stipulation | ˌstɪpjuˈleɪʃn | n. 约定，规定，（条约、合同等的）款项，条款，自愿协议，（双方辩护律师的）协议书，〔罗〕正式合同 |
| stock | stɑːk | n. 祖先，世系，家族，人种，（公司的）资本，股本，证券资本，股票<br>adj.〔美〕股票的，证券的，库存的，管理存货的，现有的，常备的 |
| storage | ˈstɔːrɪdʒ | n. 储存，仓储，栈租，存仓费，保管，仓库，储存量，保管费，仓库费 |
| streetcars | ˈstriːtkɑːrs | n. 有轨电车（streetcar 的复数） |
| struggle | ˈstrʌgl | v. 斗争，奋斗，努力<br>n. 斗争，奋斗，努力 |
| subjected | səbˈdʒektɪd | v. 使遭受；使从属；受…影响（subject 的过去式和过去分词形式） |
| submit | səbˈmɪt | v. 使服从，使受到，呈交，提交，认为，主张，建议，服从，忍受 |
| subordinate | səˈbɔːrdɪnət | adj. 下级的，次要的，从属的<br>n. 部属，部下，下级，服从者 |
| substance | ˈsʌbstəns | n. 实质（体），物质，使人上瘾的药物，毒品，本质（体），主旨，要义，资产（金），财产（物），内容 |
| substandard | ˌsʌbˈstændərd | adj. 标准以下的，低于标准以下的，不合标准的，（语言等）不规范的 |

续表

| 单词 | 国际音标 | 词性及中文意思 |
|------|----------|----------------|
| substantial | səbˈstænʃl | adj. 真实的，实体（质）的，物质的，有重大价值的，内容充实的 |
| subversion | səbˈvɜːrʒn | n. 颠覆，灭亡，败坏 |
| sued | suːd | v. 要求，请求（sue 过去分词形式） |
| suffer | ˈsʌfər | v. 遭受，惩罚，被处死刑，受损失（害），患病，允许，容许 |
| sufficient | səˈfɪʃnt | adj. 充分（足）的，足够的 |
| superstition | ˌsuːpərˈstɪʃn | n. 迷信（行为） |
| supervision | ˌsuːpərˈvɪʒn | n. 监督，监察，管理 |
| supervisor | ˈsuːpərvaɪzər | n. 监督者，管理者，监察人 |
| supplementary | ˌsʌplɪˈmentri | adj. 增补的，补充的，追加的<br>n. 增补者（物），补充者（物） |
| supply | səˈplaɪ | n. 供应品，（生活）用品，储藏，（储备）物资，补给<br>v. 供应，填补，弥补，补充，提供，代理，暂代 |
| support | səˈpɔːrt | vt. 支撑；撑扶；托住；支持 |
| supreme | suːˈpriːm | adj. 最高的，最重要的 |
| surgery | ˈsɜːrdʒəri | n. 外科 |
| surrender | səˈrendər | n. 屈从（权力等），让步，放弃（权利、主张），解约，退保，缴还（保险单），投降，屈服<br>v. 解约，退保，投降，自首，引渡，（要塞）陷落，放弃，让与 |
| surveillance | sɜːrˈveɪləns | n. 监视，看守，监督，管理 |
| survey | ˈsɜːrveɪ | n. 评估（价），考察，视察，调查，政府（或官方）测量机构，民意测验，问卷调查，（船舶）评估书，勘定，逐点说明，全面地评述，概括地评述 |
| susceptible | səˈseptəbl | adj. 易感的，易受影响的，能容许的，受影响的 |
| suspect | səˈspekt | n. 犯罪嫌疑人，疑犯<br>v. 嫌疑，怀疑 |

| 单词 | 国际音标 | 词性及中文意思 |
|------|----------|----------------|
| suspected | səˈspektɪd | adj. 嫌疑的，涉嫌的 |
| suspended | səˈspendɪd | adj. 缓期的 |
| swindle | ˈswɪndl | n. 骗取（财产），欺骗，骗术，骗子<br>v. 骗取（财产），骗人 |
| symbol | ˈsɪmbl | n. 象征，标志，符（记、代）号，信条，教义 |
| syndicate | ˈsɪndɪkət | n. 企业联合组织，财团，理事会，董事会 |
| syphilis | ˈsɪfɪlɪs | n. 梅毒 |
| system | ˈsɪstəm | n. 制度，体系，体制，系统 |
| tablets | ˈtæblɪts | n. 药片；便笺 |
| tampers | ˈtæmpər | vt. 夯实，砸实；填塞 |
| tap | tæp | n. 随时可买的证券（或国库券、债券），可供应的国债券，定价供应（证券），窃听（器）<br>v. 开发，挖掘，搭线窃听，安装窃听器 |
| tapes | teɪps | n. 录音带，胶纸带；条带，边带 |
| targets | ˈtɑːgɪts | n. 目标，靶子，批评或嘲笑的对象<br>v. 规定为指标，为指定目标，作为目标，对准 |
| taxpayer | ˈtækspeɪər | n. 纳税人，租金仅够支付地产税的临建房屋 |
| technical | ˈteknɪkl | adj. 严格根据法律或规则的；技术的，工艺的，人为的 |
| technological | ˌteknəˈlɑːdʒɪkl | adj. 技术上的 |
| telecommunica-tion | ˌtelikəˌmjuːnɪˈkeɪʃn | n. 电信 |
| telegrams | ˈtelɪgræms | n. 电报（telegram 的复数） |
| televised | ˈtelɪvaɪzd | adj. 被电视播放的<br>vi. 电视播放（televise 的过去式、过去分词） |
| tenders | ˈtendərz | n. ［贸易］投标（tender 的复数）<br>v. ［贸易］投标（tender 的第三人称单数） |

| 单词 | 国际音标 | 词性及中文意思 |
|---|---|---|
| term | tɜːrm | n. 术语，（合同）条款，约定，条件，期限，（法庭的）开庭期 |
| termination | ˌtɜːrmɪˈneɪʃn | n. 结束，终止 |
| territorial | ˌterəˈtɔːriəl | adj. 领土的；区域的；土地的；地方的 |
| territory | ˈterətɔːri | n. 领土，领域；范围；地域 |
| terrorism | ˈterərɪzəm | n. 恐怖主义 |
| terrorist | ˈterərɪst | n. 恐怖分子，恐怖主义者 |
| testify | ˈtestɪfaɪ | v. 证明（实），作证，提供证据，确言，宣称 |
| testimony | ˈtestɪmoʊni | n. 言辞证据，证言，（刻在两块石碑上的）摩西十诫 |
| theft | θeft | n. 盗窃行为，偷窃（罪） |
| threaten | ˈθretn | v. 威胁，恐吓，预示恶兆，使有受害之虑 |
| tomb | tuːm | n. 墓穴 |
| torture | ˈtɔːrtʃər | n. 拷问，刑讯，痛苦，折磨，歪曲 |
| trademark | ˈtreɪdmɑːrk | n. 商标 |
| trafficking | ˈtræfɪkɪŋ | n. 贩卖，私自买卖 |
| traitor | ˈtreɪtər | n. 叛徒，叛逆者，背信者，卖国贼 |
| trampling | ˈtræmplɪŋ | n. 践踏；踩踏<br>v. 踩躏（trample 的现在分词） |
| transaction | trænˈzækʃn | n. 处理，执行，会计项目，来往项目，交易，具体事务，业务，和解协议，事项，议价，安排 |
| transfer | trænsˈfɜːr | n.（所有权的）让与，（物权、产权等的）转让，过户，汇兑，（会计）转账，调动，转移，<br>v. 转移，让渡，交付，变换，过户，调职 |
| transgress | trænsˈgres | v. 超越（范围或限度），违犯，违反法律，有罪 |
| translator | trænsˈleɪtər | n. 译员，翻译者；翻译家 |
| transmission | trænsˈmɪʃn | n. 传送（递），转递，传播 |

| 单词 | 国际音标 | 词性及中文意思 |
|---|---|---|
| transportation | ˌtrænspɔːrˈteɪʃn | n. 流刑，放逐，（客运或货运）运输（工具、费用），输送，交通业 |
| treasury | ˈtreʒəri | n. 国库，金库，资金，（国家或机关）所拥有的款项，（大写）财政部 |
| treatment | ˈtriːtmənt | n. 处置，处理，待遇，治疗 |
| treaty | ˈtriːti | n. 条约，谈判，协商，合同，合约，转保协议 |
| trial | ˈtraɪəl | n. 审判 |
| trick | trɪk | n. 奸诈，欺诈手段，恶作剧 |
| troops | truːps | n. 部队；军队（troop 的复数） |
| trustor | ˈtrʌstə | n. 财产授予者，信托人，信托者，设立信托资产者，委托人 |
| truthful | ˈtruːθfl | adj. 真实的，说实话的，诚实的 |
| tunnel | ˈtʌnl | n. 隧道，地道 |
| twist | twɪst | vt. 捻；拧；扭伤；编织；使苦恼 |
| unauthorized | ʌnˈɔːθəraɪzd | adj. 未经授权，未经批准（许可、公认）的，无根据的，越权的 |
| undergo | ˌʌndərˈgoʊ | v. 经受，经历，忍受，遭受（苦难等） |
| undermine | ˌʌndərˈmaɪn | v. 暗中破坏，损害 |
| undertaken | ˌʌndəˈteɪkən | v. 从事；开始进行（undertake 的过去分词） |
| undisclosed | ˌʌndɪsˈkloʊzd | n. 未泄露的，不公开的，保持秘密的，身份不明的，隐名的 |
| undue | ˌʌnˈduː | adj. 不当的，过分的，非法的，未到期的，未到支付期的 |
| unfair | ˌʌnˈfer | adj. 不公平的，不正直的，不正当的，不合理的 |
| unforeseeable | ˌʌnfɔːrˈsiːəbl | adj. 不能合理预见的，无法预料的 |
| unification | ˌjuːnɪfɪˈkeɪʃn | n. 统一，一致，联合，标准化 |
| uniform | ˈjuːnɪfɔːrm | adj. 统一的，一致的 |

续表

| 单词 | 国际音标 | 词性及中文意思 |
|------|----------|----------------|
| unlawful | ʌnˈlɔːfl | adj. 非法的，不合法的，不正当的，违法的，不道德的，私生子的 |
| unqualified | ˌʌnˈkwɑːlɪfaɪd | adj. 不合格的，不适当的，无条件的，绝对的，无资格的 |
| unsettled | ʌnˈsetld | adj. 未决的，未偿付的，未结账的，法律上未作处理的，无秩序的，有待进一步讨论的 |
| urgent | ˈɜːrdʒənt | adj. 紧急的，急迫的，加急的 |
| urine | ˈjʊrɪn | n. 尿 |
| usable | ˈjuːzəbl | adj. 可用的，便于使用的，有效的 |
| utilize | ˈjuːtəlaɪz | vt. 利用 |
| valuable | ˈvæljuəbl | adj. 贵重的；有价值的；可估价的 |
| value-added | ˈvæljuː ˈædɪd | n. 增值 |
| vandalizing | ˈvændəlaɪz | vt. 肆意破坏（尤指公共财产） |
| venereal | vəˈnɪriəl | adj. 性交的；性病的；由性交传染的 |
| vent | vent | n. 出口；通风孔；（感情的）发泄 |
| verification | ˌverɪfɪˈkeɪʃn | n. 证明；证实 |
| verify | ˈverɪfaɪ | vt. 核实；查证 |
| version | ˈvɜːrʒn | n. 译文；版本；[医] 倒转术 |
| vertebrate | ˈvɜːrtɪbrət | n. 脊椎动物 |
| vessels | vɛslz | n. 容器；船舶；血管（vessel 的复数） |
| vicinity | vəˈsɪnəti | n. 近，接近，密切 |
| vicious | ˈvɪʃəs | adj. 恶的，邪恶的 |
| victim | ˈvɪktɪm | n. 牺牲者；受害人；牺牲品 |
| video | ˈvɪdioʊ | n. 磁带录像，录像 |
| vile | vaɪl | adj. 卑鄙的；低廉的；肮脏的；邪恶的 |
| violate | ˈvaɪəleɪt | vt. 违反，违背 |

续表

| 单词 | 国际音标 | 词性及中文意思 |
|------|----------|----------------|
| violence | ˈvaɪələns | n. 激烈；暴力；侵犯；歪曲 |
| virus | ˈvaɪrəs | n. 病毒 |
| voided | ˈvɔɪdɪd | adj. 有空间的；废弃的；中心区空白的 |
| voluntarily | ˌvɑːlənˈterəli | adv. 志愿地 |
| voter | ˈvoʊtər | n. 选举人，投票人；有投票权者 |
| voucher | ˈvaʊtʃər | n. 证人；保证人；证明者；收据 |
| waive | weɪv | vt. 放弃；搁置 |
| ward | wɔːrd | n. 监视；保卫；病房 |
| warrant | ˈwɔːrənt | n. 授权证；许可证 |
| wartime | ˈwɔːrtaɪm | n. 战时 |
| waste | weɪst | n. 浪费；滥用 |
| waterway | ˈwɔːtərweɪ | n. 水路；航道；排水沟 |
| weaponry | ˈwepənri | n. 兵器，武器（总称） |
| wharves | wɔːvz | n. 码头；停泊处（wharf 的复数） |
| whenever | wenˈevər | conj. 每当；无论何时 |
| whorehouse | ˈhɔːrhaʊs | n. 妓院 |
| wildlife | ˈwaɪldlaɪf | n. 野生动植物 |
| withdraw | wɪθˈdrɔː | v. 取回 |
| withheld | wɪθˈheld | v. 保留；扣留；抑制（withhold 的过去时） |
| witness | ˈwɪtnəs | n. 目击者；证人 |
| womb | wuːm | n. 子宫；发源地 |
| woods | wʊdz | n. 森林 |
| workforce | ˈwɜːrkfɔːrs | n. 全体员工 |
| wrongful | ˈrɔːŋfl | adj. 不正当的；不讲道理的；不合法的 |
| youngster | ˈjʌŋstər | n. 孩子；少年；青年；年轻人 |
| zone | zoʊn | n. 地带；地区 |